International Migration in Cuba

MARGARITA CERVANTES-RODRÍGUEZ

With a Foreword by Alejandro Portes

International Migration in Cuba

Accumulation, Imperial Designs, and Transnational Social Fields

The Pennsylvania State University Press
University Park, Pennsylvania

Library of Congress Cataloging-in-Publication Data

Cervantes-Rodríguez, Ana Margarita.
International migration in Cuba : accumulation, imperial designs,
and transnational social fields / Margarita Cervantes-Rodríguez ;
with a foreword by Alejandro Portes.
p. cm.
Includes bibliographical references and index.
Summary: "Examines the impact of international migration
on the society and culture of Cuba since the colonial
period"—Provided by publisher.
ISBN 978-0-271-03538-3 (cloth : alk. paper)
ISBN 978-0-271-03539-0 (pbk : alk. paper)
1. Cuba—Emigration and immigration—History.
2. Cubans—Migrations—History.
3. Immigrants—Cuba—History.
4. United States—Emigration and immigration—History.
I. Title.

JV7372.C473   2010
304.8097291—dc22
2010009667

The Pennsylvania State University Press
is a member of the Association of American University Presses.

It is the policy of The Pennsylvania State University Press
to use acid-free paper.
Publications on uncoated stock satisfy the minimum
requirements of American National Standard for Information Sciences—
Permanence of Paper for Printed
Library Material, ANSI Z39.48-1992.

CONTENTS

FIGURES AND TABLES

Figures

Tables

The island of Cuba occupies a peculiar and unique place in the Americas. It was the first territory of any size met by Cristóbal Colón and his companions, who thought that, after their long Atlantic voyage, they had arrived in Cipango (Japan). Colón himself undertook the first mapping of Cuba's coast before returning to Spain. The first immigrants to Cuba were Spanish soldiers, fortune seekers, and priests who settled Cuba right after their first foundation in the new continent, on the nearby island of Hispaniola. Hernán Cortés, formerly mayor of one of Cuba's larger towns—Santiago—left the island for his famous conquest of Mexico. The Spanish settlers proceeded to subject the native Taíno population to such a harsh work regime in their mines and farms that, in a few years, the Taíno were exterminated, with lasting consequences for migration to the island in the coming centuries.

Cuba is peculiar for two reasons. First, its large size for an island—over 110,000 square kilometers—gave it the space and resources to become a significant colony on its own and subsequently a viable country. Unlike most of the other islands dotting the Caribbean, it was not just a landing spot. Second, it has a privileged location, situated at the entrance of the Gulf of Mexico and in relative proximity to the South American northern coast, the Central American isthmus, and the North American mainland. Spanish sailors were the first to designate Cuba as the place of encounter for the fleets bringing mineral treasure from the mines of Peru and Mexico. The excellent harbor of Havana became the chosen spot, and the small village grew as the "Fleet-of-Fleets" City, adding to its population a steady sediment of adventurers, sailors, and other human cargo brought aboard the ships.

The size and location of the island, in turn, meant that a substantial export economy could be developed. Agriculture was first stimulated by the need to feed the sailors when the fleets converged in Havana's harbor. The discovery of sugar and tobacco as valuable export crops in the eighteenth century led to a quantum leap in agricultural development: not only did these crops find fertile soil on the big island, but they could also be readily exported to Europe through its fine port facilities. For the rest of the colonial period, the entrepreneurial and labor demands of these industries marked the course of migration to Cuba. Europeans—mostly Spaniards, but later the French—came in search of fortune in the sugar, tobacco, and subsequently, coffee plantations. Unlike Mexico or Peru, Cuba had no more native labor to yield, and this forced the second major wave of immigrants—black slaves from Africa brought into Havana's harbor at the last leg of the "Triangular Trade."

The ups and downs of the agricultural export economy continued to drive the course of immigration during the nineteenth century. When the slave trade became forbidden and then effectively persecuted by the British Navy, planters turned to Chinese coolie labor, and Cuba became the main recipient of this new flow. Fearing the excessive "blackening" of the island and, hence, the possibility of a successful slave revolution, as in nearby Saint-Domingue (Haiti), the Spanish crown encouraged further migration, filling the islands with new flows of migrants from Galicia, Asturias, and the Canary Islands.

The wars of independence brought about the first significant outflows from the island as those opposed to the Spanish colonial regime left in droves to exile in Key West, Tampa, and New York, as well as the newly independent Latin countries in the Caribbean and Central America. These outmigrations, ending with formal independence in 1902, marked another distinct peculiarity of Cuban migration history: the island has been the recipient, but not the source, of major labor flows. The two great waves of Cuban outmigration have been political—first in opposition to the Spanish regime, and then to the communist one imposed by the advent of the Castro brothers to power in 1959. The result is that, unlike Mexico and the surrounding countries of the Caribbean, Cuba has never had a sizable labor diaspora. The consequences of this fact, in terms of the relationship between the nation and its expatriate community and the singular forms of Cuban transnationalism, are examined in this volume.

Margarita Cervantes-Rodríguez has written a book that needed to be written. Until now, studies of migration to and from the island have been segmented and largely descriptive. Cuban scholars, such as Fernando Ortiz, Jose Antonio Saco, and Julio Le Riverend, wrote at length about the colonial period and about African migration. There were, subsequently, voluminous Cuban and American literatures on the war of independence years, including the role of the large exile communities of the time. There was then a large hiatus until 1959, with the exodus of the Cuban upper and middle classes in the wake of Castro's revolution. This book aims to bring these segmented literatures together and to do so under an overarching theoretical framework constructed on the basis of both historical and sociological concepts bearing on the secular development of the world economy. It is an ambitious idea.

Cervantes-Rodríguez is to be commended for this extraordinary effort of synthesis. Her book will be read with much profit not only by specialists on Cuba but also by those seeking to make sense of the complex waves of migration during the history of capitalism. Because of its geographical position, Cuba represents a strategic site for pursuing such study.

Alejandro Portes
Princeton University
May 2009

My interest in approaching international migration in Cuba from a historical perspective started some years ago in Havana, when I was first captivated by compelling studies that dealt with the immigration of certain groups to the island and the enduring impact of immigration on Cuban society. I started exploring the topic when I produced a comparative study about international migration in Nicaragua and Cuba in my doctoral dissertation. However, as I moved into the transnational experiences of the migrants, my focus switched to Nicaraguans, since it was logistically more feasible to conduct fieldwork in the Central American country. Eventually, the contrast between the Nicaraguan and Cuban cases, in terms of broad historical trends, shaped the novelty of the study. It was not until a few years later that I could focus on the topic of this book. By then, my personal experiences and my familiarity with the narratives and experiences of other Cubans in different societies had become what, borrowing from Miguel de Unamuno, one might call the *intrahistoria* that nourished and brought a sense of purpose to the formal scholarly account presented here.

This work aims to tie up the loose ends of an extensive yet dispersed body of scholarly literature as well as alternative sources of information through a coherent historical narrative. Yet many issues remain unexplored, and some ends remain loose. I hope, nevertheless, to have shed light on relevant aspects of the process and the social forces shaping it. I believe that a historical perspective on international migration in Cuba holds lessons that are useful for the present and the immediate future of Cuban society. It sheds light on pervasive structures, fluid relationships, and changing contexts and invites a debate on pressing issues.

During a national meeting organized in 1993, Cuban bishops produced the document *El amor todo lo espera* (Love Hopes All Things) in which they referred to emigration as a major issue affecting Cuban society and called for an understanding of why so many Cubans from different walks of life—manual workers, professionals, athletes, members of the military, artists—wanted to leave their homeland. In early 2009, the religious magazine *Vitral* published an article entitled "La emigración, fenómeno alarmante" (Emigration: An

Alarming Phenomenon), which addressed this issue more poignantly in light of the difficult conditions in which most Cubans live today.

Many countries of the periphery and semiperiphery have lost qualified workers to more prosperous societies. Many of them have acknowledged the economic impact and socioeconomic role of their diasporas, and some have even developed incentives for migrants to put their experiences, knowledge, and material resources in the service of their homeland. Presidents, ministers, and other officials frequently make presentations in the countries where their emigrants concentrate in order to invite them to contribute to social and economic projects. Another trend points to the formation of associations and professional organizations by migrants to assist in the development of infrastructure and social programs in their localities of origin. Cuba is out of sync with all these trends. Furthermore, Cuban migrants today have fewer opportunities to unleash their economic and social potential in their homeland than immigrants in Cuba did a century ago. Many migrants who arrived in Cuba in earlier periods formed associations and contributed to their hometowns in many ways, such as through the building of schools, cultural and recreational centers, and health care institutions and by making investments there. Some developed such projects after having returned, while others participated in them while keeping homes, jobs, or investments in Cuba.

Today, many Cuban households are transnational households by definition—if only in the narrow sense that at least one of the economic providers, usually the main provider, does not reside in Cuba—and remittances constitute a major source of income both micro- and macroeconomically. Yet in times of greater global interconnectedness and expanding transnational relations, the Cuban government's restrictionist approach to migration and its bias against private entrepreneurship by Cubans impose insurmountable barriers to the development of strategies similar to those launched by migrants elsewhere for the benefit of the society of origin. Such barriers have led to a situation in which policies and regulations have secured the unilateral transfer of talented entrepreneurs and highly skilled workers to other societies. Cuba's current dominant discourses and policy interventions on migration fail to recognize the needs (or potential) of a society that has become increasingly transnationalized.

As this book moves into the final stage of the production process, the governments of Spain and the United States have made major announcements that directly affect Cuban migration. On December 29, 2008, the Spanish government enacted Disposition No. 7 related to the Law 52/2007, also known as Ley de la Memoria Histórica (The Historical Memory Law). This ruling opened the door for thousands of Cubans to acquire Spanish citizenship: "people whose father or mother were Spanish by origin" and "the grandsons and granddaughters of Spaniards who lost or had to give up their Spanish citizenship as a result of their exile" could apply for citizenship within a two-year period after the enactment of the law.[1] Since then, more than 130,000 Cubans have made appointments to present their cases before the Spanish authorities.[2] This announcement by the Spanish government derives from a law that was shaped by the commitment to recognize, even if retroactively, the rights of thousands of exiles and other Spanish emigrants by allowing their descendants to return to Spain. It conveys a sense of restitution, a humanitarian perspective, a sense of social justice toward Spanish migrants that were forced to leave their country under exceptionally difficult circumstances. And on April 2009, the administration of President Barack Obama started to lift existing restrictions on family visits to the island and the sending of remittances. The announcement by the Obama administration with respect to the Cuban immigrants in the United States also conveys the ideal of social justice. The approach of the current administration to this issue shows that only when the migrants cease to be seen either as allies or enemies, and start to be seen through compassionate, humanitarian eyes, can misleading and unjust regulations be eliminated. Thousands of Cuban migrants in the United States and elsewhere have demonstrated that they are beyond the Cold War discourse. They are ready to contribute to their society as many migrants around the world do. However, twisted ideological positions and entrenched interests and biases are acting as formidable impediments, preventing this from happening.

ACKNOWLEDGMENTS

The encouragement and dedicated support of many people saw me through the writing of this book. The late Enrique Baloyra was very encouraging and helpful when I presented him with the idea of writing a book on international migration in Cuba from a historical vantage point. The professional guidance of Alejandro Portes, and his own work, was decisive for me when I started the study of international migration more systematically. His encouragement was crucial as I moved into the final stages of the manuscript. The works of many scholars from several countries who have made significant contributions to the understanding of international migration, Caribbean migration, and Cuban migration in particular were inspirational and enlightening. I only hope to have made good use of their valuable insights throughout this work. Some of the contents of this book were presented in academic conferences and seminars and some discussed in my courses on international migration as the manuscript wended its way toward the final draft. The invitations of colleagues Martín Rodrigo, Nina Glick-Schiller, Ramón Grosfoguel, Laura Oso, Alejandro Portes, and Consuelo Naranjo to discuss my papers at events and panels gave me great opportunities to receive feedback and further expand my knowledge. I would like to express my deepest appreciation to them all.

I have talked with many Cubans about their migration experiences in several countries throughout these years. I appreciate their time and the candor with which they shared their experiences. All these exchanges were very enlightening and helped me shape the manuscript. I also thank the colleagues and staff of several institutions: the Department of International Studies and the Cuban Heritage Collection at the University of Miami and the Center for Migration and Development at Princeton University figure prominently among them. I would also like to thank the staff at the New York Public Library and the Biblioteca Nacional de Madrid. My appreciation also goes to Spanish scholar Laura Oso, who gave me pointers for finding data in Spain and invited me to participate in a project on immigrants in Spain, which allowed me to gain greater understanding of the migration experience of Cubans there. I thank Fernando Sánchez, who generously opened the doors of the books and documents collection at the information center of the Immigration Archives at the Department of Labor in Madrid and provided useful contacts. I would also like to thank Christopher Barrueta for producing the design for the cover of this book. My special appreciation goes to Sandy Thatcher, the former director of Penn State Press, and his team for their dedicated, professional guidance throughout the production process.

My immense gratitude goes to my family and friends for their encouragement, love, and care. The greatest gratitude goes to my mother, who taught me to appreciate knowledge and to be compassionate to those in need—and above all, who made sacrifices. She never wanted to move to El Norte. However, as with many other Cubans, one day she was confronted with the difficult decision of whether to leave her beloved island, where friends and family members remained. The stories about my Spanish grandparents walking in the snow to learn English and build "a new life" in New York at an advanced age, when they were supposed to start harvesting the fruits of their immigration experience in Cuba, had an enduring impact on me as well. They taught me at close range that for many individuals and families who once landed on Cuban shores, the island would not be the last stop. My grandmother Fefita, who never left Cuba, deserves a special place in my acknowledgments. She was the one who first explained to me what labor leaders in the sugar industry were fighting for when she was young. Her interesting conversations concerning social issues began when she was still introducing me to the intricacies of the Spanish verbs. She seemed to have known that she did not have much time. And in fact, sadly, she eventually left us early. I dedicate this book to her memory and to my mother. My special gratitude to my dearest Lu, whose loving encouragement and careful reading of the first draft meant so much to me. My deepest appreciation also goes to Eduardo, Kyle, Gail, Mathew, María Luz, Luisito, Stefan, Armando, and Carlos, and other members of my family and extended family, including good friends who have encouraged and supported me throughout this process, always in loving ways. The image of individuals and families arriving in Cuba or departing from it under difficult (and at times even inhuman) circumstances in different periods stayed with me as I wrote this book. My deepest sympathy goes to these migrants throughout the centuries.

Introduction

Objectives

Historical analyses of international migration in Cuba have tended to focus on either specific groups of migrants or major aspects of the process associated with specific periods. Notwithstanding their significant contributions, the literature lacks comprehensive appraisals of the dynamics shaping international migration, the inner workings of the process, and its major implications from the colonial period to date. This book tackles these issues by pursuing several interwoven goals. One of the goals is to explore the dynamics of the process of international migration in Cuba associated with major structural transformations—globally, regionally, and in Cuban society—and during periods characterized by important, albeit less sweeping, changes that nevertheless affected the demand for labor or the social and political aspects of the migration process. Another goal is to explore the role played by specific social actors (such as the state, the migrant family and their enterprises, transnational corporations and workers, labor unions, and other politically influential groups) in shaping the migration process. A third, related goal is to explore the role of the migrants in articulating Cuba with the global structures of capitalism. These goals are pursued under some premises that are grounded in historical-structural and transnational perspectives on migration: capitalism is a global system that operates in the *longue durée* through pervasive (but not immutable) social structures and fluid social relationships that overflow specific societies; "the migrants" constitute a highly diverse group of people that occupy different "social locations" and include subjugated groups as well as dominant ones; although more frequently than not they have been forced to move across societies, they have not been passive actors in the global scenario;

they have played an important role in shaping societies, transnational relations, and the social history of capital. This book also seeks to shed light on the particularities of the Cuban case with respect to other societies of similar socioeconomic and geopolitical locations in the international system at different historical junctures.

Thus, in the present inquiry, I explore how international migration in Cuba has been molded by the interplay of structural and behavioral dynamics that operate at different temporal and spatial scales. These include cycles of accumulation, imperial designs, colonial projects and anticolonial struggles, regime change, nation-building projects, labor-capital relations, immigration policies, strategies of accumulation, and the pursuing of livelihoods, among others. Central to this inquiry is the exploration of the synergies between the structural processes shaping international migration in Cuba during the most critical periods of the process and the expectations, values, identities, and ideologies of specific social actors who were involved either directly or indirectly in the migration process. Thus, the issues examined throughout this work cannot be grasped under a single theoretical paradigm even when a particular conceptualization of history guides the inquiry.

I formulate the terms of investigation according to an analytical schema that allows us to see the continuum between the internal dynamics of Cuban society, those of other societies, and larger social structures. It provides the basis for a systematic inquiry into the continuities and discontinuities of the migration process. I specifically forge conceptual and methodological connections to bridge the gap between Fernand Braudel's *longue durée* conceptualization of history and what I call a comprehensive perspective on transnationalism. Other conceptual frameworks are employed wherever necessary to refine the inquiry.

Historical Antecedents

Several factors related to Cuba's multiple functions within the Spanish colonial system contributed to an increase in immigration to the island from the onset of the colonial period to the mid-eighteenth century. However, the process intensified in the last decade of the eighteenth century and throughout the first decades of the nineteenth century, primarily as a result of the arrival of massive numbers of people escaping turmoil and as Cuba emerged as a major producer of sugar for the world market. Between 1791 and 1810, an interval the historian Julio Le Riverend called "the French period in immigration to Cuba," thousands of migrants, many of them French nationals, sought refuge in Cuba from the revolution in Saint-Domingue (currently Haiti) and the subsequent waves of violence that reached other areas of Hispaniola, and when Louisiana was transferred to the United States, among other geopolitical scenarios. By then, the introduction of African slaves had begun to escalate, and Cuba eventually became one of the epicenters of the slave traffic in the Americas. Between 1847 and 1874, it was the main recipient of Chinese indentured laborers in Latin America and the Caribbean.[1] It was also the main recipient of immigrants from Spain in the nineteenth century. Jordi Maluquer de Motes summarizes the role of Cuba as a magnet of immigration to Latin America in the nineteenth and early twentieth centuries in the following terms: "Once we take into consideration the dimensions of this phenomenon and its numerical relevance with respect to the total population, Cuba surfaces as the only Latin American society that receives a massive number of immigrants throughout the nineteenth century and into the first third of the twentieth century."[2] Major aspects of the migration process during the second half of the nineteenth century were strongly linked to the expansion of trade, investment, labor, and monetary flows across the Atlantic and between Cuba and the United States—and, to some extent, other areas of the Americas—and the intensification of the political struggle against Spanish colonialism.

The first decades after the Spanish-American War were characterized by the development of a strong immigration regime associated primarily with the expansion of the sugar industry. Spanish immigrants were either returning from societies where they had settled during the independence war or arrived for the first time, often through aggressive recruitment by employers. Immigration to Cuba was linked once again in the Spanish popular imaginary with prospects of social mobility and quick accumulation, which in conjunction with family reunification and an overall positive reception toward members of the group also strengthened the migration ties between Spain and its former colony. Caribbean laborers, the second-largest group arriving on the island at that time, also were massively incorporated into the labor circuits generated by the expansion of the sugar industry through various modalities of labor recruitment. Chinese workers and entrepreneurs once again gravitated toward Cuba, while migrants from other areas of the world also arrived, prompted by the dramatic transformations that were taking place in the island and elsewhere.

International migration in Cuba from the last decades of the colonial period to the first three decades of the twentieth century reflected the juxtaposition of patterns of capitalist expansion on a global scale that heavily relied on migration. One of these patterns pointed to large-scale migrations from Europe to colonial and former colonial areas, which redistributed European workers and entrepreneurs across different areas of the capitalist world economy, with the United States as the major recipient society in the Americas. The other pointed to the growing use by the United States of a non-European workforce through migration processes by importing labor from societies beyond Europe, while the United States also started to rely more heavily on the redistribution of the workforce within the periphery for accumulation purposes.[3] These dynamics directly affected Cuba at that time. The import of labor and entrepreneurship from Cuba as a result of the expansion of accumulation in the United States was first intertwined with the exodus of people from the island related to the anti-colonial struggle there, while during the first decades of the twentieth century, accumulation in the United States benefited primarily from Cuba's transformation into a regional magnet of labor from the Caribbean along with its continuing role as a magnet of workers and entrepreneurs from Spain, and, once again, the arrival of a large number of Chinese workers.[4] The national and transnational involvement of migrants of different backgrounds played a key role in the expansion of Cuba's economy and in securing the transfer of value, understood in economic terms, but also facilitated the flow of social values, norms, and ideologies upon which the new imperial designs and further capitalist penetration, and the rise of counterhegemonic projects in labor-capital relations and beyond, were built.

When the notion of migrants as subjugated subjects under capitalism is complemented by a more nuanced approach to this complex social group, and the state-centric way of explaining U.S. hegemony in Cuba is reexamined in light of an inquiry into the social history of capital, we are in a better position to shed light on the role of specific actors and social forces that go beyond state-to-state and labor-capital relations in shaping Cuba's articulation with the world through migration. The approaches to power and transnationalism used in this work allow for the incorporation of insights about the different strategies and projects, some of which were carried out throughout generations, through which the migrants have historically articulated Cuba with other societies and global structures. The study of the migrants as social subjects of different social locations (e.g., those related to class, gender, politics, and culture) also sheds light on the complex impact that migration had on Cuban society in different periods. While migration and transnationalism exacerbated labor exploitation, labor-capital tensions, and social inequalities and facilitated economic dependency, migration and transnationalism were also instrumental in the unfolding of complex political currents, strategies to resist oppression, the advancing of progressive social programs, and the achievement of certain levels of socioeconomic progress. There are periods in Cuban history where immigration surpassed emigration in impressive ways and others in which the opposite happened. Although this work addresses these general trends, their causes, and their major consequences, it also calls attention to the fact that in most such periods the participation of migrants in transnational social fields remained fluid and scrutinizes the rationales under which such involvement took place.

Immigration to Cuba experienced a sharp decline after the late 1920s as a result of global, regional, and local transformations. Some of these transformations were on their way and had impacted migration and the debates on immigration even earlier than that. Although the island continued to receive immigrants from different areas of the world until the thresholds of the revolution of 1959, it never regained the high levels of immigration it exhibited in the nineteenth and early twentieth centuries. The growth of emigration to and temporary relocations in the United States (and to some extent other societies), as a result of strategies of labor market participation and accumulation, overlapped with the declining trends in immigration. From the 1930s to the late 1950s, Cuban migration to the United States and the transnational processes associated with it became more relevant than immigration to the island from other areas as mechanisms of support of the accumulation process in the United States. In addition, the practices associated with transnational political involvement, which had been an important aspect of the migration experience toward the end of the colonial period and surfaced sporadically in times of turmoil in Cuba, continued to be relevant during this period.

The synergy between geopolitical processes associated with the Cold War and major politico-economic and social transformations brought about by the revolution of 1959 had a dramatic impact on migration. The fact that emigration reached unprecedented levels was just the tip of the iceberg. Certainly, the migration process acquired new quantitative and qualitative dimensions with respect not only to regime change but also to structural transformations involving the disarticulation of the private sector, and the revamping of the class structure of the society upon a radical change of values, norms, laws, and policies that redefined property rights, labor rights, social and citizenship rights, developmental strategies, and the emergence of new identities and recycling of others. At the core of these transformations was the realignment of Cuba in world politics, and the whole restructuring of the relationship with the United States became central to the migration process once again.

In a matter of a century, Cuba transitioned from being a major labor-importing society to being a major refugee-generating and labor-exporting society in the Americas. Some of the dynamics of the migration processes since 1959 point to important discontinuities with respect to both previous time periods in the island and other societies with similar locations in the world economy. Others, however, point to important continuities in relation to the underlying processes shaping migration globally. Exploration of how the general manifests through the particularities of this case is an important aspect of the study, which explores major continuities and changes in the process of international migration in Cuba since the colonial period, from the arrival of the Spaniards and with them the *bozales,* to the current period, marked by the ongoing departure of the *balseros.*

Bozales and Balseros

Imported from the Iberian Peninsula, where it was widely used to refer to the slaves recently brought from Africa, the term *bozales* could often be heard in the entry ports of Cuba as early as the sixteenth century. In *El engaño de las razas,* Fernando Ortiz explains that *bozal* referred to African slaves recently taken from their homeland, as well as to domesticated animals, mainly livestock, and to the muzzle employed to prevent domesticated animals from biting. Ortiz further specifies that "Bozal also meant stubbornness, lack of intelligence or being idiotic" [Bozal quiso también significar necio, bruto o idiota] (1975, 53). Works in linguistics tend to use *bozal* to refer to the particular way African slaves spoke Spanish—when establishing differences between "Black Spanish" and "White Spanish."[5] Fernando Ortiz adds that the term *bozalón* was employed to refer to a black person with a low level of Spanish proficiency: "Bozalón se dijo en Cuba al *negro que comenzaba a darse a entender algo, chapurreando el castellano.*"[6] In a work on African slavery in the Americas published in 1879, José Antonio Saco noted that as early as 1510, there was a preference to use the term *bozales* instead of *Ladinos* ("Spanish-speaking Christianized Negroes from Spain") to emphasize precisely their lack of familiarity with and vulnerability to the culture within which they were forced to live.[7]

By the end of the twentieth century, and under different circumstances, common Cuban parlance introduces another term, *balseros* ("rafters," or those who leave the island on rafts), to refer to a particular type of migrant who uses precarious means and risks his or her life to escape from the homeland. The symbolic violence that dwells in the term *bozales* is not found in the term *balsero*, insofar as the social conditions that led to forced migrations under the institution of slavery differ greatly from the present conditions that induce the *balseros* to leave their homeland. Unlike the *bozales,* the *balseros* are not slaves, nor do they arrive in the ports of Cuba, but rather depart from them. However, the two terms evoke some similarities in terms of human experience and some historical continuities that are worth bearing in mind. Both the *balseros* and the *bozales* travel under perilous conditions, with important levels of violence associated with their journeys. Like the *bozales,* many *balseros* never make it to the shore. Ultimately, the two traumatic journeys point to a common thread; from the arrival of the Spaniards and the *bozales* to the departures of the *balseros,* the process of international migration in Cuba has been molded by labor processes, power relations, and systems of hegemony associated with competition and domination, and has involved significant human degradation and despair.

Structure of the Book

Although the issues of agency and structure, determinacy and contingency, the general and the particular, and continuity and discontinuity are equally relevant throughout this inquiry, the issue of continuity and discontinuity takes precedence for the organization of the book given the period of time covered. The process of international migration in Cuba has evolved since the sixteenth century through phases that reflect major shifts in Cuba's articulation with the world economy, including its corresponding interstate system, hence the importance of organizing this inquiry along chapters that capture these general dynamics.

Chapter 1, "The Theoretical Framework," presents the analytical schema employed. This schema relies on the assumption that a historical approach to the role and place of international migration in Cuba's articulation with the global structures of the capitalist system presupposes a global perspective and a comprehensive transnational perspective. These three perspectives—the historical, the global, and the transnational—are constructed as a unit in this work. The transnational perspective in migration studies invites us to examine how migrants participate in the development of transnational social networks and social fields in relation to their involvement in two or more societies.

Notwithstanding its relevance, this perspective is still limited in terms of grasping the manifold dimensions of migration in relation to transnational processes. Acknowledging this limitation, I build on several approaches to transnationalism.[8] I emphasize how the interaction of migrants and nonmigrants and the coalescing of migration strategies and policies with others not directly linked to migration enable the formation and sustainability of the transnational social fields in which the migrants operate. A comprehensive perspective on transnationalism allows us to account for the multiple (and sometimes overlapping) roles played by the migrants (as laborers, merchants, bankers, owners of enterprises, heads of households, members of clubs and associations, and so on) in their interactions with other migrants and nonmigrants as important aspects of their transnational involvement.

The historical perspective on migration, as presented in this work, engages a particular conceptualization of history, one that is rooted in Fernand Braudel's conceptualization of the *longue durée,* which involves a series of interrelated notions and concepts.[9] Frequently, the *longue durée* is used to emphasize how the pervasive global structures of capitalism and related geopolitical forces shape events and processes occurring in specific social formations in specific periods of time. Although this interpretation underlies my use of the concept, I also emphasize the centrality of "the plurality of social time" to Braudel's conceptualization of history. The idea of "breaking history into successive levels" to account for "the multiplicity of times" that every social process involves—a key aspect of Braudel's historical conceptualization—has particular importance for the study of migration, a process that is molded by the intertwining of social structures and forces that have different durations and operate on different spatial/temporal scales. As Braudel notices, while "the long time span" has "exceptional value" for the historian, it is the complementary notions of "multiplicity of time" and the understanding of history as the "history of a hundred aspects" that engage the attention of the social sciences.[10] Hence, his notion of the "plurality of social times" offers a theoretical tool to incorporate the various perspectives on migration and transnationalism employed in this work, which stem from the social sciences and a coherent historical narrative.[11]

Chapter 2, "Accumulation, Colonialism, Modernity, and Imperial Rivalry," grounds what follows by examining major causal links, characteristics, and implications of the process of international migration in Cuba under Spanish colonialism. The chapter shows how the gradual increase in the arrival of transients and migrants was related to Cuba's strategic importance to Spain, the expansion of Cuba's port economy, and an overall expansion of the division of labor related to these and other activities. It documents the importance of imperial wars and territorial seizures, enslavement, anticolonial struggles, and other violent processes in the Caribbean, Latin America, Europe, the southern United States, and other areas of the world in shaping migration in Cuba throughout the colonial period. Chapter 2 also addresses the synergy between migration and the production of tobacco, coffee, and sugar in relation to large-scale accumulation schema and individual strategies. It discusses how migration impacted the transformation of the urban space in Havana, its articulation with other major cities, and the beginning of patterns of spatial inequalities that still exist.

It examines the entanglements of the debates on migration in the nineteenth century and other debates, such as those pertaining to the sustainability of the slavery system, the technological transformation of the sugar industry, the political status of the island, and the desired racial makeup of the population, as defined by the Spanish authorities and influential members of the Creole elite. It also discusses specific immigration rules and incentives designed to attract Spanish immigrants, their impact on the growth of immigration from Spain, and how these approaches were guided by the interplay of geopolitical, racist, and economic rationales. The growth of the migration links with the United States by the end of the Spanish colonial rule in the island is examined as well.

Chapter 3, "Migration and Other Transnational Processes in the Colonial-Postcolonial Transition," focuses on the role and place of migration in the expansion of the transnational social fields that linked the island with other societies in the second half of the nineteenth century and throughout the unfolding of Cuba's postcolonial society.[12] Emphasis is placed on types of transnationalism related to immigration from different regions of Spain and U.S.-bound migration.

The chapter documents the role and place of the migrants in the development of transnational social fields, across the Atlantic and regionally. It calls attention to the centrality of migration in the transnationalization of the Spanish-origin capitalist class, the evolution of family enterprises, and the role of marriage, investment, and other strategies in their survival and even expansion across generations. The chapter also examines the links between migration and the transnationalization of labor-capital relations and the expansion of commercial activities, the banking industry, and social and political projects, including those sustaining "long-distance nationalism." The analysis of these issues involves exploring both material exchanges and particular interests and their links to the construction of identities and loyalties related to ethnicity, class, gender, and political affiliations, which were forged across the Atlantic and regionally by the migrants.

Chapter 4, "Migration Within the U.S. Sphere of Influence," examines the interplay between international migration and Cuba's economic and political repositioning globally and regionally from the early twentieth century to 1958. Cuba's unfolding as a postcolonial society under the shadow of U.S. hegemony occurred within the global transition from the British-led systemic cycle of accumulation to the one led by the United States.[13] The global transition was marked by the intensification of competition between Britain and the United States for global economic spaces in the early twentieth century, the Great Depression and "final collapse of the nineteenth century world order in the 1930s," and the subsequent rise of the United States as the global hegemon after World War II.[14] The chapter examines major structural changes and social forces through which these developments impacted migration in Cuba. As in the other chapters, the issue of migrants' incorporation is discussed in relation to labor market incorporation, transnational livelihoods and accumulation strategies, and political involvement. Chapter 4 also includes an analysis of the evolution of the foreign-born population from the beginning of the twentieth century to the threshold of the revolution of 1959.

Chapter 5, "Cuba's Cold War Revolution and Migration," sheds light on how the migration process was affected by the geopolitics of the Cold War, political processes in Cuba, and the political economy of the Cuban revolution since 1959. The role played by the bilateral relationship with the United States in shaping migration is a relevant aspect discussed in this work. However, attention is also called to the political economy of the transformations undergone by Cuban society within the sphere of influence of the Soviet Union and during the post-Soviet era, as well as Cuba's gradual rearticulation with the structures of capitalism since. It is shown how migration associated with labor processes and the temporary participation of Cubans in labor markets outside the island have been fundamental aspects of such rearticulation. The chapter discusses various characteristics of the migration process and its demographic and socioeconomic implications in Cuba and the United States, particularly South Florida. It also discusses the reversal of the historical pattern of migration from Spain and contrasts some of the characteristics of the migration process and the incorporation of the migrants in Spain with respect to the United States.

Chapter 6, "Transnational Social Fields Between Cuba and the United States at the Beginning of the Twenty-First Century," focuses on how the collapse of the Soviet Union impacted the expansion of transnational social fields between Cuba and the United States and the central role played by migration in this development. It shows that transnational processes operate in truncated ways in this context because of the nature of the bilateral relationship and major characteristics of the migration policy and policy toward the emigrants in Cuba, and other dynamics related to the Cuban political system. However, the chapter also shows that since the 1990s, there has been a growing involvement of Cubans and non-Cubans in transnational relations between the two societies. It documents how transnational practices by migrants and nonmigrants since then have both supported and challenged forms of control and hegemonic designs stemming from the two governments involved. The chapter discusses the particularities of the transnational involvement of Cubans in light of other experiences involving the United States and labor-exporting societies of the region and beyond. It also discusses how certain ideological positions, identities, interests, and strategies currently shape transnational involvement and its implications.

The Conclusion emphasizes that in Cuba's most crucial transitional periods, the process of international migration has not been weightless for Cubans, Cuba, and the global powers directly involved there in one capacity or another. It further argues that Cuba is currently going through one such moment. It engages a discussion about the tensions between current policy approaches to migration and the global structures and forces shaping the process.

Research Methods and Strategies

This work incorporates evidence from an array of secondary sources spanning several countries and languages, and various emphases and perspectives, over two centuries. Such wealth in the sources attests to the centrality of the process of international migration in Cuba's society since the colonial period and its key importance in articulating Cuba with the world. Such dispersion, however, called for a synthesis under complementary theoretical perspectives in order to reveal some of the enduring features and major transformations of the migration process in Cuba, its particularities as they have been shaped by global trends, and the historical interface between social structures and social agency under changing conditions.

I consulted a wealth of journals, books, government documents, nonacademic periodicals, reprints of historical documents, and occasionally original documents. Access to documents and studies available in the Cuban Heritage

Collection at the University of Miami; the manuscripts section of Guildhall Library, London; the Rare Books Collection of the New York Public Library; the Immigration Archives at the Ministerio de Trabajo y Asuntos Sociales in Madrid; the London School of Economics; and the Biblioteca Nacional de España was very helpful. I also discuss evidence from informal conversations and everyday observations related to my own experiences among Cubans in South Florida and New York, formal interviews with Cubans in Barcelona, and observations and informal conversations with Cuban migrants in other areas of Spain and in France, Mexico, the Dominican Republic, Puerto Rico, and Canada.

In Spain, I conducted a formal preliminary exploration of the migration strategies and aspects of the incorporation process of Cubans through eleven interviews in the summer of 2005 with Cubans living in Barcelona, ten of whom were enterprise owners or operators; a formal interview with a Spanish immigration attorney in Barcelona whose firm has a large Cuban clientele; and participation in a focus group organized by the community organization Debat a Bat in the Església de Sant Agustí in Barcelona, a church known for having provided sanctuary to undocumented immigrants. I interviewed the attorney and participated in the focus group in order to gain a clearer perspective on the migration context in Barcelona. In addition, I talked to several Cubans whom I met in social events and gathering places, such as Cuban restaurants, in Madrid and Barcelona. Although one cannot claim that the evidence gathered from these interviews and my informal conversations is representative of the entire group, it has helped me understand and compare some aspects of the migration experience of Cubans in Spain with that of Cubans in the United States, including their migration strategies, the ways in which they carry their transnational practices, and their sense of social distance from and proximity to the homeland. These interviews and my observations, combined with information from alternative sources, allowed me to take a glance at one of the most pressing, albeit less studied, issues pertaining to current international migration in Cuba: how gender, class, and racialization interface in Cubans' migration and adaptation strategies, and, in general, their incorporation into other societies. This book calls attention to the relevance of this issue and the need to study it more systematically in future inquiries. My visits to Spanish cities in recent years and my living experiences in the United States also gave me firsthand knowledge about the experiences of other Latin American and Caribbean groups in these societies and how migration from Cuba is part of general historical processes that include them all.

The least conventional methods of inquiry, such as informal conversations with Cubans residing in other societies and discussions with colleagues and other people from those societies about societal perceptions about Cubans, were instrumental in grounding my understanding about their migration experiences in recent decades, the challenges they face, the continuities and discontinuities in Cuba's government strategies concerning the insertion of Cubans into labor markets abroad. Differences in terms of the perceptions of the migrants about their migration experience based on the years in which they departed from the island and the countries in which they live were also observed. They also allowed me to improve my understanding of the complex social structures of the Cubans who reside abroad and the different ways in which they are linked to their homeland.

A recent visit to Cuba has also informed this work, particularly the chapters dealing with the current conditions in Cuba and the involvement of Cubans in transnational livelihood to cope with them, how remittances are used, and the specific forces shaping emigration today. Extensive conversations with friends and my systematic communication with my relatives in Cuba have kept me abreast of the human implications of policies that have been frequently designed based on political calculations, entrenched interests, ideologies, and fears rather than by taking into consideration the pressing needs and legitimate aspirations of Cubans on the island and abroad for a better future for their families and their homeland—and the potential for realizing such aspirations.

ONE

The Theoretical Framework

Existing Gaps in the Study of International Migration in Cuba

Given the multiple repercussions of international migration in Cuba's society, a wealth of analyses on the subject can be found not only in studies that focus on migration but also in Cuban historiography in general. However, the study of international migration has followed an unprecedented path since 1959. The works addressing different aspects of the migration process in Cuba published in the last fifty years can be classified by whether they were produced by scholars living in Cuba or abroad and by whether they refer to migration before 1959 or after. These distinctions shed light on existing links between the periods covered and the loci of enunciation associated with political contexts, cultural affinities, and institutional choices as they have shaped the production of knowledge on international migration in Cuba since 1959.

A glance at the literature reviewed for this study in light of these parameters indicates that the vast majority of studies on international migration in Cuba conducted by historians and social scientists working in Cuba itself after 1959 have tended to focus on specific groups of migrants or different aspects of the migration process during periods before 1959.[1] These works, many of which are cited throughout this work, constitute an invaluable source. In sharp contrast with this trend, until the 1990s, scholarly institutions in Cuba largely avoided inquiries about the process of international migration after the revolution of 1959.[2] By focusing until recently on aspects of the migration process before 1959, the most substantive body of literature produced by Cuban scholars working from the island since then has complemented the literature produced outside Cuba covering the colonial and "the republican" periods.

Although several influential works on different aspects of the migration process in the pre-1959 period have been produced by scholars in the United States, their contribution has been more noticeable in the study of immigration from Cuba since 1959. To be sure, it is from the United States that Cuban scholars have produced the vast majority of scholarly studies referring to international migration in Cuba in the post-1959 period with a focus on U.S.-bound migration. Their contributions have also been invaluable sources for this work.

Thus, a sort of unintended division of labor between scholars in Cuba and the United States prevailed until recently in the studies on the forces shaping migration and its major social consequences: history—understood as antecedent or prerevolutionary history—prevailed in the inquiries produced in Cuba in the post-1959 period and the Cuban American experience in inquiries produced in the United States. In neither, however, has a historical perspective made a significant inroad in the sense of accounting for how past and present are tied in complementary and contradictory fashion in the shaping of migration in Cuba. The result has been a neglect of a wide range of themes pertaining to the understanding of the continuities and discontinuities between past and present, and the general aspects and particularities of the Cuban case with respect to other societies of the periphery. For example, the issue of how the dramatic changes Cuban society underwent during the first decades of the revolution affected first- and second-generation immigrants in the island and triggered a new cycle of displacement related to physical relocation and social repositioning as experienced by many families remains largely unexplored. Studies on the slave trade and slavery and its long-term social repercussions have paid little attention, for example, to the possibility of a continuum between past and present in the form of "structural displacements"[3] among Cuban blacks. Alejandro de la Fuente (1998) notes that "despite the demographic weight of African groups and their descendants in Cuba's total population, and known inequalities and discriminatory practices related to skin color, Cuban historiography has devoted very little attention to the black population and the social participation of this group in the republican and revolutionary periods."[4] It should be added that the manifestations of structural displacement among Cuban blacks are to be found not just in Cuba but are also part of the migration experience, a topic that has not been systematically addressed either.[5] The significant exodus of professionals (and qualified workers in general), and the issue of the geographical dispersal of Cubans who do not gravitate toward the United States, are other chapters of the migration process that merit deciphering in light of historical trends inclusive of the present. Nor has the relationship between internal displacement and international migration or the participation of migrants in transnational social fields that link Cuba to other societies been sufficiently studied. In general, the existing lacunae in the study of international migration in Cuba suggest that the call for "the making of the history of people without history"⁶ remains largely unanswered.

Dividing migration studies at 1959 reflects the dramatic nature of the changes brought about by the revolution and has allowed researchers to shed light on their impact on migration. Unfortunately, however, understanding this rupture as ontology introduces a historical bias that prevents us from grasping the *longue durée* of the migration process in relation to labor processes, geopolitical designs, and even intergenerational dynamics within families, enterprises, and other collective actors that have been central to the migration process.

Common sense dictates a consensus according to which any hypothetical number of migrants and temporary workers arriving in Cuba since 1959 would pale if contrasted with the massive exodus since then. However, even though *leaving* Cuba, not *arriving* in Cuba, is the definitive feature of the migration process since 1959, the relative insignificance of temporary movements and even permanent migration to the island does not necessarily imply absolute irrelevance from a sociological standpoint. Anecdotal evidence suggests that people from different areas of the world have arrived to work, study, or even live on a permanent basis on the island since 1959. These arrivals range from professionals who were enthusiastic about the revolutionary project mostly throughout its first years and wanted to contribute their expertise and eventually stayed to escapees from right-wing regimes of Latin America, temporary workers and immigrants from the former Soviet Union and other countries of the Soviet bloc who married Cubans, and students and temporary workers from Africa and other areas of the periphery. Even if their numbers are much lower than those of Cubans living elsewhere, their demographics, the rationales of their arrivals, issues pertaining to their modalities of incorporation into the labor market and society in general, when and under which conditions they arrived and returned, and their involvement in transnational practices related to their continuing personal and institutional ties to Cuba are chapters of the most recent history of international migration that remain in absolute obscurity. Another critical issue that requires a systematic exploration of migration beyond the dichotomy "emigration" and "immigration" is the link between migration and marriage strategies and work-related strategies in relation to the opening up of Cuba to temporary worker programs and tourism with some countries, such as Spain, Venezuela, Mexico, and Italy, among others, since the collapse of the Soviet bloc and the development of transnational livelihoods and the lifestyles associated with them. Anecdotal evidence also calls for inquiries about whether and how the emergence of new sources of wealth and status within the Cuban population relates to different access to transnational livelihoods and even accumulation strategies by different social groups. Along these lines, it seems relevant to explore to what extent enterprises that appear to be "ethnic enterprises" run by Cuban immigrants in Spain, Mexico, and other societies are related to and even controlled by the state apparatus in Cuba.

Filling existing research gaps will require the concerted efforts of teams of scholars and years of ethnographic research; in some cases, it will also require access to reliable statistical data gathered by governments and other institutions. Thus, the most we can do at present is to call attention to these gaps and cover some of the aforementioned issues in preliminary ways.

The Influence of "Methodological Nationalism"

Arguably, while works heavily influenced by "methodological nationalism" have advanced our knowledge of certain aspects of the process, they have also framed the study of the migration process in ways that tend to overlook its global and transnational dimensions. In their critical appraisal of the influence of this tradition in the social sciences, Andreas Wimmer and Nina Glick-Schiller define "methodological nationalism" as "the naturalization of the nation-state by the social sciences" and the corresponding understanding of "the web of social life" as being spun "within the container of national society."[7] Thus, methodological nationalism relies on the assumption that "countries are the natural unit for comparative studies," the tendency to "equate society with the nation-state," and the conflation of "national interests with the purpose of the social science."[8] In historiography, methodological nationalism has gone hand in glove with the propensity to narrate the history of societies through discrete events ("the history of events"[9]), although the later two propensities should not be confounded. Wimmer and Glick-Schiller further clarify that historically, methodological nationalism grew in the shadows of and fed political projects related to "the nationalizing of societies and states" and show how its influence has been widespread across Western societies since the twentieth century, shaping much of the production of knowledge about social phenomena in general and international migration in particular.[10]

Louis Pérez (1995a) and Nicola Miller (2003) shed light on the strong links between political nationalism and Cuban historiography. They explain that the entanglement of Cuba's historiography and social sciences and nationalist projects in politics grew strong during the republican period and that this link was further reinforced by the political conditions under which the revolution of 1959 unfolded. The link between historiography and "the national question" is acknowledged by Cuban historians. However, the argument that this trend corresponds mainly to Cuba's experience with different forms of extra-territorial domination[11] neglects the influence of methodological nationalism in western historiographies, the generalized propensity associated with it to narrate history (whether political or otherwise) as centered in the nation-state, and as Miller (2003) has suggested for the case of Cuba, the political value of the corresponding idea that the state is the main agent of change. As Glick-Schiller (1999) shows, this influence can be found in historiographies throughout the twentieth century as political nationalism, the formation of national identities, and methodological nationalism reinforced each other.

The study of international migration in the Caribbean and Cuba has been influenced by what is called "social history." Furthermore, it has also been molded by the tendency among students of the insular Caribbean to look at the particularities of these societies as part of broader social structures.[12] Báez Evertsz (1986) argues that this kind of analysis is taken to a higher level by Ramiro Guerra, whose work he cites as a forerunner of the dependency theory. To be sure, Guerra's invaluable contributions have constituted an important building block in Cuban historiography and offer a good example to illustrate both its advantages and limitations. However, even in cases in which such traditions have been embraced, the entanglements among historiography, nationalism, and methodology have not been erased. Guerra's influential *Sugar and Society in the Caribbean* is precisely a case in point. As is frequently noted, Guerra's insightful analysis of the sugar plantation in the Caribbean establishes important parameters for historical inquiries into the demographic processes, the social institutions, the forms of land tenure, and the labor exploitation systems that supported capitalist production in the Caribbean in relation to their external links. His work also sheds light on how the asymmetric relationship with the United States shaped structural imbalances in Cuba. However, his analysis does not escape the representation of these phenomena in a fragmentary way, spinning different colonial systems of social relations within "the container" of each society without attention to broader articulations.

In the case of international migration, his argument ultimately invokes the container model of society, explicitly characterizing "the U.S. economy" as "virtually closed." In the particular case of migration, he overestimates the role of U.S. customs in reaping "the savings" that immigration represented for "the Cuban economy": "When during this century [the twentieth century], *Cuba* managed to reduce production costs by obtaining higher yields, opening up new farm lands, giving less sugar in payment to the colono, and importing cheap labor from the other islands, all our savings disappeared in the United States customhouses" (Guerra 1964, 113). By focusing on the role of the two nation-states in forging the links between Cuba and the United States, in this account Guerra neglects the fact that tariffs were not the only, or even the main, mechanism through which labor migration to Cuba functioned as a vehicle for the transfer of value ("savings from imported cheap labor") from the island to the United States. Often most of the labor used in the sugar fields was not brought in "by Cuba," and the value added was not "Cuban" even before the products reached the United States. Most of Guerra's methodological premises and theoretical apparatus would be improved by the progress made by historical structural perspectives in the analyses on labor migration in Cuba and the Caribbean. Even by the time *Sugar and Society* was published, some influential Cuban intellectuals, including Fernando Ortiz, were also concerned with issues pertaining to the ways of understanding and narrating history as a result of complex social and economic processes that operated through social structures that transcended Cuban society. In an insightful account of the intellectual traditions that informed Fernando Ortiz's work, José Antonio Matos (1999) calls attention to the influence that not only Malinowski's anthropology but also Durkheim's structuralism and the French contributions to social history, including the emerging Annales school, had in Ortiz's explorations of Cuban society. Such background, Matos argues, allows Ortiz to criticize some Cuban historians' (including Guerra's) piecemeal approach to processes such as the formation of latifundia in Cuba and the propensity to miss the social relations in the agricultural sectors in their connection to broader processes, such as industrialization. In *Contrapunteo cubano del tabaco y el azúcar*, Ortiz criticizes the understanding of latifundia as the origin of the importation of cheap *braceros* (day laborers).[13] For Ortiz, both the import of cheap labor and latifundia were the result of the concentration processes under capitalism: "Land and braceros concentration," he argued, "are identical phenomena" that respond to the "capitalist concentration" that derives from Cuba's industrial development.[14] Ortiz's structuralist argument about the bracero phenomenon did not eliminate the "methodological nationalism" bias insofar as the new links that he emphasized did not imply a theoretical proposition about capitalism as a system structured beyond Cuba. However, he set important foundations in place to diminish such bias, as he starts unveiling the links between industrial processes and commercial networks that transcended Cuba and shaped immigration to the island, and the fusion of cultures (in the broad sense as ways of producing, speaking, behaving) that made up the Cuban nation as a result of an intense exposure to several migration streams. He prefers his concept of "transculturation" over "acculturation" (the dominant one in narratives on immigrant incorporation) to emphasize the rich cultural and material heritage that make up Cuban culture as a result of multiple transitions "from one culture to another," a process that involves the formation of a new quality instead of a linear process of assimilation to the dominant culture.[15] In this respect, Walter Mignolo (2000, 168) argues that Fernando Ortiz's concept invites us to explore cultural processes related to colonialism beyond racial considerations, which cannot be achieved through the concept of *mestizaje*, while allowing us "to map a complex, transcultured history instead of the homogeneous imagined community." However, he also notes that "national history, rather than the location of Cuba's history in the larger picture of the modern world system, was at the center of his concern."[16] Jorge Duany (1997) has forcefully argued that neither the concept of transculturation nor the associated image of "el ajiaco cubano" (the Cuban straw)—developed by Ortiz to characterize the mélange of cultures that make up Cuban society and its fluidity—has challenged the centrality of the notion of "national territory" in the way of rationalizing national identity and Cubanness, despite the fact that major political notions and projects about the Cuban nation have been constantly remade transnationally since the nineteenth century.

From a historical perspective, Ortiz's *Cuban Counterpoint* can also be read as a work on "the life and history," as Ortiz puts it, of the production of sugar and tobacco in Cuba, read in his case through the social relations, identities, systems of beliefs, and worldviews and the constructs related to them, and how all these were molded by and molded social structures over the long term. This kind of narrative, which found the highest aesthetic expression in *Cuban Counterpoint,* builds upon and further cements the tradition of narrating Cuban history in relation to "the history" of major products and resources: population, sugar, tobacco, and coffee. This legacy—which has been influential beyond Cuba as well—continues in several studies on specific groups of immigrants to the island in relation to the evolution of the demand for labor in major productive activities and related cultural processes.

Manuel Moreno Fraginals's *El ingenio* reflects an approach to the *durées* of Cuban products as a way of capturing Cuban history while it advances the understanding of labor migration in terms of accumulation and political processes that were not confined to Cuba. *El ingenio* provides detailed descriptions of the whole process of sugar production, from the technologies and social relations involved to the conditions for profit realization in the market, as part of the structures and dynamics of capitalism, a system that he understood in its global projection. His analysis of the structural changes leading to changes in how particular forms of labor exploitation were either promoted or transcended is particularly insightful for understanding the migration process. Moreno Fraginals, like other Cuban scholars concerned with social history, had exposure to the Annales school.[17]

In "The Absolution of History," Nicola Miller notes that the idea of narrating history as social history—as opposed to emphasizing prominent individuals, diplomatic history, military history, and other branches of political history that focus on discrete events and the role of states and individuals as the agents of historical transformation—had already made some inroads among influential Cuban historians who had been exposed to the Annales school. By the 1940s this trend had shaped not only scholarly works but also policies on how to teach history.[18] In addition, the studies of the structural aspects of underdevelopment under historical structural perspectives and world-systems analysis, a tradition that contains elements of the former and establishes a methodology and conceptual framework for the study of social processes and social change in relation to the world-systemic nature of capitalism,[19] were influenced by and would influence Cuban scholars. The impact of the above-mentioned traditions are noticeable in Cuban scholars working at the fringes of history and the social sciences, such as Moreno Fraginals, Pérez de la Riva, López Segrera, and Julio le Riverend, who have advanced our comprehension of the links between migration and other processes and social forces that articulated Cuba with the structures of capitalism.[20] This foundational thread—the inclination to see the structures of capitalism as globally and hierarchically organized, and the ability to see the imbrications between capitalism, colonialism and neocolonialism—places their works as an important gateway through which the *longue durée* conceptualization of history and world-systems analysis would have made significant inroads into historical narratives in Cuba. However, this legacy found a bumpy road on the island. Notwithstanding these antecedents and the growing global influence of the Annales school in the 1960s and 1970s, and world-systems analysis from the 1970s onward, Cuban scholars fell short of embracing critical thinking and holistic approaches with respect to the Cuban case in what Nicola Miller (2003) calls "a dialectical movement to the present" inclusive of the post-1959 periods. Miller suggests that this "dialectical movement to the present" was truncated because the new context of abundant anticapitalist rhetoric and orientation did not promote interest in Marxist methodologies: "The rich academic historiography produced by the many highly-talented Cuban historians working on the island under the revolutionary government has barely touched upon the post-1959 period. Virtually all available material has been written by academics and activists from abroad" (N. Miller 2003, 149). It is hard to overemphasize the influence that biases stemming from "methodological nationalism" in the context of Cuba's totalitarian system had in this outcome.

Methodological nationalism has also influenced scholars working in the United States. In the case of Cuban American scholars, it has been filtered through a new mode of rationalizing nationalism from exile in conjunction with the influence of discourses and research agendas that point to the links between migration and nationalist projects (as related to national security, to the political relations among ethnic minorities and between them and the dominant group, to immigrant incorporation understood mainly from the perspective of the container model of society, and to assimilation). The simultaneous influence in Cuba and the United States of two equally strong (albeit antagonistic) nationalist political agendas that until very recently had virtually prohibited all types of transnational ties among households and still constrain transnationalism has also contributed to the prevalence of methodological nationalism in the study of Cuban migration. Certainly, the very conditions that have encouraged this methodological orientation continue to shape our academic inquiries. Hence the issue is not whether a given inquiry is being permeated by some of the aspects of methodological nationalism, but to what extent the recognition of its limitations and the adoption of an alternative conceptualization of history and alternative methodologies allow us to overcome important biases and pitfalls introduced by the tradition in question and, in the process, move our inquiries forward.

The Global, Transnational, and Historical Perspectives

The Legacy of Historical Structuralism

Even though Cuban scholars interested in migration issues have not embraced world-systems analysis for the study of the Cuban case, Cuban American sociologist Alejandro Portes figures prominently among those scholars who advocate interrogating migration processes under the lens of world-systems analysis. In their seminal work *Labor, Capital, Class, and the International System*, published in 1981, Portes and North American scholar John Walton forcefully advocate the use of basic methodological premises and theoretical insights stemming from the world-systems perspective as an alternative to the modernization perspective in migration studies. They also see the potential of a focus on migration to improve world-systems analysis: "The lack of concern with concrete subprocesses has slowed down the application of the new general perspective [world-systems analysis] to specific research topics. There is at present a manifest disjuncture between general theory, where the world-system perspective has become dominant, and the myriad lower-level focused studies—national, local, and thematic—based on the earlier modernization model."[21] They define the purpose of their work as twofold: "first to explore the interface between labor processes, class structure, and the global requirements of accumulation as a necessary complement to the analysis of capital and dominant institutions," and "second by focusing on this interaction to clarify some of the apparent contradictions and bring the general models in line with empirical reality."[22] Although Portes's influential works on Cuban migration owe more to other traditions than world-systems analysis, his early works on undocumented migration, brain drain, and other aspects of the process were prominent among authors who did not fully embrace the world-systems perspective to the extent of becoming world-systems analysts yet effectively incorporated some of its core concepts and methodological assumptions in ways that led to a serious challenge to the paradigmatic assumptions of neoclassical economics and modernization theories in migration studies from the late 1970s and throughout the 1980s.[23] Rooted in methodological individualism, neoclassical economics and modernization theories ultimately examine migration as a product of cost and benefits calculations by individuals or their motivations, while migration is broadly understood as an equilibrium-restoring mechanism for markets or societies in general. One of the basic tenets of world-systems analysis is that capitalism is a global social system that comprises units (or social formations) that are functionally and hierarchically articulated through a dominant mode of production, a global division of labor, and core hegemonic projects that sustain the necessary institutional arrangements for the endless accumulation of capital.[24]

Such an understanding opens up new horizons for migration studies. Historical structural perspectives and world-systems analysis in particular further advance our understanding of how migration is bound and shaped by forces that operate over relatively prolonged periods of time through accumulation and geopolitical processes before they yield a given migration pattern.[25] In addition, the holistic methodology of world-systems analysis allows us to explore related structural processes and the interrelations of migration types, such as documented and undocumented migration, internal and international migration, and the mobility of manual workers and professionals, links that have been neglected in works influenced by the modernization theories.[26] However, Patricia Pessar (1997) emphasizes that while some "bimodal approaches" inherited from modernization theory were overcome under the new paradigmatic umbrella, the structural interpretation of the links between migration and global processes often created others, such as "the settler-sojourner model," while a tension still permeated the analysis of "historical structural processes" and "social agency." In relation to this, "the incorporation of the migrants" referred for the most part to the incorporation into the "host" or "receiving" society which neglected the transnational lifestyles developed by migrants. It has also been argued that migration continued to be reduced "to labor migration and migrants to workers, eliminating all discussion of the many different racial, ethnic, or national identities that shape people's actions and consciousness."[27]

The Transnational Perspective in Migration Studies

The transnational perspective in migration studies invites us to understand migration processes and the migration experience as the result of relationships, social repositioning strategies, interests, and identities that extend beyond the borders of particular societies usually identified with nation-states. The perspective in question focuses on people "who migrate and yet maintain or establish familial, economic, religious, political, or social relations in the country from which they moved, even as they also forge such relationships in the new state or states in which they settle."[28] It also calls our attention to the fact that the migrant's incorporation frequently implies "simultaneous incorporation" into two or more labor markets, political systems, and societies in general. Building upon this tradition, some authors have advanced the transnational perspective in migration studies from several disciplinary backgrounds. They have shed light on issues relevant to this study, such as those pertaining to the construction of identities, material transfers and the dissemination of norms and values across societies, political involvement, the development of transnational enterprises by migrants and the role of families and other collective actors in sustaining transnational social ties, among other issues.[29]

In migration studies, transnationalism is thus understood as "the process by which immigrants forge and sustain multi-stranded social relations" that connect localities and are bounded with the global capitalist system:

> When we join a global level of analysis with a scrutiny of particular histories of peoples . . . we can better understand the movements of labor at specific points in time. We are able to link the wave of migration into the advanced capitalist countries in the last twenty-five years to new forms of capital concentration and global investments. Although conditions of labor and production processes in core areas in certain respects are coming to resemble those in the peripheries, in developing an overview of the dynamics of global political processes, the terms "core" and "peripheral" still have a great deal of analytical power.[30]

The concept of transnational social fields is central to the transnational perspective in migration. The concept has its immediate antecedents in Pierre Bourdieu's use of the concept of "fields" (*champs*) as a way of addressing power relations when examining social relations in specific fields of action (*champs d'action*). In his usage, a social field is a site of conflict among individuals who are seeking to either preserve or modify their social positioning in general and social status in particular through means that may or may not challenge the status quo.[31] Building upon this and other traditions, anthropologist Nina Glick-Schiller has placed this concept at the core of the transnational perspective in migration studies. This perspective emphasizes that social networks constitute an important aspect of the morphology of social relations and how they are structured by and enable power relations that extend beyond the boundaries of nation-states. Norman Long argues that when examining the role and place of migrants in the development of transnational social fields, the researcher should also bear in mind that "central to the concept of networks and organizing practices is the concept of livelihood." The concept of livelihood "best expresses the idea of individuals and groups striving to make a living, attempting to meet their various consumptions and economic necessities, coping with uncertainties, responding to new opportunities, and choosing between various value positions." Building upon Sandra Wallman (1982), Long clarifies that the pursuit of livelihood has material, normative, and identity-building aspects, which include "wide-ranging interpersonal networks" and multiple activities in which people are typically engaged, including those that transcend the (nation-) state setting.[32]

The Cuban case serves to illustrate how the transnational livelihood and accumulation strategies of people who migrated worked synergistically (not without antagonisms) in the expansion of the social fields that tied Cuba with Spain and the United States in critical periods of Cuba's articulation with the structures of capitalism. Thus, the distinction between transnational livelihood and transnational strategies of accumulation is relevant because while the first reinforces the idea of migration as the exclusive realm of subjugated groups trying to make a living, the distinction sheds light on how the migration process can be structured by accumulation designs launched not only by corporations, states, and other actors that are easily identified as the power brokers of capitalism, but also by migrants themselves through their multiple class locations and social roles.

Another important aspect of migrants' involvement in transnational social fields explored in this work refers to "long-distance nationalism" or "a claim to membership in a political community that stretches beyond the territorial borders of a homeland," a claim of membership that "generates an emotional attachment that is strong enough to compel people to political action."[33] Understanding migration in relation to the pursuit of livelihoods, accumulation strategies, and political involvement in two or more societies sheds light on the formation and fluidity of identities and loyalties related to ethnicity, class, gender, political affiliations, and familial and economic strategies that were forged across the Atlantic and regionally by migrants arriving in Cuba or departing from the island at different historical junctures.

The people immigrating to or emigrating from Cuba since the inception of colonialism have systematically constituted a highly heterogeneous group in terms of social class, ethnic background, political affinities, gendered experiences, and their corresponding social positioning with respect to specific hegemonic projects. As the number of migrants and their origins and destinations increased, many more migrants and migrant families were actively involved in different social milieus and occupied different social positions, either simultaneously or throughout their lives, even across generations. While for some the migration experience was a source of upward mobility, others remained entrapped in a structural cycle of displacement characterized by lack of mobility or even downward mobility. Some enjoyed greater margins of freedom in choosing their migration paths; for others, their destinations were brutally forced upon them. Many migrants were engaged in political activities, transnational strategies of livelihood, or even large-scale capital accumulation and played a key role in the development of transnational social fields. Even for many slaves, some kind of direct involvement in transnational social fields eventually became part of their life experiences in Cuba. By tracing these nuances, this work seeks to shed light on how the social agency of the migrants resulted from and played into the building up of the structures of capitalism, colonialism, and imperialism, including counterhegemonic forces as they became involved in transnational social fields that linked Cuba with other areas of the Americas, Europe, and other regions of the world.

Notwithstanding their role in advancing our knowledge of migration through their critique of methodological nationalism and their emphasis on social agency, theoretical insights on migration and transnationalism within migration studies do not provide all the conceptual tools necessary for understanding the role and place of the migrants in the development of transnational social fields and in shaping the articulation of specific societies with others and with global structures. For starters, the efforts to overcome the shortcomings introduced by the emphasis of historical structural analyses on labor processes have neglected such processes. Recent studies have advanced our understanding of the involvement of migrants in transnational economic activities under the umbrella of economic sociology with an explicit interest in how migration relates to "global capital," but they have not engaged a coherent debate on labor-capital relations. The category of capital, understood as both means and expression of accumulation and also a social relation under capitalism as the dominant mode of production and a set of categories that are logically articulated with it, such as finance capital and alienation (to mention just two examples), has been excluded from the analyses stemming from this tradition. As a result, current debates on socioeconomic aspects of the migrants' transnational involvement have tended to emphasize the migrant as family member, member of a given ethnic group, or transnational entrepreneur. Yet they tend to neglect the migrants as workers—producers of value—and consequently miss the ways in which their labor is subsumed by capital. Social networks, not the structures of capitalism, tend to be emphasized as "the broader social structures" in which migration is embedded, while entrepreneurship, not labor, is narrated as the basic variable structuring the reproduction of the work force. There is even reluctance to examine remittances as monetary flows that are bound up with production processes, the maintenance and reproduction of the labor force, and the mobilization of labor and capital on a global scale. Concerning power relations, the migrants tend to be portrayed as transnational subjects that operate "from below" vis-à-vis "global capital" as purveyors of power relations. This perspective overlooks the nuances of power relations associated with labor-capital relations.

Alienation—a key concept for understanding the resulting impact of class relations on workers, including migrant workers—has been neglected as a result. Alienation refers to the separation of workers from their labor once the labor power is sold in the market. It means, Wennerlind (1995, 1–2) clarifies, "a process of human degradation" and "a strategic instrument in the valorization process," a process "that takes on a strategic role within the dynamics of class relations." This process is compounded by the physical separation of the migrant workers from their families for many years.

Marx defines alienation differently from other influential non-Marxist writers, such as Simmel and Hegel. For example, Simmel discusses alienation as part of his general interest in "the social and cultural preconditions and consequences of the emergence of the mature money economy" (Dodd 1994, 46). Thus, while alienation is also understood to be based on objectification, it refers to the irreversibility of alienation of culture associated with modern life (Harvey 1990; see also Dodd 1994). Broadly defined, it is understood as "instability, disorder and dissatisfaction" (Dodd 1994, 48). In Marx, the concept of alienation is central to his critique of capitalism (Mészáros 1970). Murray Smith emphasizes that in the Marxist paradigm, alienation is neither an anthropological condition that manifests across time and space (Hegel's formulation of alienation as the material objectification of human capacities) nor the representation of a tension between material and ideal, objectivity and subjectivity, which reaches a climax in modern life (Simmel's formulation). It represents a condition associated with specific relations of production that convey class antagonisms; labor belongs to others and, therefore, is external to the worker (Smith 1994, 113). Although Marx's concept of alienation does not emerge from his theory of value, it is one of its cornerstones, and as such, it is a part of a conceptual framework employed to examine the inner connections among accumulation, exploitation, human degradation, and labor reproduction under capitalism.

The Transnational Perspective in International Studies and Political Economy

The transnational perspective was first conceptualized in International Relations, or "international studies," in the early 1970s.[34] In contrast with the so-called state-centric perspective, which tends to focus on state-to-state relations, the scholars advancing the transnational perspective focus on the involvement of nonstate actors in political and cultural projects, economic transactions, social networks, value systems, and discursive practices that span borders; how such involvement relates to state agency; and how it shapes politics and political-economic processes within and beyond the confines of nation-states. Like any attempt to grasp complex patterns of social relations, the transnational perspective in international studies stems from several traditions. Some are inscribed into the "interdependence" framework,[35] while others stem from critical thinking in international studies and include a wide range of approaches from neo-Marxist to postmodern theories. Yet others theorize power relations from the fringes of political economy, political sociology, world-systems analysis, and critical international studies.[36]

Critical thinking on transnational relations in international studies and political economy is rooted in the Gramscian perspective. From this perspective, power is constructed as a "fluid social process," not one "determined" by the "accumulated capabilities" (such as the diplomatic or military capabilities) of the state. This constitutes a basic tenet of critical thinking in international studies:

> The Gramscian meaning of hegemony . . . joins the ideological and intersubjective element to the brute power relationship. In a hegemonic order, the dominant power makes certain concessions or compromises to secure the acquiescence of lesser powers to an order that can be expressed in terms of a general interest. It is important, in appraising a hegemonic order, to know both (a) that it functions mainly by consent in accordance with universalistic principles, and (b) that it rests upon a certain structure of power to maintain that structure. The consensual element distinguishes hegemonic from nonhegemonic world orders. It also tends to mystify the power relations upon which the order ultimately rests.[37]

This perspective also brings to our attention the interaction between state and nonstate actors in the building up of power relations transnationally by shedding light on the class dimension of transnational relations. It calls attention to the rationales involved in the rise of global hegemonies, and how they are constituted by a social continuum of inter- and intrastate approaches to leadership and dominance:

> World hegemonies . . . can only arise if the pursuit of power by states in relation to one another is not the only objective of state action. In fact, the pursuit of power in the inter-state system is only one side of the coin that jointly defines the strategy and the structure of states qua organizations. The other side is the maximization of power vis-à-vis

subjects. A state may therefore become world hegemonic because it can credibly claim to be the motor force of the general expansion of the collective power of rulers vis-à-vis subjects.[38]

This approach to hegemony is advanced by Giovanni Arrighi through his conceptualization of "the three hegemonies of historical capitalism" and their "systemic cycles of accumulation."[39] According to Arrighi, the global hegemonies of capitalism, successively led by the Netherlands, Britain, and the United States, have left specific imprints on the hierarchical structure of the interstate system, accumulation regimes, and the use of labor and its territorial mobility. Some of the main features of British hegemony, defined by Arrighi as "settler colonialism, capitalist slavery, and economic nationalism," and major aspects of U.S. hegemony, such as an extensive reliance on the transfers of labor and entrepreneurship from peripheral areas of the world to core areas, are particularly relevant for the historical analysis of migration in Cuba. Furthermore, Arrighi's "breaking down" of world capitalism into cyclical history or more "manageable units of analysis" than the world-system as a totality is relevant for understanding how specific systems of hegemony and accumulation cycles impacted the global flow of people. A caveat is necessary, though. This model, as its author acknowledges, "is not meant to tell us what goes on in the lower layers."[40] As way of closing this gap, this book supplements Arrighi's model with the insights stemming from political economy, international studies, and migration studies concerning hegemonic and counterhegemonic practices associated with the global expansion of capitalism as it has affected international migration.

The emphasis that the Gramscian approach to hegemony as derived from class conflict is important for the purpose of this analysis. However, it is also important to acknowledge the limitations of such an emphasis. Some works on transnational political involvement by migrants, advocacy groups, and so on have shed light on the manifold forms that power relations can take transnationally and the multiplicity of interests and social locations of the actors involved.

Other Approaches to Transnationalism and Power

In their pathbreaking work *Nations Unbound: Transnational Projects, Postcolonial Predicaments, and Deterritorialized Nation-States,* Linda Basch, Nina Glick-Schiller, and Cristina Szanton Blanc highlight alternative aspects of hegemony (broadly understood also as relations of dominance established through consensus) to improve our understanding of migration as the result of social agency that involves conflicts related to labor-capital relations as much as it involves tensions derived from the formation and fluidity of identities, the use of racial constructs, and cultural citizenship as part of "the political maneuverings" of state and nonstate actors to advance hegemonic and counterhegemonic agendas. Other approaches to transnationalism and power have shed light on how grassroots movements come into being and on how the voluntary associations and advocacy networks that are formed by the migrants to channel resources transnationally may lead to their empowering or may even have unintended consequences that put downward pressures on their economic and social status.[41] They also pinpoint how the "supranational" and the "national" are framed by "configurations of hegemonies" found in gender relations, social interaction within the household, the labor market, and other realms, or what feminist theory has termed "scattered hegemonies." Studies of how transnational practices shape or are shaped by gender identity, citizenship, and gendered exploitation, such as the use of women in the transnational sex market,[42] are also relevant for the purpose of this study, particularly for understanding the two major stages of the transnational sex trade that have dramatically affected Cuba: first, the transatlantic *trata de blancas* (white female trafficking) involving many European women, including Spaniards, and more recently the exploitation of migrant women, including Cubans, in transnational sex markets. Thus, as this work tries to emphasize, no single paradigm, author, or theory can account for the complex system of power relations associated with the transnational processes associated with migration.

The concept of hegemony in the Gramscian tradition as employed in critical thinking in international studies and world-systems analysis allows us to explore other dimensions of the power relations that have unquestionably impacted the migration process in Cuba in relation to global cycles of hegemony. The Foucauldian tradition, on the other hand, invites us to examine at close range the synergies between technologies of governing and subjects of power. For example, in her work on the Chinese diaspora, Aihwa Ong calls our attention to how the transnational strategies of the migrants involve "flexible" approaches to nationality and citizenship. She defines "flexible citizenship" as "the cultural logics of capitalist accumulation, travel, and displacement that induce subjects to respond fluidly and opportunistically to changing political-economic conditions." She further clarifies that "in their quest to accumulate capital and social prestige in the global arena, subjects emphasize, and are regulated by, practices favoring flexibility, mobility, and repositioning in relation to markets, governments and cultural regimes."[43] Although Ong draws her definition of flexible citizenship from the Chinese experience in the context of the current conditions of accumulation globally, I argue that the transnational involvement of Spanish and other migrants in Cuba and from Cuba showed that "flexible citizenship" was a feature of capitalism much earlier. As David Harvey reminds us, "the power nexus" formed by "the intersecting command of money, time, and space" was significantly altered with the expansion of trade and investment in conjunction with innovations in transport and communications in the second half of the nineteenth century.[44] These developments triggered social dynamics associated with transatlantic migration that were similar to what Ong calls today "flexible citizenship." Cuba and the United States together expanded after the end of Spanish colonial rule. The exploration of the Cuban case under the lens of the concept of "flexible citizenship" also leads us to ask whether and, if so, how this concept applies to the most recent context in which Cubans open up to "the cultural logics of capitalism" and the procurement of venues of social mobility and prestige and even capital accumulation increasingly account for the launching of transnational strategies among them.

For Michel Foucault, governmentality involved the transformation of the administrative state of the fifteenth and sixteenth centuries through the mutual conditioning of "sovereignty-discipline-government." This triadic relationship, he clarifies, "brings about the emergence of population as a datum, a field of government intervention, and as an objective of governmental techniques." The separation of the economy "as a specific sector of reality," the use of biopower as a direct (usually scientific) modality of control of the population by dividing it into biologically identifiable strata, the use of "a whole series of specific government apparatuses," and "the development of a whole complex of knowledges [savoirs]" for the purposes of controlling and disciplining the population are all constituents of what he calls "governmentality."[45] The bilateral context in which Cuban migration has taken place since 1959 operates through fields of governmentality that overflow specific societies. In her work on Cuban exiles, María de los Angeles Torres illustrates the systematicity and complementarity of the mechanisms of control established by the Cuban and the U.S. governments with respect to Cuban migrants and their links to the strategies of Cuban exiles for accessing symbolic and political capital through the formation of a dominant faction.[46] In congruence with this approach, it has been noted how certain discursive practices have ideologized the development of enterprises by Cuban Americans by presenting their "entrepreneurial proclivity" almost as a natural characteristic of the members of the group when referring to their incorporation as a success story, an observation that is also in tune with Ong's insights on the Chinese diaspora.[47] By the same token, the discourses deployed by the Cuban government have also tended to ideologize enterprise development by Cuban Americans by equating it with mafia behavior.

For half a century, both the U.S. and the Cuban governments have developed fields of governmentality that facilitate their capacity to control Cuban migrants and potential migrants. As I discuss in greater detail in Chapter 5, this context has led to the constant remaking of countercultural narratives and strategies of social repositioning that have been highly influenced by the transnational media and interpersonal relations. The regulatory interventions of the United States into the migration process in Cuba can be traced to the short, albeit important, period of direct military control of the island. By then the efforts to bring the former Spanish colony into tune with habits, norms, and interests that prevailed in the United States involved an unprecedented level of bureaucratization of the migration process. This included the inauguration of a processing and detention center in Havana, similar to the one in Ellis Island, and the extensive use of statistics for the administration, organization, and differentiation of the migrant population by race, occupation, and health status among other characteristics. The heavy-handed control of the migration in Cuba by U.S. bureaucrats reflected the manifold technologies of governing deployed to control the Cuban population through the enactment of laws and regulations that were advanced through narratives that equated Americanization with modernity and progress. These technologies of government were not applied exclusively in Cuba nor would they be applied only once. The handling of the *marielitos* in 1980 and the rafters during the rafter crisis of 1994 by the Cuban and the U.S. governments also illustrates at close range how migration becomes an important field of government intervention involving constructs for the purpose of exclusion and biopolitical methods as well.[48]

The Longue Durée *Conceptualization of History*

The transnational perspective represents a step forward in the attempt to overcome the constraints imposed by "methodological nationalism" on the understanding of migration as a global process. Nonetheless, even a comprehensive approach to transnationalism is no substitute for a global perspective:

rather, the two presuppose each other in the historical inquiry developed here. In this account, a comprehensive approach to transnationalism rooted in complementary approaches to power relations builds upon and nourishes a world-historical perspective.

The theoretical coherence of the *longue durée* conceptualization of history and recent developments in the study of transnational processes is shown with particular clarity in migration studies where scholars whose works have been influenced by world-systems analysis, mainly the basic tenet that migration occurs not as the resulting interactions between two societies exclusively but "as part of the internal dynamics of the same overarching unit" (Portes and Walton 1981, 29), have tended to embrace the transnational perspective as well. The works of Alejandro Portes, Nina Glick-Schiller, Saskia Sassen, and Ramón Grosfoguel, whose work explicitly builds upon Braudel's concept of *longue durée,* attest to this propensity. The propensity to bridge world-systems analysis—including an explicit emphasis on the concept of *longue durée* —with theoretical insights stemming from the transnational perspective is found also in works that do not theorize migration yet make significant contributions to its understanding as resulting from the synergy between structural and relational dynamics that work at several scales and temporalities (see, for example, Robinson 2003). World-systemic approaches to migration from within world-systems analysis have emphasized the importance of the concept of the *longue durée* in inquiries on migration. Ramón Grosfoguel's work has been instrumental in advancing migration studies under the lens of the *longue durée* by emphasizing how pervasive structures that are readily observable at a systematic level shape events and processes occurring in particular social formations and affecting specific social groups that operate in certain locations and even transnationally.[49] It is widely acknowledged that the incorporation of certain groups of migrants into labor markets and societies in general is usually affected by multiple "structural disadvantages." However, the *longue durée* conceptualization of history allows us to see that such disadvantages can be traced not only to domestic processes in the United States but also to several processes that include and transcend the specific society and time in which they are manifesting themselves and even manifest transnationally.[50] This approach to the incorporation of migrants relies on a greater sensitivity to the way incorporation is filtered through relations of domination and power regimes rooted in structures that operate systemically and over the long term. The concept of "coloniality of power" emphasizes precisely this aspect.

The concept "coloniality of power" (*colonialidad del poder*), as developed by Peruvian sociologist Anibal Quijano and further refined by Walter Mignolo, is explicated as a global pattern of power that controls labor and its products, gender relations, and many other aspects of social life and has advanced our understanding of the interplay of capitalism, colonization, and modernity as mutually reinforced projects.[51] Like the postmodern and feminist approaches to power that have built upon the Foucauldian tradition, this approach to power relations also emphasizes the role of discourses on race, gender, and culture in shaping ideologies and imaginaries that sustain relations of domination, although the concept "coloniality of power" emphasizes "the recognition of the colonial difference from subaltern perspectives."[52] This conceptualization of power is relevant for the study of international migration and particularly the Caribbean experience, since it sheds light on how a global pattern rooted in colonial structures, including its symbolic aspects, has affected Caribbean migration and the migrants' experiences, the centrality of the "racialization" and "Africanization" of some immigrant groups, and their incorporation into labor markets and society in general.[53] A complement to this line of reasoning is found in postmodernist and feminist narratives on colonialism, modernity, and imperialism, which tend to unveil the nuances of this triad. From this perspective, "colonialism" is not explicated in opposition to modernity but as "a modernist institution, fundamentally a practice ... of producing modern citizen-subjects in metropoles as well as colonies."[54] Concepts such as "culture," "race," and "sexuality" are at the core of the designs of policies related to modernity, colonialism, and imperialism.[55] These approaches tend to rely (either explicitly or implicitly) on a reading of the conceptualization of the *longue durée* that emphasizes the links between the current situation of racialized groups, including members of the migrant population, in relation to colonial and transnational experiences.

Braudel emphasizes "the dialectic of duration" as well as the limitations of choosing a single path when narrating history: "For me, history is the total of all possible histories—an assemblage of professions and points of view, from yesterday, today and tomorrow. . . . The only error, in my view, would be to choose one of these histories to the exclusion of all others."[56] His explanation of the concept of *longue durée* shows a theoretical distance from totalizing linear narratives. This becomes more apparent when he explains that the concept of *longue durée* conveys two interrelated meanings. On the one hand, it refers to the idea of the "permanence of particular systems" (which includes, for example, "the entire lifetime of the capitalist system" and even "civilizations"). On the other hand, *longue durée* refers to a particular approach to history: a way of examining history "as a long duration" by looking at historical time through "the breaking down of history" into "successive levels" to account for "the multiplicity of time."[57]

Braudel's conceptualization breaks down the *durées* into the "short time span," the "cycle," the "intercycle," and the *longue durée*. The "short time span . . . [is] proportionate to individuals, to daily life, to our illusions, to our hasty awareness."[58] There is "the conjuncture . . . the cycle, and even of the 'intercycle,' covering a decade, a quarter of a century and [beyond]."[59] And there is the *longue durée*, which "cuts across the most diverse societies, worlds, and psyches . . . the old habits of thinking and acting, the patterns which do not break easily."[60] The assertion that the value of explanations "depends fairly heavily" on their "implied duration"[61] is important for the analysis of the processes and social forces that shape migration. Building upon Braudel, Immanuel Wallerstein has argued that the cycles of history represented in *l'histoire conjoncturelle* can operate through "the cyclico-ideological TimeSpace."[62] The concept of "cyclico-ideological TimeSpace" emphasizes not only "cyclical time, the times of alternating rhythms" in historical accounts, but also "ideological space." By "ideological space" Wallerstein means "a division of the world that is political, military, cultural, and above all ideological." By using the "East-West" coordinates as a particular case, he further clarifies that such alternating rhythms "are explained by, and in turn explain, major economic, political, and social thrusts that are in some sense 'medium term' in time span."[63]

Giovanni Arrighi's conceptualization of the three hegemonies of capitalism and their corresponding accumulation cycles is built upon the notion of *l'histoire conjoncturelle* (or "cyclical history") and, like Wallerstein, he also clarifies that the representation of "cycles" and "inter-cycles" do not have to have the same durations; some may stretch over several decades, and others over a century, yet all have distinctive economic, geopolitical, or ideological traits that provide continuity.[64] These approaches provide a sense of global and regional contextuality that allows us to examine not only migration patterns but also what have been called "patterned migrations" by focusing on how regional and global geopolitical and ideological configurations can shape migration simultaneously in different societies and their transnational activities.[65] This kind of analysis can also be found in Grosfoguel's abovementioned works on migration in the Caribbean and his contribution to the analysis of the "global logics" of Caribbean urban structures, which shed light on processes affecting Caribbean migrants by building upon the concepts of *longue durée* and cyclical history in relation to global geopolitical and ideological configurations in conjunction with transnational practices and identities. Arrighi's conceptualization of global hegemonies and systemic cycles of accumulation—which further advances world-systems analysts' contributions to the study of Kondratieff-style global cycles—is relevant for the study of systemic processes affecting global patterns of accumulation in relation to migration.

The understanding of migration in relation to capital accumulation requires specification of the functions of the social formations in the periphery and the core in relation to the international division of labor, and even the phases specific regions and societies go through in the organization of production processes, the specific types of labor supply systems employed and their interrelations, and so on.[66] Sassen-Koob (1980) offers a typology of the ways in which historical cases of major labor imports relate to stages in the global expansion of capitalism. She identifies four ways in which this process takes place. First, the capitalist mode of production expands in the periphery by producing the surplus value there. The historical cases she places under this category are the production of coffee and tea in Ceylon (currently Sri Lanka) for international markets, which led to massive immigration from southern India; the import of slaves to the sugar plantations of the Caribbean, the slaves' transformation into free laborers, and the subsequent import of indentured laborers from India; and the import of African slaves to work in the plantations and mines in Brazil who would be replaced by waged labor, including free laborers from Southern Europe (mainly Italy), who tended to work in the coffee plantations, which they often alternated with their work on their small parcels. All of these cases illustrate how the redistribution of the workforce within peripheral areas of the world economy played a role in the transfer of surplus value to core areas. Workers from distant tribes who worked in the plantations and mines of Africa also fall into this category. Her second type refers to labor imports associated with intense accumulation in the periphery and offers the example of large-scale labor imports in the United States from the late nineteenth century to the early twentieth century as a typical example. What distinguishes this type from the previous one, Sassen-Koob explains, is that massive imports of labor were associated with large-scale accumulation and not surplus value transfers to the center. The third type refers to labor imports associated with intensive accumulation in core areas, and the examples given are the import of Irish workers to England, which had reached a peak by 1850, and the import of labor by the most advanced economies of Europe after World War II. And the fourth she accounts for is large-scale immigration of workers not so much related to expansive cycles of accumulation but to the dominance of capital over labor, which facilitates profit making in some firms and serves as a cushion against unfavorable cyclical trends.[67]

In addition to its methodological value as an illustration of how intermediate processes affect the link between capital accumulation and labor migration, Sassen-Koob's typology has theoretical value for the study of international migration in Cuba in relation to capital accumulation. The Cuban case confirms the importance of distinguishing the dual role that migration in and from the periphery has had in accumulating processes in core areas. Thus, the different types of forces that shape migration through cyclical history are interrelated in real life. However, our theoretical understanding of how they operate has benefited from different theoretical emphasis. For example, the following works, among others examined here, have made significant theoretical contributions to the understanding of how productive and specialization cycles affect the demand for imported labor, the incorporation of the migrants, and, in general, the relocation of labor throughout the world economy: Amin 1974, Wallerstein 1974, Sassen-Koob 1980, Portes and Walton 1981, Richardson 1989, and Robinson 2003. Cuban historiography and studies specifically devoted to international migration have advanced our theoretical understanding on how the above links have worked in this particular case. See, for example, López Segrera 1973, Le Riverend 1974, de la Riva 1975, Moreno Fraginals 2001, García Alvarez 1990, among others. Yet other works, some of which have addressed the Cuban case, have shed light on how cycles of violence, regime change, shifts in global hegemonic designs, and ideological reconfigurations have affected migration and the incorporation of the migrants. See, for example, Pedraza-Bailey 1985, Loescher and Scanlan 1986, Bach 1988, Deive 1989, Zolberg, Suhrke, and Aguayo 1989, Domínguez 1992, Mitchell 1992, and Grosfoguel 1999b.

Understanding specifically how capitalism and its "global logics of accumulation" and patterns of power frame the territorial mobility of people throughout the world—and that, as neo-Marxist approaches tend to emphasize, international migration is inherent in patterns of core-periphery specialization that are inclusive of multiple societies—requires understanding of the multiple rationales, scales, and temporalities involved in the shape of these links. This calls for understanding the complex, often contradictory roles and interests that the actors involved in these dynamics, including the migrants, play in the social history of capital. The term "migrants" signifies a heterogeneous group of people that, under capitalism, has historically included not only members of the working class, colonized, racialized, and subjugated groups in general, but also members of the capitalist class and other dominant strata of society. The role of migrants has not been limited to that of providers of cheap labor. The migrants have historically played multiple roles in the expansion of capitalism through their involvement in labor, trade, investment, monetary and cultural flows across societies, and through their political involvement.[68] By building upon the perspectives discussed in this chapter, this study invites exploration of these issues at close range, and sheds further light on the role of international migration in Cuba in the social history of capital.

TWO

Accumulation, Colonialism, Modernity, and Imperial Rivalry

Seen retrospectively, the interval between the arrival of the first European expeditions on American shores and the transformation of the Caribbean into what Ramiro Guerra called an "imperial frontier" was not long. The establishment of the Caribbean as an imperial frontier has been linked to what is called "the first modernity," or a historical process that condenses the material, symbolic, and intersubjective aspects of the expansion of European powers "through world hegemonies" which were built upon the economic basis "of the modern world system," in conjunction with "the Indian Question" and the establishment of the institution of slavery in the Americas.[1] The foundations of the imperial interventions and colonial histories in the Americas had a turning point when by conquering Jamaica, England "broke up the Spanish design to control the entire Caribbean" and reached new stages as other European powers made significant inroads into the Caribbean.[2] The imperial designs and the accumulation paradigms associated with them yielded several forms of land tenure, various labor exploitation systems and productivity paradigms, patterns of exploitation of natural resources, and multiple kinds of commercial activities that pointed to both unity and difference across the insular Caribbean. The complex, traumatic, and gradual articulation of these societies with the global structures of capitalism of which they were key constitutive elements filtered through cultural paradigms, such as those that encompassed the imposition of European languages and the resulting emergence of bilingualism and multilingualism, the use of pidgins, the evolution of Creole languages, and patterns of "language asymmetry" as reflections of hegemonic and counterhegemonic practices. It is upon these historical foundations that Cuba is drawn with particular intensity to "the

Atlantic economy" (Braudel), "the Black Atlantic" (Gilroy), and other geosocial axes of the modern capitalist world-system as colonialism made its inroads into the island under the Spanish rule.[3]

Early Colonial Society and Migration

Although Spanish expeditions reached Cuba as early as 1492 and then 1494, the first expedition sent for the purpose of conquering the island arrived in 1510, from the neighboring island of Hispaniola. Sooner rather than later the indigenous inhabitants were subdued, and several strategic points along the coast fell under Spanish control. By 1513, the Spanish monarchs had already instituted the first sets of rights and obligations of the Spanish settlers and established specific procedures for dealing with the conquered populations.[4] Those early years brought about an exodus that has been characterized by Leví Marrero as the first waves of "refugees," as the atrocities and disruptions induced by the Spanish conquerors forced part of the indigenous population to seek safety within Cuba away from the occupied territories, and in neighboring islands. Tens of thousands died in the confrontations with the Spaniards, from exposure to diseases and other causes, including a drastic reduction of fertility levels associated with the brutality of what has been represented as "the encounter." It has been estimated that by 1542, there were fewer than one thousand indigenous inhabitants remaining on the island, a significant population loss when contrasted with the estimated 127,000 inhabitants Cuba had in 1512.[5] It has been argued that much earlier than 1542, the Spanish authorities had shown concern about the rapid depopulation of the island, and the crown had authorized the introduction of 1,000 African slaves and Indians from Yucatan.[6] Bishop Sarmiento, a Spanish bishop brought to Cuba by Hernando de Soto, reported that only 1,749 inhabitants were counted in the six major population settlements in 1544: 112 Spaniards, 744 African and Indians slaves, and 893 Indians.[7] In any event, the growth of the population at that time was nothing compared to its decline.

The population decline of the early colonial period was not counterbalanced by the slow arrival of certain groups, among them official representatives of the Spanish crown, Spanish subjects in search of new opportunities, African slaves, Indians brought through the Mexican port of Campeche as slaves (which intensified during the period of gold extraction, circa 1511–24), women who were said to be traveling "on their own" or "escaping from their husbands" ("huidas de sus maridos"), as the governor of the island put it in

1578, members of the clergy, and prisoners of war.[8] Although different groups settled in the island, for most of the sixteenth century Cuba was used by the Spaniards as a transient point in a path that took them either to other areas of America as new sources of wealth were discovered, or on their way back to Europe, while others did not stay longer than the time necessary to service the fleets.[9] Strategies involving transatlantic mobility and/or involvement in economic and political projects that transcended Cuba were not that infrequent among the free immigrants even during the early colonial period. This issue will be addressed later on.

Pérez de la Riva (2004, 100) estimated that in the seventeenth century, Cuba's population grew from ten thousand to fifty thousand inhabitants. In a recent estimate, de la Fuente (2008, 107) indicates that the city of Havana had a population of between seven and ten thousand in 1610. Similarities and discrepancies in the estimates involving migration abound in the literature because it is impossible to accurately estimate the portion of the population movements that took place without documentation and to assess the accuracy of what documentation does exist. Issues of methodology matter also. However, if we disregard the issue of precise estimates and focus on the trends, we can see that population estimates suggest certain socioeconomic dynamism throughout the seventeenth century, when immigration grew at a greater pace, yet not quickly enough to make up the population lost during the previous century.

The demographics of the city of Havana spoke of the relative economic dynamism experienced during the last decades of the sixteenth century and into the first years of the seventeenth century. Alejandro de la Fuente indicates that "as early as 1575 one of the town's *alcaldes* [mayors] reported that Havana was 'much grown' in terms of population and that each year the fleets brought many more people to it," and that "in 1602 the town council not only reported that the city had experienced 'very rapid growth' during the previous eight years but confidently asserted that it was going to grow even more in the near future" (2008, 107). Concerning immigration, after a period of stagnation or even decline between 1540 and 1550, the arrival of Europeans, mainly Spaniards, increased between 1585 and 1610. Of them, 77 percent are estimated to have come from Spain. The three main sources of Spanish immigrants were Andalusia (41.8 percent of the total number of people from Spain), the Canary Islands (23.5 percent), and Castile (14.4 percent). Catalonians, one of the main groups of immigrants in the years to come, represented at the time a modest 2.1 percent of all Spanish immigration to the city (ibid., 87). As for the African slave population, it went "from a few hundreds in the mid-1580s" to more than four thousand in 1610 (ibid., 103).

The seventeenth century was still part of the formative period of Cuba's articulation with the Atlantic economy as a strategic colony for the Spanish crown, yet several interwoven developments impacted the demographic trends, such as the growing importance of the port economy, the service economy related to it, the island's growing strategic role for Spain's defensive system, and the gradual growth of agricultural production and a division of labor that simultaneously differentiated and integrated the port economy, agricultural activities, and craft making and emerging forms of manufacturing that reinforced the formation of an incipient urban economy in the most prominent towns.[10] Even though the Spanish colonies, including Cuba, did not experience the "sugar boom" that some of the British and French colonies experienced in the mid-seventeenth century nor the types of productive links associated with the production of tobacco that the colonies of rival powers had developed earlier, the demand in Spanish markets and smuggling toward other markets acted as incentives for the production of these two products in Cuba at that time.[11]

Throughout the seventeenth century and for most of the eighteenth century, African slaves were introduced at an increasing pace and Spaniards continued to arrive. Despite the restrictions on migration to the colonies that had been imposed by the Spanish crown, which excluded people based on their regional and national origins, religion, etc., Spanish Catholic subjects from various regions of Spain and groups that did not fit the desired classifications, such as nationals from other European areas, Muslims, and Jewish migrants, settled in Cuba at that time under various provisions of the existing rules and frequently by giving up (or pretending to give up) their religious beliefs and embracing the Catholic faith. Immigration continued to grow gradually with the increasing demand for labor. In that period, the production of sugar did not have the status of Cuba's "produit moteur"—that is, the product with the greatest impact on social relations of production, labor-capital relations, the creation of wealth, and the formation of stratification systems—and its role in propelling immigration was very limited. The demand for imported labor and entrepreneurship and the arrival of administrators and members of the military grew instead in relation to various types of economic activities and geopolitical developments that started to underscore Cuba's growing articulation with and vulnerability to the world-system.[12]

Immigration: The Centrality of Havana

Originally known as La Villa de San Juan Cristobal de la Habana, the settlement that led to what is now the city of Havana was established in 1514 on the southern coast of the island. It was moved to the northern coast in 1519 to take advantage of the newly discovered Gulf Stream. Havana had become the de facto capital of Cuba by 1553, although the Spanish crown did not officially designate it a city until 1592, or recognize it as Cuba's capital until 1607.[13] By the end of 1515, the Spaniards had already founded several towns in Cuba—Baracoa, Bayamo, Trinidad, Sancti Spiritus, and Santiago de Cuba—all of which would become important cities in the future, albeit of different positions in the urban structure and in terms of their respective global projections. They had been founded close to rivers in the expectation that gold would be found in addition to the need to have access to drinkable water. The first villas were intended to function as nodes in the commercial networks that linked Spain and its territories in the Americas and to perform security functions as well. Commercial activities, service functions linked to the maintenance of the fleets, agricultural activities associated with the production of tobacco, sugar, and other crops, and cattle raising were the main sources of subsistence for the newly formed towns. As the few gold mines available were depleted by about 1525, copper, which was abundant in the eastern part of the island, became another source of wealth.[14]

The vulnerability of Havana to pirate and corsair attacks soon worked against the growth of the incipient urban settlements and Cuba's demographic growth in general. In 1537, 1538, and 1555, Havana was plundered and razed by French corsairs and pirates and suffered other attacks. However, after a period of net population loss followed by slow recovery, Havana's population grew to become the epicenter of the promising demographic pace exhibited by the island between 1580 and 1620, which ultimately reflected the city's growing strategic importance for imperial Spain. By the mid-sixteenth century, the Spanish monarchs had already assigned a number of functions, mostly administrative, commercial, and military in nature, to Havana. Among the strategic constructions for economic and defensive purposes was the construction of Havana's aqueduct, La Zanja, which was completed in the last decade of the sixteenth century. La Zanja supplied water to the fleets and the garrisons in addition to the comfort it brought to the service economy in general. A church, convents, and other public facilities were built during the sixteenth century or their construction started at that time while private residents' applications for construction permits had also increased. After the attack of 1538, Spain ordered the construction of a fortress in Havana, which resulted in the Fortaleza de la Fuerza Vieja, completed circa 1540. The construction of a series of fortresses would follow after another major attack, launched by Jacques de Sores in 1555, reduced the town to ruins. A major fort, Castillo de la Real Fuerza, was completed in 1577; the fortresses Castillo San Salvador de la Punta and Castillo de los Tres Reyes del Morro were completed circa 1630. The fortresses of La Chorrera and Cojímar (both finished by circa 1646), San Lázaro (circa 1665), and La Muralla, "the Wall," a defensive wall around the city, the construction of which ended in the eighteenth century, literally cemented the central role of Havana in the Spanish transatlantic trade, naval, and military systems. The fortress San Carlos de la Cabaña (1763–74), the Aróstegui Castle (also known as the Castle of the Prince, circa 1767), and the fortress of Atarés (1763–67) were added to the defensive system after the occupation of Havana by the British in 1762.[15]

Spain had also built fortresses and public facilities in other major bay areas by the end of the century, although not at the same pace. Santiago de Cuba, where Spaniards had found abundant copper mines, reinforced its strategic military role in the beginning of the seventeenth century when the British, the Dutch, and the French started to aggressively look for possessions in the Caribbean. Havana, Santiago, Matanzas, and other port areas offered a maritime base and the supplies needed by the fleets that carried precious metals and other products from Spanish America to continue the long journey to the Iberian Peninsula. In addition, they supplied the fleet and kept it apprised of the comings and goings of smugglers and pirates. Equally relevant for Spain, they also reinforced the defensive capacity of Florida, a strategic zone in its own right, as a deterrent to the British southward expansion in North America. The port and, in general, the city of Havana were at the core of all these strategic functions.[16]

By the early 1620s, the port of Havana functioned as "the prime center of shipbuilding in the Americas . . . where an increasing proportion of the Spanish fleet was being built" and "a nodal point" in the emerging global shipbuilding commodity chain.[17] As the port economy and the urban economy continued to expand, more Spaniards were drawn toward Cuba's port areas. Even though shipbuilding had some ups and downs from the seventeenth to the nineteenth centuries, Cuba's shipyards were highly regarded in the Atlantic economy: "Beginning in the 1720s Havana built more durable ships more cheaply than any port in Spain. Indeed the revival of the Spanish navy in the early eighteenth century owed much to the success of the Havana *astillero* [shipyard]."[18] The expansion of shipbuilding and the constant refurbishing of the arriving vessels, among other activities associated with the port economy, the development of certain types of agricultural production linked to the internal demand and some for external markets, and the gradual growth of the urban economy in general increased the demand for factors of production, including labor. As mentioned before, the number of people from the fleets and transients in general could be significantly high in Havana in certain periods. Even though they were neither immigrants nor producers, as consumers and merchants they played a key role in activating the economy of the city and of intraregional exchanges within Cuba. Toward the end of the seventeenth century, local groups linked to the production of tobacco and the port economy (either through formal operations with territories under Spanish control or through smuggling operations with the British islands) provided some of the sources of credit that further backed these economic activities.[19] The expansion of backward and forward linkages between the port economy and other types of economic activities was of key importance for the growing demand for imported labor. Angel Bahamonde argues that "the port economies and their impact on urban services made up the set of economic factors that attracted immigration flows from Spain" (1992, 110; my translation). He notes that Havana offered Spain "a more dynamic, aggressive, and cosmopolitan trade context than the one working in the metropolis" since "the ports [of Cuba] meant openness, connections, and contacts with other more developed commercial environments, such as the British." Bahamonde further argues that eventually, immigration from Spain to Cuba would help forge "the largest part of the Spanish overseas economic elite" (120; my translation).

There was no unitary form of labor exploitation; the wage regime and the slavery regime coexisted with other modalities of labor exploitation, such as the use of indentured laborers. The economic activities and defensive projects launched during the first centuries of the colonial period relied on a combination of labor sources that included slaves, the *negros horros* (free blacks), prisoners of war, and Spanish workers, among others. Given the incipient development of the production of sugar, the slavery system in Cuba remained weakly articulated with the slave trade circuits that linked other areas of the Caribbean with Europe.[20]

Throughout the seventeenth century, in addition to the introduction of slaves and manual laborers from Spain and other areas, entrepreneurs, artists, architects, and other professionals arrived at the island more regularly, either to settle there or to work for a period of time, and contributed to the construction of churches, housing, fortresses, and the overall expansion of Havana's architectural environment and service infrastructure. By the end of the seventeenth century, the economic position of local producers and merchants had strengthened, and the most powerful groups imitated European elites in their choice of lifestyle and their consumption of ostentatious material goods. As the eighteenth century advanced, not only the *criollos* and their descendants (the *rellollos*) but also immigrants of different socioeconomic backgrounds were claiming and appropriating greater economic, social, and political spaces within the colonial structure as Havana's cultural projection transcended the confines of the island. Even African-origin groups, despite the inhuman conditions and forms of discrimination and prejudice they were subjected to, were finding ways to culturally and socially express their resistance through the development of associations and their greater participation in the urban economy, even as operators of small enterprises, as much as the limitations of Cuba's slave society would permit. Havana experienced significant social and cultural dynamism, much of which was related to the consolidation of the Creoles and their descendants as a distinct social group with a class of increasing economic affluence and political voice. The contributions made by African slaves and Spanish and other immigrants to Cuba's society extended beyond the economic realm yet within the social limitations and contradictions of a slave society.[21] Plazas, *paseos,* theaters, and other recreational and cultural facilities; the first university; technical and art schools; churches and medical institutions; and exorbitant mansions for the *negreros* (those involved in slave trafficking) were built during the eighteenth century. It also became increasingly appealing for wealthy Creoles to travel or to study and live abroad for a number of years, which further connected the elite with the flows of ideas and ideologies and productive and social paradigms in vogue in Europe. Havana was the epicenter of these dynamics. It is in Havana that the first printing shop in Cuba was opened in 1734, presumably by Carlos Habeé, a French national. *La Gaceta de la Habana,* Cuba's first daily newspaper, was founded in 1782. Havana also had the service infrastructure necessary for the organization of the first census in 1774, and the Sociedad Económica Amigos del País (SEAP), was founded in 1793, replicating a model already implemented in Spain and some of its colonial possessions.[22] Throughout its existence during the colonial period, influential Creole and Spanish intellectuals and other members of the elite with alternative points of view on several issues, from technological innovation in the sugar industry to medicine, trade, and immigration policy, participated in the debates, which were frequently published in periodicals that enjoyed significant prestige among professionals and intellectuals. Like similar institutions in other colonial societies, SEAP was influenced by Eurocentric ideas about the role of science and technology in social progress.[23]

Thus, an intellectually and politically alert city with a busy port and growing cosmopolitan flair was being built on the shoulders of the slaves, the *negros horros,* and other subjugated groups, including segments of the immigrant population, upon the foundations of a highly stratified society. A French visitor to Havana captured the shocking contrasts of the city in a moving way: "I came back full of worries with my unhappy thoughts. That contrast between el Paseo and the *barracones,* that opposition between extreme wealth and extreme poverty, such a proliferation of material goods at the expense of the sweat and tears of so many unlucky ones, all that confusion of pleasure and hurt, of pride and abjection, of justice and injustice, of mildness and ferocity. They all nourished my imagination and filled my soul with sinister impressions."[24] Cuba's capital reflected by then in a vivid way the complex synergy among accumulation, imperial designs, colonialism, slavery, and modernity. This synthesis would reach a climax with the emergence of sugar as Cuba's "produit moteur."

By the end of the eighteenth century, the production of sugar and tobacco was not only highly profitable but also culturally emblematic—and a magnet for immigration. Cuban historians, inspired by Fernando Ortiz's classic work *Cuban Counterpoint,* have tended to emphasize that these two products, sugar and tobacco, had an external orientation not only because for the most part they were produced for world markets but also because they relied heavily on imported labor. Immigration increased dramatically in the last decades of the eighteenth century and in the early nineteenth century because of the expansion of the production of sugar for the world market and the arrival of people escaping different waves of political turmoil. The growing articulation of Cuba with transatlantic and regional labor, commercial, and investment circuits spurred significant demographic and urban changes in Cuba in general and transformed Havana into one of the faster-growing urban areas in the Americas. This trend was not unique to Cuba, although its "efficient causes" were. Other Latin American societies whose economies became major nodal points in the articulation of the region with the Atlantic economy experienced similar demographic growth: "The incorporation of the Atlantic Coastline with world commercial currents favored the development of real urban nuclei. Thus, Havana, Caracas, and Buenos Aires, trading centers in developing export zones, grew phenomenally."[25] By the time most of Latin America had achieved independence, Havana was the region's third-largest city. This rank in the urban structure of the region is impressive if we take into consideration the size of Cuba compared to the other countries where the major cities were located. According to census data, Havana's population in 1817 was approximately 84,000 inhabitants. This meant that it was surpassed only by Mexico City (168,846 by 1820) and Rio de Janeiro (135,000 by 1822), and was followed by Buenos Aires (55,416 by 1822) and Caracas (42,000 by 1812).[26] By that time, the infrastructure of the city and its social life were growing in complexity as a result of the unprecedented economic dynamism generated by the sugar industry.

The first steamboat arrived in Havana in 1819; in 1837 the railroads expanded the connections of the city with eastern and southern areas of the island. These two developments were crucial for the expansion of the economy and the increase in the demand for labor. While these innovations facilitated urban growth and the integration of the rural and the urban sectors of the economy, the social relations of production in which their workings were embedded also boosted territorial inequalities as the concentration of capital, wealth, and prestige gravitated toward the western part of the island, and within it, Havana.[27] The most impressive demographic dynamics resulting from immigration took place in the western part of Cuba, which reportedly had 408,537 inhabitants in 1827 (Havana and Matanzas were the most dynamic areas within this region), while the eastern part had only 131,453. The population grew 27 percent between 1817 and 1827 in the west, but only 3.6 percent in the east for the same period.[28] The destination of the migrants reflected and further emphasized existing spatial inequalities as Havana absorbed most of the external and internal immigrants throughout the nineteenth century. The origins of the inequalities between Havana and the rest of the island can be traced to structural gaps that originated much earlier yet were cemented during the expansion of the sugar industry.[29]

Imperial Rivalry, Anticolonial Struggles, and Migration

Endless Accumulation and Conquest

When greediness prevails in the pursuit of wealth, violence, exercised either through the use of brute force or through symbolic means, becomes intrinsic to the process. The enslavement of Africans to force them to work in the plantations of the Americas is one of such moments in which capital accumulation and violence become intertwined with particular intensity. Other groups were also forced into Cuba to meet the requirements of endless accumulation. They were forced in "by the circumstances" and saw their lives languishing year after year without much hope for their future and that of their families, some members of which they would never see again. In this respect, violence was always already intrinsic to the migration experience. However, violence directly linked to political turmoil drove tens of thousands of people in need of protection to Cuban shores while a number of people were driven away from the island for similar reasons.

The tensions between the Spanish and the Dutch were instrumental for the consolidation of Dutch hegemony and the subsequent establishment of the modern interstate system and the furthering of long-distance financial and commercial networks.[30] Such rivalry was transplanted to the Caribbean with particular intensity. Kennedy (1987) and Arrighi (1999) argue that the United Provinces of the Netherlands, whose moral authority in Europe and military strength owed much to its thirty-year struggle for independence from Spain—a process that culminated with the Peace of Westphalia of 1648—managed to keep Spain under constant check not only in Europe but also in the Caribbean. The French and the British, "latecomers" in the colonial enterprise in the Americas, would soon challenge the Spanish, Portuguese, and the Dutch by developing their own technologies of imperial expansion and colonial control. The British, Arrighi further argues, carried out the endeavor through the establishment of a global pattern of "settler colonialism, capitalist slavery, and economic nationalism," no element of which, he clarifies, they invented. Forms of settler colonialism and the use of slaves in the colonies to cope with the demand for labor were common practices of the Spanish and the Portuguese in their colonial possessions. Conversely, some of the institutional aspects of economic nationalism, Arrighi clarifies, had a direct antecedent in the provisions of the Treaty of Westphalia and the resulting norms regulating the rights of governments over their exclusive possessions and the protection of property and commerce in time of war. A remote antecedent can be found in some of the practices and norms of the Italian system of city-states. Yet the British took the core practices associated with settler colonialism, slavery, and economic nationalism to a systemic level and transformed them into structural features of their accumulation regime on a world scale, although important heterogeneities persisted in terms of the ways in which they were implemented and worked in specific contexts (Arrighi 1999, chap. 1). These pillars of the global expansion of capitalism impacted Cuba through a system of hegemonies that included Spanish colonialism, the overshadowing of the British imperial designs (which led to Britain's direct ruling of the city of Havana for almost a year), and, eventually, U.S. imperial designs in relation to the Caribbean. The dramatic impact of the British on the structures of accumulation at a world-systemic level was mediated by the escalation of imperial conflicts in the Caribbean. These became even more acute among Britain, Spain, and France once the United Provinces of the Netherlands was dismissed as a hegemonic power. These conflicts were typically associated with the strategic goals of building up imperial strongholds, generating violence and turmoil and forcing population displacements as a result.

Soon after the conquest, "Cuba found itself in the frontline of Europe's wars, as the frontiers of the old continent extended themselves across the Atlantic and into the Caribbean."[31] The takeover of Jamaica by the British in 1655 was the beginning of the end of Spanish imperial aspirations. Spain's imperial ambitions and possessions had survived the Peace of Westphalia and the Anglo-Dutch Wars of 1648 and 1652, but losing Jamaica irreversibly eroded Spain's hegemony in the insular Caribbean and southeastern areas of the North American mainland.[32] The advancement of other hegemonic projects in the area reinforced the strategic role of Cuba for Spain, which in part explains why the waves of violence and political turmoil that affected the populations of the insular Caribbean, the continental territories facing the Gulf of Mexico, and some areas of eastern Florida had a direct impact on immigration to Cuba and, occasionally, emigration from the island.

The Takeover of Jamaica and Havana, and More Violence

Approximately ten thousand Spaniards fled to Cuba when the British took power in Jamaica.[33] Political conditions in Europe during the end of the seventeenth and into the early eighteenth century led to more forced migrations through wars and shifting alliances that resulted in territorial claims. By the beginning of the eighteenth century, the War of the Spanish Succession, resulting from the claims of the Austrian-controlled Hapsburgs (supported by the British and the Dutch) and the French-controlled Bourbons over the Spanish crown, also impacted immigration in Cuba. The war ended in 1713 with the Peace of Utrecht, after which the Bourbons lifted some trade barriers and favored the production of certain products such as coffee and cotton in some colonies, including Cuba. The alliance of France and Spain under the Bourbons also allowed for greater flexibility for French nationals to move to the Spanish colonies, provided that certain conditions were met. This period of concord ended when hostilities erupted between Spain and France over control of Hispaniola, which paved the way for continuing immigration of

French nationals, mainly coffee growers, albeit on a much larger scale this time.[34] The occupation of Havana by British forces from August 1762 to July 1763 also impacted migration directly—as the occupation generated an exodus of people in search of protection, like those moving to Veracruz from the occupied territory,[35] and through the introduction of more slaves than would normally have been introduced in Cuba at the time—and indirectly, through a series of intermediate processes and policies that reinforced Cuba's articulation with trade and investment circuits that connected the island with the soon-to-be-independent Thirteen Colonies and with Great Britain. Estimates of the number of African slaves brought by the British during the occupation period range from 4,000 to 10,700.[36] It has been pointed out that it was during the occupation period that the Cuban *hacendados* dealt with British slave traders directly for the first time: "During the British occupation the merchant from Liverpool places its slaves in Havana, by moving them directly from his slave warehouses in Jamaica. . . . According to a pamphlet of the time, at the very moment in which the surrender of the city of Havana was being signed there were slave shipments waiting in the external area of the port, waiting for a signal to come in."[37] The British presence in Havana led to the opening of trade avenues for Cuba as a result of both actual trade and the boosting of "the trade and plantation mentalities" among members of the Spanish and Creole elites, while it opened the doors for a more direct engagement of economic agents in Cuba in slave trade.[38] However, it has been contended that the occupation only made visible and legal what was previously a covert slave trade.[39] In general, there is consensus that even though Spain rushed to reinstate certain protectionist measures after it recovered Havana, the participation of Cuba in trade circuits expanded as a result of the British occupation, including some trade routes linking the island with the Thirteen Colonies. Alternative productive approaches and technologies were also introduced in the sugar industry that would indirectly fuel the import of labor. In addition, the British occupation reinforced the Spanish mentality of settling the island with Spanish loyalists, while the agreement that put an end to the British occupation included a concession of the Spanish territories in East and West Florida to Britain in exchange for Havana. As a result many Spaniards from Florida resettled in Cuba.[40]

The war for independence in the Thirteen Colonies of North America and its aftermath boosted direct commercial (legal and clandestine) activity between Cuba and the emerging United States of America. By the end of the eighteenth century, trade between Cuba and the United States included consumer products and building materials and other productive inputs from the United States in exchange for slaves. The imperial war of 1793–95 between Spain and France also led to an increase of commerce with the United States and England as the neutrals, since communications with Spain were severely curtailed by the war.[41] As mentioned before, the British occupation of Havana spurred fortress building, and so did the independence in North America and the escalation of hostilities with France. Considerations regarding the balance of power among the British, Spain, and France were instrumental in shaping the final peace treaty leading to the recognition of independence of the Thirteen Colonies in 1783. Among the clauses of the agreement was the restoration of Spanish sovereignty over Florida, which also reinvigorated the economic corridor between North America and Cuba. The early national period (1789–1860) in the emerging United States of America led to a series of confrontations, negotiations, and declarations of intent concerning territorial claims and the strategic role of Cuba for securing slavery in the Southern territories. All these events, in addition to spurring immigration directly, also had an indirect repercussion on immigration through various intermediate processes. The most remarkable ones included the War of 1812, which made transparent the expansionist intentions of the United States, the signature of the Adams-Onís Treaty in 1819 under which Spain renounced to its claims in West Florida and ceded East Florida to the United States, and the tensions between the United States and Britain concerning Cuba during the design of the Monroe Doctrine between 1822 and 1823, and the production of "the Ostend Manifesto." The so-called Ostend Manifesto was originally supposed to be a confidential diplomatic dispatch resulting from a meeting of the U.S. ministers to Spain, France, and Britain in Ostend, Belgium, in 1854 with the approval of U.S. president Franklin Pierce. The communication in question encouraged the purchasing of Cuba by the United States because of its strategic value for securing slavery. In case of Spanish refusal, the document stated: "then by every law human and divine, we shall be justified in wrestling it from Spain, if we possess the power."[42] The publication of the document in question in 1855 provoked an embarrassment among diplomatic circles in the United States and the Pierce administration took certain steps to distancing itself from it. Even though the argument did not lead to a confrontation, it reinforced the perception in Madrid of the imminent danger posed by the expansionist intentions with respect to Cuba by influential politicians in the United

States.[43] These developments further reinforced Madrid's efforts to populate Cuba with Spaniards based on geopolitical considerations.

Revolution in Haiti and the "French Period"

It is no coincidence that Cuban historian Julio le Riverend used to refer to the period between 1791 and 1810 as the "French period" in immigration to Cuba.

By the end of the eighteenth century, the Caribbean witnessed several incidences of political turmoil. The most acute occurred on the island of Hispaniola, where a major revolution unfolded in Saint-Domingue (the Haitian revolution). The French revolution boosted pro-independence movements in Saint Domingue. Violent confrontations beginning in 1790 between monarchists and those sympathetic to the revolution (mostly wealthy landowners) became more widespread to involve groups that were fighting under different rationales, including African-origin groups who played a major role in the revolutionary process.[44] The first stage of violence in Hispaniola brought some merchants to the eastern cities of Baracoa and Santiago de Cuba. Between 1794 (the year of "Terror"), and circa 1808–10 (the end of the period of extreme violence), the conflict spread to other areas of Hispaniola. There were widespread revolts and a revolution in Saint-Domingue, and armed opposition by anti-Spanish coalitions in what was known as "La Reconquista," when forces favoring Spain attempted to keep a grip on the western part of the island. The Basilea Treaty, signed in 1795, ended the imperial dispute between Spain and France over the Hispaniola. Under its provisions, the Spanish part of Hispaniola was ceded to France. A Spanish Royal Decree signed in 1799 ordered the removal of the Audiencia de Santo Domingo (Spain's main governing body in the region) from Hispaniola and its reinstallation in Cuba. All these events, working in concert, led to large-scale emigration of French and Spanish subjects to Cuba, including wealthy landowners, merchants, professionals, free laborers and a number of slaves who were working mostly as servants.[45] Some brought as much money and material goods as they could, although many arrived penniless, in addition to transplanting to Cuba their know-how in the production and commercialization of coffee, and to an important extent sugar. This process was officially encouraged from Madrid by the granting of land titles in favorable terms, among other incentives, aimed at taking advantage of the experience, material resources, and commercial networks this extraordinary wave of immigrants landing on the island. In addition, some immigrants also forged economic links with moneylenders in Cuba and some worked as administrators in enterprises there.[46]

Carlos E. Deive (1989) breaks down the exodus from the Hispaniola to Cuba at that time into the following stages: From 1795 to 1801, those leaving were mainly wealthy French-origin *hacendados* and other members of the moneyed classes. Following the turmoil of 1801, which spread the conflict to the eastern part of the island, there was a new period characterized by the massive exodus of people that included artisans, small landowners, and professionals as well as slaves and agricultural workers. This period of emigration, "the great exodus," reached a high point in 1803 as the peak of the revolution (1804) approached. In 1805, turmoil escalated again, which also contributed to the exodus. In all, from 1795 to the end of the Haitian revolution, between 20,000 and 30,000 people, most of them French nationals, had fled to Cuba both from Hispaniola and even directly from France.[47] The acquisition of Louisiana by the United States in 1803 brought not only Spaniards but French immigrants as well to Cuban shores.[48]

The migration process of French-origin groups to Cuba was relatively prolonged and encompassed not only massive arrivals (according to the demographic levels of the time), but also a number of departures, the subsequent return of some groups to Cuba, and the development of commercial and other transnational links with the United States and France. Many French immigrants did not stay in Cuba. It has been argued that this was in part due to the prejudices and barriers affecting their incorporation, which was influenced by the fact that they were subjects of a European power that had invaded Spain and that many of them were supporters of the French revolution and the republican system, not the monarchical one that prevailed in Spain.[49] As a result of such tensions, the French-origin groups suffered from prejudice and discrimination by the pro-Spanish authorities and groups between 1793 and 1795 and even from a system of surveillance and deportation when Spain was invaded by Napoleon in 1808. Cuba's official records of that time show that 8,800 French nationals were deported in 1809, most of whom went to New Orleans.[50] If many French-origins groups were driven to leave Cuba when the conflict between Spain and the Napoleonic forces intensified, many returned in 1812, when Bonaparte was defeated in Madrid and Cadiz. Among the arrivals after the defeat of Napoleon were not only French nationals who had lived in Cuba (returnees) but also others who were heading toward the island for the first time. Some aimed at recovering their possessions and reestablish their networks; others were in search of new opportunities; most were escaping prejudice and the discriminatory practices to which they were subjected in Louisiana and their problematic economic incorporation there. Other French-origin groups would arrive in 1830, as a result of the

French-Mexican hostilities. And some would depart from the island in the early 1840s when several factors, including the diminishing returns for coffee producers and slave revolts in Cuba, pushed a number of French families back to France, mainly Southern France; their main region of origin.[51]

The migration of French nationals and French colonial subjects to Cuba is perhaps the most telling in terms of how the entanglements of the expansion of capitalism, imperial rivalry among European powers, and violent anticolonial struggles shaped not only the migration process but also the incorporation of the immigrants and its enduring consequences. In this particular case, the migration context unleashed the forces that shaped the growth of commercial and investment activities involving ports in Cuba, France, and the United States: "We shouldn't forget the French merchants from Bordeaux, for example, settled in Cuba frequently after their transit by ports of the Atlantic coast of the United States, such as Philadelphia, Baltimore, or Charleston. The Guestiers, Foussats, Changeurs, Dutilhs, who moved from Saint-Domingue to the United States, could have certainly been in Santiago de Cuba or Havana at the end of the eighteenth century."[52] Certainly, Cuba was the second most important destination (after Argentina) for the passengers leaving the French port of Bordeaux for the Americas between 1825 and 1827, and remained in the second rank (after New Orleans) between 1836 and 1837.[53] The role of French-origin migrants in Cuba in expanding the social fields that connected the island with Saint-Domingue, Louisiana, and France and their long-term impact on Cuba's economy and society cannot be overstated.

Decolonization in Latin America, Cuba's Independence War, and the Spanish Militarization of Cuba

The militarization of Cuba through the actual deployment of Spanish forces in the island gained increasing centrality in Spain's imperial designs as Spain faced both the pressures stemming from other European powers and the crumbling of its colonial system in Latin America. The wave of decolonization that swept Latin America between 1810 and the 1820s brought Spanish and Latin American immigrants to Cuba. Mexico was a typical case of this phenomenon. Following its independence in 1821, "many families both Spanish and Creole who were linked to the ousted colonial regime in the Viceroyalty of New Spain emigrated to Cuba which was already used by Spain as a base of operations for the recovery of its possessions in the Americas."[54] The turbulent period brought about by the French intervention in Mexico and the Porfiriato also brought a number of Mexicans to Cuban shores. Notwithstanding the efforts of Spain to open the doors of Cuba for the loyalists of the former colonies, independence in Mexico, Central, and South America also brought pro-independence activists to the Cuban shores. In addition, once most of Latin America achieved independence, the Spaniards faced regulations that banned their emigration to the emergent Latin American republics, which lasted between 1848 and 1853, and also drove many of them to Cuba and Puerto Rico, Spain's only remaining colonies in the Americas.[55] Decolonization in Latin America and Cuba's anticolonial struggles prompted the militarization of the island, which indirectly albeit not insignificantly impacted on immigration.[56]

Since the eighteenth century, Spain's imperial designs already emphasized not only the construction of fortifications in Cuba but also the populating of the island with members of the army.[57] Militia units sent to strategic areas of Cuba in the eighteenth century were relatively large by standards of those times. In Havana alone, they numbered 2,457 men in 1740 and by 1760, 6,346 had been added to the regular forces.[58] In the nineteenth century, faced with the challenges posed by decolonization throughout Latin America, and Cuba's own pro-independence movement, the Spanish crown sent thousands of members of the army to the island and enacted a series of rules and laws aimed at organizing and strengthening the Spanish military establishment there.[59] It has been estimated that approximately 600,000 Spanish soldiers arrived in Cuba during the nineteenth century, many of whom married or became involved in civilian activities that allowed them to stay on the island.[60] The involvement of Spain in confrontations in Europe, including its own domestic wars, also led to an increase in the number of Spanish immigrants of draft age who used emigration to Cuba to avoid conscription for wars elsewhere. The strategies these young people used included legally buying their way out of the military, being deployed to Cuba in the hope that they could eventually work in civilian activities there, or emigrating to Cuba secretly, which enabled them to avoid activation in both Spain and Cuba.[61] In addition to the indirect impact that the militarization of Cuba, particularly during the independence war had on migration, the war (or wars)—which started with The Ten-Year War in 1868 and unfolded through various stages that encompassed several periods of intense armed confrontation, truces, periods of economic recovery and others of deep crises, until its culmination in 1898—prompted emigration to the United States, the Hispaniola and other neighboring societies, as well as Spain and other societies in Europe. Several processes, which will be examined later, unleashed both immigration and emigration and the expansion of the transnational links between Cuba and other societies. The economic impact of the émigrés from Cuba was another major consequence of this turbulent period. The United States, which benefited from the transfers of labor, raw material and entrepreneurship from the island—mainly to the cigar industry in Key West, Tampa, New York and Philadelphia—and the Dominican portion of Hispaniola, where the sugar industry flourished as a result of heavy transfers of capital as well as know-how from Cuba, are cases in point. In addition, the cigar industry in Mexico also benefited from the arrival of immigrant entrepreneurs and workers from Cuba in the last decades of Spanish colonialism on the island.

Accumulation, Colonialism, Racism, and Migration

The story of the complete decimation of the indigenous population in Cuba has been challenged by contemporary critiques.[62] However, compared to Mexico, Central America, and most areas of South America, the indigenous population in Cuba was not that numerous, and for the most part it was massacred, escaped, or succumbed to diseases during the first decades of the conquest. Only a demographic minority survived and stayed, some of whom were regionally displaced and formed enclaves in remote areas. The demographic shortage was a major reason that both the *encomienda* and the *repartimiento* systems of labor exploitation were employed in Cuba without either of them becoming dominant.[63] Soon the importation of labor to cope with the demand became a common practice. Enslaved groups were brought primarily but not exclusively from Africa. The Yucatan Peninsula, Peru, Central America, and neighboring islands also functioned at different junctures as sources of enslaved labor. European settlers came mainly from the Iberian Peninsula, and particularly Spain, but despite restrictions placed by Spain on these matters, not all were of Spanish origin or Roman Catholic. Since the beginning of the colonial period, Spain had a restrictionist approach to immigration to the colonies that excluded many groups, among them, people professing non-Roman Catholic religions or from areas of Europe in conflict with Spain (unless they were taken to the colonies by force as prisoners of war), people from areas where the basic principles of the monarchical system had been challenged, and even certain slaves. Thus even though certain groups, such as Jews and Arab Muslims, had been arriving on the island since the onset of colonization, their relatively low demographic and social profiles, which were in many cases influenced by their religious conversion, kept most of them off the official records.[64]

At some point, Spaniards comprised the highest proportion of the work-force employed in the shipyards, even though the port economy as a whole increasingly used enslaved and freed Africans. Eventually, many Spanish im-migrants would be in charge of or employed in activities related to the cultiva-tion, factory production, and commercialization of leaf tobacco, snuff, and pipe tobacco, for which Cuba would be well known in world markets, even though factory workers also included nonmigrants and freed slaves.[65] Spanish investors and farmers would dominate the production and commercialization of tobacco until well beyond the colonial period. Even though Cuba was a major supplier for the expanding markets of tobacco products, because of the limitations of the demand and the monopoly/monopsony arrangements (*estancos*) imposed by Madrid, its production did not yield the kind of eco-nomic expansion that sugar production later secured. These arrangements restricted manufacturing in Cuba and provided incentives to the export of tobacco leaf to Spain as a way to protect Spanish producers in the Peninsula. They were instituted through the Factoría del Tabaco as the legal entity in charge of buying the product was called, by a Royal Decree signed in 1717, and were suppressed and re-instituted again until they were suppressed by the Royal Decree of June 23, 1817.[66]

The production of sugar had started relatively early in the colonial period, but competition stemming from the French colonies, particularly Saint-Dom-ingue, which by the end of the eighteenth century had emerged as the world's main exporter of sugar and coffee, was hard on the sugar producers in Cuba. Saint-Domingue lost most of its markets between 1792 and the early 1800s, while the production of sugar also dropped dramatically in Martinique and Guadalupe, also related to political turmoil that in their case included British invasions. Although all these factors led to an extraordinary increase in the demand for Cuba's sugar, Moreno Fraginals (2001, 81–86) argues that the Cuban producers faced not only opportunities but also obstacles before Cuba could cement its status as the main exporter on a world scale. While the world markets opened up for Cuba's sugar, the Spanish commercial fleet's limited capacity represented an obstacle for the exporters. Faced with this difficulty, Spain granted licenses to trade with "the neutrals" in 1778, and would use such mechanisms again, when needed. The aggressiveness of the planters and merchants and the political will of the Spanish crown to open up Cuba's sugar to world markets, More Fraginals further argues, moved Cuba from its rank as a "discrete producer of sugar" in 1760, to the third producer in the world in the early 1790s, by which time the island was experiencing what has been called its first "danza de los millones."[67] The economic dynamics resulting from a boom in the sugar industry powered Cuba's labor absorption capacity in various productive activities that went beyond the sugar plantation and the sugar mill, including construction, transportation and various activities within the service economy. As a result, the demand for imported labor continued to grow at unprecedented pace.

Slave Trafficking and Slavery

As mentioned before, the African presence in Cuba goes back to the early years of the colonial period. The exploration of African territories from the Iberian Peninsula in the fifteenth century yielded slave trafficking between the two areas prior to the discovery of the Americas, and the use of African slaves for the production of sugar and other products or in domestic service and port activities was common practice in places like the Canary Islands, Madeira, Lisbon, and Seville before the first Spanish conquerors arrived in the Americas.[68] Once the first navigation circuits between the Iberian Peninsula and the Americas were traced, Spain put in place some restrictions concerning the transportation of African slaves from Spain to the newly conquered areas. However, it was not infrequent to see slaves shipped to Cuba as "part of the normal complement" of the first colonizing expeditions, while "the wealthier settlers" brought them when needed.[69] As the colonial project advanced, African slaves were brought in larger numbers to work in various activities related to the port economy, the construction of fortresses, domestic service, and agricultural production. From there on, they would be used virtually in all sorts of economic activities. The demand for slaves reached a peak in the late eighteenth century, as the demand for labor in the sugar industry grew at an unprecedented pace; although it has been noted that the expansion of slavery-based coffee plantations during the first decades of the nineteenth century, controlled mainly by French-origin groups, also played an important role in the introduction of slaves.[70]

Cuba's first census, conducted in 1774, indicates that the population of "color" had reached approximately 75,180, or 44 percent of the total population, of which 25 percent were reportedly slaves.[71] That much of the slave trade was "underground" means that this is probably a significant undercount and may explain the disparity of the estimates in the literature. It has been pointed out that the estimate of 75,000 slaves introduced between 1700 and 1760 "might well be low rather than high,"[72] while estimates of the number of African slaves brought to the island by the British during the occupation period range from 4,000 to 10,700,[73] as mentioned before. Nicolás Sánchez-Albornoz (1974, 126, table 4.6) indicates that between 1811 and 1860, 489,400 slaves were introduced to Cuba, with the highest numbers (more than 110,000) between 1821 and 1860, and the highest numbers in that period between 1831 and 1840, when approximately 126,100 slaves were brought to Cuba. Based on several estimates, the average number of slaves introduced in Cuba between 1774 and 1865 has been placed at 700,000.[74] All in all, it has been estimated that Brazil and Spanish America imported approximately 40 percent of the total number of slaves brought to the Americas, and that most of the slaves taken to Spanish America were taken to Cuba.[75]

Most Africans were brought to Cuba through trafficking networks that were controlled by European companies that were not Spanish. Initially, when the Portuguese controlled most of this profitable activity, Spain issued licenses mostly to private individuals and companies to transport slaves to its possessions in the Americas. As the Dutch, the British, and to a lesser extent the French challenged the Portuguese control of the slave trade, the Netherlands West Indies Company, the Company of Royal Adventurers (among whose investors were members of the European nobility, including French and British queens and princesses and Carlos II of Spain), the Royal African Company, the British Hudson Bay Company, and the French West Indies Company negotiated for the right to sell slaves in the Spanish possessions through the Casa de Contratación de Sevilla, which by granting the rights through *asientos* (contracts) reinforced its monopolistic position.[76] The relative marginalization of Spain in this profitable business, which had been sealed by the defeat of the Armada in 1588, meant that Spain increasingly relied on British companies. By the mid-eighteenth century, Spanish-origin slave traders bought mainly from British traders or from smugglers.[77] One of the main objectives of the Real Compañía Mercantil de la Habana (The Havana Royal Trade Company), created in 1740, was to take control of the slave trade. The Company proved unable to meet the increasing demand for slaves, and between 1760 and in 1789 Madrid tested several other approaches to keeping the slave trade under its control until it finally allowed both Spaniards and non-Spaniards to sell slaves in several ports in Cuba, a flexible arrangement that lasted until 1802. However, even though in the late eighteenth century the Spaniards had become more active in transatlantic slave trade, "interisland trade" became a common practice to keep pace with the demand.[78]

Starting in the second decade of the 1800s, the British championed the emerging international anti–slave trade regime, which was supported by several international actors and conventions; from the Treaty of Vienna of 1815, to the highest hierarchy of the Roman Catholic Church, which had condemned slavery in Pope Gregory XVI's Bull (*In Supremo*) in 1839.[79] In addition, an international patrolling system was deployed to deter slave trade. It has been noticed that "if the British wished to abolish the slave trade, they simply sent the navy. By 1840, no fewer than 425 slave ships had been intercepted by the Royal Navy off the West African coast. . . . A total of thirty warships were engaged in this international policing operation."[80] However, the international anti–slave trade regime was not so clear cut, and it did not prevent its champion, the British, from continuing to be major beneficiaries of the slave trade, despite the official rhetoric and the policing operations. As Moreno Fraginals has pointed out, long after the end of the legal slave trade, when Britain needed sugar, "slave sugar" from Cuba found its way to British shores, where the British also "dressed with slave-grown cotton" and "smoked slave-grown tobacco" (2001, 212). The bifurcation between "legal" and "illegal" forms of slave trade has led to the portrayal of the colonial economy on the island as a dual system constituted by two circuits: one that implied a "fluid" and "regulated" link with the metropolis and other areas of the world, and another that was "extra-imperial" insofar as it relied on corsair and smuggling activities.[81] However, it has been documented that corsair and smuggling activities, including slave smuggling, were not necessarily "extra-imperial" in the sense of being conducted outside imperial designs; for European powers found them useful at times, and even backed them when pressures from producers mounted.[82] Thus, it is no surprise that even when Spain decided to formally sign agreements of cooperation against the slave trade, neither the Spanish concessions nor the British patrols stopped the smuggling of slaves to Cuba. They were brought by "English privateers," "French contrabandists," and in vessels under the U.S. flag, until "treaties between Britain and France (1831), Spain (1835), and Portugal (1839) left only the American flag as a useful disguise."[83] Smuggling had several causes, ranging from the closing of formal trade avenues and the rising prices of the slaves, to specific variations in the supply and demand in certain periods and places. There is consensus, nevertheless, that most African slaves were introduced in Cuba between 1820 and 1873, precisely after the establishment of the anti–slave trade regime.

The use of the African workforce was never embedded in a "pure" system of labor exploitation in Cuba. Since the first decades of their introduction to the island, the slaves who had been recently taken from Africa (*bozales*) were incorporated into a labor regime that also included the freed blacks (*negros horros*) and escapees (*cimarrones*), among others. Herbert Klein (1967, chap. 9) argues that "the policy of manumission" and the "coartación institution" were important mechanisms through which the enslaved groups coexisted with the freed ones. The first, Klein clarifies, was a mechanism to purchase freedom that resulted from an attitude toward the slaves that was to a great extent shaped by Spanish traditional customs and laws, and existed in Cuba since the sixteenth century. He also sheds light on the gender differences in manumission, as African-origin women had greater access than men to work in towns and different patterns of miscegenation from the men. The second refers to a practice that was fully developed in Cuba by the late seventeenth century, according to which slaves could purchase their freedom on an installment basis. *Coartación* was backed by the Royal Cédula of 1789, which mandated the improvement of the slaves' living conditions and sanctioned the purchasing of freedom through installments. These two aspects of the process of freeing the slaves, Klein further argues, created a nuanced social continuum between the slave society and the free society and set the foundations for the integration of blacks not only in the economy but also in the military service, more specifically the "volunteer militias."[84]

Moreno Fraginals captures the complexities of slave society in Cuba by the 1860s as follows:

> First, there was the "pure" slave who was obligated physically to work in the sugar mill. The *esclavo contratado* [hired slave] followed. He was subjected to completely different conditions: corporal punishment was prohibited, and he received part of the money that was paid to him on a contractual basis. Then there was the *jornalero* [day laborer], a variant of the previous one, this is the slave that was hired personally by a sugar mill for a fee, and who, frequently, gave part of his salary to his nominal owner. . . . There was also the "salaried slave" (a common type at the time) who usually received from 50 to 70 percent of the salary of a free man. (2001, 482; my translation)

Rebecca Scott (1985) argues that the understanding of African slaves in Cuba as active members of society transcends the issue of their economic and political incorporation as functional to the Spanish dominion and global capitalism and brings us to the issue of their active role in shaping the transition into emancipation and free labor. Adding to the nuances of the life of Africans and persons of African descent in Cuba was the fact that African slaves had been brought from several source areas and created institutions that sustained their ethnic identities based to a great extent on a sense of awareness and a strong sense of pride concerning the *nación* from which they had come. At the onset of slave trade in the Spanish colonies, the source areas of Africa were very limited, but these expanded later on. As a result, the African groups in Cuba by the mid-1800s included numerous subgroups from several regional and cultural backgrounds, such as the Lucumies (Yorubas), Carabalies, Congos, and Mandingos (a multiethnic group), among others.[85] The African-origin ethnic groups in colonial Cuba founded societies and other organizations as way to keep their cultural heritage and reinforce their human dignity in the adverse conditions of a slave society. This was not a new phenomenon. The founding of confraternities and other associations by African-origin groups as a way to reinforce their identities, provide mutual assistance, and celebrate certain holidays was part of the African experience in the Iberian Peninsula before the sixteenth century. In Lisbon, black groups had founded the Confraternity of Our Lady of the Rosary in the late fifteenth century, and in Seville there were two operating under different parishes.[86] It has been documented that "by the early 1600s there were two such confraternities in Havana, one devoted to Our Lady of the Remedies and the other to the Holy Spirit," and that even earlier than that "free blacks frequently gave alms in their wills to either all or some of the confraternities in the city," and some might have even accepted them as members.[87] In her study of the forms of organization of African-origin ethnic groups in Cuba, Carmen Montejo Arrechea (1993) shows that they formed associations of mutual assistance, and for recreational and religious purposes, which became highly syncretized. The *cabildos de nación* (associations organized around African ethnic groups, sometimes inclusive of several African ethnicities) reflected the efforts of the Africans brought to Cuba to keep a sense of identity and human integrity. They also gathered around *cofradías* or brotherhoods, secret societies, and other forms of associations that, Montejo Arrechea argues, reflected the complex ethos and complex religious and material conditions of their everyday lives. Religious festivities or celebrations were a main component of these forms of organization, even though during the colonial period they had to be disguised as devotion to a Catholic saint. As Montejo Arrechea explains, the *cabildos* were frequently depicted as inferior forms of associations. For example, *cabildo* had been formally defined as "a place where the black *bozales* of different African origins gather; a gathering of inept people where chaos reigns."[88] The application of the Spanish Constitution in Cuba in 1876 called for the conversion of the African associations (*cabildos* and *cofradías*) into societies for instructional and recreational purposes, more in tune with the modern Spanish model. The new rules were particularly critical of the continuous performance of dances and the re-creation of other customs of "the savage African tribes."[89] Montejo Arrechea reminds us that such a transition was part of a more comprehensive plan to reorganize the institutional and political basis of the Spanish regime in Cuba at the peak of the pro-independence movements, which also encompassed the promotion of mutual assistance associations and other associations among the population, including those founded by Creoles and Spanish immigrants. However, in the case of African groups, it also responded to a comprehensive plan oriented toward their Hispanization for the purpose of political control. Some used this relatively favorable context for the advocacy of many social-justice causes, including the education and advancement of "women of color." As Scott points out, associations that focused on religious activities and mutual assistance were not merely mechanisms that allowed Africans to adapt without offering resistance; rather, they involved both accommodation and resistance in nuanced ways.[90] Resistance from slaves in Cuba was influenced by the immersion of "people from the sugar-cane plantations" in transnational flows of information: "This kind of interrelationship with external places and peoples had been a key ingredient of the Caribbean plantation since its inception. But by the late 1800s the Cubans were receiving and sending out goods, people, products, and news in a continuous circulation not only to Spain but to neighboring colonies and the states throughout the Americas. These information flows, significantly, were not limited to the Cuban elite but included slave men and women as well."[91]

Slavery was formally abolished in Cuba on February 13, 1880, although many slaves had been freed before, including those who had fought in the Ten Years' War on either side. However, many slaves remained under the patronage of their owners until freed. *Patronato*, as this practice was known, allowed the owners to continue using the services of former slaves as "sponsored subjects" or "apprentices" after abolition. The law included clauses concerning the *patronos'* representation of their subjects in civil and judicial affairs, the stipend to be paid to the subjects depending on age, and the basis for gradually ending the *patronato* relationship eight years after the promulgation of the law. Under *patronato*, the masters retained substantial prerogatives. They regulated the physical limits of the city and the farm, and where their sponsored subjects could move in their everyday lives, and the hours and conditions of labor. Until 1883, the issue of corporal punishment was still loosely regulated. It was not until 1886, and only after strong social pressures for actual abolition, that *patronato* was legally terminated. A Royal Order signed on October 1886 dictated: "The Government is hereby authorized to promulgate, in short, freedom for those who are currently sponsored subjects in Cuba, within and under the jurisdiction of the law of 1880."[92]

Some of the practices of exclusion and human degradation of slavery were carried on for generations beyond its abolition on both sides of the Atlantic, which reflected a global pattern of "structural displacement"[93] that is historically traceable to colonialism and the institution of slavery but extends into the *longue durée* of a geosocial continuum that remains framed in racism. The first manifestation of this phenomenon in Cuba took place after emancipation, when social exclusion and economic hardships, including high levels of unemployment, affected the black population in the most dramatic ways.[94] Cuba abolished slavery almost a century after abolition had taken place in Haiti and after the practice had been legally banned in most of Latin America, the British Caribbean (1830s), and the United States (1863). It remained a society of large-scale immigration from the metropolis (and would remain so for many more years after abolition of slavery), which had profound implications for the racialization of certain groups and for interethnic relations in Cuban society beyond the slave society and the colonial period. Institutional and attitudinal forms of discrimination pointed to racism as a major legacy, while discursive practices including the legal frameworks concerning immigration would continue to reinforce the goal of Hispanization as explicitly contrasted with Africanization.

The Centrality of Blanqueamiento *in the Colonial Paradigm*

Racism, "the matrix that permeates every domain of the imaginary of the modern/colonial world system," and Occidentalism, "the overarching metaphor around which colonial differences have been articulated and rearticulated through the changing hands in the history of capitalism and the changing ideologies motivated by imperial conflicts,"[95] found dramatic expressions in the approaches to immigration in Cuba in the nineteenth century. The debates about slave trafficking that proliferated by the early 1840s were contemporaneous with the debates about human dignity, individual rights, and social progress that permeated Western societies following the French and the American revolutions. However, Walter Mignolo (2000) reminds us that the paradigms for social progress and the principles of human dignity and individual rights that inspired the French and the American revolutions were not meant to be applied equally to all members of society. Certainly, there was no indication that the principles of human dignity, equality and justice applied equally to Spaniards (regardless of social class and region of origin), light-skinned Creoles, and the black population in Cuba. In Cuba as in other slave societies in the Americas, the Haitian revolution, which claimed human dignity for blacks, was openly and systematically rationalized as so unacceptable that fear of a slave revolt prevented any inclusion of African groups in the conceptualization of human dignity, social justice, and individual rights.[96] The rationales that shaped the policies on the introduction of slaves and immigration in general, in addition to the economic interests of the *hacendados* for most of the nineteenth century, were rooted in "the scientific validation" of the existence of superior and inferior races. By the time abolitionist movements reached their peak globally, Cuba remained both a slave society whose elite was inclined to echo pro-Western racist ideologies and a colony of a European power, albeit one that, as Paul Kennedy put it, had already lost its bid for mastery. The idea of a "desired racial make up" for Cuba, which carried the imprints of "the purity of the blood" ideology that had unfolded in Spain during the conflicts with the Arabs—long before the colonization of the Americas—was reinvigorated after the Haitian revolution and led to strong opposition to slave trafficking by some influential members of the Creole elite and the Spanish crown.[97] Thus, racism was present both in arguments in favor of slavery and arguments opposing it. Furthermore, opposition to slave trafficking did not always mean opposition to the institution of slavery. Raúl Cepero Bonilla (1948) assertively pointed out that security concerns related to the growth of the black population, and even concerns that the British could force Spain to abandon slavery in Cuba if Madrid did not take further actions against the growing clandestine trading of slaves, were major motivations for some of the organic intellectuals linked to the Cuban sugarocracy to oppose slave trafficking. Some of the most outspoken intellectuals among those opposing slave trafficking were ultimately defending the institution of slavery. These ideological undercurrents led some to propose to counterbalance the introduction of slaves and even replace it with immigration from Spain and the use of other sources of labor, such as Chinese coolies. These efforts were not free from resistance based on the conflicts of interest among social agents with a voice in the matter, including wealthy landholders for whom making a profit was inalienably linked to the constant availability of "young and healthy" African slaves.[98]

The Haitian revolution certainly empowered African slaves in Cuba. Tensions in the *barracones,* those large living quarters where the slaves were kept locked after their workday, grew stronger and slave revolts more numerous as news of the revolution by slaves in Haiti became widely known in Cuba. Juan Pérez de la Riva (1978) argued that even though the *barracones* were not invented in Cuba, their widespread use to control the slave population after the 1830s and even their architectural design, which severely limited the possibility of escape, were in many respects unique to Cuba. Several courses of action were proposed to contain potential revolts, including both repressive measures and humanitarian ones. Initially, brutal repression against slave revolts was combined with a reduction in the number of slaves imported from Africa, an increase in the number of black women in sugar mills, education for the children of slaves (including religious indoctrination), and the development of colonizing projects to bring people from the Canary Islands and Mexico.[99] In 1843 slave insurrections occurred in sugar mills, railroads, and other production sites in the western provinces. In addition, hundreds of people, mostly free blacks and mulattoes, were charged with illegal conduct for acting or conspiring to act against Spain. The whole process included the Conspiración de la Escalera, a "conspiracy" that has been recorded in history as having been possibly induced by the Spanish authorities to control the slave revolts and crush the political activism of people of color, among whom there were some distinguished intellectuals and political activists who opposed slavery and colonialism. There is a widespread perception that this situation eventually played into the hands of "the annexionists," those who believed that the political incorporation of Cuba into the United States would solve Cuba's economic and political problems. This political current was instigated in the United States by political agents who supported slavery and opposed the Spanish presence in the Caribbean. Another major conspiracy against Spanish domination was La Conspiración de los Rayos y Soles de Bolívar, which was led by "white nationalists" inspired by the newly independent Latin American republics, yet nevertheless was ambiguous, at best, concerning the role that the black population could have in the anticolonial struggle or openly opposed arming freed slaves and other Afro-Cubans who, once armed, could potentially turn against the wealthy white Creoles.[100] Many of the so-called reformists—members of a political movement that opposed independence via revolutionary upheaval and did not challenge Spanish hegemony in the island—were actively involved in supporting white colonizing projects as a way to head off a radical revolution. This scenario also reinforced some existing tensions between those who favored the introduction of free white laborers and *colonos* from Spain and those who opposed it. However, the introduction of white colonizers had been an important aspect of Spain's colonial design since much earlier.

As early as 1732, there was some debate and experimentation with "white settlers" as a way of containing the relative growth of the black population in certain localities.[101] This was the antecedent of what some decades later would become an overtly racist population policy, one framed by Spain's geopolitical interests, heated debates, the creation of advocacy and policy groups, and the enactment of royal ordinances and decrees. Although they were systematically addressed by the end of the eighteenth century, the propositions leaning toward an increase in the European (Spanish) portion of Cuba's ethnic composition to prevent the risks associated with having a nation that was predominantly "colored" became increasingly popular after the slave rebellions of the 1830s–1840s. The goal of *blanqueamiento,* or "the bleaching out" of the population, was placed at the top of the metropolis's agenda for the political control of the colony and was supported by influential members of the Creole elite, whose various forms of "proto-nationalism" were rooted in racist doctrines. Although focused on specific domestic concerns, the debates on abolition and *blanqueamiento,* and the ways they shaped immigration policies in Cuba, reflected the development of a complex set of interrelated global and regional changes. They included the collapse of the slave trade globally and the increasing economic and political costs associated with the maintenance of slavery; the independence of Spain's colonies in most of Latin America; Spain's shrinking space in the world economy and the erosion of its geopolitical leverage; the search for alternative sources of labor in Asia for the Atlantic economy; and conditions in Europe and the Americas that propelled transatlantic migrations from Europe, including Spain. Such changes went hand in hand with the consolidation of Eurocentric imaginaries and the racist ideologies associated with them, claimed to be supported at the time by "scientific evidence" about racial differences that supposedly manifested in different patterns of behavior and intellectual abilities that either accelerated or slowed down the path to progress.[102] In this context, the debates on immigration sprang up throughout Latin America and framed unprecedented transatlantic migrations to the region, mainly South America, at the time in which nation-building projects gained momentum there. Certain interest groups in the postcolonial societies of Latin America favored immigration of European *colonos* as a way to supply labor and entrepreneurship in the rural and urban sectors. The prevailing ideology in Latin America was "gobernar es poblar" (to govern is to populate), yet populating with "the right population stocks"—that is, white Europeans—was seen as the most effective strategy to achieve social progress. The idea was to strengthen "the population stocks" both quantitatively and qualitatively by attracting white people, who were frequently portrayed as being better suited for the introduction of new technologies. Systematic efforts to attract European migrants were codified in major pieces of legislation throughout Latin America, most of which employed overtly racist language; consular efforts were also launched to recruit the "right" population stocks.[103] The migration business, itself largely carried on through smuggling, also accounted for an important part of the European transatlantic immigration.[104]

Notwithstanding the influence that global and regional contexts concerning immigration had on Cuba, the fact that it was still a colony of Spain and a slave society immersed in debates concerning immigration, abolition, *blanqueamiento*, the population of imperial frontiers, and the issue of Cuba's status vis-à-vis Spain, complicated the issue of who was in favor of a given immigration policy and why. That the introduction of slaves in Cuba continued to be encouraged while the slavery regime was disintegrating worldwide has been attributed not only to the profit-making rationale of the proslavery planters and slave traders but also to Spain's interest in maintaining control over the supply of labor to the sugar industry, one of the most important pillars for its dominance over Cuba.[105] In any case, influential Spaniards or Creoles were by no means of one mind on slavery and immigration, and the clashes within these groups and between them and the central government in Spain on these matters were frequent. Thus, the efforts at building up consensuses on these issues in order to guarantee Spanish hegemony were at the core of Spain's strategies to deal with them. In principle, the immigration of white Europeans would be primarily from Spain; therefore, immigration from other areas of Europe were not expected to have (and in fact did not have) either the same demographic magnitude or the same social repercussions in Cuba as it did in other societies of Latin America.

The slogan "Cuba será africana o española" (Cuba shall be either African or Spanish) was frequently used in heated debates on immigration in the late 1830s[106] and resonated in the colonizing plans that forcibly pushed for *blanqueamiento* and the overall Hispanization of the island. There was both support for and opposition to this kind of project. While the support tended to rely on racist arguments, the opposition sometimes also conveyed a racist twist, as the following passage of an essay published in 1839 indicates:

> Not many years ago, an enlightened patrician enthusiastically announced the initiative of an owner of a sugar mill (Sucrerie) to try to bring 30 or 40 fellow countrymen from Old Castile, his homeland, in order for them to plant sugar cane in his farm for a basic wage. A few days after the publication of the advertisement, another Castilian wrote a note in the newspaper insulting the hacendado, telling him that the

honest harvestmen of Seville were not so degraded as to lower themselves to the position of working together with the black slaves of the Cuban island.[107]

Since the time of Luís de las Casas, governor of the island in the last decade of the eighteenth century, the issue of *blanqueamiento* was a clear mandate from Madrid. In 1796, a commission was established in Madrid that implemented the policy of populating certain territories of Cuba with white settlers and creating more fortresses. In 1817, the Junta de Población Blanca (White Population Board) was created under the initiative of Spanish bureaucrat Alejandro Ramírez, financial superintendent of Cuba, with the support of influential Creoles. A Royal Ordinance of October 21, 1817, stipulated the need to increase the white population through a colonizing schema in order to counterbalance the growth of the black population generated by the introduction of slaves. It was published in Spanish, English, and French in 1818 under the title "Real Cédula del 21 de Octubre de 1817, Sobre Cómo Aumentar la Población Blanca de la Isla de Cuba" or "Royal Ordinance of October 21, 1817, On How to Increase the White Population of the Island of Cuba." The document described Cuba as an "under-populated precious possession where vast areas of uncultivated lands were available." It also stated the desired profile for immigrants: white Spaniards from the Peninsula or the Canary Islands, or if they were not available ("y a falta de esta [población]"), Catholics from allied powers of Europe ("con Europeos católicos de las potencias amigas") willing to settle on the island and be loyal to Spain. It established prerequisites for granting Spanish nationality to foreigners who resided on the island for at least five years. Other provisions addressed the naturalization of their offspring, both those brought with them and those who were born in Cuba, the possibility and requisites for returning to their areas of origin, and the conditions under which such return could take place within the first five years of residence, including what returnees would be allowed to take with them.[108] The Real Cédula also included certain provisions concerning the types of economic activities that the would-be *colonos*[109] could perform before acquiring Spanish nationality. An ultimatum was given to foreigners who were de facto residents on the island, with the exception of transients from the fleets or cargo ships, to either regularize their residence or naturalize, a measure aimed at encouraging the regularization of the white immigrants already established in Cuba. Influential members of the Creole and Spanish intelligentsia welcomed the ordinance; for them it represented both a modernizing prospect and a defense against the potential racial turmoil the increasingly antagonistic slave society of the island could witness at any time. A prominent intellectual stated that the ordinance in question "will be forever regarded as a document that enhances the honor of the Spanish government, and as such it was welcomed by the authorities, the corporations, and the neighbors of the island."[110] Of course, "the neighbors" to whom the statement refers were mostly the white Spanish and Creoles who had long advocated the establishment of white colonizing programs.

After the enactment of the Royal Ordinance of October 21, 1817, various experiments were carried out to bring *colonos* to populate agricultural areas. The incentives included the granting of land, credit, and other forms of support, which would be funded from private as well as public sources. One of the first was the formation of the settlement Fernandina de Jagua, a southern port area. Alejandro Ramírez, the Spanish governor in charge of applying the Royal Ordinance on white colonizing projects, and Luis de Clouet, a French-origin immigrant who arrived in Cuba among those who left Louisiana after it was sold to the United States by France, were in change of the project. De Clouet brought the first families to Fernandina de Jagua—about forty-five French families from the region of Bordeaux. More white settlers, mainly from a few cities in the United States, arrived later to the Villa de Cienfuegos, which would eventually evolve into Cienfuegos, currently one of Cuba's most picturesque cities. In 1824 the settlement had more than 1,800 inhabitants, according to its first census.[111] Although this project may appear to have ben a success, some assessments produced at that time indicated that it largely proved to be a costly experiment that did not lead to the expected results.[112] Other colonizing projects that were active by the early 1830s were in the port areas of Nuevitas and Guantánamo. Land was also either purchased by the Spanish administration or donated by private owners for the purposes of establishing white settlements in other areas, such as Santo Domingo and Nueva Gerona.[113]

The Junta de Fomento (Development Board), which was organized in 1832, made one of its primary goals the immigration of white families to the island. The Development Board advanced several proposals to further the goals of "la colonización blanca," such as the transport of *braceros* and *colonos* from the Canary Islands, Galicia, and other regions of Spain. Bringing immigrants from these areas was meant to expand the base of support by introducing groups that were loyal to the colonial establishment, while it kept the white sector of the population growing. By 1845, a system of labor recruitment based on contracts had been developed in the northern areas of Spain. Recruitment efforts, combined with an intense famine in Galicia, and the social networks developed by the migrants themselves led to the transportation of the impressive number of two thousand families to Cuba in 1853.[114] From there on, Spain would also be more systematic in the enforcement of the international treaties on slave trade. Since independence movements had succeeded throughout Latin America, support for the introduction of alternative sources of cheap labor in Cuba ultimately corresponded with the metropolis's objective of political control not only through economic means but also through ethnic, linguistic, and cultural hegemony. It was in this context that Spanish immigrants, including Spanish women, were encouraged to move to Cuba, either with their families or alone. As was happening with many other European women, Spanish women were also targeted by those involved in the *trata de blancas* (the smuggling of women migrants for the sex trade). Simultaneously, immigration itself had matured enough that it had become a major force shaping the social fields that tied Cuba and Spain; the flow of information concerning job availability and living and working conditions and the possibilities for entrepreneurial strategies was facilitated as well, which encouraged more women to move across the Atlantic. As a result, the rate of growth for female emigrants from the Peninsula as well as the Canary Islands between 1846 and 1852 surpassed the rates of growth for the male Spanish population.[115]

The recruitment of non-Spanish European immigrants as *colonos* and laborers was part of the immigration-*blanqueamiento* formula. However, efforts to bring white immigrants from other areas beyond Spain to colonial Cuba were not as systematic as they were in some independent republics, such as Argentina and Uruguay. Some of the incentives for prospective immigrants included, as mentioned before, exempting farms sold to new *colonos* from property taxes and allowing the immigrants and their offspring to enjoy the rights of the native-born Cubans. In the 1830s, 378 workers from Ireland, Prussia, Scotland, and other parts of Europe—together with workers from the United States, who tended to have different national origins—arrived in Cuba to work on the first stage of the construction of the railroad system. It has been noted that these workers were adversely affected by the working conditions in Cuba and did not establish immigrant communities on the island.[116]

Like other immigrants from Europe and beyond, the presence of Italian immigrants since the first centuries of colonization was obscured by the shifting of political alliances and their related territorial readjustments in Europe, as well as Spain's assimilationist policies. In addition to participating in commercial fleets, an important number of Italian architects, other professionals, and artists were hired to work on Havana's urban projects. Others arrived when the urban life of the city had become more sophisticated. It was fashionable among certain religious and governmental institutions in Cuba to hire instructors in plastic arts and professional painters directly from Italy for the frescoes of the cathedral, churches, and other buildings. Some of the professionals and artists stayed in the island. There was at least one official attempt to develop an Italian settlement as part of the *blanqueamiento* policy of the nineteenth century, but the results, in terms of attracting Italians, were modest. By the end of the nineteenth century, however, the Italian presence in Cuba already was significant enough to merit the formation of associations by Italian-origin groups.[117] In 1884, Italians founded the Sociedad de Socorros Mutuos (Society for Mutual Aid), and in 1891 they founded the Sociedad Italiana de Beneficencia (Italian Welfare Society). Similar societies and others with greater political orientation (such as the Antifascist Italian Society) grew during the first half of the twentieth century as Italians continued to arrive in the island, albeit in modest numbers.[118] Sometimes the Italian immigrants in Cuba opposed the prevailing regimes in Italy, but other groups were parts of migrations fostered by the Italian government, for after the beginning of the twentieth century the Italian government began actively launching strategies of support for the growing Italian diaspora in the Americas, principally the United States and Argentina, since it had become vital to Italian society.[119] In sharp contrast with independent Latin American countries that were receiving a large number of Europeans at that time—prominently but not exclusively Argentina—the Spanish administration in Cuba did not encourage large-scale immigration from other European areas. The main strategy used Cuba was the retention and productive incorporation of European immigrants who had already settled on the island. This approach was employed particularly in the eastern provinces, where a large number of French entrepreneurs had settled and become actively involved in agricultural production, such as coffee and indigo, that did not compete directly with the sugar industry.[120]

The censuses conducted during the colonial period classified the population into "white" and "nonwhite," and "nonwhite" further into "slaves" and "free of color." As in other slave societies, the gathering of statistics was biased by the use of race as an important "political category" associated with geopolitical control.[121] Ramón de la Sagra's longitudinal analysis of the four censuses conducted between 1774 and 1827 indicates that the white population in 1774 was 96,440, which represented 56 percent of the total population (171,620), yet the proportion of the white population had significantly dropped to 49 percent in 1792 (133,599 out of 272,301), and by 1827, it represented 44 percent of the total (311,051 out of 704,487).[122] He also specifies that the group with the highest growth rate in each intercensus period was African slaves. Census estimates from 1841 on indicate that the population of color reached its peak in 1841, when it represented almost 60 percent of the total population. By 1861 the white subgroup had recovered the demographic majority (56 percent), a trend that would be reinforced throughout the republican stage of the postcolonial period, when the "whites" were consistently 70 percent or more of the population. Reportedly, in 1907 it was very close to 70 percent already.[123] Thus, the official data suggest that the ideological tension of *africanización* versus *españolización* had been settled demographically in favor of the latter. Yet the battle for *blanqueamiento* did not end when the last Spanish soldier left the island and the U.S. military administrator set foot on it. The immigration policy of the postcolonial period would favor immigration from Spain as a natural course of action, given the existence of sustained family and business links between Spaniards living in the island and elsewhere, the demand for labor and capital, and prejudice against other groups. The advantages of such migration were emphasized in modernist discourses deployed by the U.S. military government that pointed to the supposed superiority of Spaniards vis-à-vis other groups, including native Cubans. In addition, the Cuban bureaucracy had inherited the mission of not letting the demographic supremacy of the white groups diminish. Even when Anglo-Saxon capitalists insisted on bringing in black *braceros* from neighboring Caribbean islands, they faced opposition based on multiple foundations, one of them being the always already established fear of having a predominantly black society.

Immigration from the Metropole: General Trends

Although emigration from Spain to the Americas was significantly lower than emigration from the British Isles, Spain was the second major metropolitan source of immigrants to colonial areas in the Americas. Immigration from Holland and France was considerably lower, since the latter groups gravitated instead toward their colonies in Asia and North Africa.[124] It has been estimated that by the end of the eighteenth century, there were approximately 4 million Europeans in Latin America and 4.5 million in North America. The estimates suggest that European settlements in the Americas, which to a lesser extent also included immigrants from Portugal and other European societies, constituted one-third of the population from Newfoundland to Tierra del Fuego.[125]

Cuba gradually became a magnet for Spanish migration. It has been argued that between 1560 and the end of the sixteenth century, approximately two thousand Spaniards had settled in Cuba, although other estimates point to more modest numbers.[126] Though the estimates vary, accumulation strategies, political turmoil, modern projects rooted in racist rationales, and the need to populate imperial frontiers drove an array of groups from Spain to Cuba throughout the colonial period. For analytical purposes they are frequently classified as government officials, members of the clergy and the army, *colonos,* convicts, deserters from the armada and the commercial fleets, entrepreneurs, urban workers, and agriculturists, among others, although in real life some of the categories overlapped—not only because they combine immigration status and occupational descriptors but also because of the overlapping of occupations and the fluidity of some of the occupations individuals held.

Spain had established tight controls on immigration to the Americas out of geopolitical, religious, racist, and economic considerations. The prospects of wealth in other areas of the Americas, epidemics, and attacks had kept the growth of the Spanish population of the island at relatively modest levels until 1655, when an estimated ten thousand Spanish settlers moved from Jamaica to Cuba after the British takeover of the former. Until the 1760s, bans on immigration affected people from different regions of Spain. Catalonia, a possession controlled directly by Aragon rather than Castile, is a case in point. Occasionally, special licenses were granted, and people from restricted source areas were allowed to travel and even stay in Cuba following certain provisions. The waiver system included an ample range of people in categories that sometimes overlapped—among them, Spaniards and other Europeans escaping political turmoil, mainly in areas neighboring Cuba; *colonos;* investors; experts in leading industries; and laborers. When the most rigorous stage of the restrictionist period ended, a licensing system was established that tended to privilege the immigration of certain individuals.[127]

The transatlantic migrations of Spaniards were at the core of Spain's colonial and imperial designs when Cuba and Puerto Rico remained its last two colonies in the Americas. Immigration to Cuba manifested with particular intensity given the capacity of its economy to absorb a much larger number of immigrants. However, Spain also experienced significant levels of emigration to the former colonial areas, which also peaked between the 1880s and throughout the first decades of the twentieth century. Labor recruitments in general and the recruitment of members of the military for the two colonies prompted migration; the development of social networks driven by work, kinship, and friendship reinforced the process, while deep economic crises, turmoil, and all sorts of disasters in the metropole prompted sporadic increases in the number of transatlantic migrants moving to the colonies and the postcolonial societies. By the end of the colonial period in Cuba, Spanish immigration was propelled by socioeconomic, geopolitical, and technological dynamics that further reinforced the flow of commodities, people, information, and capital across the Atlantic in the last decades of the nineteenth century. This occurred in a context of accumulation that combined the importation of cheap labor from Europe and growing entrepreneurship in the Americas. Epidemics and agricultural crises, mainly in northern Spain, were other major forces shaping emigration from an array of localities in Spain. Key actors involved in the migration process included the migrant families, the state, and private actors with a vested interest in migration (such as labor recruiters and those involved in human trafficking).[128]

Available estimates indicate that the population movement from Spain to the Americas grew from 300,000 in the sixteenth century to over 3 million at its peak between 1882 and 1930.[129] The data gathered in Spain on passengers indicate that 3,297,312 Spanish civilians crossed the Atlantic to the Americas between 1882 and 1930; of them, 1,118,968, or approximately 40 percent, went to Cuba. An estimate based on Spanish official records indicates that of the more than 600,000 Spaniards that embarked for the Americas between 1882 and 1889, 46 percent went to Cuba. All the available estimates indicate that between 1882 and the early 1900s, Cuba was the main recipient of Spanish transatlantic migration. Even though Cuba was the second major destination for Spanish migrants after Argentina in the entire period between 1900 and 1930, it momentarily recaptured first place between 1916 and 1920, receiving almost 60 percent of Spanish emigration to the Americas when the demand for immigrant workers in Cuba's sugar industry peaked. The arrival of members of the military, many of whom would stay in Cuba, was reinforced between the 1860s and 1898, as the independence movement and armed confrontations related to it proliferated across the island. Between 1895 and 1898 alone, Spain sent 220,285 soldiers to Cuba—which is said to have been the largest army to cross the Atlantic before World War II.[130] Contrary to what happened in most of the newly independent republics of Latin America, Cuba remained a colony until 1898 and, as discussed above, retained institutional frameworks that were not only friendly to immigration from Spain but also induced immigration from the metropolis based on an array of interrelated logics.

The "Chinese Coolies" and the "Californios"

Most Chinese laborers, usually referred to as "Chinese coolies," brought to Latin America and the Caribbean between 1847 and 1874 went to Cuba.[131] Like *bozales,* the term "Chinese coolies," while ideologically charged and an embodiment of symbolic violence, involves some semantic complexities as well. Pierre Trolliet indicates that the term "coolie" is not from China. He argues that the term results from "a phonetic transcription, influenced by English, of the Tamil *kúli* (salary), unless it originated in the Turkish *kuli* (slave)."[132] In its most common usage it was applied by non-Chinese people to classify Asians who were incorporated into global labor circuits, often through deceptive migration schemes.

Chinese laborers were introduced in Cuba at the height of the official efforts toward *blanqueamiento*. Official estimates indicate that more than 40,000 "coolies" landed in Cuba between 1847 and 1859. By 1874, 141,391 Chinese had embarked from China's shores to Cuba; of these, 16,576 died during the trip, and an additional 53,502 died in Cuba shortly after arriving.[133] As with the African slaves, many Asians died during the trips on what were frequently called "floating hells," and others would become terminally ill in Cuba, where they could not survive the harshness of the work regime, the personal degradation, other psychological pressures, and epidemics. Approximately half a million Asians were transported to the Americas between 1847 and 1874, the year in which the Chinese government prohibited banned departures under labor contracts.[134] It has been estimated that of them, just over a quarter of a million, or approximately 45 percent, headed toward areas other than North America; of them, "roughly 125,000 or 48 percent went to Cuba," followed by Peru (38 percent) and the British West Indies (8 percent), with Panama, Brazil, and the Dutch and French possessions, among other areas, receiving the remaining 6 percent.[135] The points of origin in China were clustered around the Pearl River Delta. The ports of Macao, Shantou, and Xiamen were major exit points for Asian migration to Cuba and other areas in the circum-Caribbean.[136]

It is impossible to sort out the root causes of the rise of emigration from Asia to the Americas during the nineteenth century without taking into consideration the deepening of the military and economic involvement of Great Britain in Asia after 1840. The incursions of what Paul Kennedy refers to as "the Western man"—their interventions in Asia through disruptive mechanisms, including the Opium Wars—were at the core of the British imperial designs in Asia. The Opium Wars unveil the link between capitalism and coloniality of power as important components of Britain's global hegemonic designs in relation to Asia. According to Niall Ferguson,

> The Opium Wars of 1841 and 1856 were, of course, about much more than opium. The *Illustrated London News* portrayed the 1841 war as a crusade to introduce the benefits of free trade to yet another benighted Oriental despotism. . . . Yet it is very hard to believe the Opium Wars would have been fought if exports of opium, prohibited by the Chinese authorities by 1821, had not been so crucial to the finances of British rule in India. . . . It is indeed one of the richer ironies of the Victorian value-system that the same navy that was deployed to abolish the slave trade was also active in expanding the narcotics trade. (2002, 167)

Where Ferguson sees "ironies," one can see a logical sequence in the history of global strategies of capital accumulation and their supporting material and symbolic mechanisms. While the international regime against slavery was closing the doors, at least formally, to what until then had been a profitable form of labor exploitation, the Opium Wars opened the doors to the global flow of "indentured laborers" from China and India. The use of indentured labor was not a new modality of surplus value appropriation. As noted above, it had coexisted with slavery since the beginning of the colonial enterprises in the Americas. However, it reached unprecedented levels when Asian immigrants were forced as cheap laborers into the global labor flows, while many European migrants were also crossing the Atlantic as indentured laborers.

After the Treaty of Nanking (1842), which concluded the first Opium War and led to the British takeover of Hong Kong, five ports were opened to the trade of "coolies." Trolliet (1994) indicates that the bans imposed on the slave trade, the economic dynamism of certain areas of the Americas, the spread of European imperial designs in Asia, and economic recession in some areas particularly affected by commercial imbalances (such as those related to the contraband of opium), when coupled with war compensations, political turmoil, and even natural disasters in Asia, set in motion the largest-ever migration movement from Asia to the Americas, and within it, the largest emigration stream from China to Cuba. In the Americas, the Chinese immigrants, mostly working as indentured laborers, were involved in the sugar industry and other types of activities, such as mining, the development of the railroad, and other construction projects. In the context of heated debates about the end of slave trade and of abolition and the need for alternative sources of labor, the idea of bringing laborers from Asia found widespread reception among the Cuban elites:

> In March 1846 . . . [a] proposition was made to import 1,000 Asians under contract to work for 8 years at $4 a month, plus food, clothing and the assistance commonly given to slaves. For this service, the [importing British] Company was to receive 170 pesos for each coolie delivered. . . .
>
> The treasury superintendent, the Count of Villanueva, agreed for 100,000 pesos to be taken from the White colonization fund for use in importing coolies. Thereafter the Coolie trade was considered officially as White colonization and a subscription list was started for prospective purchases of Chinese.[137]

The trading of Chinese indentured laborers became a very profitable activity: "On arrival in Havana . . . a single labor contract could be sold for anything between $250 to $500. Total net profit on a single voyage could run as high as $85,000 on a sale of two hundred and seventy contracts."[138] The first groups were sent primarily to work in the sugar industry. As they improved their command of Spanish, they were assigned to other tasks in the sugar mills, which were experiencing technological and industrial improvements by that time. Many also were employed in the construction of the railroads and other construction projects, and some worked in personal services in the private housing compounds of the sugar mills, the cities, and the cigar factories.[139] Bans imposed by China on the departure of Chinese workers from Chinese ports created a hiatus that lasted until 1853, when the traffic was resumed. Most Chinese immigrants arriving in Cuba in the nineteenth century had come from Canton and originally settled in the regions of Matanzas and Las Villas, although a number of them moved to other places as they found opportunities elsewhere. Some were brought directly via Santiago de Cuba after 1853, where they worked mostly in the copper mines.[140]

For several years Chinese immigrants were incorporated into a labor regime that overlapped with slavery and in some respects resembled it. It has been extensively documented that more often than not, working conditions made the line between free labor and slavery hard to draw, and this was particularly true in the case of Chinese laborers. The way the Chinese workers entered this system put them in a position similar to that of the African slaves in many respects: "The problems of indentured Asians on the plantations, it should be noted, were similar to those of the slaves. This is especially reflected in the death rate and their propensity to escape."[141] The typical Cuban contract for the indentured laborers from China had clauses that specified that they acknowledged that their "stipulated salary" could be much lower than the compensation received by other free laborers and even the slaves in the island. They had to sign a clause that stated: "I consider the difference compensated by the other advantages which are to be allowed to me by my employer."[142] Such "advantages" referred mainly to recruitment mechanisms that in reality tied them to their contracts for years under a labor regime that was closer to semi-slavery than free labor, such as their indebtedness related to the costs of their voyages, initial installation expenses, and so on. The system of punishment that they acknowledged themselves to be subjected to, in case they were not "industrious" or "obedient" enough, included "lashes," "being put in irons," and "made to sleep in the stocks." Similar punishments were stipulated for runaway Chinese indentured laborers, in addition to the denial of salary payments and deduction of expenses related to capture from future compensation.[143] It has been argued that the Chinese resistance to the labor regime to which they had been subjected manifested itself in several forms, including the numerous suicides they committed, their direct confrontations (sometimes involving violent acts) against the employers, their escape from the plantations, and their prominent participation in Cuba's independence wars.[144]

The use of Chinese indentured labor in agricultural and construction activities was a major feature of their incorporation in North America and Central and South America. In Cuba, as noted above, Chinese laborers worked in the construction of the railroad, which had started in 1837. By the time Spain opened the doors for the introduction of thousands of Chinese workers to be exploited in the plantations, construction sites, and elsewhere in Cuba, the British, the French, and the Dutch were involved in the importation of workers from the Indian subcontinent. In 1838, the British Colonial Office had opened the doors for the transportation of indentured laborers to the Caribbean from India under five-year contracts. Between 1838 and 1917, over 400,000 men and women who were recruited in Calcutta and Madras were reportedly brought to work on British Caribbean plantations (mainly in British Guiana, Trinidad, and Jamaica). By the same token, the French and the Dutch put in place labor schemas that led to the shipment of tens of thousands of workers from India to their colonies—Guadeloupe, Martinique, French Guiana, and Suriname—between the 1850s and 1917.[145]

Chinese immigrants of greater economic means started arriving in Cuba from California in the mid 1860s. The "Californios," as the members of this group are frequently referred to in the literature, arrived as opportunities grew in Cuba and discrimination and prejudice against Chinese immigrants grew in the United States (which would eventually enact the Chinese Exclusion Act in 1882). By 1870, a social distinction had been made in Cuban society between the Chinese laborers who had arrived as "coolies" and those who had arrived with economic means.[146] The penetration of capitalism through imperial designs in Asia coincided with what has been called the rise of "Orientalism" in "the second modernity,"[147] and the whole process is inseparable from what Aihwa Ong (1999), building upon the work of other authors, refers to as "the naturalization of the transnational imaginaries" about Chinese "race, culture, and economic activities," although she emphasizes current times. In this context, the growing demand for Chinese labor eventually merged with a growing demand for Chinese entrepreneurs and "exotic Oriental products." José Baltar Rodríguez documents that the first import outlet dedicated to Chinese products opened in Havana in 1870. It was backed by three Chinese investors who had put together 50,000 pesos for that purpose. The Chinese also invested in the sugar industry, banking, and an array of other economic activities. In addition, the arrival of Chinese with greater economic means also affected the development of some cultural and social associations, including those providing some safety nets and social representation, such as the Casino Chung Wah, founded in 1893, which encompassed a broad range of Chinese-origin groups.[148]

The Arrival of Other Immigrants

Immigrants and temporary workers also came from North America in the nineteenth century. Their class and occupational backgrounds were diverse: they were investors, managers, technicians, and other skilled workers. Some had been born in the United States; others were immigrants of various origins, such as Ireland and Italy; still others were returnees from Cuba who had acquired American citizenship.[149] The complexity of the migration links with the United States only grew after the 1840s, when Creole and Spanish groups, including prominent political figures who had opposed Spanish colonialism, settled there either after deportation, under pressure from Spanish authorities, or by their own initiative. This trend intensified during the 1860s as a result of the independence wars. By that time, many U.S. citizens were also crossing the Florida Straits, but in the other direction, in search of opportunities, and some established their permanent residence on the island, mainly in Havana and other western areas. Reportedly, the average trade-related floating population from the United States had reached 32,000 persons per year in the

1880s. There were tourists as well, who as early as 1850 numbered approximately five thousand. In addition to the transient groups and those visiting or staying for a certain period of time, there were also U.S. citizens establishing residence in Cuba, mostly in Havana and across the northern coast.[150]

Between 1846 and 1862, the U.S.-born population in Cuba grew from 1,260 to nearly 2,500.[151] The later movement of people from the United States to Cuba as a result of "the panic of 1893," as the major economic event of that year is remembered, has been portrayed by Louis Pérez as an "immigration rush" that was taking place simultaneously with the emigration *from* the island of Cubans escaping their own economic hardships and the uncertainty and violence related to their anticolonial struggle: "It was now the turn of North Americans to escape hard times. They migrated to war-ravaged Cuba by the thousands, shipload after shipload in successive waves, each larger than the one before, people of all social types . . . in search of opportunity and fortune, in flight from one of the most devastating depressions of U.S. history" (1999, 22–23).

There were an estimated 2,496 U.S. citizens residing in Cuba in 1861; that number had risen to 6,444 by 1899. Many who were born in the United States had moved to Cuba to work. Merchants and other entrepreneurs from the United States were a significant presence in highly dynamic areas of Cuba, including some port areas, by the end of the nineteenth century.[152]

Immigrants also arrived from the areas that would relatively soon be unified as Germany. Their migration responded to several intertwined dynamics that included not only some attempts at attracting white immigrants from Europe to the island but also growing mobility of merchants, bankers, and industrialists across the Atlantic—a trend that in some cases involved physical relocation. Along with those who emigrated to the United States, German migrants were establishing communities in South America, primarily Brazil, Argentina, and Chile, by the 1830s and 1840s. It has been documented that what primarily brought members of this group to Cuba were the economic links developed by German entrepreneurs, which included trade, finance, and certain aspects of the port economy, such as the insurance of commercial vessels. Rolando Alvarez Estévez and Marta Guzmán Pascual (2004) show that investment opportunities were a major facilitator of the settlement of a number of Germans before 1871, the year of the political unification of Germany as a federation of principalities, and again after that year, when the emergent nation-state became aggressively involved in imperial designs that were supportive of the overseas economic involvement of their nationals. Contributing to this trend were Spain's more flexible policies concerning trade and invest-ments in the colony and the efforts to attract white settlers. In the long run, Alvarez Estévez and Guzmán Pascual argue, even though immigration from Germany never reached significant demographic levels, those who settled in Cuba made important contributions in the production and commercializa-tion of tobacco and the beverage industry, mainly the production of beer; they were involved in trade; and they also worked as technical personnel in industrial activities related to the sugar industry and mining. H. Upmann cigars were developed in the 1840s by two brothers from Bremen who, by 1868, had extended their investment portfolio to the banking industry. Ger-man experts in the brewing industry provided technical assistance with the foundation of La Tropical (still renowned in Cuba) in 1888 (ibid.). At the peak of immigration in the early twentieth century, some Germans settled in Cuba. However, the census report on the foreign-born population for 1931 indicates that there were 839 German nationals living in Cuba, a number that was modest in relation to Cuba's overall immigration levels and even within the source countries from Western Europe.[153]

Indigenous groups from Yucatan were also brought to Cuba when Spanish authorities were experimenting with alternative sources of labor. However, the first settlement of Mayans from Yucatan can be traced to 1564, the year that marks the origins of the "Campeche neighborhood" in Havana (which would become known as *el barrio de Campeche*). In addition, white immi-grants from Campeche who had economic means and higher social status had also settled in Cuba by 1724; some of them married on the island (sometimes among members of their own group) and registered themselves as "Span-iards."[154] The important commercial links that were developed between Yuca-tan and Cuba encouraged both the import of laborers and the arrival of individuals with greater economic resources. By the mid-nineteenth century, those engaged in labor recruitment in Yucatan capitalized on a political situa-tion in the Yucatan Peninsula that had led to the imprisonment and deporta-tion of thousands of members of the indigenous population in relation to the "Caste War," in which some factions had demanded independence from Mexico. Eventually, the experiment of shipping Indians from the Yucatan ended: in Cuba, there were concerns about possible political involvement of the deportees from Yucatán, and the Mexican government resisted the idea for political reasons as well. However, the total number of people brought from the Yucatan under such conditions was considerable, with estimates placing it at about 2,000. Reportedly, by 1862, there were 1,046 immigrants from Yucatan in Cuba, most of them living in the western parts of the island.

Those working in the sugar mills numbered 786.[155] In the same decade, some immigrants apparently from Turkey (or having departed from Turkish territory) also arrived, in what has been portrayed as an effort either to introduce "Arab *colonos*" or to smuggle some blacks "under a fake nationality."[156]

Thus, throughout the nineteenth century Cuba emerged an unequivocal immigrant society. Hundreds of thousands of immigrants to Cuba were forced to work as slaves or under other inhumane conditions; many others arrived in the hope of increasing their wealth. Others just meant to visit—to work or to make an investment, a "hit-and-run" type of escapade—yet found conditions inviting enough to stay and develop a new life. Even in the final decades of Spanish colonialism, when emigration peaked as a result of armed struggle, increasing repression, and political turmoil, there were immigrants arriving, following different (and sometimes overlapping) logics. Cuba suffered a net population loss at the very end of the colonial period, when repression intensified and living conditions became unbearable for large segments of the population. Both an increase in the number of deaths and a negative migration balance contributed to this demographic outcome. Nevertheless, Cuba would continue to be a strong magnet for immigrants in the postcolonial years to come.

THREE

Migration and Other Transnational Processes in the Colonial-Postcolonial Transition

Spanish Migration and Transnationalism

Capital Accumulation, Family Strategies, and Transnational Livelihoods

Spanish migrants played a central role in the development of the social fields that connected Cuba with Spain (and other societies) since the early stages of the colonial project. As Alejandro de la Fuente notes, "Immigrants maintained active ties with their hometowns. Doing so with Seville or other Andalusian towns was particularly easy from Havana, given the active communications that existed between Havana and Seville since the mid-sixteenth century. Some of the immigrants from Andalusia used the opportunities that Havana provided to bring family members or conduct business from afar."[1] Referring to Díaz Pimienta, an immigrant from the Canary Islands, de la Fuente (2008, 90) observes that he "never settled in Havana, although he obviously spent long periods of time there conducting his business. His commercial interests in the city were served by his son-in-law, Captain Alonso de Ferrera, also from La Palma, who apparently came first to Havana in 1599. Like his father-in-law's business, Ferrera's commercial ventures covered a large variety of products, although as always with merchants from the Canaries, wine and naval stores figured prominently among them."

Although the forging of transnational links between Spain and Cuba was a constitutive aspect of the migration experience since the sixteenth century, the participation of Spanish migrants in transnational economic, cultural, social, and political strategies and projects acquired new qualitative dimensions by the second half of the nineteenth century and into the first decades of the twentieth. In Cuba, this time frame marks the transition from the colonial period to the post- or neocolonial period. Internationally, it marks a period that has been termed "the path to globalism" or "the first globalization wave" because of the unprecedented expansion of trade, investment, and migration and the concomitant flows of ideas, symbols, values, commodities, and capital that forged a complex configuration of social fields across the Atlantic. These developments included the emergence of financial capital as the dominant form of capital, the centrality of credit in long-distance economic transactions, corporate forms of organization of the production processes, and technological innovations that facilitated travel, communications, and the printing and distribution of news. Equally important, as David Harvey contends, such changes were rooted in (and inaugurated) new ways of viewing and experiencing space, motion, and time.[2] Regionally, the period in question points to the definitive establishment of the United States as the dominant power. With the Monroe Doctrine and Manifest Destiny as antecedents, the U.S. sphere of influence extended further over Latin America and the Caribbean. Increased Anglo-Latino differentiation, military interventions, and specific legal frameworks sustained U.S. hegemonic designs locally, as the Platt Amendment in Cuba demonstrates. It is widely accepted that the Spanish-American War played a key role in the ascendance of the United States regionally. What frequently passes unnoticed is the fact that the transnational relations and social fields that were developed between Cuba and the United States before the Spanish-American War and their expansion after it played a pivotal role in the hegemonic repositioning of the United States in Cuba and as a regional power.

Transnational entrepreneurship among Spanish migrants was entangled with entrepreneurial strategies, marital arrangements, and political affiliations that usually stretched not only across space but also beyond the first generation of immigrants and included the building of family, entrepreneurial, and political alliances, as well as an array of labor market participation strategies that included the United States. Cuban Creoles, many of whom were second-generation Spanish immigrants, were actively involved in the migration links and the transnational activities that connected the island with the United States during the final stages of the colonial period. The state and other actors, such as merchants, workers, and bankers, many of whom were migrants, performed overlapping functions in their involvement in transnational social fields that linked Cuba with other societies. Their manifold transnational involvement was instrumental for the development of commercial activities, investments, social projects, and the expansion of cultural and political links that transformed localities in Cuba, Spain, and the United States with singular intensity. The development of transnational social, educational, and cultural projects; ethnic and class loyalties; and the phenomenon known as "long-distance nationalism" and other forms of long-distance political involvement were important aspects of the transnational relations forged at that time, while the transnational dimension of the process of surplus value production and appropriation by means of migration picked up momentum during this crucial transition period.

At the peak of Spanish migration, from the late nineteenth century to the early twentieth century, return to the homeland—which often took place without severing social networks with the island—was also a key aspect of the migration process. Migrations increasingly responded to a "culture of migration" that sprang up in different localities in Spain and not only responded to the socialization toward emigration as a social mobility path but also included seasonal and circular movements.[3] The frequent traveling back and forth between areas of origin and destination for household reproduction and capital accumulation purposes is succinctly captured by a descendant of Catalonian immigrants in Santiago de Cuba:

> On my father's side we already had some family members in Santiago de Cuba in the 1830s, while my grandfather on the mother's side, who arrived in 1888 when he was fourteen, made his last trip sometime between 1922 and 1923 to sell his store "La California.". . . Between the spring of 1912 and 1916 he crossed the Atlantic several times. In 1912 he went from Santiago de Cuba to Spain to get married and in 1913 for the birth of my mother. We have records indicating that he was in Sitges [Catalonia] in October 1914. Then, he came back again when my aunt was born and he conceived my other aunt. In all, between 1912 and 1916, he made five transatlantic trips that were very productive in every sense of the word: from the business perspective and for the reproduction of the family.[4]

Certainly, strategies of accumulation and livelihood by Spaniards from Galicia, the Canary Islands, Catalonia, Asturias, and Andalusia, among other regions, involved frequent trips (for the standards of that time) to Santiago de Cuba, Havana, Matanzas, and other areas of Cuba. In some cases, such strategies also involved either temporary migration or frequent trips to the United States, other Caribbean islands, and Latin America. Spanish migrants, sometimes accompanied by family members or friends, would travel to Cuba, then other areas of the Caribbean and the United States in search of market opportunities. Sometimes they searched for seasonal jobs, while in other cases they stayed for longer periods of time in two or more societies.[5] Many Spanish families, as will be seen later, also had economic and familial ties in South America and Mexico that also implied their physical mobility across societies. These practices intensified in the early twentieth century as communication and transportation technologies became more sophisticated, facilitating the cyclical incorporation to distant labor markets: "The temporary migrations to the United States, and to a lesser extent Canada, were relatively frequent in the 1910s. A large number of Spaniards (from Asturias, Almeria, Alicante, and Galicia), who lived in Cuba and worked in activities related to sugar harvesting, moved to the U.S. from April or May until the beginning of the winter to complement their income, mainly by working in the construction of railroads and roads."[6]

In the last decade of the nineteenth century, approximately one million Spaniards crossed the Atlantic for the Americas or back to Europe, and the figure is placed at approximately six million (including duplications based on the fact that some traveled more than once in either direction) in the period between 1885 and the early 1930s.[7] Spanish migrants were also actively involved in transnational activities that did not necessarily involve border crossing—or ocean crossing, for that matter. These included sending remittances, transferring capital, and participating in trade activities that linked them to places located across the Atlantic and were carried out with the assistance of family members or associates. It is not possible to fully grasp the meaning and reach of Spanish commercial relations with Cuba in the nineteenth and early twentieth centuries without taking into consideration their embeddedness in multilayered transnational social fields that involved Spanish migrants as well as merchants and investors who never left Spain, yet heavily relied on their social networks with Spaniards residing in the Americas and returnees. Sometimes, migrants were merchants themselves, or facilitators of trade relations as lenders, or simply consumers principally but not only of "ethnic products." Thus, while trade can be seen as an "inter-national" activity (that is to say, falling into the realms of "state-to-state" relations), it can also be seen as the result of a multiplicity of transnational activities that are the result of family and entrepreneurial strategies and encompass multiple networks developed by different actors, including the migrants.

By focusing on immigration and trade links between Baltimore, Boston, and port areas that would eventually become part of Germany from 1776 to 1835, Sam Mustafa calls attention to the role of migrant merchants, including their "invisible diplomacy" in the exploration of the Atlantic as a "highway of exchange."[8] James Dunlevy and William Hutchinson (1999) examine the growth of import trade in conjunction with immigration from eastern and southern Europe in the late nineteenth and early twentieth centuries. More recently, focusing on Korean immigrants, some authors have shown the role of immigrants in promoting trade with the United States after having identified a particular market niche.[9] In general, there is widespread recognition of a strong link between trade and migration, although it remains understudied largely due to the influence of methodological nationalism, which, by naturalizing the state, tends to present societies as linked primarily through state relations.

Historical structural analyses on the expansion of the sugar industry in Cuba call our attention to the entanglements between immigration and the expansion of commercial capital in the transition of Cuba into a major producer of sugar for the world market. British, North American, Creole, and Spanish merchants who had made fortunes, mostly out of slave trafficking, would eventually become the financial agents for large-scale investments in the sugar industry.[10] When these accounts are complemented by those that focus on the microstructures of commercial activities, investments, credit, and migration, then we gain a better understanding of how the complex links between commercial activities, migration, and the transnational flows of goods, money, and capital operated in everyday life.[11]

The establishment in 1764 of the maritime postal service between Spain and the Americas opened up an important communication and transportation pathway that facilitated migration and commercial activities principally between La Coruña in Galicia and Havana, Veracruz in Mexico, and Montevideo and Buenos Aires in South America. Commercial activities between La Coruña and certain areas of the Americas encompassed periods of bonanza as well as periods of crisis caused by competition from other northern ports in Spain or Portugal and contraction of the commercial frontiers and labor markets in South America. Sometimes Galicians would return en masse as opportunities opened up in their homeland and shrank elsewhere, as when approximately three thousand Galicians returned toward the end of 1879.[12] There was also the issue of whether the growing role of La Coruña as a port for reexportation of commodities from South America negatively affected industrialization in Galicia, resulting in further emigration.[13]

Long-distance trade involving La Coruña and Cuba existed earlier, which is illustrated by a letter from a Spanish merchant in La Coruña to Frederick Huth and Company (in London) in 1826. The letter in question indicates in a detailed way that the merchant was preparing a shipment that required the involvement of other merchants, insurers, lenders, and consumer markets that operated from four different places: La Coruña, London, Santiago de Cuba, and Havana. After detailing the insurance and credit issues, the merchant indicated that his objective was to sell the merchandise in Santiago de Cuba, but if that was not possible, then in Havana. Payment could be received either in silver or gold or such products as sugar, tobacco, coffee, and so on, depending on what was available at the time.[14] It should be noted that migration figured prominently in the links that tied the merchants, insurers, and bankers to one another in the case of Frederick Huth and Company's operations. Before moving to London, Frederick Huth had established his business in La Coruña in 1805. He arrived in London a few years later where he established himself as a merchant, but his links to Spain, particularly Galicia, proved to be instrumental for the firm's strategy of transatlantic business expansion and diversification.[15]

Long-distance trade and banking relations between Galicia and Latin America would be reinforced as transatlantic migration increased toward the end of the century and reached a new peak in the twentieth century. Continuing migration for a prolonged period of time and the social networks developed across generations between localities of origin and destination created the social foundations upon which some economic relations were built beyond the nineteenth century and into the twenty-first. For example, Caixanova, a banking institution in Galicia, expanded its transatlantic operations after having established a headquarters for Latin America in Miami in 2002. The fact that approximately six hundred thousand Galicians reside in Latin America was at the core of this decision.[16] As was the case in the nineteenth century, the multiple links that currently tie Galicia with the Americas via migration go beyond trade.

The case of Catalonians illustrates the complex imbrications of immigration and "the merchants' world" in particular ways. The statement "being Catalan in Cuba meant being a merchant," popularized by historian Levi Marrero and still quoted today, captures the entrenched representation of Catalonians as merchants in modern narratives about the Atlantic economy. In Cuba, Marrero's maxim points to the fact that Catalonian migrants tended to be clustered around economic niches related to transatlantic trade and all sorts of commercial activities in the island. They were known in particular for their involvement in trade, including the slave trade, and their ownership of stores and warehouses in Cuba and Catalonia, many of which were linked through entrepreneurial associations. It has been argued that they constituted an important segment of the Spanish from the Peninsula who played a key role in the revitalization of the sugar industry between 1800 and 1840. Their economic involvement increasingly included their participation in financial operations as lenders of money to the landowners (*hacendados*) linked to the production of sugar and other profitable activities, and eventually to eventually purchase haciendas and became *comerciantes/hacendados*.[17]

Estimates based on boarding licenses indicate that between 1800 and 1835, Catalonians represented 58 percent of all arrivals to Cuba, followed by immigrants from Asturias and the Basque Country–Navarra region (approximately 14 percent each).[18] Although their proportion among Spanish immigrants had dramatically dropped by the end of the century, Catalonians continued to arrive in significant numbers, mainly from Barcelona and the port areas of Sitges and Vilanova, after 1835. They tended to settle in Havana and Matanzas and Santiago de Cuba.

The peak of emigration from Catalonia to Cuba in particular and the circum-Caribbean in general in the nineteenth century corresponded to the economic transformations that included an increase of trade activities as well as "proto-industrial" efforts in the Mediterranean economy that created some structural imbalances between the rural and urban economies in Catalonia, while changes in emigration rules, sometimes as part of such dynamics or under a combination of rationales, encouraged their departure in certain periods.[19] Throughout the nineteenth century, migrant-merchants from Catalonia participated in an array of commercial ventures that connected several ports in Spain and Cuba. For Catalonians and other Spanish migrant groups, developments contributing to the impact of migration on trade included the growing demand for "ethnic products," the identification of trade opportunities by immigrants based on their privileged access to information about different markets, and their linguistic and other cultural abilities. In addition, there was mutual conditioning between commercial activities and migration, and "domino" effects as well. The seizing of market opportunities by the migrants in their localities of origin and settlement enhanced the labor market and stimulated migration; arrivals and departures were either slowed down or accelerated depending on the effects of trade on the local economy.[20] And as in other cases, the commercial activities of the Catalonians reflected both the consumption habits of Spanish migrants and the growing demand for products from the Americas in Spain and other areas of Europe.

Martín Rodrigo argues that both "the cosmopolitan sumptuous consumption habits" of the wealthiest groups as well as more "local" and "popular" habits led to a growing demand for products and specific brands from certain regions in Spain and Cuba.[21] He has documented that Catalonian merchants in Cuba often kept a variety of products from different areas of Spain in their warehouses. Payment was made either in cash, using monetary instruments, or through commodities that could be sold elsewhere. This approach, in turn, fueled the expansion of commercial activities within the region, since not all products acquired in the Americas were taken to Spain; some were resold in Cuba's neighboring markets, such as St. Thomas, Kingston, or Curaçao. There was demand in Cuba for textiles from England, which Catalonian and other merchants from Spain also tried to satisfy.[22] By the end of the nineteenth century, "the triangular trade that encompassed Europe, Cuba, and the United States" also attracted a segment of Spanish merchants and the fleets associated with them. Piqueras clarifies that "el verdadero negocio" (the real deal) for the Spanish merchants was in the return trip, when after unloading their commodities in Cuba, they transported sugar from there to the United States and then wheat or cotton from the United States to Europe.[23] Such a triangularization also reflected the important role that Cuba played as a major source of Spanish migrants to the United States at that time."[24]

The development of commercial networks relied heavily on personal networks established between friends and family members and reflected patterns of in-group solidarity related to economic specialization. It was not unusual for the returnees to keep important investments in Cuba as they expanded their enterprises in Spain: "By the second half of the nineteenth century, a solid network that crossed the Atlantic linked the economies of Cuba and Catalonia . . . [and] some of the benefits generated by the island's economy ended up in Catalonia. This financial flow did not stop the [Catalonian] landowners from transforming and modernizing their haciendas in Cuba."[25] Simultaneous entrepreneurial presence in Cuba and Catalonia prominently included involvement in banking and real estate investments in Catalonia, the sugar industry in Cuba, and enterprises related to maritime transportation and trade (including slave trade).[26]

Birgit Sonesson documents that young Spaniards from different regions arrived in Cuba to work in "commercial houses" in Havana, Santiago de Cuba, San Juan, Monterrey, Brownsville, and on the like that had been established by family or friends. Typically, those who arrived later would stay to administer the enterprise once the founders returned to Spain to control the business from there while exploring new accumulation opportunities. Catalonians have been portrayed as being particularly efficient at developing a pattern of rotation and collaboration among extended family members and neighbors. This pattern, Sonesson argues, predated the nineteenth century but it was further reinforced in colonial Cuba and Puerto Rico as the political risk of losing assets was minimal there. The so-called migration chains played a key role.

> The "migration chains" developed through commercial relations by entrepreneurs from Sitges and Vilanova in the eighteenth century usually included a family member operating the enterprise in the town of origin and a small distilling shop administered by an employee or a younger brother, and several brothers and cousins in the islands who were in charge of importing and distribution of wine and aguardiente from Catalonia and all kinds of consumer goods. In this model of a close-knit network, the oldest son, the one who directed the whole enterprise, played a key role: how he accumulated capital reflected a symbiosis that ultimately benefited not only the main partner but also offered support to the partners in the island in times of crisis.[27]

"Those who were neighbors in Sitges, were neighbors in Santiago," was the phrase chosen by a Catalonian scholar to open an international scholarly colloquium held in Barcelona in 2005.[28] Certainly, families from Sitges used to transplant their social networks to Cuba and even tried to remain neighbors when they settled on the island. By the same token, the "Indianos reproduced in Catalonia the social networks that they had initially developed in the Antilles."[29]

While transnationalism relied on regular migration flows for prolonged periods of time and regular arrangements related to them and even a normative approach to sustaining long-distance links in cases in which the "migration culture" was fully developed, sometimes there were gaps of time or discontinuities in the transnational strategies pursued and the alliances formed. Martín Rodrigo (1998, 2004) shows, in the case of Catalonians, that some Spanish investors tended to keep their investments "quasi-dormant" on the island after having launched some investment strategies in Spain with the capital brought from Cuba.

The social networks of the migrants also extended to the state apparatus as a means to secure large-scale capital accumulation. Although this issue will be further examined in the next section, for now suffices it to say that some transnational entrepreneurs used direct leverage from state sources for capital accumulation. The making of some fortunes—most of which either originated in commercial activities or incorporated them at some point—depended to a large extent on the links developed by these individuals with the Spanish state through lending practices, marriage with members of high-profile political families, or other social mechanisms.[30] The activities of the migrant-merchants (either immigrants or returnees) encompassed shipping and warehousing as much as it encompassed transnational lending practices, money transfers, and investments. As both commerce and the Spanish-origin population in the Americas grew, so too did the need for loans for investment. In this context, a number of Spanish merchants worked as merchant-lenders.[31] In addition, their frequent travel, knowledge of the money markets, and personal ties with people on both sides of the Atlantic created the social conditions for their involvement in the remittance business, encouraged by a growing demand for that service.

Remittances, Capital Transfers, and Banking

In sync with migration, trade, and investment trends, the flow of family remittances grew during the second half of the nineteenth century and reached unprecedented levels in the early twentieth. As the Spanish-origin population of the Americas grew, the historical entanglements among remittances and social, economic, and political projects in the homeland, became more complex, while this flow of money became structurally linked to major economic developments, such as large capital transfers and the development of the banking industry.

The reception of remittances from the Americas—including transfers sent by relatives and associates, and through extended networks forged through clubs, associations, and political groups—had gained momentum in certain parts of Spain as early as the eighteenth century. María Cruz Morales Saro (1992, 58) documents that in the mid-eighteenth century the monetary transfers from the Americas to Asturias had multiple purposes and effects. They were used to help pay the pending debts of the family or enterprise, purchase real estate, and cover the expenses related to marriage, among many other family uses. They also had enduring social impact, such as when remittances were used to build infrastructure, churches, and educational institutions.

Several studies on Spanish transatlantic migration that address the issue of remittances either directly or indirectly agree that family remittances were used for an array of purposes, although their uses varied by region and period.[32] They were used to cover the basic needs of households when some of the household members had been forced to look for jobs in remote labor markets. They also assisted families and communities that had been affected by natural disasters or other crises. For example, in the case of the Canary

Islands, the remittances received from Cuba during the yellow fever plague of the early 1890s were higher than the ones received from Europe, including peninsular Spain. Remittances were also used to pay debts, to purchase land and build or rebuild houses, to pay for the exemption of family members from military service, and to help finance the trips of other migrants through kinship or friendship networks (this could also be capital investment if those traveling were doing so to work in a family business). In addition, they were employed directly for the development of small enterprises through very limited forms of capitalization. In some contexts, capital transfers were used for projects related to proto-industrialization, usually investments directly related to agricultural, fishing, and mining production for external markets, among others. Both family remittances and capital transfers were also used for improvement of the social and cultural infrastructure in the localities of origin in Spain.[33] London, Madrid, and Barcelona were the main recipients of capital transfers.[34]

The total amount of remittances received by Spaniards from the Americas between 1906 and 1910 has been estimated at more than 1.1 billion pesetas.[35] In a comprehensive regional study on remittances that focuses on those sent through Asturian banking and lending institutions, José R. García L?pez shows that, between 1881 and 1911, approximately 144 million pesetas (or an annual average of 5 million pesetas) were processed. García L?pez points out that this figure represents "more than what the Ministry of Commerce collected in Asturias from industrial, commercial, real estate, agriculture and livestock activities," and that, "measured in annual salaries," it was equivalent to "the creation of enough jobs to hire those who were emigrating at that time" (1992, 123; my translation). He also indicates that at the beginning of the nineteenth century, when financial instruments were still poorly developed, merchants and commercial houses provided the bulk of services needed to meet the growing demand related to the sending of remittances. Most remittances originated in Cuba until the end of the nineteenth century, which is in tune with Cuba's prominence as the major destination point at that time. It should be noted that by 1897, there were an estimated 200,000 persons of Asturian origin living in Cuba (66).

Emigration from Galicia to Cuba, as from other regions of Spain, was also positively impacted by the Royal Order of 1853, which liberalized movement from Spain in many respects. In contrast with emigration from Catalonia, emigration from Galicia was dramatically marked by the efforts of the Spanish crown to populate different areas of the Americas, such as the Mosquito Coast in Central America (an area under siege by the British), the borderland areas of South America threatened by the Portuguese, and Cuba. This practice had been established long before but was sanctioned by the Royal Ordinance of 1888, which further codified bureaucratic procedures to be followed by Spaniards who were using government programs to emigrate, mainly to colonial areas, and principally Cuba.[36]

In Galicia, a region that was eminently agrarian, structural problems associated with patterns of land tenure and low levels of productivity resulted in several decades of continuous emigration, beginning in the eighteenth century. The remittances sent by Galicians in the Americas or carried by returnees were rarely employed in the development of industries, large-scale commercial activities, or in promoting banking institutions, through some efforts led to these outcomes, but rather for the purchase of land, the remodeling and repair of housing, and the creation of small banking associations devoted to channeling more remittances.[37] José A. Durán (1992) argues that migrants from Galicia may also have participated in some forms of sojournerism related to seasonal labor market opportunities both in Cuba and in their localities of origin. The migration process and transnational economic strategies associated with it reflected the ups and downs of the economies of Galicia and Latin America. Between 1764 and 1818, emigration, return migration, and transnational strategies were particularly linked to trade relations between La Coruña and the Americas, and fluctuations in the labor markets on both sides of the Atlantic. Durán argues that these circumstances, compounded with the agrarian problems in Galicia, prevented merchants in Galicia from developing into a powerful commercial class similar to the one that arose in Catalonia. Instead, they tended to rely on rents from agricultural activities as a major source of income. As a result of the specific logics that propelled migration and transnationalism between Galicia and Cuba in the nineteenth century, their participation in transnational labor circuits as workers selling their labor become more prominent than their involvement in transnational investments as capitalists. The contrasts between the modes of incorporation of Galicians and Catalonians in labor markets in Cuba and their involvement in transnational social fields fed the imaginary about these groups. Although there were wealthy investors in Cuba of Galician origin, Galicians tended to invest in small family enterprises, typically small corner stores or convenience stores, with the assistance of a friend or a nephew after having spent some time selling their labor, mainly in agricultural activities. This pattern is suggested by the title of Naranjo Orovio's inspiring 1988 study, *Del campo a la bodega* (From the Countryside to the Corner Store). In the whole period between 1885 and 1930, Galicia contributed 36 percent of the Spanish immigrants to the Americas. Much of the movement was facilitated by family networks established in connection with immigration in prior years, mainly to Argentina and Cuba.[38]

Immigration from the Canary Islands to Cuba had started as early as the sixteenth century, and in 1693 immigrants from Tenerife had founded Matanzas, one of Cuba's most dynamic settlements during the early colonial period. Immigration from the islands peaked in the mid-1830s, right in the midst of colonizing experiments and the increasing demand for *braceros* to work in the sugar plantations. Between 1835 and 1843, approximately 11,500 immigrants arrived in Cuba from the Canary Islands.[39] The Spanish population of Cuba in 1859 has been estimated at approximately 83,000 Spaniards, of whom approximately 45,500 were from different regions of mainland Spain, 38,714 from the Canary Islands, and 1,317 from the Balearic Islands.[40] Cuba's census of 1862 estimates that there were approximately 45,814 people from the Canary Islands residing in Cuba: 29,944 male and 15,870 female.[41] Cuba and Venezuela were the main destinations of immigrants from the Canary and Balearic islands throughout the second half of the nineteenth century, by which time emigration from those islands had peaked. Juan Pérez de la Riva (1975, 1979) argued that *migración golondrina,* or sojournerism, between Cuba and the Canary Islands was significant and grew in the 1880s. Canary Islanders tended to work in agricultural production both in Cuba and in their homeland. In Cuba, they worked mainly as agricultural laborers or supervisors in the sugar industry or as small farmers renting small lots from the *hacendados* to grow tobacco. They also had a relatively high number of women participating in the migration process, which was related to recruitment efforts to bring entire families, the emigration of women on their own, and also the *trata de blancas.* In general there was no "feminization of migration" in Spanish transatlantic migrations during the nineteenth century and very little of it at the beginning of the twentieth century. The process was a male-dominated phenomenon. Precisely this characteristic introduced some tensions concerning the idea of protecting the Spanish nuclear family—either directly, in cases of males who emigrated after having married in Spain, or indirectly, in the cases of male migrants who emigrated at very young ages (which was very common) and would eventually return. Despite their comparatively lower levels of emigration, women played a key role in migration as decision-makers in the migrant households, even in cases where they did not migrate. The wives, daughters, and sisters of male entrepreneurs usually either took over the administration of enterprises (if the entrepreneur died without any reliable male successor in the family) or worked in partnership with the male successors. Spanish women were also key players in the tradition of incorporating marriage strate-gies at the core of capital accumulation through the mergers of wealthy fami-lies. Nevertheless, a number of women did travel across the Atlantic on their own, sometimes hiding their status as single women, or with their families.[42] It has been suggested that among Spanish migrants, a relatively high percent-age of widows (6 percent), as compared to widowers (1 percent), went to live in the United States at the beginning of the 1900s.[43] Given the role of Cuba as a major source of Spanish migration to the United States at that time, Spanish widows might have also arrived from the island.

The key role of the economic links with Cuba through labor circuits, family remittances, and other forms of transnational links for the Canary Islands' economy is succinctly captured in a mid-nineteenth-century editorial of the newspaper El Aladid: "We all hope that Cuba survives the tremendous crisis that she is facing, because Cuba was and is still our older sister, our mother, whom we help with the blood and work of our fellow islanders, while she returns such aid, our efforts toward its prosperity, with riches that have saved us from the tremendous crisis that this province faced not many years ago, without grave repercussions for our island, precisely because with the gold that came from Cuba we could pay our taxes."[44] The structural dependency of the Canary Islands on the remittances sent by the migrants was reinforced in the twentieth century. Between the 1960s and early 1970s, when migrants from these islands were not emigrating to Cuba anymore but to other areas in the Americas and Europe, remittances matched the relevance of tourism and capital imports.[45]

Thus, all these groups of immigrants from Spain, among others, partici-pated both in capital transfers and the sending of remittances to Spain. Both forms of transfers affected the Spanish economy through the development of a dense web of lending and banking institutions that participated in the busi-ness of monetary transfers. Migration shaped the flow of money and capital and the banking industry in a variety of ways, since some migrants not only sent money to cover some basic needs and minor private and social invest-ments in their localities of origin but also tended to operate as bankers them-selves in Spain, founders of banks with branches in Spain and Latin American countries, depositors of money in such banks, investors purchasing stocks in the banking industry, and agents providing commercial credits.[46]

Angel Bahamonde and José Cayuela (1992) and José Ramón García López (1992) have argued that the international prominence of Spain in banking and finance is a late-nineteenth-century phenomenon and that the economic links that the Spanish migrants established with the Americas, either as immigrants or returnees, were crucial to this development. It is widely acknowledged that the expansion of commerce between Europe and the Americas by the second half of the nineteenth century presupposed a sophistication of the financial system that other areas of Europe had achieved much earlier than Madrid and Barcelona. While there had been a long-standing tradition of credit associations and banking activity in Venice, Genoa, London, Amsterdam, and Hamburg—since as early as the twelfth and fourteenth centuries in Venice and Genoa—it took longer for Barcelona and Madrid to develop these areas.[47] *Indianos* (wealthy returnees) and Spanish entrepreneurs living in the Americas used their personal networks to advance their accumulation strategies. Such networks were sometimes conspicuously entangled with the Spanish state and backed its hegemonic projects. This was particularly true in the second half of the nineteenth century, when the Spanish government launched an aggressive strategy to use Cuba "to directly feed the peninsular financial capital."[48] Political-economy and sociological studies on the strategies of accumulation launched by the migrants, including the *Indianos,* call our attention to how the migrants were involved in projects sometimes linked to the state.

For example, the *Indiano* Antonio López y López functioned as a major investor and first president of the Banco Hispano-Colonial (BHC), a bank founded in 1875 for the mobilization of private capital to deal with the Spanish state's "lack of economic solvency" for its colonial administration in Cuba. As per its statutes, the "special object of the BHC" was "to loan the Spanish Government the sum of 75 to 85 million pesetas . . . to the urgent attention of the Treasury of Cuba."[49] Angel Bahamonde (1992) argues that participation in state projects, mainly through the lending of capital, was done with the expectation of gaining government contracts. Such contracts were typically offered by the state to help materialize its strategic investments, such as the railroads, mining, transatlantic postal service, and so on. It was through this process that Antonio López and Compañía—later called the "Transatlantic Company"—was granted a contract to carry the transatlantic post. State subvention of maritime transportation allowed the company to profit from the Spanish budget in Cuba.[50] Similarly, Juan Manuel de Manzanedo, an immigrant from Santander in Cuba, made a fortune from sugar and the slave trade and returned to Spain as a wealthy entrepreneur. Manzanedo, who has been portrayed as "a key player in Madrid's financial sector" between 1845 and 1883 and part of the "Hispanic-Antillean bourgeoisie," developed strategies of accumulation that reached the Spanish state and extended beyond Spain, mainly to Cuba. As highlighted by Bahamonde, Manzanedo "returned to

Spain in 1845 . . . but he always kept his numerous ties in Havana working" (1992, 118; my translation).

There was also the great mass of less affluent and even impoverished migrants from numerous localities in Spain who entered transnational labor circuits as providers of an important source of the surplus value upon which the big fortunes were built. They were major actors in the sending of remittances and small-capital transfers. Those who sent remittances, or took their savings to Spain, had a direct impact on the Spanish banking industry through its transnational components by fueling the remittances business and also by depositing money and value instruments. Eventually, the United States also functioned as a major originator of the monetary transfers of Spanish migrants.[51] The United States also received large sums of money and capital as Spanish-origin entrepreneurs and Cuban Creoles relocated their families and enterprises to the United States during periods of turmoil in the island.

At the beginning of the twentieth century, the most important Spanish banking houses benefiting from capital transfers and remittances were mainly in Madrid and Barcelona. Until 1910, the most important ones in Latin America were concentrated in Cuba, Mexico, and Argentina. At least sixteen institutions that carried out lending and banking practices in Cuba at the time were either directly or indirectly responsible for monetary transfers to Spain.[52] As García López (1992, 104–5) has noted, commerce and banking were still dual functions performed by many enterprises, many of which were operated by migrant families or through business partnerships that relied heavily on transnational networks based on kinship and friendship. By the end of the nineteenth century, capital transfers and remittances sent by the Spanish migrants played a role in the transatlantic expansion of monetary flows; they also illustrate the links between migration and the global integration of financial markets. For example, Blanca Sánchez Alonso (1995, 187–88) indicates that the monetary crisis in Argentina in the 1890s, related to the collapse of the Baring Brothers bank, led to a depreciation of the Argentinean peso vis-à-vis the Spanish peseta, which also reduced the value of remittances to Spain. This development, she argues, made immigration seem less attractive in Galicia and elsewhere.

The expansion of highly profitable transnational economic activities frequently involved marriage strategies, which secured the consolidation of wealth. The Banco Hispano Americano (BHA), founded in 1900 by Spanish migrants who had lived in Mexico and Cuba, was reinforced through marriages and amply promoted and backed by Spanish returnees. BHA merged with the Banco Central (founded in 1919) to form the Banco Central Hispanoamericano, which is currently portrayed as having played "a prominent role in the history of Spain's banking system in the twentieth century."[53] The Vidal Cuadras Hermanos banking house, founded in 1846 in Catalonia by wealthy returnees; the Banco Gijón in Asturias, opened by Florencio Rodríguez, a returnee from Cuba; and the Banco de Vigo, officially founded in 1900, are additional examples of the transnational imbrication of family and enterprise strategies.[54] Spanish investors in banking in Latin America competed with each other but they also established entrepreneurial and family links and formed alliances among themselves, which facilitated raising capital and ultimately coping with global competition in which British and U.S. investors and lenders figured prominently. In sum, the sociogeography of transnational investments and finance capital was built upon social networks, forged by Spanish migrants, that extended to the insular Caribbean, Mexico, several nations in South America, London, and some areas in the United States.

Political Involvement and the Creation of Social Clubs and Associations

Spanish migrants founded an array of political associations, parties, clubs, and organizations whose goals ranged from resistance projects against the hegemony of the Spanish state, such as those rooted in the struggles based on ethnic, cultural, and political identities in what today constitute Spain's "autonomous communities" (Galicia, Catalonia, and the Basque Autonomous Community, among others), to those that supported Spanish colonial and imperial designs. They were also actively involved in the organization of mutual assistance associations and developed educational and cultural projects impacting both the Americas and their localities of origin, some of which had a strong political orientation as well. Among the most influential parties were the Irmandades de Fala and the Partido Nazionalista Galego, both founded in the early twentieth century. As in the case of parties from regions of Spain with strong secessionist traditions, such as Catalonia and the Basque region, Galicians from the National Party advocated seceding from Spain's central government, recognizing Galician as the official language of the region, and preserving the regional culture and patrimony. In addition, the party advocated equal rights for women.[55] Another prominent nationalist organization created in Cuba by immigrants from Galicia was Irmandade Nazonalista Galega, whose main objectives included "the unity of Galicians to combat *caciquismo* [local leadership centered in one person] from America, a phenomenon that has victimized our beautiful region, and to make it possible for Galicia to integrate by its own right into the concert of civilized nations."[56]

In Havana, Galician immigrants printed the first newspaper published by Spanish immigrants in the Americas, *El Eco de Galicia,* founded in 1878. The newspaper generally defended immigrants' rights, denounced Cuban *hacendados'* approach to immigration, and kept immigrants abreast of major issues in Galicia. It also provided a media outlet for Galician enterprises in Cuba and for the diffusion of Galician culture in Cuba as well.[57] The involvement of Waldo Álvarez Insua, founder of the newspaper, in a dispute about the will of Fernando Blanco de Lema, a Galician migrant who had died in Havana and left a large sum of money and resources to be employed in the development of a foundation and some educational projects in Cee, his hometown, illustrates the sense of entitlement that influential institutions and individuals in the migrants' hometowns could have concerning funds promised for social projects there. In this case, the director of a local newspaper in Cee claimed part of Blanco de Lema's inheritance, saying that the migrant would reportedly have used the money for local projects. Such claims were made for "the common good" in Galicia. After what many considered an unreasonable delay on the part of the will's executors to fulfill Blanco de Lema's wishes, Álvarez Insua launched a strong campaign in *El Eco de Galicia* supporting the release of the funds that were intended to be used for the construction of two schools and the provision of free education. He justified his involvement in the matter by claiming, "I have a newspaper that is devoted to defending the interests of Galicia. Cee is a town in Galicia that is being jeopardized by the despicable conduct of [the executors of the will]. I strongly believe that it is my duty to take on their actions more aggressively since they have not paid attention to prior gently expressed requests."[58]

As was the case in the nineteenth century, the links that today tie Galicia with the Americas via migration involve politics. For example, Galician politicians campaigned in South America before the regional elections of 2005 because Argentina, labeled as Galicia's "fifth province" during election periods, has 100,857 Galician-origin registered voters, just as Venezuela and Uruguay also have large numbers of Galician-origin registered voters.[59]

Canary Islanders in Cuba also developed sustained political networks, parties, and associations that expanded across the Atlantic. The press also played a key role in the development and continuation of transnational relations and the spread of political ideas beyond the Atlantic. *El Eco de las Canarias, Las Afortunadas,* and *La Revista de las Canarias* were among the newspapers and magazines published in Cuba that had strong links to the Canary Islands.

Equally important was the influence of immigrants from the islands on Cuba's independence movement; the anticolonial struggle in Cuba also influenced social movements against Spanish hegemony in the Canary Islands. *El Guanche,* a secessionist newspaper founded by immigrants from the Canary Islands in Venezuela in 1897 following the spirit of the independence movement in Cuba, attests to such influence.[60] Asturians funded their own press in Cuba, *El Progeso de Asturias,* which would play a role in keeping immigrants from the region abreast of developments "at home." By 1900, immigrants from the area of Santander had published *Ecos de la Montaña* and *El Eco Montañés.*[61] The press, particularly in the regions of heavy emigration such as Galicia, Asturias, and the Canary Islands, was usually involved in the analysis of migration policies and labor recruitment strategies, which they were occasionally able to shape. In some cases, newspapers had representatives on both sides of the Atlantic. As such, the media became instrumental in raising awareness of both the perils and the advantages of the migration experience, and sometimes helped mold "migration culture."[62] It has been documented that between 1861 and 1898 at least ten newspapers were founded in Cuba (Havana and Santiago de Cuba) by Catalonian migrants. Some of them were bilingual (Catalan and Spanish), and others were in Spanish only. They tended to advance issues of interest in Catalonia and among Catalonians in Cuba on a wide range of topics: political, cultural, economic, and scientific.[63]

Immigrants from different regions of Spain were very actively involved in the creation of associations of mutual assistance, associations with recreational, cultural, and educational purposes, and other supporting associations throughout the Americas. It was common to find associations with multiple purposes, and in many cases the goals of an association went beyond the protection of the welfare of the Spanish-origin population in the Americas to include projects to help the populations of their regions of origin in times of natural disasters, wars, or economic crises, and also in building productive and service infrastructures there. Those were the hometown associations of the nineteenth and early twentieth centuries. Some of these associations had great social recognition by the beginning of the twentieth century. The Sociedad Montañesa de Beneficencia (the welfare society of the Cantabria region) was founded in 1883 with the aim of protecting poor immigrants, but its funds were also used to help the victims of natural disasters and other "tragedies" there. As early as 1804, Galicians founded Apóstol Santiago, an association of mutual assistance. In 1840, Catalonians founded in Cuba the Sociedad Benéfica de Naturales de Cataluña (Catalonian Welfare Society). A similar organization, the Sociedad Benéfica de Naturales de Galicia (Galician Welfare

Society), was founded by Galician immigrants in a meeting held in 1871. They also founded the Hijas de Galicia, and those from Ortigueira founded the Naturales de Ortigueira and the Unión Mugardesa de Beneficencia y Recreo (1926).[64]

Concerned about the working conditions in Cuba, immigrants from the Canary Islands founded the Asociación de Beneficencia y Protección Agrícola in 1872, whose main objective was to protect immigrant agricultural workers from the islands.[65] In 1878, the Asociación Protectora de la Inmigración Cana-ria y de Beneficencia was founded in the province of Matanzas, and similar associations would be created throughout Cuba at the beginning of the twentieth century following an unprecedented rise in immigration from Spain in general and the Canary Islands in particular.[66] The Asociación Vasco-Navarra de Beneficencia, founded in 1878, focused on helping poor immigrants from the Basque region (as well as those who needed assistance to return there).[67] The Sociedad Benéfica Castellana was founded in 1885 by Castilians. By that time, Asturians had founded the society Nuestra Señora de Covadonga Princi-pado de Asturias (Our Lady of Covadonga of the Principality of Asturias), which would eventually be split into La Quinta Covadonga and the Sociedad Asturiana de Beneficencia (The Asturian Welfare Society).[68]

In addition to those associations, there were the regional centers or clubs, which systematically promoted social, cultural, and educational activities. Although they were often linked to the associations by virtue of the social networks of their members and the coordination of programs, their functions and social reach were different. Prominent among these clubs was the Centro Asturiano (Asturian Center), which was created in 1886 as an umbrella organization for immigrants from Asturias. One of its first missions was to help people affected by floods, droughts, and other natural disasters in Asturias, while it aimed to strengthen the ties between various generations of Asturian immigrants, provide social assistance for the ill, offer instruction and entertainment, and continue to raise the profile of Asturias in Cuba.[69] El Centro Gallego (the Galician Center) was founded in 1879.[70] El Centro Vasco (the Basque Center) was created decades later out of the Centro Euskaro, which was founded in 1911.[71] These clubs and centers also helped organize religious and other festivities frequently observed in certain regions of Spain, or in Spain in general. Some of them promoted entrepreneurship among immigrants, and also the retention of language and other cultural characteristics; often, they had an explicit political agenda that favored the colonial status quo. Such a tradition resonated particularly during the last years of Spanish colonialism in Cuba and again during the Spanish Civil War, when different ideological trends were represented by an array of Spanish organizations and political parties in Cuba. Sometimes, immigrants from several regions participated in umbrella associations that included Cubans in their membership. The Asociación de Dependientes del Comercio (Association of Commercial Workers) is often referred to as the most salient example of this kind of inclusive organization. The Spanish social assistance centers that had been founded in Cuba and other Latin American societies were also replicated in the United States. For example, by the late 1920s, there were two renowned social assistance centers in Tampa that had been created mostly by Spanish and Creole migrants: El Bien Público, founded by a Spanish-origin doctor, and La Covadonga.[72]

Since before the nineteenth century, Spanish migrants of different social strata had participated in the construction of churches, plazas, and cultural and educational centers in Spain. At the local level, returnees and "transmigrants" of various socioeconomic backgrounds participated in efforts to improve the quality of life in their localities of origin, either out of altruism, or for political or economic gain, or through collective associations (which themselves had a variety of motivations). Participation in the society of origin linked ideological discourses on migration with cultural and political imaginaries sustained by the local or even transnational elites. These discourses helped frame the construction of identities related to the migration experience such as *Indiano* and *Americano*.[73]

The development of translocal associations went hand in hand with projects that transformed Cuban urban space. The influence of Spanish migrants on the architecture of Cuba tended to reflect ideas on modernity very much in vogue among the Spanish and Latin American elites in the nineteenth century. Venegas Fornias (1996) argues that in Havana, cutting-edge architects emphasized the introduction of new architectural styles that reflected a sort of "'anxiety for modernity' that pervaded the island from the 1850s on." Havana's Spanish Casino, El Centro Asturiano, and El Centro Vasco were housed in sumptuous buildings. Some of them were part of a series of landmarks built in the city from the late nineteenth to the early twentieth centuries, and, Venegas Fornias claims, would be "never surpassed in size or quality" (1996, 24). The time of the Spanish fortresses was past. The exuberant styles of the clubs, fountains, and *obeliscos* built upon the shoulders of a slave society evoked the architectural splendor of Madrid and even replicated some of its most famous landmarks, and accentuating the Hispanic flavor of the world city. In Spain, the returnees were involved in the construction of mansions and other architectural projects that even today evoke a Cuban flavor. They also built profitable enterprises that, in the twenty-first century, hide the colonial past underneath their modern corporate structures. El Corte Inglés, one of the most popular department stores in Spain (and perhaps the most famous Spanish department store outside Spain), originally founded by Ramón Areces Rodríguez, a returnee from Cuba, is perhaps the most conspicuous of all.

U.S.-Bound Migration and Transnationalism

Historical accounts of the links between Cuba and the United States have shed light on the multiple channels through which the two societies were connected. Rebecca Scott, for example, calls our attention to the fact that planters and merchants in Havana and in New Orleans tried to keep abreast of their economic performance while political activists in the two areas were aware of their actions:

> Planters and merchants in Havana and New Orleans, part of the same intertwined Atlantic world, kept an eye on each other. A record-breaking harvest in Cuba could mean lowered profits in Louisiana; a new tariff in the United States could be a blow to Cuban producers. At the same time, the Caribbean and the Gulf of Mexico opened the way to the circulation of people, information, and ideas. Political activists in New Orleans and Havana often knew of each other's campaigns and tribulations.[74]

Such ties worked regularly, yet they could become even more obvious in times of deep crisis. During the U.S. Civil War, for example, merchants operating regionally used their networks in the ports of Havana in Cuba and Matamoros in Mexico to secure commercial flows to Liverpool and London.[75] In any event, the articulation of Cuba with U.S. markets, through legitimate trade as well as smuggling, grew stronger over the course of the nineteenth century. It has been estimated that between 1841 and 1860, U.S. merchant ships handled approximately 80 percent of all merchant maritime transportation in Cuba.[76] At the threshold of the independence war, which started in 1868, the United States was receiving 82 percent of all Cuban exports.[77] After the 1860s, when the United States reorganized its own sugar industry, Cuba remained an important production center, yet the refineries increasingly gravitated toward the United States while the bulk of the financial operations took place in the exchange markets of New York and London.[78] Many U.S. merchant houses established their businesses in Cuba or repositioned themselves there at that time. Between 1850 and 1895, there were about thirty-six U.S. merchant houses operating in Cuba, eleven of them in Havana.[79] It is in this context that a segment of Spanish entrepreneurs had reinforced their transnational ties with the United States through several strategies that included relationships with other actors in London, New York, and Madrid. However, these strategies were intensified at certain historical junctures.[80] The structural transformation in the U.S. economy—framed by the post–Civil War expansion of economic relations with Cuba, which overlapped with the struggle against Spanish rule in the island that reached a peak precisely during the Ten Years' War (1868–78) and then again during the final stage of the independence wars (1895–98)—also increased the flows of commodities, ideas, information, and technology between the two societies and intensified the involvement of people in political projects that linked Cuba and the United States.[81]

At that time, emigration from Cuba included, in addition to Spanish-origin groups, Creoles and, among them, many "people of color." The class background of those leaving Cuba was as diverse as their ethnic makeup, both of which were reshaped as part of the migration experience. The exodus included not only single men but many women and entire families as well, all leaving the island toward different destinations:

> The vessels that visited the ports of the island were filled out with Cuban families and New York, Philadelphia, and New Orleans received the first category of Cuba's Independent Party; Jamaica, Nassau, and Santo Domingo hosted the second category, farmers from Oriente and Camagüey; Key West, Tampa, Charleston, and Baltimore hosted and offered jobs to craftsmen; Mexico, Veracruz, Colon, and Caracas received all sorts of Cuban migrants . . .
>
> Men, women, and children wandered around streets and plazas looking for asylum . . . the vessels from Havana have arrived, and one can see them wandering with their bags and luggage that show that they have left their homeland without the travelers' usual arrangements.[82]

Families everywhere had to adjust to new lifestyles:

> And this is the way in which the daughters of [Francisco Vicente] Aguilera lived for several years. They had been groomed only to receive compliments, nice gestures, and the courtesy of their admirers, and to worry

only about their magnificent costumes . . . now that the rescue of their homeland demanded it, they sacrificed themselves without hesitation. As emigrants, in poverty, they became manual workers. . . .

. . . Yet the Aguilera family was not the only one going through all this hardship. Distinguished families of other patriots also became manual workers in the sweatshops of New York, showing, humbly, their patriotism and their virtue as daughters of this land.[83]

Key West, Tampa, New York, and Philadelphia hosted the greatest number of immigrants from Cuba at the time. The arrivals ranged from wealthy entrepreneurs, who had well-established business relations in the United States, to those who had lost most of their assets and properties to the independence conflict, as well as workers of modest economic means.[84] These were areas in which labor, management, and capital in the cigar industries were in relatively high demand and areas in which the economic links that tied the Cuban and the U.S. sugar industries and other economic activities had expanded. It has been estimated that between 1820 and 1900, approximately thirty-eight thousand Spanish migrants landed on U.S. shores.[85]

Immigrants from Cuba in the United States developed associations and clubs that expressed their political concerns and supported their plans concerning the status of Cuba. Cuban exiles used Tampa and Key West as political as well as military bases during the last stage of the independence wars, while the headquarters of some political groups were in New York. Access to prominent politicians and lawmakers in the United States by their leaders and the increasing appeal of the "Cuban cause" in U.S. public opinion contributed to favorable conditions for members of the opposition to the Spanish colonial establishment to operate from U.S. soil. This political environment was abetted by and reinforced a long-lasting inclination among certain interest groups in the United States to either purchase Cuba or expel Spain from there militarily.

Tampa and Key West perhaps provide a paradigmatic example of the complex links between economic and political forms of transnationalism among Cubans at that time. As the Cuban-origin working-class population grew with the expansion of the cigar industry in the area, Tampa became a magnet of revolutionary propaganda and activity. El Liceo Cubano de Tampa, La Liga Patriótica Cubana, and the Ignacio Agramonte Cuban Revolutionary Club, three of the most important organizations among those involved in revolutionary activities, were based there, and they had prominent Cuban pro-independence intellectuals and veterans who lived in Tampa and other areas as members. El Club de San Carlos of Key West was among the most renowned clubs organized by the émigrés in the U.S. The émigrés that were against Spanish colonialism also developed media outlets to spread political ideas and cultivate support groups in different cities. Between 1850 and 1898 they were publishing an important number of newspapers and similar periodicals in U.S. cities. About thirty-five periodicals had been published in New York in different years, about fourteen in Tampa, and a similar number in Key West.[86]

In the midst of the long period of armed confrontation between the Spanish Army and Cuban pro-independence fighters, the latter constituted "the republic in arms" (la república en armas), a government structure established in the territories that the rebels had been able to wrest from the Spanish forces. "The republic in arms" was guided by a new constitution and laws concerning public education, civil marriage, taxation, and the links between the judiciary and the executive and the legislative bodies. During the Ten Years' War, seven presidents were elected, most of them *hacendados* (owners of large extensions of land). This parallel governmental structure in occupied territories had representatives in several countries. All important political currents in Cuba had their representatives abroad, mainly in the United States. Toward the end of the nineteenth century, an important number of civilian leaders, generals, and high-ranking officers of the independence movement and the Liberation Army had lived in the United States. Some of them had completed their education there, and some had even acquired U.S. citizenship. Some of them would occupy high positions in the political cabinets and Cuba's army years later, including the post of president.[87]

Those representatives carried out strategic functions, such as raising money to purchase arms and for other ends, shipping arms, and handling the logistics of the political offensive in foreign lands, which included organizing rallies and lobbying foreign governments to gain support for their cause. Given Spain's repression of the anti-colonial struggle in the island, sometimes the logistics of the war made those who had settled in the western part of Cuba travel to the United States before they could join the insurrection in the eastern part.[88] All sorts of political tensions existed within the Cuban communities of the United States, including those derived from class differences and the racialization of non-white Cubans. Some leaders, like José Martí, were forced to deal with this phenomenon frequently. Martí's efforts to unite Cubans in the United States can be discerned in some of his speeches at social and political gatherings of Cubans in New York and Tampa. In the midst of Cuba's war for independence, Martí founded in New York the newspaper *Patria,* a revolutionary tribune against Spanish colonialism on the island. In

1892 he also founded the Partido Revolucionario Cubano (Cuban Revolutionary Party) with the support of Cuban immigrants in Tampa, New York, and Key West. Cuban immigrants gathered in their clubs and associations in the United States. Indeed, Cubans at El Club de San Carlos in Key West and the Liceo Cubano de Tampa constituted José Martí's main audience when he delivered some of his most notorious speeches. His poetic and patriotic representations, which are still used as powerful symbols of Cuban nationalism and Cubanness both by Cubans on the island and by exiles, illustrate his efforts at uniting a community of Cubans outside Cuba. His well-known speech "Con todos y para el bien de todos" (With All and for the Good of All), referring to the integrationist character of the colonial struggle, was delivered in the Liceo Cubano de Tampa in November 1891 and stressed his efforts to unite Cubans of different social backgrounds and political trends in the common struggle for independence. In the essay "Mi raza" (My Race), published in *Patria* in 1893, he declared that "Cubano es más que blanco, más que mulato, más que negro"[89] (being Cuban is more than being white, mulatto, or black), an image that pointed to the racial tensions in the communities of émigrés, and that since then has been a centerpiece of Cuba's antiracist integrationist imaginary. Martí himself had developed what we would call today a transnational exilic lifestyle and became engaged in transnational political projects that prominently included the support of the pro-independence movement not only in Cuba but also in Puerto Rico. He was deported from Cuba to Spain in 1871 when he was only seventeen. He completed his education there. After studying in Spanish universities and traveling within Europe, he left for Latin America, where he lived in different countries until he finally moved to New York in 1880. He stayed in New York, for the most part, until 1895, when he helped organize an exile expedition to go to Cuba to fight for independence and was subsequently killed in battle. Between 1880 and 1895, he only went to Cuba twice—in 1877 and in 1879. The fact that the greatest symbol of Cuban nationalism and anti-imperialism lived most of his prolific intellectual and political life in the United States has made José Martí a symbol not only of Cuban nationalism but also of what has been called "the importance of the exile experience in shaping Cuban nationalism."[90] Cubans of greater economic means and prominent political activists had been living in exile much earlier. Among them were prominent intellectuals such as Félix Varela, who had played an important role in the process of shaping Cuba's political thought and nationalism through what we tend to call today "long-distance nationalism."

Paradoxically, the fact that the independence struggle was promoted and financed to a great extent from U.S. soil created the conditions for greater U.S. control of the independence movement in Cuba. Cuban independence fighters both hoped for support for their struggle to transform Cuba into an independent republic and feared U.S. betrayal once the Spanish had been driven from the island. In addition, while they were receiving widespread support and were even encouraged in their struggle against Spain in the U.S. Congress, influential groups were against supporting their struggle, and they were barred from launching any military expeditions from the United States. Many Cubans were imprisoned in the United States for violating this rule; prominent émigrés frequently denounced this practice as hypocritical. As in the cases of other exile groups with a special commitment to oust the government in their homeland, they were regarded by some members of the U.S. government as both an asset and a liability concerning national security. Cubans in exile would be involved in a similar situation a century later.[91]

The integration of labor and capital markets through transnational processes was expanded when Spain lifted the controls it had imposed on the distribution of cigar products, but the United States imposed its own restrictions on cigar and cigarette imports from Cuba. In this context and within the political economy of Cuba's independence struggle, some entrepreneurs opened factories in the United States. Sometimes a process of enterprise relocation took place. In this case, the cigar factory owners and many of their workers emigrated from the island. Florida was the second most important destination for Spanish migrants in the United States, after New York, by the end of the century, although in 1868, New Orleans had the largest Spanish-origin population among all U.S. cities.[92] By 1868, Spanish migrant Eduardo Gato had opened a cigar factory in Key West, and some Cuban and Spanish investors would soon follow. Both Spaniards and Creoles arriving from Cuba provided cheap skilled labor for the factories.

As production strategies became transnationalized, so too did labor-capital relations, which in the case of the confrontations between Cuban workers and Spanish factory owners were frequently tinted by the major political confrontation between those who opposed continued Spanish rule of the island and those who favored it.[93] By the end of the nineteenth century, workers in Cuba were organizing strikes to offer solidarity and support to those who were on strike in Key West and Tampa. In 1893, the largest tobacco factory in Key West, La Rosa Española, owned by a Spanish immigrant, José Arango, and a German immigrant, William J. Seidenberg, was immersed in a dramatic conflict that involved labor strikes. Such strikes had repercussions in Cuba, as the owners tried to recruit docile, Spanish-origin workers there to the detriment of Cuban Creole workers in Key West.[94] Labor conflicts also took place in Ybor City, a city in the Tampa area founded by an immigrant from Catalonia, Vicente Martínez Ybor, who arrived on the west coast of Florida in 1886. Apparently he moved his original investments from Key West to Tampa to largely to avoid such confrontations. Ybor City evolved as a factory town with strong links with Cuba. As in Key West, the factories in Ybor City imported much of their labor, capital, and raw material from Cuba. Labor conflicts similar to those in Key West soon developed there as well, where other immigrants, including Italian- and Russian-origin groups, provided a significant number of workers to the factories and the service economy.[95] The settlement of Spanish and Cuban migrants in Ybor City and other areas of Tampa continued beyond the nineteenth century, and by the 1930s, 35 percent of the foreign-born population of Tampa was of Cuban origin and 25 percent of Spanish origin, followed by Italian-origin groups.[96] Based on estimates that may represent undercounts, the Spanish-origin population, many of whom arrived from Cuba, grew from 3,764 in 1870 to 6,185 in 1890. Ten years later the Spanish-origin population had reached 7,050.[97]

As in other places where relatively large numbers of workers and investors from Cuba had settled, these immigrants formed social and political clubs and mutual assistance societies to create safety nets for their members beyond extended family links. They also joined existing associations and clubs based on their class status and the existing racist codes. How classism and racism influenced the immigration experience is perhaps no more vividly illustrated than by the case of El Club Nacional Cubano, founded mostly by cigar workers and veterans of the independence wars in Cuba in 1899. Currently known as El Círculo Cubano (The Cuban Club) and Sociedad la Unión Martí-Maceo,[98] El Club Nacional Cubano was a multiracial mutual assistance society founded under the influential normative principle that prevailed among many war veterans, according to which Cubans, regardless of their skin color, were expected to cooperate with the independence movement and participate in the war against the colonial power. In her study of this association, Susan Greenbaum (2002) documents that the members of the Club were white and black Cubans, all united as veterans of the struggle against Spanish colonialism and as Cuban families seeking to strengthen their Cubanness in Tampa through the reinforcement of cultural ties and mutual support. La Liga Patriótica Cubana and El Partido Revolucionario Cubano, of which José Martí had been a member and founder, respectively, had set important examples of multiracial integration among Cubans for the purposes of fighting against

Spanish colonialism. These immigrants from Cuba held attitudes concerning race and national unity that softened the racism permeating Cuban society. However, by the end of 1900, dark-skinned Cubans had left El Club Nacional Cubano and created their own society, La Sociedad la Unión Martí-Maceo. Greenbaum explains this outcome in part as a result of the challenges imposed by the strict segregationist rules in the South during the Jim Crow era. As she emphasizes, the history of these two institutions captures a story of identities that have been constantly remolded by the synergies among prevailing discourses on race in the United States as well as discourses and imaginaries about national identity among Cubans and their enduring efforts to preserve Cubanness. Thus, ultimately, the Sociedad la Unión Martí-Maceo has come to represent what Greenbaum (2002) has referred to as "the definition and negotiating" of identities related to both blackness and Cubanness as core aspects of the Afro-Cuban experience in Tampa.

Migration and Enterprise Development Across Generations

The evolution of enterprises founded by Spanish immigrants and their descendants in Cuba in the nineteenth and early twentieth centuries typically relied on a combination of business and marriage strategies for capitalization and diversification purposes (see Appendix A).[99] Marriages within the group—which, in the case of the Spaniards, tended to mean not only marrying someone of the same social class but from the same region of origin in Spain—and intermarriage between Spanish immigrants and wealthy members of the local elite were central aspects of the reproduction of the Spanish enterprises and the Spanish-origin elite on the island. Most of the immigrants started with investments related to commercial or agricultural activities. Some would move to the most profitable investments in the sugar and the cigar industry and went on to diversify their investment portfolios, some even within the first generation—although in most cases, full-fledged diversification, encompassing highly profitable financial and industrial activities, was not reached until the second generation.

The increase in diversification and margins of profit usually went hand in hand with the establishment of political connections forged in Cuba and often transnationally. As mentioned before, "the Hispanic-Antillean elite" enjoyed contracts and other enterprise concessions by virtue of their links with the Spanish state. This was also true to some extent for Spaniards of modest origins who first accessed land and other properties and started their first investments by virtue of their loyalty to Spain, for example, during the independence wars in Cuba. Thus, the entanglements between enterprise formation and expansion and political ties cannot be ignored as a factor propelling entrepreneurship among certain Spaniards who arrived in the nineteenth century. Both family and political links would become more complex among Spanish-origin entrepreneurs from the first and second generation as their links with power brokers in Washington and Havana became more relevant than their links with Madrid. Spanish immigrants and their descendants, whose enterprises benefited from their transnational social networks, largely reached the United States and Spain but also embraced societies in the circum-Caribbean as well as London and, to a lesser extent, other European and Latin American societies. As mentioned before, some companies in Spain, including companies that would eventually have a global reach, were not directly linked to migration (insofar as they did not have migrants as founders or as the main investors), still tended to have strong links with Spaniards overseas and with returnees who impacted such companies as investors or by facilitating access to clients, suppliers of inputs, or markets.

The social aspects of these processes and relationships are presented in a schematic way in Annex A in which they are seeing through the evolution of family enterprises and aspects of their social embeddedness within and beyond the first generation. Annex A also includes some enterprises that were not immigrant enterprises yet had strong links with the migrants and certain aspects of the migration process, such as capital transfers.

FOUR

Migration Within the U.S. Sphere of Influence

General Trends

Toward the end of the nineteenth century, the relationships between Cuba and the United States had grown in complexity, albeit within a context that clearly pointed to an asymmetry. At the core of the relationship were some key links, such as trade and the flows of labor and capital between the two countries. The expansion of communication and transportation infrastructure connecting the two societies facilitated the flow in both directions of people, goods, ideas, and symbols, as well as the gradual integration of labor reproduction processes on the island with the labor market in the United States, mainly through the incorporation of the migrants into certain economic niches. The Monroe Doctrine, Manifest Destiny, and the Mexican War, followed by the growing U.S. economic and political involvement in the Caribbean and Central America in the second half of the nineteenth century were part and parcel of the U.S. strategy to reign as the undisputed regional power. However, by the end of the nineteenth century, Latin America was still an area in which "no one power [was] predominant," and, as a result, each power had to "exercise restraint in its actions."[1] Yet Spain lost its last two strategic possessions in the Americas to the United States in the Spanish-American War, and subsequent military interventions in the Caribbean and Central America were definitive steps to establish Latin America as the geosocial area in which the United States exerted predominant influence.[2]

From the end of the Spanish-American War until 1902, the United States ruled the island through the establishment of a military government that gave some participation to Cubans who had fought in the independence wars against Spain. After 1902, when Cuba had its own civilian government with a

Cuban president, U.S. control continued to be effective; it focused on the economic positioning of U.S. companies and the control of key aspects of the accumulation process by controlling trade, labor-capital relations in the strategic industry, and the political environment in general under the stipulations of the Platt Amendment. Among other things, the Platt Amendment granted the United States the right to use military force on the island whenever Washington deemed it necessary. This right was fully exercised in 1906 and 1917, and since then U.S. military deployment became imminent whenever there was political turmoil. The U.S. government provided the army that kept control of the island and, in particular, backed the transnational corporations' aims at controlling labor in the strategic industry, including imported labor.[3] The direct participation of the U.S. government in the elaboration of migration laws and regulations in Cuba, or its attempts to influence them, evolved in this context as an important mechanism that enabled U.S. control over labor and its products as part of the strategy to control accumulation processes and its own borders. Even after the repeal of the Platt Amendment, the United States continued to influence migration processes in Cuba, mostly by extending the principle of national security extraterritorially to prevent the use of Cuba as a transit point for anarchists, communists, and other groups that were excluded by U.S. immigration laws in different periods.[4] Closer attention to the role of labor-capital relations, and the actions and expectations of the actors with vested interests in migration, from the Cuban government to labor unions, Cuban American investors, and U.S. multinationals, suggests a complex scenario of policy bargains and tensions that we miss if we focus only on the state as the main (and a unitary) actor. By the same token, although immigration was the prevailing aspect of the process as the sugar industry expanded at the beginning of the twentieth century, a longer view sheds light on the overlapping of immigration and emigration, return migration, cyclical movements, and the participation of the migrants in transnational social fields as Cuban society moved into the U.S. sphere of influence without the constraints imposed by Spanish colonialism.

After the U.S. occupation following the Spanish-American War, there was a two-way movement between Cuba and the former metropole: while a number of Spanish migrants returned to Spain, many more arrived in the former colony. Official Cuban statistics place the total number of arrivals to the island between 1902 and 1933 at approximately 1.3 million, of whom 785,000 were from Spain (61 percent), 198,000 from Haiti (15 percent), 115,000 from Jamaica (9 percent), and the rest, approximately 15 percent, from different origins, including Puerto Rico, the United States, and China, among others.[5] Even though these figures may represent a dramatic undercount, the one-million mark in the number of arrivals is impressive if we take into consideration that the absolute growth of Cuba's total population between 1904 and 1934 was around 1.9 million.[6] Between 1899 and 1931, the number of Spanish nationals living in Cuba grew to approximately 625,500.[7] This figure was influenced by the official designation of both those who were born in Spain and their Cuba-born children as "Spanish nationals." Thus, the role of immigration from Spain in augmenting the Spanish-origin population of Cuba is best accounted for by the number of arrivals discussed above. Cuba, Argentina, Brazil, and Uruguay received approximately 90 percent of the total number of immigrants during the peak of Spanish transatlantic migration between the end of the nineteenth century and the first decades of the twentieth.[8] The first peak in immigration to Cuba in the twentieth century occurred between 1900 and 1906. Argentina received 34 percent of the total number of Spanish immigrants to the five major destination countries at the time, and Cuba approximately 23 percent. The second peak corresponded to the years between 1919 and 1921, when the island was absorbing the largest share of immigration from Spain to a single country.[9] By 1930 Argentina had recovered its position as the main recipient of Spanish transatlantic migration. Although most immigrants were single men between fourteen and forty-five, the numbers of women gradually increased, and women also exhibited lower levels of return migration. In the case of Cuba, return migration from the United States and Spain was also an important factor contributing to immigration at the beginning of the twentieth century.[10]

These two peaks of immigration corresponded with two major expansions in the economy of Cuba as shaped by global changes. From 1902 to 1920, the economy expanded overall, principally as a result of the rise in the global demand for sugar throughout most of the period, which included the inflationary trends brought about by World War I. This demand encouraged increased production, which reached a record high of more than 5 million metric tons in 1925 and caused what has frequently been called an overproduction crisis, which drove prices down to their lowest level since 1914. Thus, from the early 1920s through the early 1930s, the overall economic situation in Cuba worsened because of the fall in the price of sugar and, eventually, the immersion of Cuba in the global depression through its strong links to the depression's epicenter: the United States. As a result, there was a drastic reduction in the labor absorption capacity from 1921 to 1933.[11] Toward the end of this period there was a surge in grassroots nativist movements in Cuba, a restrictive approach toward immigration, and within this context, the enactment of legislation that clearly differentiated between nationals and foreigners concerning hiring practices, labor rights, and other issues. This scenario, which took place in the context of the global depression and war in Europe, contributed to the drastic reduction in immigration levels between 1919 and 1943. Immigration dropped from 598,906 immigrants between 1919 and 1931 to 20,505 between 1931 and 1943.[12]

Accumulation and Immigration in the Early Twentieth Century

Spanish Migrants

After the Spanish-American War, the Treaty of Paris protected basic rights of Spaniards in Cuba, such as the right to stay and keep their Spanish nationality and patrimony, although it was careful to limit the rights of Spanish-origin people who continued to work for the Spanish government to serve in the public sector in Cuba. In the section "Orders, Modifications and Changes in Existing Laws of the Civil Report," the U.S. military governor of Cuba, Major General John R. Brooke, officially sanctioned a positive approach to the Spanish-origin population based on a discourse that emphasized modernization with a racial twist: "A very large part of the wealth, intelligence, refinement and commercial enterprise of this Island is among those who were born in Spain, but who are waiting to acquire a new citizenship whenever such is available."[13] An overall positive approach toward immigration from Spain prevailed. The immigration law of 1906 approved a budget of up to 1 million Cuban pesos for the formulation and implementation of immigration and colonizing plans for bringing immigrants from continental Europe and the Canary Islands, among other areas.[14] Parallel to the state legislation was private recruitment through advertisement in the local press in Spain, among other strategies.

Many Spaniards in the island were organized around influential groups that favored immigration from Spain. The Spanish migrants' clubs and associations of mutual assistance, as well as groups interested in recruiting laborers from Spain, lobbied in the Ministry of Commerce to create a favorable climate for immigration. Representatives of the associations usually brought letters from family members to the incoming immigrants and tried to recruit them for their associations. The Liga Agraria, an organization that represented the interests of labor recruiters, created an immigration office to handle issues such as assisting immigrants while they were held in the Triscornia immigration detention center. The Office of Immigration of the Agrarian League was authorized by the government to establish contact with immigrants before private recruiters did. These groups also lobbied for a reduction of the immigrants' transportation expenses and even the underwriting of Spanish emigrants' cost of passage to Cuba, under certain conditions. (This practice of "assisted migrations" had been used before, albeit under a different set of circumstances; for example, in 1886, the Spanish government offered to underwrite the cost of Spanish emigrants eager to work in Cuba.)[15]

Eighty percent of the immigration budget approved under the 1906 law was destined for immigration from continental Europe and the Canary Islands. The remaining 20 percent was to be used to bring *braceros* from places "approved by the current law."[16] The budget provided for payment for the trip for families from these areas to settle on the farms of *hacendados*. It supported *colonos* and those with work contracts while stipulating family reunification provisions. In addition, it opened the doors for employers, mainly from the sugar industry, to negotiate with the government concerning the number and origin of the *braceros* to be introduced. Part of the budget "was explicitly set to bring immigrants and *braceros* from Switzerland and Norway, as well as Denmark and Northern Italy."[17] Such stipulations in the immigration law replicated both the quota system of the United States, which at that time privileged the immigration of people from northern Europe, and the efforts of Latin American countries to attract immigrants from western Europe. However, the growing labor pool available from Spain and the Caribbean would be the main sources of cheap labor to Cuba. Many Spanish immigrants arriving during the first three decades of the twentieth century were attracted by the positive investment climate and overall economic bonanza the island was experiencing. A number of them were entrepreneurs who came principally from Spain and the United States to profit from the new business opportunities in the sugar industry, the growing service economy, and other areas. Many of those who arrived to work in agricultural activities eventually moved to urban areas to open their own small enterprises or work in other activities of the expanding urban economy. As noted above, while commercial relations with the United States intensified, so did economic transnationalism among Spanish migrants and their descendants.

Despite the fact that Spanish immigrants experienced a generally positive reception, they were not insulated from a general prejudice against imported labor that worsened in times of economic uncertainty. Spanish immigrants and the Spanish government voiced their concerns over immigration during the economic crisis of 1921 and 1922 as well as in successive crises. An official document produced by the Spanish consulate in Havana entitled "Memoria sobre la emigración correspondiente al año 1930" even complained about how the availability of imported labor from the Caribbean worsened the situation of Spanish laborers: "The economic crisis to which we constantly allude and the immigration in large scale of workers of color—principally blacks—have contributed to the lack of consideration toward the rights and interests of the laborers from the Peninsula and the [Canary] islands."[18] The statement emphasized that the introduction of *braceros* from the Caribbean was being used to control the working demands of Spanish immigrants.

Immigrants and Seasonal Laborers from Neighboring Islands

The Caribbean laborers came mainly from Haiti and Jamaica, but also from Barbados and other "British islands." McLeod observes that "approximately two-thirds of the British West Indian immigrants came from Jamaica, with more than one-half of the remainder from Barbados and the rest from the Leeward Islands such as Grenada, St. Kitts, and Nevis" (1998, 15). Puerto Ricans, Dominicans, and workers from other areas of the region were also pulled into economic activities as the demand for *braceros* soared. By the time of their growing incorporation into Cuba's sugar industry, workers from the Caribbean also supplied cheap labor to the Panama Canal Zone. From Panama, some moved to the banana plantations of Central America, and as the availability of construction jobs in Panama shrank, some West Indians with work experience there moved to Cuba and the Dominican Republic to work in the sugar plantations.[19] In the case of Cuba, many worked seasonally. Among those who stayed on a more permanent basis, most tended to settle in the eastern parts of the island. The Caribbean workers were used to keep not only the production costs low but the political risks in control in a context characterized by escalating labor-capital conflicts and greater class consciousness and political organizational skills among the workers of the sugar industry. Not only were formal and legal channels used to recruit workers from the Caribbean, but the production companies resorted to smuggling operations as well. Many workers went more than once to the island to work on a seasonal basis. Therefore, it is hard to estimate precisely how many individuals from neighboring territories were recruited at that time. Juan Pérez de la Riva estimates that they numbered well in excess of a half million.[20] Based on Cuba's official statistics, it has been estimated that between 1914 and 1928, immigration from the Caribbean went from 26.7 percent of the total number of immigrants to 41.6 percent. During the entire period from 1902 to 1934, Caribbean migrants represented approximately 25 percent of the immigrant population, second only to Spanish immigrants, who constituted 57 percent of the total.[21] The transformation of Cuba into a major importer of labor within the circum-Caribbean meant a greater fluidity in the cultures and identities that made up Cuba's society, more contact among speakers of different languages, and other processes related not only to immigration but also to the growing transnationalization of the livelihoods of thousands of migrant households. In general, labor migration was framed by a series of events that marked a closing of one politico-economic cycle and the beginning of another in the articulation of Cuba with the world economy under U.S. hegemony.

The incorporation of workers from neighboring Caribbean islands into the sugar industry, other agricultural activities, domestic service, and the urban economy was framed by racist rationales. These workers were subjected to all sorts of discriminatory practices and prejudices because of their African ancestry, and they were further judged by their respective national origins and sociocultural characteristics. Marc McLeod (1998) forcibly argues that racism and prejudice related to ethnicity, national origin, and class background shaped different attitudes toward the workers from the Caribbean in Cuba. While their labor was in high demand in the sugar companies, their arrival was met with political resistance. The efforts by recruiters to bring laborers from the insular Caribbean faced legislation that reflected an exclusionist attitude toward the members of these groups that was due to the combination of social prejudice against blacks and the resistance by representatives of the native laborers to the recruitment of foreigners. In the early part of the twentieth century, the political elites were still trying to control the racial makeup of the Cuban population through immigration laws, although populist approaches to labor concerns framed policymaking at that time as well. More than once, the U.S. government mediated the resolution of conflicts between local labor and transnational capitalists, mainly when such tensions threatened sugar production and the profits of U.S. companies.[22] From the U.S. perspective, vital economic and national security interests were at risk if the export of sugar produced in Cuba plummeted at a time in which the global demand had skyrocketed. At times, organized labor went on strike and adopted defiant positions at different production and distribution sites to express their opposition to the salary levels and their working conditions, including their overexploitation in times of high demand. (One of the main complaints raised by the workers following a boom in the global demand for sugar was that many of them were forced to work twelve hours per day.)[23]

Violent confrontations occurred in some areas. In response, the U.S. government sent in the Marines, while some of the most powerful companies tried to bring in more *braceros* to reduce production costs and ameliorate labor-capital conflicts. The tensions generated from the opposition to the introduction of cheap workers from neighboring islands would eventually surface more forcefully.

The United Fruit Company (UFCO) and other companies with an interest in the introduction of cheap labor had been trying to lobby the Cuban government to open the door, at least partially and temporarily, to *braceros,* first from the Canary Islands, and then, as the demand rose, from the Caribbean. They relied on certain provisions of the Immigration Law of 1906 to negotiate for the introduction of *braceros* from the Caribbean as temporary workers, although they also resorted to the use of undocumented laborers and even became involved in smuggling.[24] In Decree No. 743 of 1910, the Cuban government authorized the employment of *braceros* from areas other than the Caribbean islands only during the peak of the sugar harvest. Thousands of Spaniards took advantage of the new regulation to emigrate to Cuba on the pretext of going there as temporary workers.[25] It was not until 1913, however, that the Nipe Bay Company, a subsidiary of the UFCO, was granted the first-ever government permit given to any private company operating in Cuba to bring a large contingent of *braceros* (a thousand initially, a limit that was eventually increased to three thousand) from neighboring islands. In August 1917, another law was signed that authorized private parties to introduce *braceros,* although certain restrictions were imposed and the government reserved the right to repatriate them when necessary.[26] The "reciprocity treaty," which came into effect in 1903, granted Cuba's sugar and other products privileged access to U.S. markets, with which the United States secured the supply not only of final products but also raw materials that would be further processed in the United States, where more value would be added to the products. The treaty also secured Cuban markets for U.S. manufactures. While economic trade instruments regulated specific transactions, the Platt Amendment created the enabling political environment upon which the expansion of production processes in relation to the expansion of accumulation in the United States was taking place. By that time, like Cuba, the United States was also relying on a strong immigration regime to expand production processes. However, while large-scale immigration and large-scale accumulation were central to the political economy of the United States at that time, large-scale immigration did not imply large-scale accumulation in Cuba, since all the instruments of domination were in place for the transfer of a significant share of the surplus value generated by immigrant workers in Cuba to the core of the world economy, including its rising star a few miles from Cuban shores.

Chinese Migrants

The military government that administered the island from the end of the Spanish-American War to 1902 established a comprehensive system to control the immigrant population, regulating customs and sanitation programs and reinforcing forms of state racism through discourses on modernity that explicitly targeted the Chinese. Biopower continued to play a role in the laws and policies framing the reception, regulation, and specific mechanisms of control for immigrants and temporary workers, including not only Africanized Caribbean groups but Chinese migrants as well. The "Orders, Modifications and Changes in Existing Laws of the Civil Report" by the U.S. military governor of Cuba stated: "By circular No. 13 Division of Customs and Insular Affairs, Washington, April 14, 1899, the laws and regulations governing immigration in the United States were declared to be in effect in the territory under government by the military forces of the United States, and collectors of customs were directed to enforce these laws until the establishment of immigrant stations in such territory."[27] By that time Chinese immigrants had experienced the rigors of the Chinese Exclusion Act in the United States. The report specified the intention to also apply restrictions to Chinese immigration to Cuba once specific instructions were given; in the meantime, Chinese immigrants, referred to as "people from that race" in the document, were arriving in Cuba "without restrictions." It continued, "they come directly from Hong Kong, viséd through the United States, where they are not allowed to stop."[28] Several decrees, military orders, and official memos would regulate Chinese immigration to Cuba during the period of the U.S. military government and beyond. Section VII of U.S. Military Order No. 451 of May 15, 1902, explicitly prohibited the immigration of Chinese laborers and established fines for the "masters of vessels" who violated the restriction, and section VIII specified that such restrictions did not apply to diplomatic personnel, merchants, or "tourists with certificates."[29]

A circular signed on October 12, 1903, that established visa requirements for immigrants from China specified that its use of the term "Chinese people" meant "any individual of the yellow race, subject to be identified as an individual from China based on his ethnic characteristics."[30] The same year, a circular dated October 16 established passport and visa requirements for people from Asia. Decree No. 237 of August 11, 1904, authorized the entry of

Chinese people from third countries, provided they brought with them official documentation certifying their lawful stay and exit from the government of their last country of residence and paid a bond before leaving the port of origin for Cuba. At that time, an increasing number of Chinese immigrants were arriving from the United States; among them were entrepreneurs who were attracted to the economic opportunities on the island and were leaving the United States because of anti-Chinese discrimination. Decree No. 268 of July 5, 1905, also regulated Chinese immigration to Cuba. It established that Chinese nationals either had to pay US$1,000 in currency or gold, to be deposited in a bond through a company, or indicate support from a reputable merchant in Cuba. A similar provision was ratified on February 2, 1907, with two important modifications: the government of China would cooperate in identifying immigrants from China, and a bond from a Chinese entrepreneur would suffice for admission. The owners of vessels transporting undocumented Asians, or Asians who did not or could not post the required bond, were subject to severe penalties that included either monetary fines or responsibility for returning the passengers or both.[31]

Juan Jiménez Pastrana (1963, 113–14) points out that despite efforts by U.S. and Cuban authorities to replicate U.S. regulations concerning Chinese immigrants, the growing labor absorption capacity of Cuba, combined with the exclusionary approach toward the Chinese in the United States—and the fact that Cuba was known by Chinese immigrants in general and those facing exclusion from the United States as a potential destination—contributed to an increase in the Chinese population on the island. The turning point in Chinese immigration came after 1914, when Cuba's sugar production capacity was expanded as a result of the increasing demand in global markets. Decree No. 1707 of 1917, which established the opening of immigration doors for *braceros*, provided that the workers would be sponsored and not represent any threat to national security or the welfare of the population. This law also fostered the arrival of Chinese workers (ibid., 112). As with other migrants, the arrival of Chinese migrants in Cuba also involved smuggling operations. In this case, more than one smuggling scandal involved labor recruiters, representatives of the Cuban and the Chinese governments, and even prominent members of the group in question. Many would also try to use Cuba as a transit country to reach U.S. soil.[32] Decree No. 559 of May 1924 provisionally suspended issuance of visas to holders of Chinese passports, unless they were members of the diplomatic service of China, and Decree 573 of 1926 partially revoked the one of 1924 and limited the residence status of Chinese to two years (ibid, 113). As the Communists gained control of China a few decades later, many Chinese fled to the Americas. Cuba received more Chinese immigrants then, but not at the levels experienced before.

Chinese migrants sometimes entered Cuba as students, merchants, or tourists to circumvent the restrictions of the immigration law. Cuba's censuses indicate that the Chinese population went from 11,217 in 1907 to 24,674 in 1931, the year in which the Chinese population of Havana (11,148) outnumbered for the first time the combined Chinese population of Las Villas and Matanzas (6,165), which had been major destinations for Chinese immigrants during the colonial period.[33] The last census before the revolution of 1959, conducted in 1953, indicates that 74 percent of the total Chinese population was concentrated in the western part of Cuba.[34] While Chinese immigration to the Americas began in the nineteenth century and continued to grow in the first decades of the twentieth century, Cuba, followed by Peru, remained their main destination in the Americas outside the United States throughout the entire period.[35] A consistent pattern among Chinese immigrants was the extraordinarily high proportion of men. All the Cuban censuses from 1861 to 1970 show that men represented more than 95 percent of the Chinese population, with women never exceeding 4 percent for a single census—a percentage reported in the census of 1970, the first taken after the revolution. That census counted 5,800 Chinese people, indicating that a drastic reduction of the Chinese population had taken place since its last peak in 1931. The most impressive growth of the Chinese population in the twentieth century took place in the 1920s. By 1930 it was estimated at 24,600. It is precisely in the mid-1920s that Havana's Chinatown emerged as an economically vibrant and culturally picturesque neighborhood of the area called Centro Habana.

Havana's Chinatown and the development of multiple associations by the Chinese immigrants attest to the relevance of the Chinese community in Cuba. José Baltar Rodríguez (1997, chap. 2) refers to the correspondence between the development of Chinese associations in Cuba and their associations elsewhere. He distinguishes several types: clan-based associations, regional associations, corporative and trading associations, secret societies, and societies devoted to cultural issues, politics, and sports. Members of clan-based associations, he elaborates, claimed to have common ancestry. They arose mainly in the 1920s, although some emerged much later. Members of regional associations were linked by their common place of origin, mainly in southern China (and more specifically, Canton). The ties of members of corporative and trading associations extended to mainland China, Hong Kong, San Francisco, and New York. Baltar Rodríguez argues that the latter types were oriented mainly toward the protection of Chinese enterprises. For example, they purchased commodities wholesale and then sold them to Chinese retailers at competitive prices that allowed them to keep the prices low. And the "secret societies," he argues, were mostly engaged in illicit activities and had extensive contacts abroad. He refers to the Casino Chung Wah (or "The Palace of the Chinese Colony") as the broader organization or "national society" that grouped Chinese people of different origins and social and economic status. Its leaders had direct links with the Chinese government, and eventually some supported the Guomindang (ibid.). In the 1960s, the dynamics of these and other community associations significantly changed. State bias against the private sector and aggressive schemes of expropriation of private property hit the Chinese community and Havana's Chinatown and other immigrant communities hard. Many immigrant, ethnic and religious associations vanished, while the few that survived saw their social functions and membership substantially reduced, often as a result of the exodus of many of their members. Some were disarticulated by state mandate due to their actual or alleged involvement in activities against the government; others disappeared as the social and political spaces they required for survival vanished in a context of growing suppression of the right of association and freedom of expression. Eventually, the "mass organizations" (organizaciones de masas) became the preferred and dominant form of associations by the state.

The manipulation of the concepts of culture and race were instrumental in shaping the incorporation of the Chinese immigrants in Cuba, and they were not disconnected from the perceptions about their functions in the division of labor in ways that resemble what Ong calls "naturalizing powers" of discourses that emphasize the entanglements of "Chinese race, culture, and economic activities" (1999, 68). The most dramatic antecedents of the use of the concepts of culture and race to control and exploit immigrant groups can be traced to the mechanisms deployed by the Spanish government, with the support of influential members of the Creole elite, to regulate and control the workforce of the African slaves and the "Chinese coolies." Once again, at the beginning of the twentieth century, the language of the immigration laws in Cuba specifically designed for the Chinese reflected the use of the concepts of culture and race as tools that both reflected and shaped public opinion about members of the group, and Chinese migrants were expected to perform certain economic functions in ways that were associated with their cultural heritage—choosing self-employment, working long hours, employing family members, and offering their products and services for very low prices.

Other Asian Migrants

Asian immigrants in Cuba also included approximately three hundred Asian-origin immigrants from Yucatan in 1921, most of whom were Korean. Ruz and Lim Kim (2000) document that some Koreans and their families had been recruited and brought to Yucatan in 1905, mostly to work in the *henequen* (sisal) plantations. Some of them, along with their descendants, they argue, were attracted by the rumors of job availability and the prospects of better living conditions, including greater educational possibilities for the children in the island. Some of the migrants established small enterprises, which, for the most part, were sold to pay for their trip and resettlement in Cuba.[36] They had to enter the country surreptitiously and for the most part dispersed upon arrival, but some were able to stay together on the farm El Bolo, in the province of Matanzas, where they formed what has been called "the most important Korean settlement in Cuba."[37] A number of Japanese arrived between 1915 and 1930, mostly directly from Japan, although some arrived via third countries, such as Mexico. Reportedly 380 Japanese were brought between 1924 and 1926 by labor recruiters. Between 1920 and 1931, a total of 1,007 Japanese had entered the island, according to the official reports on passengers and immigration.[38] Although these figures might include some who entered the island more than once during that period, they indicate that the Japanese arrived during the expansion of the sugar industry. They tended to work in agriculture, trade, and the construction of railroads, and more would arrive later. Although their main goal seems to have been to return to Japan after saving some money, some stayed, and more would arrive later.[39]

The Limits of the Immigration Regime

The decline of the immigration regime in Cuba has its own peculiarities. However, it cannot be fully understood if we fail to consider that to a great extent it reflected a global trend. The period between 1906 and the late 1920s was not one of continuous economic bonanza in Cuba. There were years of deep crisis and others of slow recovery as well as years of growth. Thus, even though the whole period can be characterized as one in which a strong labor immigration regime emerged in association with the expansion of the sugar industry, there were some countercurrents and even repatriation and deportation processes associated with the fluctuations of the economy.

As mentioned above, after a dramatic rise in the price of sugar in world markets associated with World War I, there was a crisis of overproduction of sugar in Cuba, which was compounded by a reduction of the demand as a result of the recovery of alternative markets and a credit crisis that originated in the United States, but affected Cuban producers. There were important signs pointing to a crisis by the end of 1920. Although the final years of the 1920s marked the end of large-scale immigration to Cuba, some signs indicating the crumbling of the immigration regime, including forced repatriations, showed as early as 1921. The issue of forced repatriation is usually discussed in relation to Caribbean migrants and frequently related to racism and the attitude toward migrant workers in times of crisis; however, many Spanish workers of modest economic resources suffered from the adverse attitudes that affected immigrant workers and the actual shrinking of economic possibilities for them as the economy became immersed in a downward spiral.

Macías Martín (2002) shows that thousands of Spaniards who had been brought to work in the agricultural sector found themselves unemployed for most of the year and deeply indebted, and many became homeless. Faced with the crisis many Spanish immigrants and temporary workers lined up in front of the Spanish consulates to request economic assistance for their return to their localities of origin in Spain. Macías Martín further documents that although some petitions had been made in 1920, this trend reached a critical moment in 1921, and the Spanish government fully intervened in the repatriation crisis that year by assisting with the return of 35,000 Spaniards who were considered to be indigent people (*indigentes*): "Real need more than discouragement reigned among Spanish immigrants; many of them did not receive the salaries they were supposed to receive for their work in the sugar cane fields, and, in addition, many were laid off. So they had no choice but to go en masse to the Spanish consulates asking to be repatriated, something for which the consulates were unprepared. It was not surprising to hear consular officials refer to this situation as a 'repatriation conflict'" (2002, 298; my translation). The crisis in Cuba certainly had repercussions on transatlantic Spanish migrations. The number of Spanish migrants going to the Americas dropped from 163,438 in 1920 to 74,585 in 1921 and 72,678 in 1922, even though the levels had remained stable among the other major recipients of migrants (Argentina, Brazil, and Uruguay).[40] In Cuba in particular, the number of immigrants from Spain dropped from 97,569 in 1920 to 24,729 in 1921, and to 22,714 in 1922. After a brief recovery in 1923 and 1924, immigration from Spain experienced a dramatic drop from 1924 to 1930—from 43,310 to only 8,284.[41] Hope was regained in Cuba by the early days of 1923 as the price of sugar recovered in world markets, and a good indicator of the economic recovery was precisely that the number of people arriving from Spain rose that year, although that would be the highest level between 1921 and 1930.[42] The economic expansion of the early twentieth century had reached a limit, and the immigration trends would reflect that.

This brief recovery was followed by the immersion of Cuba in the global depressions of the late 1920s and 1930s. As early as 1932, production and exports had dropped dramatically: "The value of total sugar exports fell from US$298 millions in 1925 to US$58 millions in 1932 with sales to the U.S. market, restricted by protectionist policies, falling from US$209 millions to US$39 millions for the same years."[43] This phenomenon had a domino effect on all sectors of the economy, particularly the banking system, and caused well-established Cuban and Spanish enterprises to declare bankruptcy while indebtedness to the United States skyrocketed. Only a handful of lending and banking institutions owned or operated by Spaniards and Cubans survived the crisis. Investment and interests in finance and the sugar industry by U.S. firms and the U.S. government grew, largely through the repossession of enterprises that cut across economic sectors—prominently, sugar production, banking, and infrastructure.[44] The public debt increased and became "socialized," resulting in a rise in unemployment and inflation and a deterioration of socioeconomic conditions among the unemployed and poorer segments of the labor force.[45] This period also saw the negotiation of a new reciprocity agreement with the United States that further opened the domestic markets for U.S. products, the end of the Platt Amendment regime in Cuba as the political core of the bilateral relationship with the United States, and the beginning of Franklin Delano Roosevelt's "Good Neighbor Policy," which called for consensus building, rather than military intervention, in the context of greater demand for new markets by American corporations and an increasingly anti-imperialist stance among many Latin American governments and influential public persons. The political scenario was convulsive, and discontent was voiced by various sectors of Cuban society whose prospects of economic prosperity had shrunk since the Depression. Discontent was also a reaction to growing corruption and the repression experienced under the presidency of Gerardo Machado. From elite organizations to trade unions, political parties, and university students, large segments of society demanded greater accountability from the representatives of the state apparatus. All this turmoil led to what has been recorded in Cuban history as the revolution of 1933.[46]

Many leaders of the organizations that participated in the social movements that preceded and followed the revolution of 1933 were immigrants who were sympathetic to various political currents. Their political involvement was informed this time by their experiences in their countries of origin, including their previous involvement in the social-democratic, anarchist, communist, and unionist movements, and their own struggles in Cuba facing exploitation and discrimination.[47] As historical accounts of labor struggles and other political struggles in different periods document, it was not infrequent to have leaders with surnames that indicated their immigrant roots. The tradition of political activism in Cuba usually extended to second-generation immigrants. Indeed, the participation of immigrants in Cuban politics has been frequently emphasized with respect to the independence wars, this particular period, and the struggle leading to the revolution of 1959.[48] Thus, between the mid-1920s and the mid-1930s, political tensions in Cuba not only reflected the immigration of politics—that is, the import of political currents and ideologies and forms of struggle by the immigrants—but was also deeply immersed in the politics of immigration. This is not disconnected from the fact that the island was experiencing the exhaustion of the growth-dependent economic model. In this context, the migrants both participated in and were the main targets of important political currents. Thus, while many immigrants were immersed in struggles that had a clear nationalist stance, some nationalists pointed to the immigrants as a major source of the problems faced by the country.

The issue of immigration was in the spotlight once again, albeit now in a political climate that had nativist discourses at center stage. Since as early as 1902, there had been incidents involving workers demanding "jobs for Cubans and not the foreigners." In that year workers in the cigar industry had gone on strike to complain that recent arrivals from Spain were taking their jobs. Anti-immigration statements by prominent public figures and even restrictive laws concerning immigration would surface at different points, motivated by different rationales. For example, in 1922 there was a bill before the Cuban parliament to employ only Cuban nationals in the ports, although it was vetoed by the president. In 1923, a bill was introduced to revoke any prior concessions granted to private companies to use the ports within their own properties to export and import (workers and merchandise), although in this case it was challenged by pressures from Washington, given its potential repercussions for large U.S. companies. In 1924, there was the proposition to deport immigrants who had proven pro-Soviet allegiances. In 1925, the pressures on migrants for their naturalization or repatriation grew while new bills for the protection of national workforce were introduced, such as the "75 percent bill," which basically stipulated that at least 75 percent of the workers of the private enterprises operating in Cuba had to be Cuban nationals. This bill did not pass either, but it had a great psychological impact and increased the pressures toward naturalization. Nationalist stances reached some of the mutual assistance associations that some immigrant groups had developed decades earlier, particularly those providing professional services to the population, such as medical services. These groups felt pressure to become subordinated to national professional organizations.[49]

However, it was not until the politico-economic crisis of the late 1920s that the agendas of capitalists, the government, and unionists converged with respect to immigration. The tense international and domestic political climate of that time also molded the new approach by establishing prohibitions against the immigration of people involved in subversive activities that the government considered threats to national security and even their deportation, if they were immigrants. The link between immigration and national security was openly discussed throughout the Americas as fascism and other political forces with manifest imperial ambitions rose in Europe. The United States, as the main recipient of European immigration, put pressure on countries in the area, including Cuba, to further reinforce their border controls and the selectivity of their immigration policies. This practice would be employed again during World War II.[50]

Political turmoil leading to the revolt of 1933 took shape through the social movements that sprang up in opposition to the Machado presidency. Machado's dictatorial style was widely resented, as were existing widespread social and economic disparities and political corruption. The struggle against Machado led to a military revolt and the installation of a succession of civilian governments, including the revolutionary government of September 1930.[51] Labor issues acquired prominence in government affairs during what is usually regarded as a short-lived revolution with significant long-term implications. Until 1933, labor issues were handled by the Department of Agriculture, Industry, and Commerce. In October 1993, the office of Secretary of Labor was created, and a law backing workers' right to free association through their respective professions, trades, or specialties was also enacted. Rules leading to the organization and governance of several professions and worker protection laws, some of which were also meant to palliate unemployment, were enacted. Decree 1703 of September 28, 1933, set the workday at a maximum of eight hours "throughout the Republic for all types of occupations and inhabitants, whatever their line of work might be."[52] However, Cuban citizenship was a requirement for union board membership. The "50-percent law" was explicit concerning the protection of nationals in the labor market. It stipulated that "worker or employee positions that vacate or are created from now on, in agricultural, industrial, or mercantile enterprises established in the Republic, must be given to native Cuban personnel."[53] The layoff policy was also regulated through a system that benefited nationals, based on a preference scale: "First, single foreigners with no dependents; second, married foreigners or those with non-native background; third, single and nationalized with no dependents; fourth, foreigners married to Cubans or with native background; fifth, nationalized and married or with native background. No layoffs are permitted in one group without having finished the process for the previous group."[54]

The Spanish embassy was involved once again in the issue of how Spanish immigrants were treated in Cuba, and once again the tone of the complaints implied that Spanish immigration was superior and more convenient for Cuba than that of "people of color." In a cablegram sent by the Spanish ambassador in Cuba to the minister of foreign relations (state secretary) of Spain in 1933, he suggested the possibility of making immigration from Spain more difficult or even prohibiting it as a bargaining tool to be able to negotiate better conditions for the Spanish immigrants and even receive compensation for it, under the assumption that while immigration from Spain was far more positive than "unwanted migrations, such as those from China and Jamaica," for the purposes of the reproduction of Cuba's population, it was not appreciated as it should have been:

> If such an agreement could be reached, and could be announced publicly, it is possible that it would cause the expected reaction in this country [Cuba], given the need they have to use our workers, mainly in the countryside, and given the fact that immigration from Spain is convenient because it helps the renovation of the Cuban population and diminishes the [negative] influence of other, unwanted migrations, such as those from China and Jamaica. It is almost certain that after a while, Cuba would request more immigration from Spain, and then we would be in a better position to negotiate an emigration treaty in which we could demand the corresponding guarantees and compensation in exchange for the Spanish workers, whose efforts are so important for the economic development of this country, even though they do not appreciate it now because we give it to them for free.[55]

The departure of foreigners, in many cases by forced deportation, reached significant levels between 1931 and 1943: 56.1 percent in the case of "blacks" and 41.5 percent for "whites."[56] Deportations became a fixture in the restrictive approach to immigration throughout the 1930s. Among all Caribbean groups, Haitians were hardest hit. Citing various sources, including secret U.S. consular correspondence, Marc McLeod (1998) reports that in March 1937 many Haitians who refused to leave a sugar cane mill located in an eastern province were rounded up, sent to a camp in Santiago de Cuba, and shipped back to Haiti, while by mid-September that year, "the Cuban authorities [had] banished nearly 25,000 Haitians." Other Caribbean migrants were also forced to leave. However, McLeod highlights several factors that placed laborers and immigrants from the British Caribbean in a better position in Cuba than Haitians, even though they all suffered discrimination and prejudice. First, the institutions of the British Commonwealth provided greater protection to the migrant workers from Jamaica and other British islands in Cuba than the Haitian institutions had been able to for the workers from Haiti. McLeod also notes that Jamaicans and other workers from the British Caribbean had a command of English, a male-to-female ratio that indicated the presence of more women, in relative terms, compared to the Haitians, who were predominantly young males (and hence Jamaicans were more likely to form families), prior work experience (which, in the case of many Jamaicans, included activities in the urban sector), and much higher literacy rates. English, McLeod emphasizes, was either the first or the second language of many managers and other people in the chain of command in the sugar industrial complex, while the maids' and other domestic servants' command of English was highly praised among the Cuban upper and middle classes, who did not hesitate to hire Jamaican women and men for their domestic services. All these characteristics to some extent softened the hardships of the incorporation of Jamaican immigrants compared to Haitians, although they also endured racism, the stereotypes that influential Cubans and Spaniards and the local press held against them, and even deportation.

In the overall picture, the early 1930s signaled the collapse of the strong immigration regime of earlier decades, with the assistance of its official dismantling through a restrictive approach to immigration. The total number of immigrants dropped dramatically to a little more than 20,500 between 1931 and 1943. Between 1946 and 1958, the number of immigrants was only 19,871. Between 1946 and 1958, Cuba absorbed only 3.55 percent of all Spanish immigration to Latin America, which by then had Argentina (40.14 percent), Venezuela (31.03 percent), and Brazil (15 percent) as the main destinations.[57] The significant decline in immigration was also related to changes in economic and political conditions in Europe and other source areas. Emigration to the

Americas became logistically difficult during the wars and for most of the interwar period. Many countries in the Americas also became more selective in their immigration policies. Although some, including Cuba, accepted groups escaping persecution and turmoil, Cuba moved away from being amongst the main recipients of immigrants in the Americas. As will be seen later in this work, parallel to the sharp decline in immigration, U.S.-bound emigration started taking a more prominent position.

Other Groups Arriving Until the Late 1950s

Expanding trade, communication, and transportation links with the United States since the nineteenth century were reflected in the growing presence of U.S. citizens in Cuba, either as temporary visitors or permanent residents. Although a number of Cubans had acquired U.S. citizenship (and, therefore, it would be inaccurate to state that all U.S. citizens living in Cuba lacked Cuban ancestry), a growing number of U.S. citizens with no Cuban ancestry arrived on the island in the last decades of the nineteenth century. Some worked there mainly as technicians and professionals, such as engineers and chemists; others worked for or owned enterprises that had representation on the island; still others were investors in real estate. There was also a floating population, mainly made up of personnel from trade vessels that were anchored in Cuba's ports for several weeks and even months at a time during the sugar harvest season. Before the peak of immigration in the second decade of the twentieth century, more U.S., British, French, Italian, and German citizens arrived on the island than any other group, with the exception of the Spaniards.

The convulsions in Europe, including the Russian revolution and the violent dissolution of the Ottoman Empire, had important repercussions on transatlantic migrations during the first decades of the twentieth century up to World War I, by which time the exodus receded, only to grow again in the years following the war. By the early 1920s, thousands of people from the Middle East and areas that had been under Ottoman control had moved to the Americas, as had many eastern Europeans. People from Poland, Russia, Lebanon, Syria, Palestine, Armenia, Egypt, and Iraq, among others, escaped political turmoil and the redrawing of borders by crossing the Atlantic. Such a massive movement of people had an impact on Cuba, not only because of its labor absorption capacity and relative political stability, but also because of its proximity to the United States, which made it a favorite transit country.

The expansion of industrial activities and search for capital accumulation venues also fomented the development of transnational entrepreneurship rooted in migration and the growth of merchant diasporas, such as the Jewish, the Indian, the Chinese, and the Lebanese Christian, all of which (with the exception of the Indian) created important communities in Cuba.[58] Members of some of the Middle Eastern groups arriving in Cuba were frequently classified in Cuban statistics depending on the travel documents they carried. While *los polacos* (Polish) was a label employed to classify immigrants from eastern Europe and Jewish immigrants, *los turcos* (Turkish) typically referred to Middle Eastern immigrants. Margalit Bejarano argues that in some cases, such labels reinforced perceptions about their entrepreneurial abilities, but at the same time, they meant that certain identities that were still relevant for their self-identification, such as those based on national origin, ethnicity, and religious beliefs, were being transcended in light of the new identities that were being forged. She further argues that the labels employed to classify immigrants could be very deceiving in many respects. Those who carried Turkish passports were not always Turks. Nor were all the owners and operators of "Polish stores" actually Polish. However, occasionally it worked for the immigrants to adopt these new sources of identity as a strategy for adapting and surviving in the new environment.[59] "Las tiendas de los polacos" (Polish shops) multiplied in certain areas of Havana, and they opened in other provinces as well. "The Polish" were known as owners and operators of small outlets that sold accessories for women as well as fabrics, clothes, and other products for men, women, and children. Like the Spanish, Chinese, French, and other immigrants, they tended to capitalize on their belonging to merchant networks to bring their "ethnic products" to the island. These groups and others contributed to Cuba's urban landscape through the opening of business outlets and their income-generating practices, which included street vending, and by opening their places of worship and societies. They also contributed to literature and other cultural manifestations and enriched Cuban cuisine and musical traditions. The small and mid-sized enterprises of immigrants from eastern Europe and the Middle East complemented those owned and operated by Chinese migrants, who were well known for their *fondas* (small eateries) and small fruit and ice cream outlets and shops, and for running the labor-intensive forerunners of what are known today as laundromats.

Immigrants from different national origins not only specialized in certain economic activities, contributing to the development of enterprises within a given economic niche, but they also developed businesses that were more "mainstream," such as factories, educational institutions, hotels and motels, bookstores, drugstores, printing shops, law and accounting firms, and many other enterprises. Immigrants from eastern Europe and the Middle East participated in both what we now call "ethnic economies" and in mainstream business venture (see Bejarano 1996), while the entrepreneurial involvement of the Chinese immigrants included both small investments in the service economy and large investments in commercial activities, which was reflected in the associations they formed (see Baltar Rodríguez 1997). Other immigrants' contributions to Cuba's entrepreneurial environment tended to be more specialized, such as the case of Germans' contribution to the brewing industry (Alvarez Estévez and Guzmán Pascual 2004). The Spanish group, the largest and most complex, had a large-scale long-term impact on almost all types of entrepreneurial activities, from the *bodega* to the bank. This trend had some continuity as more immigrants continued to arrive, although not in such large numbers from the 1930s onward. Thus behind the label "immigrant/entrepreneur" we find a disparate group of people. What Bejarano (1996) assertively notices for the case of many Middle Eastern and eastern European immigrants in Cuba also holds true for other groups. Many immigrant/entrepreneurs were, in fact, street vendors and door-to-door vendors who could barely support their families. Others were owners of enterprises that were functioning only by going further into debt and eventually went bankrupt. Self-employment and entrepreneurship in such cases did not denote economic success but pointed to economic uncertainty and long working hours, sometimes in a family enterprise for little or no pay, all sorts of economic hardships, and ultimately a very hazardous incorporation into the island's labor market.

Arab and Jewish groups were among the streams of migrants that arrived on the island in the first half of the twentieth century. Their arrival was precipitated by historical milestones that ranged from the fall of the Ottoman Empire, the spread of Zionism, the rise of authoritarian and totalitarian regimes in Europe, and the religious wars in the Middle East. Although many of those who arrived settled in Cuba, others used the island as a stepping-stone to enter the United States and, to some extent, South American countries.[60] Restrictions against entry to the United States by some of these groups at different times, as well as xenophobic attitudes there, also led to indirect immigration. Rigoberto Menéndez Paredes (1999) places the number of Arab immigrants arriving in Cuba between 1870 and 1900 at approximately two thousand. As in the case of other groups that were classified as Turkish or Polish, some groups were classified as "Arab" based on the country of previous residence or the country issuing the passports and the main language spoken. In addition, Arabs from French colonies had migrated to Cuba under French nationality. Menéndez Paredes also argues that the classification system was misleading in many respects and created some overlapping estimates of Jewish and Christian groups. Roughly, the Arab population living in Cuba in 1916 was estimated at between nine and ten thousand, with Syrians constituting the main group (approximately 65 percent), followed by Palestinians and Lebanese. The fact that they did not tend to concentrate in Havana exclusively, combined with their intermarriage with Cubans and the heterogeneity of these groups in terms of their class background and religion, he further argues, made it hard to keep track of their demographics as time passed.

According to Robert Levine (1993), by 1919, there were approximately two thousand Jews on the island, but the growth of the Jewish population was fueled by their migration toward the Americas between the Bolshevik revolution and the aftermath of World War I. Jewish immigration to Cuba reached a peak after World War I, "when large numbers of Sephardic Jews from Turkey and North Africa and Ashkenazi Jews from Eastern Europe came to the island."[61] By the end of 1924 the Jewish community in Cuba had reached approximately twenty-four thousand; most of them were from Russia and Poland.[62] Levine identifies several stages in the immigration of Jewish groups. The Sephardic Jews of Spain and Portugal, who had accumulated capital either in Spain or the Americas, were among the first groups arriving in the colonial period. Even though they were not conspicuous demographically, they had a significant economic impact. Another group was made up of the American Jews who arrived during the military occupation by the United States in 1898. They also brought capital, or were managers or experts that were typically incorporated into the higher ends of the job market. Sephardic Jews continued to arrive at the beginning of the twentieth century from North Africa and the Ottoman Empire, though their class origins were more modest than those of the first groups. In the 1920s and early 1930s, there was another influx that included both working-class people and intellectuals, some of whom had strong socialist or communist political backgrounds.[63] According to an official report produced by U.S. authorities, most of the arrivals from eastern Europe, Armenia, Palestine, Turkey, and Syria to Cuba were of Jewish extraction.[64] Bejarano notes that by that time, the U.S. government had identified immigrants to Cuba from eastern Europe and the Middle East as potential migrants to the United States, and U.S. concern was reflected in policy recommendations made to the Cuban government on this matter. The political context included not only restrictions placed under U.S. pressure, but also the targeting of Jews with socialist and communist orientations by anticommunist groups.[65] Anti-Semitism affected them as well from the early 1930s to the mid-1940s, although the Cuban government occasionally displayed a very friendly approach to influential members of the Jewish community.[66]

Like other groups of migrants, Arab and Jewish groups were known for their propensity to develop associations that reflected their cultural backgrounds and social and political concerns. These included, for example, La Sociedad Siria (The Syrian Society) in Santiago de Cuba, La Unión Libanés-Siria (The Lebanese-Syrian Society), the La Sociedad Palestino-Arabe (The Palestine-Arab Society), La Sociedad Libanesa de Cuba (The Lebanese Society of Cuba), and El Centro Hebreo de Cuba (The Hebrew Center of Cuba). Some Jewish immigrants in Cuba were very actively involved in the development of socialist associations and the foundation of Cuba's Communist Party. Arab groups founded the *Diario Al-Faihaa* in 1931, the weekly newspaper *Al-Hoda,* the newspaper *El Sayf,* the magazine *Cercano Oriente,* and a cultural center, Al-Etehad, all of which served immigrants from Lebanon, Syria, and Palestine.[67]

Other, less numerous groups were also involved in transnational political projects. Koreans are a case in point. Koreans were far from being as numerous as the Jewish and Arab groups in Cuba, but recent insights on members of this group in Cuba highlight important and particularly relevant aspects of their migration experience and context. Like other groups, they developed lasting networks rooted in ethnic cohesion and solidarity conducive to the organization of groups and associations for social, cultural, economic, and political purposes. And they were also involved in matters concerning Korean politics.[68] It has been documented that the most prominent organization developed by Korean immigrants in Cuba was the Korean National Association, which openly resisted the attempt of the Japanese consulate in Havana to integrate them as subjects of Japan while Japan occupied Korea. The Korean National Association listed, among its goals, "supporting the political ideas and progressive trends of Korea, in full compliance with the laws of the [Cuban] Republic" (Ruz and Lim Kim 2000, 59). The emphasis on the fact that the dominant political position of members of the group was in tune with the Cuban government's concerning the Korean question denotes not only a typical case of what we now conceptualize as "long-distance nationalism" but also the interest of immigrants from a country that was perceived to be problematic from the perspective of the geopolitics at that time to avoid suspicion by taking an unambiguous position on an issue that affected their incorporation into Cuban society. As mentioned above, the United States was not indifferent to the origins and the types of immigrants who were landing on the neighboring island, many of whom were perceived as potential migrants to the United States. Therefore, the triple role of Cuba—as a major immigrant society in the Americas and a close neighbor and political ally of the United States—added political weight to the issue of the perceptions about certain immigrant groups and their own political self-representation.

Scattered evidence from works that focus on various aspects of Cuban history suggests that Latin Americans from different societies arrived in Cuba during the period of economic expansion and at other junctures. However, the visibility and impact of these groups seems to be veiled not only by their relatively small numbers when contrasted with other groups but also by their cultural affinities with the Cuban population, and perhaps even their integration with Cuban families or greater propensity toward return migration.

The United States, England, France, and Italy had become major sources of immigration in the first two decades of the twentieth century. However, like other groups, their demographic representation in Cuba's population had significantly shrunk by the early 1940s. Based on statistics on the country of birth provided by the 1943 census, the number of people who were born in those countries had dropped in absolute terms. Among all the source countries for which information was made available, only the German-origin group had experienced a slight increase between 1931 and 1943.[69]

The Foreign-Born Population from 1940 to the Early 1950s

Prior to the Constitution of 1940, the law classified those who were born in Cuba of foreign parents as "foreigners" unless they opted for Cuban citizenship upon reaching adulthood. After 1940, anyone born in Cuba was automatically considered a Cuban regardless of the citizenship of their parents, including those previously classified as foreign-born.[70] Thus, based on the prevailing law at that time, the census of 1931 included in the classification of "foreigners" 443,197 persons who had been born in Cuba, which raised the total of "foreigners" to 850,413. When these figures were adjusted to account for the effect of the changes in the law, the foreign-born population in 1931 was 407,216 and had fallen to 198,689 by 1943.[71] Another important change between 1931 and 1943 was the significant growth in the number of foreigners who opted for Cuban citizenship through naturalization. The 1943 census estimates that in 1943, 19 percent of the total number of people living in Cuba with Cuban citizenship had been born in other countries, while the percentage was 6.4 percent in 1931.[72] The growth in the percentage of naturalized people is closely related to the immigration context of the late 1920s and beyond, which, as seen before, brought about important changes in attitudinal and institutional approaches to immigration that created incentives toward the acquisition of citizenship. The main group contributing to the growing naturalization trend was the Spanish group.

The city and the province of Havana attracted the highest numbers of migrants and had the highest share of the foreign-born population. While the foreign-born population of Cuba constituted 4 percent of the national total in 1943, in the city of Havana it constituted 9 percent of the population and 6 percent in the entire province. The other province in which the percentage of foreign-born population was higher than the national level was Camagüey, with 5 percent. The Spanish-origin population tended to concentrate in Havana, while "other Americans," which included *braceros* from the Caribbean, gravitated toward the agricultural regions of Camagüey and Oriente. Among the foreign-born groups in 1943, the Spanish group was estimated to be 157,527 persons, 121,227 of whom lived in Havana, followed by Las Villas with 52,733. The next province concentrating more Spaniards was Camagüey. The population born in the areas of the Americas other than the United States was estimated to be 47,240 in 1943. Of them, 85 percent concentrated in the provinces of Oriente (22,430) and Camagüey (17,839), followed by Havana with only 10 percent.[73] Among those born in China (15,822), 49 percent lived in Havana and 29 percent in the province of Oriente, followed by Las Villas (11 percent). People born in the United States constituted the next largest group. The 1943 census counted 3,800 U.S.-born people living in Cuba; 2,627 or 69 percent resided in Havana, and 14 percent in Oriente, followed by Camagüey (7 percent).

These data are congruent with the fact that most of the immigrants who had come from areas of the Americas other than the United States came as workers for the plantations, and therefore tended to settle in the eastern provinces of Camagüey and Oriente, where there were many sugar plantations and a heavy investment in the sugar industry. The fact that almost 50 percent of the Spanish-born people concentrated in Havana—and many others in other cities at that time—reflects a continuous pattern of high level of urbanization among Spanish immigrants in Cuba, who tended to be incorporated primarily in the urban economy. Although a number of them worked as *colonos,* peasants, or in the sugar mills and in other rural activities, many Spanish immigrants came to work and live in Havana and other cities or moved there after having worked in rural activities for a few years.[74] A similar pattern is found among the Chinese. Immigration (both from abroad and from other areas of the island) to the cities, mainly Havana but also to other expanding cities, contributed to the Cuba's urbanization rate, which, according to census data, was about 51 percent in 1931 and about 55 percent in 1943. Even after the decline of immigration, the cities continued to grow, which resulted to a large extent from internal migration streams and also, indirectly, as a result of the immigration of previous years. The census of 1953 indicates that by that year 57 percent of the population was urban.

The division of the foreign-population by sex indicates that in 1943, among the Spanish-born group, 70 percent of the population was male and 30 percent female. In the case of the population born in areas of the Americas other than the United States, 78 percent was male and 22 percent female. In the case of the Chinese, almost the entire group (99 percent) was male. These data reflect the fact that mostly men tended to immigrate to Cuba, although the number of women participating in the immigration process had substantially increased in the case of the Spanish group (compared to decades earlier), a trend that is not found among the Chinese. Until the census of 1931, the foreign-born population influenced the age structure of the total population mainly through the immigration of young people. However, the impact of the foreign-born population on the age structure of the population in 1943 was less relevant since the immigration levels were much lower, while a larger percentage of the foreign-born population had been residing on the island for many years.[75]

The economic incorporation of the foreign-born population, according to the census categories, shows that almost 42 percent engaged in activities related to agriculture, fishing, and livestock, followed by commerce (19 percent), manufacturing and related industries (9 percent), personal and domestic services (7 percent), and professional services (2 percent). Other activities (mining, construction, government, finance, and so on) absorbed 1.5 percent or less of the total foreign-born workforce.[76] When compared with the participation of the native population, the foreign-born population had much higher levels of involvement in the area of commerce (9 percent of the native workforce compared to 19 percent of the foreign-born) and slightly higher levels in activities related to personal and domestic services (which absorbed 5 percent of the native workforce and 7 percent of the foreign-born) and agricultural and related activities (41 percent of the native workforce and 42 percent of the foreign-born). The analysis by occupation indicates that approximately 55 percent of the foreign-born labor force toiled either as agricultural workers or farm administrators (37 percent) or as unskilled workers (18 percent). These proportions are similar to those of the native workforce (38 percent and 17 percent). An important difference between the native and the foreign-born workforce is found in the percentage working as "propietarios, gerentes y altos empleados" (owners, managers, and high-ranking employees): while 19 percent of the foreign-born group worked under this category, only 8 percent of the native population did.[77] This overrepresentation of managerial and entrepreneurial activities in the foreign-born population is arguably an indicator of the involvement of immigrants in activities related to commerce, since under "proprietors" we find the owners of the enterprises in the area of commerce as well. It also indicates the climate of investment that had prevailed since the times of the boom of the sugar industry, which had attracted not only capital but also immigrants willing to invest in certain industries. These figures roughly indicate that while migrants working as agricultural and industrial workers made a significant contribution to the working class (urban and rural) and the peasantry in Cuba, other migrants had contributed to the expansion of the middle and upper classes. Some of these trends started earlier, but as shown by the data of the 1943 census, although large-scale immigration had dried up, they still existed. It should be noted, however, that the context in which the census was taken distorted some estimates.

Statistics by major employment type (owners, self-employed, employees), by racial categories, and by citizenship show that members of the workforce, irrespective of citizenship, were predominantly represented in the "self-employed" category. This was attributed in the census to three factors: the importance of agriculture in the Cuban economy and, more specifically, that of the independent farmer as opposed to employees of agro-industrial complexes; the preponderance of commercial activities in which small independent merchants had a significant share; and the fact that the census was conducted during the *tiempo muerto* (off-season). As indicated in the census itself, had the census taken place during the harvest period, reports would not have shown such a gap in favor of independent farmers over the number of employees and agricultural workers.[78] The same source provides data that allow us to control for major employment type (owner or self-employed; employed or employee) and major occupational categories (professionals, administrators, sales and clerical workers, and so forth). The proportion of "white" people working as "self-employed" among the foreign-born population (50 percent) was higher than in the case of "white Cubans" (45 percent). However, 62 percent of the "colored foreigners" and 52 percent of "colored Cubans" were also working as self-employed persons.[79] These data also reflect the elasticity of the term "self-employment." One meaning of the term suggests the existence of an enabling institutional environment that tended to benefit immigrant entrepreneurship among certain groups with capital and entrepreneurial skills, such as well-to-do immigrants. The other meaning—framed by ostensible prejudice, discrimination, and concomitant barriers to entering the labor market and experiencing upward social mobility—signaled the growing participation of immigrants of various national origins in diverse activities as "self-employed," a means many used to escape unemployment. The census of 1953 indicates that the foreign-born population represented only 2.6 percent of Cuba's total population at that time. This was the lowest level since the beginning of the century.

U.S.-Bound Migration and Transnationalism

As seen above, by the second half of the nineteenth century, migration and transnationalism between Cuba and the United States were linked to a complex situation that included the escalation of violence associated with the wars of independence but also greater economic exchange; an increase in trade; the participation of workers from the island in U.S. labor markets, a heavy transfer of entrepreneurship and labor to the U.S. cigar industry; and U.S. investments in Cuba, which by the end of the century included not only the sugar industry but even public utilities and other key infrastructures. By the mid-1800s Cuba already occupied a significant position in U.S. trade relations: "At mid century the Cuban trade accounted for as many U.S. merchant vessels as were engaged in the total trade with England and France: 1,702 in 1850 and 2,088 in 1856; only trade with Canada and England exceeded the total tonnage of U.S. trade with Cuba."[80] This context had made sugar producers and exporters on the island more dependent on their economic links with the United States. The links were both horizontal, in the sense of being developed through enterprises that operated transnationally, and vertical, insofar as they also involved acceptance of and even pleas for some form of political tutelage by the United States to counterbalance Spanish protectionism.[81] The links with Cuba were reinforced by continuous efforts by the United States to expand its markets. In the early 1890s, there was a substantial increase in U.S. exports to Cuba, which "accounted for just under half of the total of American exports to Central and South America," and an equally impressive increase in Cuban exports to the United States (from $54 million in 1890 to $79 million in 1893).[82] The trade links went hand in hand with Cuba's increasing technological dependence on U.S. firms and the U.S. government for the expansion of certain industrial activities and the generation of energy. Such dependence grew in the early twentieth century, when Cuba became a U.S. protectorate. The modernizing projects launched under direct U.S. control after 1898 encouraged a plurality of links that included, but were not limited to, emigration of labor from Cuba and the development of certain patterns of consumption and lifestyles among the middle and upper classes that included making the United States a major destination for tourism, shopping, and the education of their children. Table 1 contrasts the foreign-born population from Latin America and the Caribbean residing in the United States for the years 1900, 1910, 1920, and 1930. The data on the specific areas of origin include the Caribbean and the Latin American regions in general and Cuba and Mexico in particular, plus the regions of Central America and South America. Table 1 shows that the Cuban-origin foreign-born population of the United States grew 26.78 percent between 1900 and 1910.

In 1900 the Cuban-origin population of the United States was approximately 11,100.[83] This number is significant, in relative terms, within the context of U.S.-bound Latin American migration. Excluding Mexicans, Cubans represented 18.62 percent of the entire Caribbean and Latin American–origin foreign-born population of the United States at that time, while in absolute terms it outnumbered the foreign-born population of Central and South American–origin combined. Although emigration to the United States continued, in the decades when Cuba's sugar industry and investment capabilities were expanding aggressively, the levels of emigration were not that significant. Between 1910 and 1920 the Cuban-origin population of the United States experienced a net reduction (see Table 1).

Table 1 also shows that the Cuban-origin population grew from slightly over 11,000 in 1900 to 18,493 in 1930—the lowest rate of growth among all foreign-born groups represented in the table. Thus, while in 1900 the Cuban-origin population represented 8 percent of all the Latin American groups in the United States, its proportion dropped to only 2.34 percent in 1930. A greater reduction is found with respect to the Caribbean. While the Cuban-origin population represented about 44 percent of the Caribbean-origin population in 1900, it only represented 17 percent in 1930. To be sure, Cuba's emigration to the United States was not as pronounced during the first decades of the twentieth century as in the case of other Caribbean societies. It should be noted that the Cuban-origin population in the United States experienced the lowest percentage of growth between 1900 and 1930 when compared

Table 1 Foreign-born population in the United States, 1900–1930 (by selected areas, subperiods, and countries of origin)

	Foreign-born population				% of growth			
	1900	1910	1920	1930	1900–1910	1910–1920	1920–1930	1900–1930
Latin America	137,458	279,514	588,843	791,840	103.35	110.67	34.47	476.06
Caribbean	25,435	47,635	78,962	106,241	87.28	65.76	34.55	317.70
Cuba	11,081	15,133	14,872	18,493	36.57	−1.72	24.35	66.89
Cuba as % of Caribbean	43.57	31.77	18.83	17.41				
Cuba as % of Latin America	8.06	5.41	2.53	2.34				
Central America	3,897	1,736	4,912	10,514	−55.45	182.95	114.05	169.80
Central America as % of Latin America	2.84	0.62	0.83	1.33				
South America	4,733	8,228	18,551	33,623	73.84	125.46	81.25	610.40
South America as % of Latin America	3.44	2.94	3.15	4.25				
Mexico	103,393	221,915	486,418	641,462	114.63	119.19	31.87	520.41
Mexico as % of Latin America	75.22	79.39	82.61	81.01				

SOURCE: U.S. Census Bureau 1999.

to the foreign-born population from the whole Caribbean region, South America, and Central America (see Table 1).

By the 1950s, Cuba showed a greater relative importance as a source country of emigration to the United States. Among the independent republics of Latin America, the island was second only to Mexico in immigration to the United States. This can be seen in the number of Cuban immigrants, nonimmigrants, and naturalized persons compared to the rest of the Caribbean, Central America, and South America between 1950 and 1959 (figs. 1, 2, and 3). The number of immigrants admitted, nonimmigrants admitted, and naturalized persons from Cuba grew between 1950 and 1959. Cuba consistently had more nonimmigrants and naturalized immigrants admitted than any of the three regions in all the years represented. The gap in the number of Cuban immigrants was similar to the number of immigrants from the rest of the Caribbean increases substantially between 1954 and 1958, while an important gap exists in that period with respect to the other source regions as well. The growth in the number of naturalized immigrants in those years reflects the cumulative effects of emigration in prior years, since naturalization occurs a number of years after arrival. The category "immigrants admitted" also reflects cumulative effects, since it refers not only to new entries but also to those adjusting their immigration status to permanent residency in a given fiscal year. Thus, the "immigrants admitted" category gives us an idea of the trends in a series of years like the ones represented. In absolute terms, immigrants admitted from Cuba grew from 2,179 in 1950 to 11,581 in 1958, with a

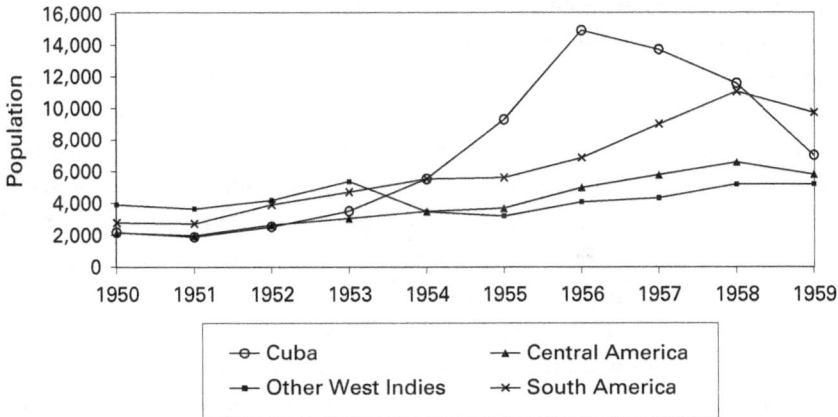

Fig. 1 Immigrants admitted to the United States, by selected areas of birth, 1950–1959
SOURCE: Compiled from U.S. Department of Justice, INS Annual Report (1959, 1961).

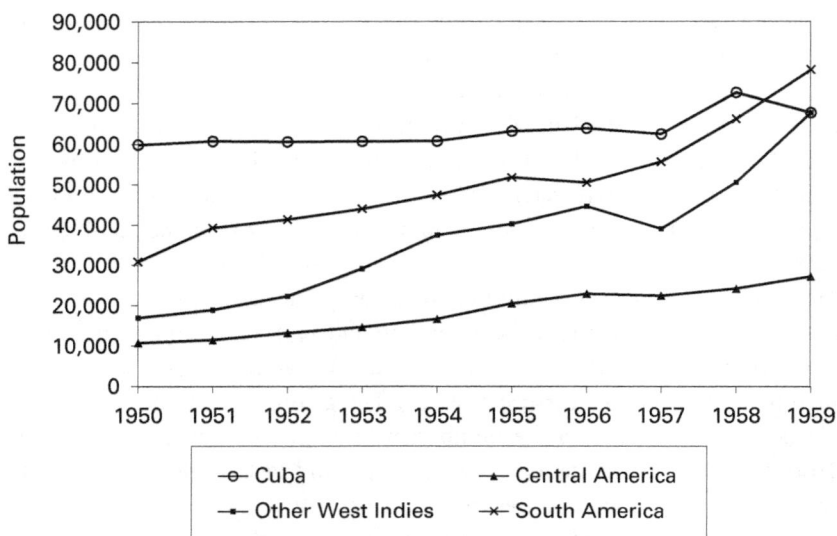

Fig. 2 Nonimmigrants admitted to the United States, by selected country of origin, 1950–1959

SOURCE: Compiled from U.S. Department of Justice, INS Annual Report (1959, 1960).

peak in 1956, when the number reached almost 15,000, followed by a total of 13,733 Cuban immigrants admitted in 1958. In 1959, the number dropped to 7,021, which is consistent with the fact that during the first year of the new government there was no massive exodus. Quite the opposite: many Cubans returned, and 1959 became Cuba's last year to date with a positive net immigration rate. The number of nonimmigrants grew from 1950 to 1958, although not as significantly as in the case of the number of immigrants. The number of nonimmigrants admitted from Cuba was exceptionally high, compared to the regions included for most of the 1950s, which suggests that Cubans may have been using channels other than immigrant visas to emigrate to the United States. This is a reasonable assumption, taking into account that using nonimmigrant visas such as those issued for students, investors, tourists, and even temporary workers, is known to be a strategy employed to emigrate to the United States or work there on a temporary basis. Cubans requested and were issued an unprecedented number of nonimmigrant visas in the turbulent years 1958 and 1959. Toward the end of the 1950s, other Caribbean groups and South Americans had caught up with Cubans as petitioners for nonimmigrant visas to reach U.S. soil.

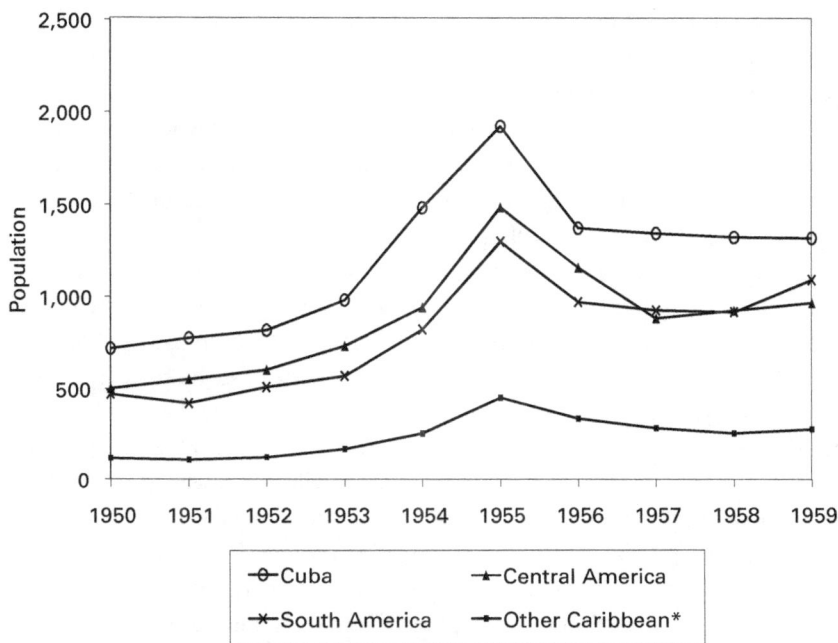

Fig. 3 Naturalized persons in the United States, by selected former areas of allegiance, 1950–1959

SOURCE: Compiled from U.S. Department of Justice, INS Annual Report (1960).

A breakdown by more specific admission categories, based on data from the Immigration and Naturalization Service (INS), shows that in 1958, Cuba and Mexico constituted the major sources of temporary visitors for business, study, and pleasure (in addition to representatives of foreign news media arriving from Latin America).[84] The distribution of immigrants by declared occupation indicates that Cubans represented a significant share (more than 30 percent) of the "operatives and kindred workers" and "sales workers" coming from "Other West Indies," Cuba, Mexico, Central America, and South America. Concerning nonimmigrants' declared occupations, in 1958, South America contributed almost 45 percent of all professional and technical people from the areas included in the comparison, followed at a distance by Cuba with approximately 19 percent. These two groups were ahead in the "managers, officials, and proprietors" category as well. Cubans led in the "sales workers," "operators," and similar occupations. Mexicans exhibited the highest percentage (37 percent) in the "farmers and farm managers" category, with Cuba in second place, with 17 percent. Mexicans contributed the highest percentage of "agricultural workers," with Cubans ranking third behind the "Other West Indies" groups.[85]

Such trends indicate that although not many agricultural workers and low-skilled laborers traveled from Cuba to the United States at the time, either as immigrants or nonimmigrants, the socioeconomic background of Cubans moving north was not so homogeneous either. To be sure, by the 1950s a growing number of Cubans were looking for job and investment opportunities abroad, including investments in real estate—as second homes, when possible. Although the United States was the main destination, many Cubans were also searching for opportunities in other societies, such as Mexico. The mobility of people toward other countries was reinforced by the escalation of political turmoil as the 1950s advanced and the exodus of people who opposed the Batista government increased. It included intellectuals, whose exodus became more apparent after 1957.[86] However, contrary to state-centric analyses that tend to emphasize political conditionality, the travel and migration links with the United States were embedded in complex social structures and prompted by social institutions that ranged from the state and the educational system to the family. As the republican period advanced, a growing number of Cuban children and adolescents, mainly of the upper and lower strata of the middle class, were being raised to expect a U.S. education and to live and work "the American way." "The North" was where many Cubans went or were expected to go "to make something of themselves and return 'made,' appropriately formed by the North American experience and prepared to succeed in Cuba."[87] Capitalist penetration, mostly through U.S. transnational corporations, went hand in hand with a pattern of cultural and political hegemony that transformed the act of living, studying, and working in the United States into an integral part of that hegemony. As Louis Pérez emphasizes, "the experience in the United States was one of the primary ways by which identity was arranged to assimilate North American normative structures as part of self-definition" (1999, 417).

In Cuba, the political situation had worsened after a coup led by Fulgencio Batista in 1952. He gained political ascendance as a member of the "Sergeants' Revolt" in 1933, and with U.S. endorsement became president of Cuba in 1940. Once he completed his first four-year term (1940–44), he orchestrated a coup in 1952 and a successful electoral move in 1954, which legitimized his transition into his second term as the officially elected president. An eclectic political opposition had been organized by then, which would include the insurgent 26th of July Movement, organized by Fidel Castro and other members of the opposition in 1955. Following a tradition in Cuban history since the independence wars, the regimes facing the greatest opposition from the civilian population from 1902 to 1959—the Machadato (as the government headed by Gerardo Machado was known) and the Batistato (the one led by Fulgencio Batista)—also faced organized resistance from members of the Cuban-origin population of the United States. The Directorio Estudiantil Universitario, an organization that played a leading role in the overthrow of Machado and the reorganization of the state apparatus during the revolution of 1933, had two highly outspoken *cédulas* (chapters) in the United States: one in Miami, and the other in New York. During the critical period of the Machadato (late 1920s–1932), issues concerning the future role of the organization and its position regarding possible U.S. intervention to settle the political crisis were debated in local newspapers such as the *Miami News* and the *Miami Herald*.[88] During his presidential visit to Washington in 1942, ten years before attempting a second term through a coup, Fulgencio Batista was given a warm welcome in Miami Beach by members of the Cuban community while receiving military honors. In 1957, the rebels in the Sierra Maestra met with civic leaders to sign a unity pact called the Sierra Maestra Declaration, through which they further reinforced the role and legitimacy of the guerrilla movement in the struggle against Batista. That same year, Cubans in Miami signed the "Miami Manifesto," which also called for unity in the struggle to reestablish civic order on the island.[89] Thus, the Cuban community in Florida continued to be politically active and involved in Cuban affairs, as it had been since the turn of the nineteenth century, although its political epicenter had moved to Miami in the twentieth century.

Based on these circumstances, a problematic emphasis is occasionally placed on the political nature of emigration from Cuba at the threshold of the revolution of 1959. A comprehensive assessment of the main forces shaping the migration links with the United States since the 1930s does not point to a political overdetermination, if by "political" one means turmoil and escalating violence. The forces that shaped not only emigration (the aspect of the process that tends to be emphasized) but also the circular mobility of labor and involvement in transnational activities, in conjunction with the long-term development of family and economic networks by certain sectors of the population and the development of transnational lifestyles, reflected multistranded relationships with the United States, which were framed, nevertheless, by a structure of domination and subordination in the political sphere as well as economic dependency. The continuation of such secular trends was further facilitated by the increase in the availability of transportation connecting the two countries. Four international airports working at full capacity by the mid-1950s in Havana, Varadero, Camagüey, and Santiago de Cuba included scheduled flights to several airports in the United States. The maritime routes had expanded and included passengers as well as transshipment, seatrain service, freight-car ferry service, and automobile ferry service connecting Havana with seaports and airports in the United States, mainly New York, New Orleans, West Palm Beach, and Key West, among others.[90] Periods of economic crisis in Cuba, combined with increasing demand for workers as a result of economic restructuring in the United States and the transnational social networks developed by Cubans with the United States, were playing a role in both emigration and circular mobility in the 1950s. Furthermore, the Cuban economic elite increasingly preferred to invest in the United States rather than in Cuba, but many kept their residences on the island even if they had real estate investments and even second homes in the United States. In addition to real estate, their investments also included banking, among other sectors. As early as the 1930s, Cuban citizens had over 300 million dollars in short-term current accounts and long-term investments in the United States.[91]

It has been argued that many links and practices that led to greater familiarization with the United States had been encouraged by the U.S. government for the purpose of getting Cubans acquainted with U.S. lifestyles and methods, "work ethics," and prevailing worldviews there.[92] This reinforced a pattern of cultural penetration that framed economic dependency and political subordination. As Cuba's economic dynamism slowed down, members of different social classes searched in El Norte for opportunities they did not find on the island. Livelihoods and accumulation strategies associated with migration frequently involved the acquisition of U.S. citizenship. Migration before 1959 also involved return migration after having lived abroad for a given period. The procurement of livelihoods by some capital accumulation strategies of many entrepreneurs and even the advancement of numerous professionals strongly relied on their ability to live and work, if not permanently, at least temporarily in the United States, Mexico, and other societies, and their ability to develop transnational social networks. In the case of the United States, such links took shape through strong social networks that relied upon marital and business strategies and participation in committees, parties, or associations. Transnational political activism had grown by the second half of the 1950s to become a key force fueling the social movements inside Cuba.

FIVE

Cuba's Cold War Revolution and Migration

The Global and Regional Contexts

During the Cold War, immigration from Latin America and the Caribbean to the United States was propelled by several processes and social forces. Pervasive social and economic gaps between the countries of the region and the United States, working in concert with global economic restructuring, increased the demand for labor in the United States, which shaped migration. Political and military conflicts generated large numbers of refugees. In addition, as migration grew, the transnational social networks developed by the migrants played an increasing role in giving continuity to the process. Throughout the 1960s, 1970s, and 1980s, millions of Latin Americans were forced to cross land and maritime borders in search not only of a "land of opportunity" but, more often than not, just a safe haven.[1]

These dynamics explain why 84 percent of the total number of immigrants legally admitted to the United States from Latin America and the Caribbean, from the beginning of the twentieth century to 1990, was admitted after 1950.[2] In the case of Central America and South America, the percentages were even higher: 96 percent and 90 percent, respectively. Even though immigrants from Mexico and the Caribbean had been arriving in relatively large numbers since the early twentieth century, 86 percent and 74 percent, respectively, of those admitted between 1901 and 1990 were admitted between 1951 and 1990. Of all the Central Americans admitted as immigrants in the United States in the whole period between 1901 and 1990, as many as 42 percent were admitted just in the decade between 1981 and 1990. This period was particularly violent in that region because of the Nicaraguan revolution, the spread of guerrilla warfare, the proliferation of death squads in some societies, and the militarization of the region associated with the involvement of the U.S. and the Soviet Union and their allies. The 1980s are also known as Latin America's "lost decade." The "lost decade" was characterized by a drop in the per capita gross domestic product and the minimum and median real wages for most countries of the region, a rise in the number of people living in conditions of extreme poverty, a decline in per capita social expenditures, an increase in capital exports (mainly to the United States), a worsening of the terms of trade, and a dramatic increase in the external debt, in conjunction with the rise of political turmoil and armed conflicts.[3] During the 1980s, the proliferation of *maquiladoras* and export-processing zones in certain areas of Mexico, Central America, and the Caribbean, which were presented as sources of employment that eventually would slow emigration from those areas, created conditions that ultimately reinforced rather than halted emigration. This was basically the effect of "the Caribbean Basin Initiative," a comprehensive foreign policy approach launched by Washington in the 1980s as a response to economic restructuring in the United States, as a strategy to contain communism in the region, and also as a way to halt immigration from it. Continuing migration from Latin America and the Caribbean to the United States after World War II also reinforced the social aspects of the migration process. Migration was increasingly shaped by the development of social networks among the migrants themselves and their relatives and friends in their homelands, which facilitated the spread of information about labor markets in the United States and immigration laws.[4] From the 1950s until the end of the 1980s, these processes and rationales, which shaped what is known as "periphery-to-core migration," ran parallel to and in some cases overlapped with those associated with East-to-West migration. During the Cold War, the term "East-to-West migration" called attention specifically to the migration of people from the Soviet bloc to the industrial democracies of the West.[5] Emigration from Cuba at that time evolved at the intersection of these two patterns.

The links between the political economy of the Cuban revolution and the geopolitical scenario in which it was embedded shaped migration in singular ways through the specific policies adopted by the Cuban government in political, economic, and other realms—and the reaction of the Cuban population to these interventions. Unintended consequences of specific policies or processes also shaped migration indirectly. The hostility of the bilateral relationship with the United States since the first years of the revolution was a major overarching force within the geopolitical context of the Cold War. Thus, the geopolitical context, structural inequalities, and the bilateral and domestic realms of policy interventions were entangled in complex ways as they shaped migration in Cuba since 1959. An emphasis on any of them at the expense of the others sheds light on specific causal links. However, it would provide a limited account of the complex forces shaping migration in Cuba since 1960. To be sure, the hostility of the bilateral relationship has had a strong direct impact on Cuban migration through a series of policy interventions by the two governments, designed to use migration as a foreign policy tool and as a way to control domestic political processes in each society. However, specific policies adopted by the Cuban government as it reengineered a new system of international alliances, revamped the social relations of production, and reconfigured the political structures and spaces of society to build an alternative system shaped the migration process in specific ways. Underlying the forces that have impacted migration since the 1960s, one finds the structural aspects of the process that are traceable to Cuba's location in the world economy in the *longue durée,* and, therefore, despite its significant specificities, some aspects of the process converge with aspects found in other Latin American and Caribbean societies.

The Political Economy of the Revolution and Migration

The links between certain developments in Cuba's political economy and emigration do not tend to be straightforward; the lack of qualitative studies addressing this issue further limits our understanding of the mechanisms through which these links operate. In addition, laws and regulations that have banned or severely restricted the emigration of certain groups in different periods have obscured the effect of politico-economic processes on emigration. These have ranged from outright bans to temporary restrictions on emigration by young men of military draft age, physicians, and professionals working in areas considered strategic by the state; difficulties related to obtaining an entrance visa from the government of the destination society; and obstacles to obtaining an exit permit, or the *tarjeta blanca,* from the Cuban government. These regulations have contributed to the usual gap between the desire to emigrate and the realization of the goal. The political stigma of and concomitant social risks for the individual or the family intending or attempting to emigrate have also contributed to this gap.[6] These factors, and the abrupt opening and closing of doors for potential migrants to the United States, have made it impossible to analyze how domestic policies and socioeconomic changes have impacted emigration in specific periods. However, the political economy of the revolution has played a key role in shaping continuous emigration, and any effort to understand the causes of the process should take this into consideration.

Economic Centralization, Redistributive Policies, and Political Control

On May 17, 1959, the new government sanctioned the first agrarian reform, which provided for the establishment of a private-ownership ceiling of 400 hectares of agricultural land, with the possibility of doubling this amount for highly productive farms. The explicit objective of the law was the elimination of latifundia by the distribution of land "to those who worked it."[7] Studies on the agrarian reform in Cuba agree that one of the most important issues during the first stages of the reform process was whether to distribute expropriated lands in the form of cooperatives or as "granjas estatales de todo el pueblo" (people's state farms). At the end, as one expert explains, the solution was "neither to divide the expropriated lands, nor to give them to the workers in the form of private property," but to form "Economic Units under the central administration of the state," many of which eventually became cooperatives.[8] It is usually argued that the decision to stimulate the creation of state farms was politically viable in Cuba because of a lack of "hunger for land" in the countryside at the time of the revolution, a phenomenon that has historical roots in the creation of a rural proletariat of significant size, mainly made up of workers accustomed to moving between rural areas and the cities in search of jobs during the *tiempo muerto* in the sugar industry.[9] The argument goes that this sort of proletarian mentality had reached an important segment of the Cuban peasantry, and they were ready to settle for "either land or work."[10] This context was favorable for launching aggressive strategies of collectivization of agricultural production via the incorporation of privately owned farms into the state sector through state farms, "collective plots," and cooperatives, or their absorption by the state.[11] By the beginning of 1963, 52 percent of the cultivated land in Cuba was owned by the state, 23 percent privately by peasants, and 25 percent by small capitalists. Further agrarian reform laws and further land appropriations by the state put 80 percent of the land in the hands of the state by 1983, while individual peasants were left with only 9 percent and state-controlled cooperatives retained 11 percent of arable land.[12] Small and medium-sized farmers continued to play an important role in the production of beans, vegetables, cattle, and tubers, among other agricultural products, but the state controlled most of the agricultural sector. Even if the agrarian question, historically understood among influential intellectuals and politicians as the elimination of latifundia, had been resolved in the first years of the revolution, an array of problems persisted in the spheres of production, distribution, and consumption of agricultural products.[13]

The policy approaches to agrarian reform, agricultural production, and the distribution of consumer goods and social services went hand in glove with a systematic hostility toward the private sector. While some segments of the population from the rural areas benefited by receiving small parcels of land or jobs in state-run enterprises, others, such as the owners of farms whose properties were confiscated or whose parcels were gradually incorporated into the state system through coercive mechanisms, had a very different experience. Sometimes individual farmers were given the opportunity to exchange their isolated rural dwellings and parcels of land for small apartments equipped with refrigerators in government-built housing projects in town areas. While some liked the idea, there was also some social compulsion to take the offer. Nevertheless, some owners of private parcels viewed it as a bad exchange: land got them not only small apartments in crowded buildings, where public utilities were not provided efficiently, but also a whole new lifestyle that was not necessarily suited to their traditional attachment to the land.[14]

During the periods of land reforms and aggressive measures against the private sector, many of those whose property had been confiscated or could be confiscated at any time chose "exiting," mostly in the form of emigrating to the United States, over "voicing" their discontent as the more viable survival strategy.[15] However, some alliances were formed to oppose the new regime. These included owners of large farms and haciendas as well as small private producers and agricultural workers, most of them of modest economic resources. The subversive activities ranged from sabotaging the supply of productive inputs in agricultural activities (sabotaging productive activities also took place in the urban economy) and the burning of sugar fields to strategies of guerrilla warfare, like the guerrilla war in the Escambray Mountains. A number left the island after their failed attempts to undermine the new government, often after having been in prison for a number of years.[16] After the Escambray movement and other social movements in the countryside, the strategic importance of rural areas became more obvious to the government, which launched several strategies to relocate the population.[17] The government also planned to repopulate certain rural areas, some of which were being urbanized. Such plans have been modified over the years, and new ones have emerged. The government's strategies in urban and rural planning and its efforts to reduce the developmental gaps between rural and urban areas entailed a comprehensive approach; the desire to improve the living conditions of the population was entangled not only with a new vision of the reduction of social inequalities but also with political strategies associated with security concerns. In such a context, the developmental rationale included the revamping of forms of land tenure and new administrative schemes in production processes, the construction of housing projects, the improvement of the social infrastructure in rural areas, and the creation of the social infrastructure to group the population into "mass organizations" (organizaciones de masas).

All these dynamics led to a dual process of urbanization and concentration of the population in secondary cities and new towns and the absolute decline in the population classified as rural between 1970 and 1980, a period in which all the provinces, with the exception of the province of Havana, experienced an absolute decrease in rural population.[18] The province of Villa Clara lost 77,000 rural inhabitants between 1970 and 1980, which represented 24 percent of the national reduction of rural population in that period.[19] The province of Camagüey, which had traditionally specialized in the large-scale production of sugar, livestock, and citrus fruit, among other crops, was the most affected. The percentage of its rural population with respect to the total population dropped from 45 percent in 1970 to 28 percent in 1980. Most immigration to the province was to its urban areas.[20] When migration and the natural increase of the population are factored in, the absolute loss in Camagüey's rural population was about 40,000 persons in that period. In her study on urbanization in Cuba between 1970 and 1980, Xiomara Franco concluded that "if we take into consideration Camagüey's high degree of specialization in agricultural activities as well as its current high degree of urbanization . . . it seems like a contradictory movement is taking place, one that is not favorable to the social and economic development of this province."[21]

It has been argued that during the first decades of the revolution, urbanization was not primarily the result of the internal mobility of the population to already established urban areas but to the emergence of urban nuclei as infrastructure such as schools, medical dispensaries, electricity, housing, and roads were brought to a number of rural areas. In fact, rural-to-urban migration went from 1.4 percent between 1943 and 1958 to 0.6 percent between 1958 and 1970, and 0.4 percent in the period between 1970 and 1975.[22] Concerning the role of the developmental approach in such outcomes, Carlos García Pleyán (1980) argued that if during the 1960s and early 1970s investments were directed mainly toward the agricultural sector as the engine to propel economic growth and future industrialization, the growth in the industrial output was a top priority during the so-called first five-year plan of 1976–80.

As a result of the complex entanglements among policies oriented toward the generation and distribution of social services beyond the main cities in each province, developmental strategies in general, and the population displacements induced by the government as a result of security concerns, by the early 1980s, the secondary cities and towns, primarily those located at the main areas within each municipality (*cabeceras municipales*), were major poles of attraction for internal migrants. While the city of Havana received 34 percent of the internal migrations in the period between 1958 and 1970 and only 12 percent between 1970 and 1981, the secondary cities absorbed 35 percent and 26 percent, respectively, and the towns received 10 percent and 33 percent, respectively, in these two periods.[23]

Labor Shortages, Underemployment, and the Mobility of the Population

Labor shortages in the production of sugar, and in the harvesting of coffee and other crops, have been a structural feature of Cuba's economy since 1959. However, in sharp contrast with previous acute labor shortages in agricultural production, mainly the sugar industry, this phenomenon has not been related to an impressive expansion in production but to a chronic absolute or relative reduction in the number of workers. A combination of factors explains this outcome. They range from the bias against the owners of small farms and the peasantry and their traditional livelihood—which had historically relied on the cultivation of small parcels of land for self-sufficiency, the private ownership of land and means of production and even the occasional hiring of labor—to population displacements; a sudden increase in social mobility opportunities available to sectors of the rural population, including young men and women, as educational opportunities increased together with employment in the service economy; the expansion of the military; and rising expectations regarding job mobility and educational training. The Cuban government has addressed labor shortages through the voluntary and forced (mainly through political mechanisms) recruitment of university students, young men serving compulsory military service, Young Workers' Brigades (Brigadas Juveniles del Trabajo), Young Military Workers' Army (Ejército Juvenil del Trabajo) and other people to cut sugar cane, harvest agricultural products, or participate in any other stage of agricultural production. Seasonal labor shortages in the production of tobacco, coffee, citrus fruits, and other crops have been filled by male and female students from high schools and universities, including students from Africa and other areas who have been granted education in Cuba in exchange for their labor and as part of a broader foreign policy strategy focused on creating allies globally. The use of "brigades" constituted of workers and students for what Carmelo Mesa-Lago (1982) calls "the transfer of urban labor surplus to the agricultural sector" have played an important part in ameliorating chronic labor shortages in the agricultural sector. Sectoral labor scarcity in professional activities has also become a structural feature of Cuba's political economy since 1959, and has increased with the growing exodus of professionals. This phenomenon has been approached by combining an aggressive educational policy to be able to replace those who left and restrictions on emigration based on age or professional expertise. Labor shortages in some sectors ran parallel to relative labor surpluses in others, including mostly urban activities, given the stagnation or poor performance of the latter. Thus seasonal and sectoral labor shortages have become inextricably linked with underemployment and disguised unemployment.[24] In this context, the Cuban government has implemented labor-exporting strategies through "internationalist brigades" and more formal "guest-worker" types of agreements signed with other governments, either bilaterally or multilaterally, in which the Cuban government has exchanged labor for currency, goods, or political capital. These strategies were put in place during the first years of the revolution and still exist. They have encompassed qualified workers and professionals in occupations related to construction, health, and education, among others, and areas as diverse as Latin America and the Caribbean, northern and sub-Saharan Africa, and western and eastern Europe.

Statism in the Urban Sector and the Declaration of the Official "Marxist-Leninist" Ideology

Important changes that took place in the urban sector since 1959 also had important repercussions for the labor market and internal and international migration. Since the 1960s, the state has established mechanisms to control industrial activities, the service sector, and foreign trade. The Ley de Reforma Urbana (Urban Reform Law) of 1960 ended private practices in the real estate industry by banning speculation and declaring the state the sole entity entitled to lease real estate.[25] By the end of 1961, the year in which the "Marxist-Leninist" ideology was proclaimed official , the state controlled the wholesale, banking, foreign trade, and education sectors in Cuba, and by 1963, more than 95 percent of the industrial, construction, and transportation sectors. In 1963, private entrepreneurs still controlled 25 percent of retail trade, although this changed in 1968, when the state gained control of these sectors as well.[26] That year was known as the year of the first "ofensiva revolucionaria" (revolutionary offensive), which gave definitive control of urban enterprises to the state. A major outcome was the confiscation of 55,636 midsize to small enterprises. They have been classified as follows: approximately 30 percent were "retail food outlets" (such as corner groceries, butcher shops, vegetable and food stands, and so on), and approximately 26 percent provided "consumer services" (such as laundromats, dry cleaners, lodging and boarding houses, auto repair shops, and so on). Food and drink businesses made up approximately 21 percent of the confiscations; 17 percent were retail outlets that sold garments, shoes, furniture, books, flowers, hardware, and so on; and small handicrafts manufacturing made up 5 percent.[27]

Many Cubans who owned or were administrators of enterprises, including transnational ones, professionals (including a number who worked for transnational corporations, local enterprises, or educational institutions) and physicians, some of whom ran private practices, left Cuba during what would be known as "the golden exile" period (1959–62) as a result of the initially vertiginous pace of the expropriations and other transformations that had negative repercussions for them. Since the first decades, the exodus was shaped by a series of regulations and state actions directly targeting migration and migrants (see Appendix B). Between January 1959 and October 1962 (the year that marked a closing of migration doors during the Missile Crisis), approximately 215,000 Cubans left for the United States.[28] Between 1960 and 1962, the exodus included approximately 14,000 unaccompanied children and adolescents under the age of sixteen who were sent by their parents as part of "Operation Peter Pan." In October 1965, the Cuban government announced that Cubans with relatives in the United States would be allowed to leave from the port of Camarioca. The Camarioca experiment, which brought about 5,000 Cubans to U.S. shores, was followed by bilateral talks leading to a memorandum of understanding to regulate the exodus. As a result, 74,000 more Cubans entered the United States. After the memorandum of understanding was signed in November 1965, which allowed direct flights between the two countries from December 1965 to 1973 (the "freedom flights") brought more than 340,000 Cubans to the United States. Between 1959 and 1973, then, approximately 630,000 Cubans had arrived in the United States.[29] During these first stages of the exodus, many Cubans also left for Spain, Mexico, and Venezuela, among other countries.

By the time of the "freedom flights," the educational and occupational backgrounds of the people leaving Cuba had become more diverse. By then, many owners of small and mid-sized enterprises that had been expropriated, as well as manual workers, were leaving the island in larger numbers. Like the previous "waves," this one also included individuals who were born in Cuba and immigrants who had been living on the island usually for a relatively long period of time, even several decades. In terms of political affiliation, a greater number of former political prisoners and their relatives arrived at that time as well. The exodus of members of the foreign-born population from Cuba mirrored that of the population at large. It first encompassed mainly the exodus of immigrant families that owned large enterprises and members of the moneyed elite in general, and then it included many more immigrant families of lesser economic means who had developed small enterprises or were members of the working class. It has been estimated that "some seventy percent of the Jewish residents in Cuba—most of them nationalized Cuban citizens—left as part of the exodus of the middle and upper classes to the U.S. mainland" during the first years of the revolution.[30] The Spanish, Chinese, Eastern European, Middle Eastern, and other immigrants who shared a history of enterprise development on the island left during this period as well. The binary representation "capitalists and proletarians" prevailed in the discourses on the abolition of private ownership under the new regime, thus eclipsing the social nuances of private ownership. According to such an oversimplification, the Spanish or the Chinese immigrant who had saved enough money to develop a family enterprise (such as a small fruit stand or a small store on a street corner) fundamentally belonged to the same "class" as the owner of the largest transnational corporations that operated in the country, and his or her means of production had to be expropriated. The vast majority of the first- and second-generation migrants leaving the island had developed their enterprises after years of sacrifice as low-paid workers or self-employed people subjected to prejudice and even discrimination (and to some extent still endured such attitudes and practices) or were workers of modest socioeconomic background. For many of them, emigrating to the United States, Spain, Mexico, Venezuela, and other countries meant that they would have to "start from scratch" once again. Although the vast majority of the initial exodus consisted of light-skinned persons of Spanish descent and other light-skinned Cubans, some people of color emigrated at that time as well. Some of them had achieved prominent positions as entrepreneurs or in their respective professions, in the arts, and so on, even though many came from families that had endured discrimination and barriers to social mobility for generations. The exodus was triggered by a complex set of factors that included changes in the material conditions of life as well as some of the intangibles of the revolution, such as the curtailing of individual civil, economic, and political rights. The gradual Stalinization of the society and the surveillance mechanisms and repressive forms associated with it created a social environment in which "exiting" rather than "voicing" dissatisfaction was perceived by thousands of Cubans as the most promising path toward individual development for them and their children. Under these circumstances, "widespread violence, social indoctrination, and [a] general climate of suspicion and harassment . . . proved to be the decisive factor causing many people to leave."[31] The top of Cuba's political elite has been ruling the country for a half century, and the technologies of governing that they have deployed to keep tight control have not varied substantially. All these intangibles continue to shape the process of international migration today.

Economic Dependency and Cuban-Style Developmentalism

The "second five-year plan" (1981–85) defined a new set of goals that brought Cuba closer to the Latin America developmentalist agenda without abandoning the substance of Cuban-style state-centrism. "Import substitution" and the increase of exports as a way to reduce "external dependency" gained popularity among the Communist Party cadres, although, as is frequently noticed, by the end of the 1970s the economic relations with the Soviet Union pointed to a level of dependency that could hardly be overcome in five years.[32] Soviet subsidies have been estimated to represent 23 to 36 percent of the national income between 1980 and 1987.[33] The Soviet Union paid a yearly average between 1986 and 1990 for the sugar imported from Cuba that was much higher than the average price in the world market for those years, which was US$752 million.[34] The products and services the Soviet Union provided to Cuba at artificially low prices included oil, military equipment and arms, foodstuffs, some manufactures, and technical assistance. Cuba's approach to import substitution in the early 1980s was focused on consumer goods and light industry, a strategy that further reinforced its subordinated position within the Council of Mutual Economic Assistance (CMEA) system.[35]

The economic support received from the Soviet bloc, mainly the Soviet Union, for more than three decades constituted a central piece of Cuba's developmentalism, including its social policies. Economic assistance from the CMEA was instrumental for the success of key social programs launched after 1959. The expansion of certain social services, both in number and in terms of their territorial reach, mainly related to education and health care, established the legitimacy of regime among vast segments of the population. Before the revolution, Cuba had already reduced the infant mortality rate from 124 per thousand in 1945 to 79.4 per thousand in 1955. After the revolution, it was further reduced to 19.3 per thousand in 1979 and continued to decline. Life expectancy grew from 58.8 years in 1950–55 to 72.8 years in 1975–80.[36] Despite a long-term trend that pointed to sustained improvements in the overall standard of living of the Cuban population, albeit with significant gaps among social classes, it has been argued that the improvements in social indicators after the revolution reflected the universal coverage of the health care system, as well as more sophisticated approaches to prenatal and neonatal care.[37] Similarly, the substantial reduction of the illiteracy rate, which was claimed to be close to zero in just a few years after the revolution, and the actual boom in enrollment and educational programs for all the segments of the population, had much to do with the policy of universal access to education and the creation of an infrastructure in semirural and rural areas and new social norms concerning education. These benefited hundreds of thousands of Cubans who otherwise would have remained marginalized from the educational system or would have been forced to abandon it at younger ages.

Despite the benefits of these revolutionary changes for vast segments of the population, the radical nature of such changes, the political environment in which they unfolded, and their unintended consequences also generated widespread economic and social dislocations and dissatisfaction among people who were negatively affected by them, those who felt they were benefiting in some respects but had been negatively affected in others, and those who had risen socially after 1959 yet whose growing expectations could not be fulfilled in Cuba. Many peasants benefited from the new legislation on land ownership and the creation of cooperatives and new sources of employment, yet the passage of such laws did not resolve these issues satisfactorily, while new social, economic, and political tensions and problems surfaced, such as those associated with the laws that suppressed some of the farmers' entrepreneurial traditions. Traditional forms of livelihood that many Cubans, including immigrant families, had sustained for several generations were wiped out in a traumatic fashion—and they were not always replaced with more favorable living conditions or economic prospects for the families. There were tensions between the government, which had taken control of the land and the means of production, and groups within the rural population who had lost it. As part of the process of alleviating the seasonal unemployment problem while boosting political loyalty, the state's farm policy included assigning to each farm technical and administrative personnel who were chosen mainly for their loyalties rather than their expertise, which also created dissatisfaction and political stress: many experts were marginalized because of their disagreement with the new policies. Those who openly opposed the revolution—or any particular initiative, for that matter, such as "la zafra de los diez millones" (the ten-million-ton harvest) initiative of 1970—were either forced into exile or were ostracized professionally, regardless of their expertise.[38]

The conflict between the growing demand of the Cuban population for agricultural products and the government's systematic attempts to control the private initiative in agricultural production and keep the profits made by independent producers at low levels was (and remains) at the core of Cuba's problems in agrarian productivity and outputs. Even though several market experiments have alleviated issues related to the supply of food, chronic shortages of certain products still exist, and the prices are well above the purchasing power of ordinary Cubans. The dissatisfaction generated by chronic shortages in agricultural products, which grew across the island since the 1960s, is still a major source of frustration among Cubans.

As the state-centric model of agricultural production grew increasingly dysfunctional by the late 1970s, the idea of developing *mercados libres campesinos* (farmers' free markets), or MLCs, was welcomed by influential members of the political elite. They were implemented in May 1980, but despite their immediate positive impact on the availability of foodstuffs in the internal markets, they were criticized, further regulated, banned, and reinstated by the government on several occasions during the 1980s.[39] The MLCs have been described as "a limited market-economy experiment" that was encouraged along with limited liberalization of self-employment opportunities in products and services such as craft-making, street vending, and minor repairs that state economic enterprises were unable to supply.[40] Albeit restricted and highly regulated, some entrepreneurial activities were allowed by the government after it realized that they were preferable to the potential political repercussions of chronic shortages caused by the low productivity of state-controlled farms.[41] Food and other agricultural products had been rationed since March 1962, when the *libreta de abastecimientos* (rationing card) system was established for the purchase of basic items, such as rice, sugar, beans, cooking oil, salt, vegetables, meat, eggs, fish, soap, detergents, and so on. The MLCs were expected to improve the availability of products outside the rationed distribution system, as the establishment of "the parallel market" had intended before.[42] However, while the prices of items available with a rationing card were strictly controlled, inflation outside the rationing card system skyrocketed while salaries stagnated. Opposition to this experiment grew within the policymaking apparatus, a faction of which had always been reluctant to support free-market reforms, as well as among the groups of peasants who were active members of the state-controlled peasant organization, the Asociación Nacional de Agricultores Pequeños (National Association of Small Agricultural Producers, or ANAP). Eventually the experiment collapsed, and MLCs were banned by the government in 1986. This development was part of a set of drastic measures taken against small producers operating within the private sector and middleman traders as part of the "proceso de rectificación de errores y tendencias negativas," the so-called rectification process, from 1986 to 1990. The main criticism on the part of the government was that the individuals working in such activities were re-creating patterns of conspicuous consumption and profit-making that corresponded to "bourgeois" patterns of behavior, and as such, they threatened the egalitarian principles of the revolution and upset the "revolutionary masses." The "rectification process" of the late 1980s was a comprehensive ideological approach that included not only attempts to overcome the shortcomings of previous economic policies, but also sanctions and other disciplining mechanisms toward individuals and groups that ostensibly deviated from the main ideological principles and modus operandi sanctioned by the government. As such, its forms of repression targeted groups as diverse as university students exhibiting "deviant" behavior (including homosexuality), bureaucratic cadres who defied the main ideological principles of the revolution, peasants who were trying to maximize their profits, and people who were openly opposed to the government, among others.[43] If the "battle" against the "capitalists" had affected many Cubans at the beginning of the revolution, the persistent battle against "petit bourgeois trends" and other "deviant" behaviors has had negative repercussions for a wide range of people, many of whom had been largely supportive of the government. Thus, permanent "ideological battles" and cyclical "revolutionary offensives" have adversely affected many Cubans who have seen emigration as the only solution to their problems. Direct repression has figured prominently as one of the factors shaping the migration process, since the government has systematically targeted not only members of particular groups or members of the opposition with alleged alliances with external destabilizing forces, but also those whose critiques of governmental policies were meant to be reformist, not antisystemic; people who have challenged heterosexual male dominance and even racism that prevail on the island and manifest from gaps in access to certain jobs to access to top political positions; advocates for a free press; and people who have felt marginalized and excluded because of their religious beliefs even when they have not been involved in political activities against the regime, among others. The *marielitos*—those who left during the "Mariel exodus" of 1980, when 124,769 Cubans abruptly left the island[44]— represent a cross section of the social backgrounds and sources of frustration among those willing to leave the island, even on short notice. This specific "wave" of migrants also captures, in a magnified way, the various forms of violence (from symbolic forms to physical attacks) that have systematically been applied by the pro-government forces or under government pressure to many individuals who proclaim their intention to leave the island.

Step Migration: A Missing Link

The lack of studies on "step migration" linking internal and international migrations makes it more difficult to study the links between politico-economic changes, the implementation of certain policies in Cuba, and emigration. The literature tends to suggest that since the beginning of the exodus in the 1960s, most immigrants have come from Havana. For example, it has been estimated that the province of Havana contributed almost 69 percent to the emigration rates between 1960 and 1964, 64.3 percent between 1965 and 1969, 54.4 percent between 1970 and 1974, and almost 65 percent between 1975 and 1979.[45] Cuba's official statistics corroborate that Havana was the main source of emigration to other countries in the year 2006: the net emigration rate of the city of Havana (7.7 per 1,000) was well above the national average (3.1 per 1,000), while the second-largest rate is found in the province of Havana (3.7 per 1,000 for the same year).[46] The same source indicates that the city and the province of Havana stand out as the main sources of emigration throughout the whole period between 2001 and 2006. It should be noted, however, that scattered suggestions throughout the literature and anecdotal evidence suggest that a number of emigrants leaving from Havana and other major cities had moved to these cities before leaving the country. Reportedly, 32 percent of those who emigrated legally from Cuba between 1985 and 1989 had first migrated internally, usually to Havana, before leaving the country.[47]

As the living conditions of the population outside the capital worsened as a result of the acute crisis of the early 1990s, many individuals and families decided to move to Havana in search of economic opportunities. They built precarious dwellings in what was officially termed "irregular settlements" (or shantytowns) using very flimsy construction materials, and sometimes settle in areas without access to electricity or potable water. In April 1997, the government officially banned the residents of areas outside Havana to move into the city unless specific criteria were met. However, the tendency to look for economic opportunities in Havana during the special period has extended to today.[48]

Transnational Fields of Governmentality and Migration

The hostility of the bilateral relationship between Cuba and the United States and the "systemic and systematic" interventions of the two governments in migration issues have been major forces shaping the process both quantitatively (in terms of numbers of migrants during a specific period) and qualitatively (in terms of the incorporation processes) since the early 1960s.[49] This explains to a great extent why most chronologies of the exodus from Cuba to the United States tend to be built around the notion of "migration waves," generally defined in relation to a drastic change in policy concerning migration, the size of the exodus, and specific characteristics of the group, such as occupational background.[50] The foundational chronologies covering the exodus during the first decades after the revolution in 1959, or any period within it, are usually divided into (more or less) the following five stages. The first, from 1959 to 1962, has been called "the golden exile," a reference to the Cuban refugees' relatively high level of education and their professional and entrepreneurial occupational backgrounds at that time, as well as the positive reception they were granted in the United States.[51] The second, from 1962 to September 1965, is called "the Missile Crisis hiatus" in some chronologies, because migration was suspended in response to the deep crisis in the bilateral relationship provoked by that event. The third, from September 1965 to 1971, was marked by a partial lifting of restrictions on emigration, which resulted in two operations closely monitored by the Cuban and U.S. governments—the Camarioca boatlift and the freedom flights. The fourth, from 1972 to 1979, was characterized by the negotiation of important agreements concerning migration and the opening of the doors for an unprecedented arrival of tens of thousands of Cuban Americans on the island for the purposes of visiting their relatives. The fifth, the 1980 Mariel exodus, was an equally unprecedented movement of Cubans across the Florida Straits, when, as mentioned before, 124,769 Cubans left the island in approximately three months.

The chronology in Appendix B calls attention to how major events, agreements, laws, and regulations shaped the context around Cuban migration to the United States between 1959 and 2006. It provides a close-up view of major mechanisms or "technologies" of governing employed by the two governments to control the migration process as well as the migrants themselves and other actions that, albeit unintentionally, have affected both. These include regulations, policies, and ad hoc approaches to bilateral issues, and migration in particular, that have affected individual movements, family reunifications, family visits, the sending of remittances, and other aspects of the migration process. Appendix B also illustrates that these regulations have been tied to a hostile bilateral relationship that has lasted for half a century, and that in all these years, the process of emigration to the United States has consistently crossed several realms, in a dramatic fashion, from "high politics" to family relations and humanitarian issues:

> Migration is the primary relationship that binds the two nations, even if at the same time it contributes to their further separation and conflict. Migration established a humanitarian, personal linkage between people on the Island and in the U.S. The personal and national feelings embodied in these linkages render migration a singularly sensitive issue that attracts and absorbs the slightest shifts in political emphases. Progress on the migration issue creates overly optimistic expectations about possibilities for improving relations on broader problems. Similarly, an antagonistic turn mobilizes both sides to strike at the issue that is felt most strongly by the other side—the personal importance of migration. . . . Second, migration occupies its singular significance because it is the only issue of real substance within a general context of antagonism for which there is a clear recognition of common interests among both states. It provides the only available policy tool, which either side can use to show changes in attitudes and goals without risking provocation and escalation.[52]

Soon after 1959 migration became one of the most important issues on the bilateral agenda. The migration process and the immigrants have also been controlled through social norms and mechanisms in the United States for the purpose of assimilating the group. Social and political control of the group has also intended to secure their political integration and to diminish the risks associated with the presence of a politically active exile group, some of whose members support military action against the homeland regime.[53] In the case of Cubans, specific regulations, assistance programs, and laws have framed their entry and incorporation into the United States.

The Cuban Refugee Adjustment Act of 1966: The Driving Force of Cuban Migration?

The U.S. government established the Cuban Refugee Program (CRP) and passed the Cuban Refugee Adjustment Act in the 1960s. The CRP was an indication of the U.S. government's willingness to receive Cuban immigrants as refugees and help them resettle in the United States. Government support included substantial economic assistance, employment support networks, bilingual educational programs, and programs to validate professional titles. It was also intended to relocate Cubans to different states to avoid their over-concentration in Miami.[54] Of all the pieces of legislation displayed in Appendix B, the Cuban Refugee Adjustment Act of 1966 is the foremost effort by the U.S. government to regulate Cuban migration and the incorporation process. As amended in 1976, the act states:

> Any alien who is a native or citizen of Cuba and who has been inspected and admitted or paroled into the United States subsequent to January 1, 1959 and has been physically present in the United States for at least one year, may be adjusted by the Attorney General, in his discretion and under such regulations as he may prescribe, to that of an alien lawfully admitted for permanent residence if the alien makes an application for such adjustment, and the alien is eligible to receive an immigrant visa and is admissible to the United States for permanent residence.... The provisions of this Act shall be applicable to the spouse and child of any alien described in this subsection, regardless of their citizenship and place of birth, who are residing with such alien in the United States.[55]

Under the Cuban Refugee Adjustment Act, Cubans were afforded preferential treatment that distinguished them from any other refugee group in the United States. Technically, such a privilege derived from the fact that the act did not establish a cutoff date (a fixture that is found in other refugee acts in the United States, such as the Hungarian Refugee Act and the Indo-Chinese Refugee Act). With the passage of the act, it became clear that Cubans leaving the island would be considered refugees, not only because they were escaping a regime that denied fundamental rights to the individuals who opposed it but also because of a combination of U.S. foreign policy and domestic political interests. Political concerns and foreign policy rationales played fundamental roles in the passage of the act. In this respect, the Cuban Refugee Adjustment

Act not only signified a consensus among exiles and the receiving government regarding the duration of the exodus, but also, from an ideological point of view, represented an important step forward in the construction of Cubans as refugees in the middle of the Cold War.[56] As is frequently emphasized, mainstream societal acceptance facilitated the realization of these objectives. In addition to humanitarian concerns, acceptance of the first wave of Cubans after the revolution was based on their predominant ethnicity (most were white, and of Spanish descent) as well as a widely held opinion that the newcomers were mainly professionals and successful entrepreneurs.[57] Concerns on the part of the U.S. government regarding the duration of their stay in the United States, along with foreign policy interests, led to the opening of doors to naturalization through favorable legislation as a path to assimilation. Following Robert Merton's work on "socially prescribed durations," Bryan Roberts rationalizes the Cuban Refugee Adjustment Act as an example of a piece of legislation that "includes a set of assumptions about moral obligations attending immigration; in particular, the assumption that immigration should lead to naturalization, abandoning any commitments to the country of origin, and becoming fully committed to the new country" (1995, 56). As a "normatively prescribed duration," the law established that Cubans not only were expected to stay longer than anticipated, but they were welcome to do so, given that the process involved a long-term commitment by the exile community to the values and expectations of U.S. society (ibid.).

By mistaking causes for effects, however, it is sometimes argued that the Cuban Refugee Adjustment Act has been the main force driving immigration from Cuba, particularly people coming on rafts. A glance at the data on interdictions of Cubans and Haitians (fig. 4) shows that tens of thousands of Cubans and Haitians have been risking their lives to come to the United States even though the Cuban Refugee Adjustment Act applies only to Cubans, which renders problematic any attempt at constructing the act as the main force driving the exodus of undocumented Cubans. The actual role of the Cuban Refugee Adjustment Act on the fluidity of the incorporation process is corroborated when we compare the share of the number of immigrants admitted under the Cuban Refugee Adjustment Act to the total number of immigrants admitted between 1959 and 1999. According to data from the U.S. Immigration and Naturalization Service, 68 percent of all Cuban admissions for permanent residence from 1959 to 1999 were processed through the Cuban Refugee Adjustment Act.[58]

The Cuban Refugee Adjustment Act has not driven immigration from Cuba. The synergic interplay of many forces, which are examined throughout

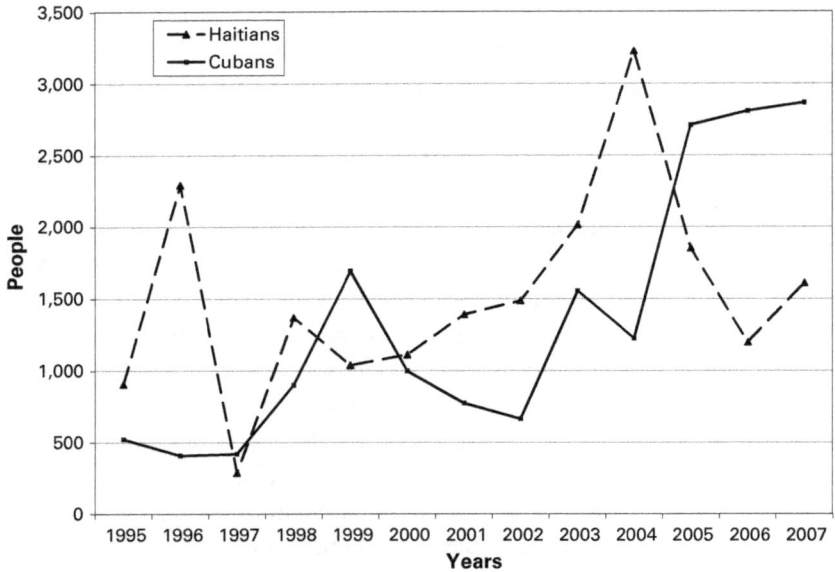

Fig. 4 U.S. interdictions of Cubans and Haitians after the "rafter crisis" of 1994
SOURCE: U.S. Coast Guard, 2008 (as of May 6, 2008).

this chapter, has. In addition to an ideological substance, the act also reflected a desire on the part of the U.S. government to manage a process that had been in the making for several years. Cubans continued to arrive from a country whose government was aligned with the Soviet Union, and therefore, Cubans were perceived, welcomed, and constructed as refugees from communism. Thus a special act was designed to benefit members of the group while managing the process, including their civic and economic incorporation. It was a tool that allowed the U.S. government to control, discipline, and assimilate the members of the group as quickly and effectively as possible. Continuing immigration after the law was passed occurred as a consequence of a set of forces that already in motion; other forces have subsequently come into play. Neither Mexicans nor Haitians have a specific act designed for members of their groups. However, they also risk their lives to reach U.S. soil, as do northern Africans to reach southern Spain through the Strait of Gibraltar and Turkish migrants to reach Germany across freezing hills. Even if the Cuban Refugee Adjustment Act was (and still is) a tool in the hands of different political factions in Havana, Washington, and Miami, the fact is that it has never been a root cause of emigration from Cuba.

The Mariel Crisis

By the end of the 1970s, a new policy toward Cubans residing abroad allowed many of them to visit their relatives on the island. The "visitas de la comunidad," or visits of members of the Cuban community abroad, had their immediate antecedent in a meeting of top Cuban officials and a small group of Cubans residing in other countries. The meeting, which was held on November 21 and 22, 1978, and hosted by the Cuban government, had the purpose of discussing issues pertaining to migration and the relationships between the Cuban government and Cubans abroad. It included topics such as the possibility that Cubans residing abroad might visit Cuba, the release and possible emigration of political prisoners ("people who are in prison because of their crimes against the revolution," in the official documents of Cuba), and family reunification, among others.[59] As a result of the new climate after what would be known as "the dialogue," more than 100,000 Cubans residing in other countries visited Cuba in 1979 as part of the "visitas de la comunidad," and these were followed by one of the most intense and traumatic episodes of emigration from Cuba: the Mariel exodus.[60] Also known as the Mariel Crisis, the exodus lasted from April to September 1980 and led to the arrival of 124,769 Cubans on U.S. shores. Among the *marielitos* were 13,000 school-aged children.[61]

It is widely acknowledged that the visits of a large number of Cuban emigrants had a "showcase" effect in Cuba, and emigration accelerated as a result of the "demonstration effect" that the visits of family members produced in thousands of Cuban households—combined with other factors, such as the continuation of the rationing card system in Cuba and the overall strains on the economy as well as the Stalinization of Cuba after the First Congress of the Cuban Communist Party in 1975. Cubans living on the island resented the special treatment given to visiting Cubans, who were patronizing hotels, restaurants, nightclubs, and stores as tourists and using dollars, which were banned for Cubans at home.[62] A popular saying in Cuba at the time perfectly captured the sentiment: "the worms," as Cubans who had left the island had been called since the first years, had transformed into "butterflies." Other factors leading to political discontent in Cuba at the time included the increasingly apparent formation of an elite in power who enjoyed privileges, such as traveling abroad and access to vacation resorts and hotels on the island that were out of reach for most Cubans.

Although, as seen above, there were important politico-economic forces underlying the Mariel exodus, the crisis was, to a large extent, crafted by the

Cuban government after a series of incidents that involved Cubans claiming asylum at foreign embassies in Cuba (especially the Peruvian embassy), spiraled out of the government's control.[63] These incidents created a crisis in the bilateral relationship; Washington had emphasized the right of Cubans to leave the island, but accepting thousands of Cubans at once was a politically delicate situation that would also put pressure on public funds at the local and national levels. The Carter administration eventually accepted most of the migrants under a special category: "Cuban entrants." In April 1980, 7,655 Cubans arrived in Key West as part of the "Mariel boatlift." The number increased to 86,488 in May, and the subsequent groups arrived in June (20,800) and from July to September (9,826).[64]

The crisis ended with the signing of a new immigration accord that included a compromise by the United States to make the visa-issuing process more expeditious. The commitment included granting up to twenty thousand visas per year to Cubans, based primarily on immigration preferences related to family reunification. The Cuban government agreed to receive 2,746 *marielitos* that were excludable under U.S. immigration laws, either because of certain health conditions or criminal records. There was also a pledge to let former political prisoners travel to the United States with their immediate relatives under a quota: up to 3,000 per year. The agreement failed to produce the expected results, however. In 1985, Havana unilaterally canceled it in response to political pressures from Washington after the development of the Radio Martí project. The project, which had received the support of influential groups in the exile community, was meant to counteract Communist propaganda on the island. As such, it mirrored previous initiatives developed in Washington to counteract communism in eastern Europe via radio broadcasting. In November 1987, implementation of the 1984 accord resumed. But by that time, many of the excludable *marielitos* with criminal records who had been held in U.S. prisons refused to go back to Cuba. To show their disagreement with the prospect of being returned to Cuba, 1,000 inmates at a federal prison in Louisiana set fire to four buildings and took more than 20 people hostage. Cuban inmates in Atlanta also created tensions. Their demand was to be allowed to remain in the United States and to have a careful individual review of their cases. The riots and the intervention of attorneys, civil rights activists, and leaders of religious organizations, many of whom were Cuban Americans, prompted the federal government's involvement.[65] As a result, although the 1984 accord contemplated the return of 2,746 "excludables," by 1992, 1,600 of them had been paroled by immigration authorities in the

United States and approximately one thousand were returned to Cuba.[66] Not all cases were resolved, and even today, there are still some cases in litigation.

These dramatic events happened in a context in which changes in laws, rules, and political actions on migration issues have been employed by the two governments to send messages to each other. Since the beginning of the revolution, the refugee exodus was frequently used by the Cuban government to send political messages to its main adversaries, both on the island and in the United States—mainly that it would not tolerate the development of an internal opposition, and that it was ready to use the migrants as political tools when necessary. Similarly, the United States government has used legislation on immigration and on the family transactions that the migrants can carry out to send messages to the government in Havana as well as Cubans on the island and in South Florida.[67] Furthermore, during the Cold War, the Cuban exodus held a "symbolic value" for the United States, as Cubans, who were ultimately portrayed as "voting with their feet," served the same ideological function as East-to-West migrants in the East-West confrontation.[68] The period between 1981 and 1993 was also one of government intervention, yet without a major crisis concerning migration (Appendix B). The main characteristic of this period was a sharp reduction in the number of immigrants admitted to the United States. However, the severe effects of the collapse of the Soviet bloc on Cuban households would shape the next major migration crisis: the "rafter crisis" of 1994.

The Collapse of the Soviet Union: Cuba's "Lost Decade" and Emigration

Precisely because of the subsides and assistance from the CMEA, Cuba was able to navigate the tides of the 1980s, Latin America's "lost decade," without having experienced the dramatic socioeconomic situations most of its neighbors went through at that time. However, such a level of dependency on the Soviet bloc (and the Soviet Union in particular) proved to be an artificial form of keeping the economy afloat, not a coherent and effective approach to development. The new form of dependency created by Cuba's ties with the Soviet Union became more apparent after the assistance and subsidies were dramatically reduced in the late 1980s and completely cut off later on, which led to Cuba's own "lost decade" in the 1990s. The worsening of relationships with Moscow was not an abrupt process. Miguel García Reyes and Guadalupe López de Llergo (1997) argue that it went through four stages: 1980–85, 1986–

89, 1990–91, and the post-1992 era. The first stage, they argue, was characterized by tensions between Moscow and Havana caused primarily by discrepancies in their respective foreign policies. However, the last stages were framed by deep transformations in the former Soviet Union until its disintegration in December 1991, which eventually led to what was officially called "the special period in peacetime" and unofficially the end of the "subsidized utopia."[69]

The Cuban economy collapsed. Macroeconomic indicators and palpable social conditions pointed to a deep crisis. There was the loss of markets and shrinking productive capacity: 80 percent of Cuba's external markets disappeared almost entirely. In everyday life, the collapse of the Soviet bloc translated into an unbearable situation for most Cubans and absolute deprivation among certain groups became apparent for the first time since the beginning of the revolution of 1959. Lack of access to subsidized oil purchases and spare parts induced a crisis in the transport system. The shortages of consumer products also reached critical levels, and items such as meat, milk, and chicken were traded mainly on the black market at prices too high for most Cuban workers to afford.[70] Although some macroeconomic adjustments were implemented to cope with the situation, overall social conditions continued to decline. A 2004 report by the United Nations Children's Fund (UNICEF) indicated that 46 percent of children under two and 28 percent of pregnant women in the third trimester had anemia. Approximately 23 percent of the population was found to have an iron deficiency. Access to potable water and sanitation was found to be a problem mainly in the eastern provinces. The report concludes that "the serious deterioration of school buildings and health installations, with the accompanying basic scarcity of teaching materials, basic medicines and diagnostic equipment, threaten the indexes achieved in education and health."[71]

The dramatic economic decline Cuba suffered after the demise of the Soviet Union forced Cuba's international reorientation to commercial, monetary, financial, and labor circuits that had not been targeted by the government at all, or at least not so aggressively. Important economic measures to cope with the crisis domestically included the decriminalization of the possession and use of dollars, the promotion of partnerships between state agencies and foreign investors through mixed enterprises, and the encouragement of self-employment, albeit for fewer than 120 types of economic activities and within the context of a highly regulated institutional framework as an alternative mode of labor market incorporation. A dual monetary system, embodied in the increasing circulation of the dollars sent by Cubans abroad, mainly from the United States, was officially sanctioned. From then on, having at least one member of the family or a close friend abroad, or any other potential source of dollars, became a valuable asset. As Ana Julia Jatar-Hausmann (1999, 55) put it, "Life for most Cubans had become unbearable. People were starving, salaries were worth nothing, and inflation in the black market was soaring. The only thing that made a difference was dollars. Those with families in exile or with access to tourist dollars could survive. Dollar holdings were still illegal, but since 1989, Cubans had learned that many laws simply did not make sense."

This is also the time in which *jineterismo,* an expression employed in Cuba to refer to prostitution, proliferated, as many young women and men saw a way to get access to dollars in the "sex market," mainly in areas frequented by tourists.[72] In addition, the Cuban government, which had encouraged supervised forms of labor through guest worker programs and "international solidarity brigades" as part of its foreign policy approach and as a palliative to unemployment, started emphasizing such methods again. Cubans have used participation in such programs as a way to stay in other countries or to use these countries as part of a "step migration" strategy that eventually takes them to the United States. Since the 1990s, however, such an approach has gone hand in hand with Cuba's revisions of certain regulations on emigration as well as work and travel abroad, some of which started in the late 1980s. Such changes have been minimal but they have allowed a number of Cubans with friends, acquaintances, or colleagues in certain countries to receive the "exit permit" from the Cuban government (still enforced as part of the restrictions on leaving the island) for them to work for a period of time abroad. This is an alternative enjoyed by only a small fraction of Cuban workers (mainly some professionals and artists with contacts abroad). Greater flexibility exists to make private trips to visit family or friends abroad. A growing number of Cubans have been using their visits to relatives in other countries, including the United States, to work there even when they do not have the appropriate permits to do so. Prior to the relative relaxation on emigration and travel rules, restrictions stipulated that only women sixty years old and over and men sixty-five years old and over could travel for such purposes and only for "humanitarian" reasons. In 1991, the age restriction was dropped to twenty and older.[73] In 2004 the Cuban government waived the "entry permit" requirement for Cubans abroad wishing to travel to Cuba, although they need a *pasaporte habilitado* (updated passport), which allows the Cuban government to filter the applicants in a way similar to when the permit was required.[74]

Since the collapse of the Soviet bloc, Cuba has also experienced an increase in the level of organized opposition to the government. Some opposition groups have developed transnational networks with human rights organizations, advocacy groups, and other groups in several countries and enjoy growing international reputation and sympathy. The Cuban government has employed a series of mechanisms to counteract such trends. These have ranged from the mass imprisonment of members of the opposition, such as during the so-called Primavera Negra of 2003, to the organization and systematic use of *brigadas de respuesta rápida* (rapid response brigades)—government-sponsored mobs organized to demonstrate outside their homes, attack them in the street, break up meetings, and the like. These violent methods have forced a number of members of the opposition and their families into exile.

The "Rafter Crisis"

Like the "Mariel crisis," the rafter crisis was a crisis that condensed the cumulative effects of political, economic, and social dynamics that directly affected the Cuban population. And, like its predecessor, the rafter crisis unfolded from a series of critical events. Cubans trying to leave the island on boats, rafts, and other devices have systematically been subject to imprisonment and other forms of punishment when captured by the Cuban Coast Guard. Although in August 2004, the Cuban government let the rafters leave and even announced that the Coast Guard would not intercept those wishing to leave the island, this course of action was announced after some violent confrontations between the authorities and the population, including "el maleconazo," a spontaneous demonstration against the government in the Malecon area. The most violent event took place a few miles from the Havana bay when more than 70 Cubans tried to leave in a tugboat (the "Remolcador trece de Marzo") and were intercepted by several government vessels that, using water hoses and other techniques, sank the old tugboat, resulting in the death of more than 40 people, including children. Once the government declared that the door was open for those who wished to leave, in the summer of 1994, more than 30,000 Cubans threw themselves to the ocean, mostly on "rafts" and other precarious vessels. By the end of the year, 38,560 Cubans had been interdicted by the U.S. Coast Guard.[75]

Contrary to what happened during the Mariel crisis, this time the U.S. government did not let Cubans reach U.S. soil. Most Cubans were intercepted by the U.S. Coast Guard and were sent not to the continental United States but to refugee camps on the Guantánamo Naval Base and in Panama, while negotiations were conducted to ask other governments to accept some refugees. At Guantánamo, which at that time had been converted into a large refugee detention camp housing both Cubans and Haitians, Cubans were placed in separate areas, and Cubans were further separated by groups based on their behavior as part of a disciplinary system. Some Cuban rafters have described the Guantánamo refugee detention camp as divided into "family tents," "male tents," "punishment areas," and other categories that indicate the use of space to control and discipline. They received visits, mainly from Cuban Americans from various organizations who aimed to support them and advised them on American ways, including some characteristics of its legal system. Miami radio stations also played a part in their socialization in anticipation of their new lives in the United States. During the first months, the Marines in Guantánamo used local radio as an instrument to deter the rafters from reaching U.S. soil, and even explicitly encouraged them to go back to their homes at a time when it was expected that bilateral negotiations would lead the Cuban government to accept those willing to return. The crisis led to a bilateral agreement that included two accords, one signed in 1994 and the other in 1995.[76]

After the rafter crisis, under the Clinton administration, the "wet feet, dry feet" rule started to be applied systematically to Cubans. The rule was based on Executive Order No. 12807, signed by President George H. W. Bush in 1992. Originally, it was designed to cope with the rise of immigration using the Florida Straits. The so-called wet feet, dry feet rule stipulates that if the person who tries to arrive on U.S. shores touches "U.S. soil, bridges, piers or rocks," he or she is "subject to go through the removal process," instead of being denied access to that process. For Cubans this has meant that if they were able to make it to the shores or any of the surfaces or areas stipulated in the rule, they would have the opportunity to make their cases for asylum, and eventually adjust their status. If they were intercepted on the high seas or before reaching U.S. soil or any of the surfaces or areas stipulated, they became "eligible to return."[77] The application of the rule to Cubans under the Clinton administration was facilitated first and foremost because of the perception that the intensity of the exodus was a threat to U.S. national security. After the 1994 and 1995 accords were signed with the Cuban government, the door was opened for the United States to send Cubans who were intercepted on the sea back to Cuba. Although the wet feet, dry feet rule has been consistently enforced since the years of the Clinton administration, apparently Cubans' ability to make landfall has also increased, which has to do with the increasing participation of Cubans in the global phenomenon of human smuggling in recent years.

The administration of George W. Bush continued the policy of monitoring immigration from Cuba very closely, and immigration policy toward Cubans has continued to be tied to domestic political considerations and a political agenda that involves inducing changes on the island. In 2004, the administration produced a five-hundred-page document that included the fundamentals of its approach to U.S.-Cuba relations. The bipartisan Presidential Commission for Assistance to a Free Cuba, created on October 10, 2003, issued the document. The report focused on how to make Cuba safe for democracy; it included "six interrelated tasks considered central to hastening change in Cuba."[78] The tasks summarized in the report were "to empower Cuban civil society, to break the Cuban dictatorship information blockade; to deny resources to the Cuban dictatorship; to illuminate the reality of Castro's Cuba; to encourage international efforts to support Cuban civil society and challenge the Castro regime; and to undermine the regime's 'succession strategy.'"[79] The document included recommendations that soon became sanctioned as new rules and laws on travel to Cuba, remittances, and the money allowances of U.S. citizens traveling to Cuba. Although this approach is further discussed in Chapter 6, it should be noted that it has made it more difficult for Cuban Americans to travel to Cuba to visit their relatives, for American citizens in general to travel to Cuba, and for American-based fully licensed remittance operators to continue their operations with Cuba. In Cuba, exchange rates and service fees allowed the government to keep approximately 20 percent of each dollar received by Cubans as a family remittance. CUCs (*el dinero cubano convertible*), or *chavitos,* as they are widely known in Cuba, became more widespread as a means to have greater state access to and control of the U.S. dollar and other foreign currencies. The *chavitos* represent a sort of intermediary currency that Cubans receiving dollars have to exchange for their dollars before being able to buy consumption items in the stores in which Cuban pesos are not accepted. The *chavitos* are purchased with dollars for a fee established by the Cuban government. From the perspectives of the individuals who send and receive dollars, this fee diminishes the dollar's purchasing power.

Thus efforts to regulate, induce, or discourage Cuban migration to the United States and to control the migrants did not cease after the Cold War. The fields of governmentality—involving the systematic use by the two governments of an array of technologies to regulate migration and control and discipline the migrant population, and even potential migrants—were instead reinforced in three interrelated ways. First, a series of systematic bilateral consultations have been held since then that have resulted in the deployment of new regulatory mechanisms (or the bilateral enforcement of existing ones) to control the process. Second, each government continues to use migration and its control of certain transnational relations (e.g., economic or political ones) to undermine the other; finally, related to this, both governments continue to use migration rules as ideological and political instruments. Such behavior is embedded in a regulatory system concerning travel and political, humanitarian, and economic exchanges between the two societies, which place significant constraints in the transnational exchanges by Cuban families. It is hard to think of a more compelling example of what Foucault called "governmentality" than how the two governments have handled U.S.-Cuban migration. Governmental control over the Cuban migrant population "is no longer essentially defined by its territoriality, by the surface it occupies, but by a mass: the mass of the population,"[80] which in this case is spread across a transnational space. There has also been an "essential continuity" between the individual, the family, and the state[81] in "the ensemble formed by the institutions, procedures, analyses and reflections, the calculations and tactics that allow the exercise of this very specific albeit complex form of power, which has as its target the population." And there has also been the preeminence of government as "a type of power," one that heavily depends on the handling of "the population as a datum, as a field of intervention of the government in that field of reality."[82]

The Expansion of the Cuban Diaspora

As a result of the politico-economic dynamics of the 1990s and beyond, the Cuban diaspora has grown in many countries throughout the world. Since the 1990s, the Cuban-origin population has increased in Mexico, Venezuela, the Dominican Republic, Panama, Nicaragua, Costa Rica, Peru, Chile, Ecuador, Argentina, Brazil, and other countries of the Americas, including Canada. Spain, Italy, France, and other countries of western Europe, as well as former members of the Soviet bloc, have also experienced an increase in the Cuban-origin population, and members of this global diaspora have also sought safe havens or greater opportunities in Africa and other regions.

Estimates based on national censuses show that in the year 2000, there were more than 6,500 Cuban immigrants in Mexico, 4,300 in Costa Rica, 3,160 in Chile, 2,200 in the Dominican Republic, 1,600 in Panama, 1,343 in Brazil, and about 1,200 in Ecuador.[83] As early as 1990, there were more than 10,000 Cubans in Venezuela. A large number of Cubans arrived in these countries after 1990; for example, the Cuban-origin population in Mexico went from close to 3,000 in 1990 to more than 6,500 in 2000. The same sources indicate that with the exception of Mexico and Argentina, males predominate among Cubans residing in other Latin American countries. The sex ratio of the Cuban population in Mexico (85.1 in 1990 and 91.9 in 2000) indicates a higher level of participation of women in the migration process and may be related to a greater tendency for Cuban women to use marriage strategies, work contracts, or some combination of the two to emigrate to Mexico. The same applies to Argentina, where the sex ratio of the Cuban population in 2000 was much lower; 79.3.[84] Recent data from the United Nations High Commissioner for Refugees indicate that the number of asylum and refuge seekers from Cuba has increased in Spain, Canada, Costa Rica, and Peru. Figure 5 shows a longitudinal cut at the number of refugees and asylum seekers from Cuba in the top four countries of destination, based on data gathered by the United Nations. The data encompass the period between 1994 and 2003, divided into five subperiods (1994–95, 1996–97, 1998–99, 2000–2001, and 2002–3). They show a growth in the number of petitions for asylum and refuge in

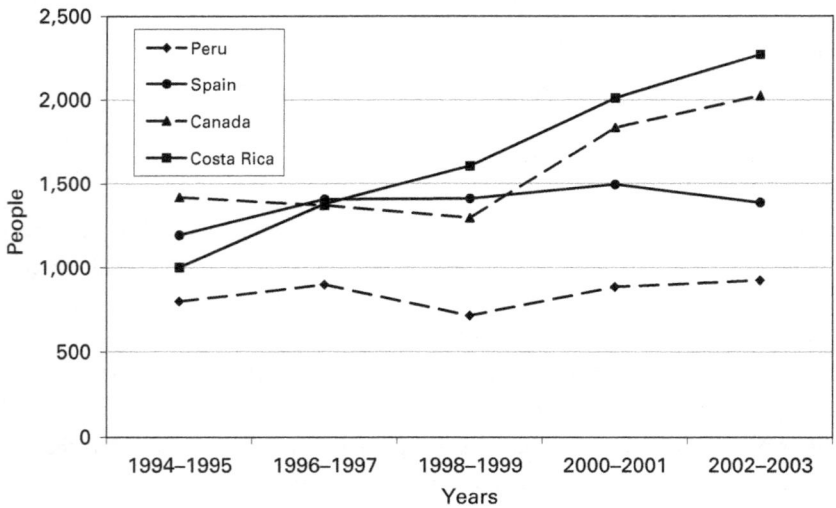

Fig. 5 Refugees and asylum seekers from Cuba, 1994–2003 (by major countries of destination beyond the United States)

SOURCE: United Nations High Commissioner for Refugees 2003.

the four countries. (The growth is more pronounced in the cases of Costa Rica and Canada.)

Anecdotal evidence also suggests that the internationalist military and civilian missions designed by the Cuban government in countries of the "Third World" in the 1980s found thousands of Cubans in those countries and in the former Soviet bloc societies during the final hours of the communist regimes in Europe. Many decided not to go back to Cuba after the disintegration of the Soviet Union. The internationalist mission of the 1990s and beyond (mainly composed of medical and construction crews) has also been used by many Cubans as a way to leave the island. It has been reported that from 1960 to 2005, 104,437 Cubans have worked in medical missions abroad. Currently, the international brigades of Cuban physicians and other medical personnel offer their services in countries in Africa, South and Central America, and areas of Asia, such as Pakistan and East Timor.[85] The working conditions of Cubans abroad are often not acceptable to the local professionals and workers. A high percentage of their salaries is kept by the Cuban government; sometimes, these Cuban workers deposit part of their corresponding portion in Cuban banks through government agencies, and the money cannot be accessed by their families until the workers return.

Cubans in Spain: A Dramatic Change in a Historical Pattern

Spain, a preferred destination for many Cubans since the 1960s, also witnessed a rapid increase in the Cuban-origin population during the 1990s, and the multiple social fields that tie Cuba and Spain expanded as a result. Emigration from Cuba to Spain is part of the global reversal of the main direction of the migration flows between Europe and former colonies in Latin America and the Caribbean.[86] In the case of Spain, previous immigration to Cuba created lines of ancestry that have encouraged emigration by taking advantage of the rules of consanguinity in Spanish immigration law. Based on official figures, it has been estimated that there were approximately 9,000 Cubans living in Spain with residence permits in 1975. The number dropped to close to 5,000 in 1985, but by 1999 it had increased to 16,556. A continuous growth followed, and by the year 2002, the number of Cubans with residency permits was 23,605. In general, the number of Latin Americans with residency permits in Spain grew from 35,894 in 1980 to 298,798 in 2001.[87] The same sources indicate that from 1987 to 2001, most Cubans tended to live in Madrid, the Canary Islands, and Barcelona. However, there has been some redistribution of the population in recent years. In 1987 Madrid had 41 percent of the Cuban residents, but from 1996 to 2001 it had less than 30 percent, dipping to 19 percent in 2001. Most of what Madrid has lost has gone to the Canary Islands, which had only 13 percent of the Cuban residents in 1987 but almost 22 percent in 2001. Barcelona has had less than 20 percent (between 12 percent and 18 percent) in most of the years between 1987 and 2001, with the exception of 1987 (23 percent).[88] As of April 2007, there were 8,804 Cubans registered as permanent residents in Madrid, although this indicator does not include all Cubans living there at the time. That same year, 43,728 Cubans were reported to be living in Spain as permanent residents.[89]

Today the level of immigration from Cuba to Spain is below the levels shown by other Latin American groups, such as Dominicans, Ecuadorians, and Colombians, among others. However, official statistics indicate that the growth of the Cuban-origin group during the 1990s was more accelerated than in other cases. Figure 6 shows the trend in the number of Cubans with permanent residence and work permits in Spain between 1990 and 2002. Even though the two categories used are usually seen as an undercount of the actual number of Cubans living in Spain, the trend points to a sharp increase in

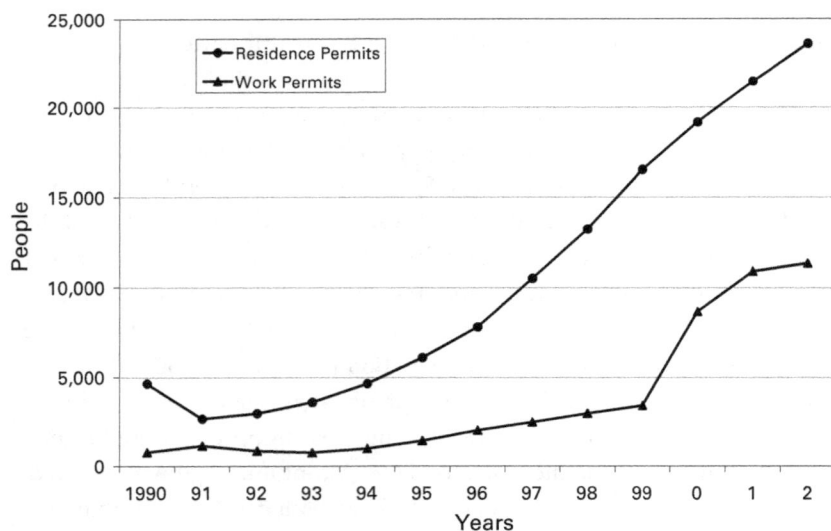

Fig. 6 Cubans in Spain with residence permits and work permits, 1990–2002

SOURCES: Ministerio del Interior, Spain, several editions; Ministerio del Trabajo y Asuntos Sociales, Spain, 2000, 2002.

immigration from Cuba since 1990. The number of Cubans with work permits more than doubled between 1999 and 2002.

Interviews and informal conversations with Cubans in Spain support the general belief that immigration to Spain is used to a certain extent as a way to reach the United States, although many of those who might have had this goal in mind have stayed in Spain because of the development of strong social ties, the command of the dominant language, the difficulties in obtaining a U.S. visa, or a combination of these factors.[90] Notably, the number of Cubans who adopted Spanish citizenship was among the highest within Latin American groups from 1980 until well into the 1990s. The propensity to acquire Spanish citizenship in the case of Cubans seems to be related to the use of consanguinity links to emigrate, the impossibility of return, and the use of marriage as a strategy to emigrate to Spain. Six of the women who were interviewed had arrived in Spain through marriage strategies or had benefited indirectly from such strategies. Three of them (one owns an antique shop and art gallery, another is a self-employed graphic designer, and a third owns a frame shop) had married Spaniards before leaving Cuba (one was from the Canary Islands, and two from Catalonia). Cubans do not necessarily use marriage with Spaniards directly as a way to emigrate, but they may benefit from this strategy indirectly. For example, an owner of a small tapas restaurant used the invitation letter of a close relative (the sister) to travel to Spain. She didn't marry a Spaniard herself, but the sister had married one before leaving Cuba. A woman who owns a small restaurant with her Cuban husband had arrived invited by their son, who had used his marriage with a Spanish woman to leave Cuba. It should be noted that is not uncommon to see middle-aged Spanish women married to younger Cuban males whom they bring to Spain; a significant age difference may also be found with respect to Spanish men and the Cuban women they marry. The importance of the marriage strategies as a way used by Cubans to migrate to Spain was confirmed by the immigration attorney interviewed: "Cubans typically use the family to come. There is a member of the family who manages to leave Cuba either by marrying a Spanish citizen—which clearly is the most recurrent strategy employed by Cubans. Someone in the family has married a Spaniard, and then they use that link to bring their parents, the siblings, or the daughters and sons. That is basically the mechanism they use."[91] The attorney also referred to political asylum as another important resource used by Cubans, and the use of consanguinity (mostly those having Spanish parents or grandparents), although the latter is a strategy that can take longer due to visa procedures.[92] Other strategies employed by Cubans to immigrate to Spain have included work contracts (e.g., the prolongation of a stay by extending work contracts becomes a way to acquire permanent status and eventually citizenship) or crossing the border to Spain from other European countries where they have been living as permanent residents, students, temporary workers, or undocumented migrants. The collapse of the Soviet bloc brought many Cubans to Spain not only from the island but also from eastern Europe, where they were studying or working. In that sense Cubans have been part of the East-to-West migration trend also.

The participation of women in the migration process reflects the increasing incorporation of women into the labor market. As can be seen in Figure 7, the proportion of women with work permits was much lower than that of men at the beginning of the 1990s. However, the gap shrank by the end of the decade. The proportion of Cuban women with work permits in Spain went from 28 percent in 1990 to 47 percent in 2000.[93]

Activities related to self-employment seem to have attracted a significant number of Cubans to Barcelona. Anecdotal evidence suggests that there is a pool of Cuban professionals who received their training either in Cuba or eastern Europe and today offer their professional services in Spain by combining self-employment with a salaried position. Another relatively well-known

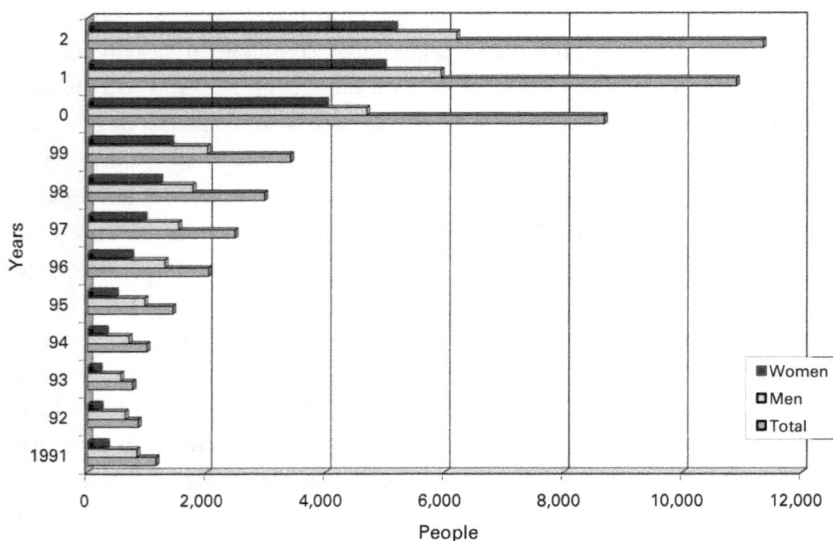

Fig. 7 Cubans in Spain with work permits, by sex, 1991–2002

SOURCE: Minsterio del Interior, Spain, various years; Ministerio del Trabajo y Asuntos Sociales, Spain, 2000, 2002.

group of self-employed Cubans in Barcelona comprise musicians and people from the entertainment industry, some of whom have work contracts in the city but keep their institutional affiliation with a workplace in Cuba. The Cuban government seems to have allowed a growing number of Cubans to travel to Spain if they have secured work contracts there, either through personal contacts or governmental contracts. Some have stayed there for several years and even become Spanish citizens. As a result, sometimes the line between immigrant and temporary worker becomes blurred. By the same token, some of what appear to be Cuban immigrants' "ethnic enterprises" in Spain could be in reality owned wholly or in part by the Cuban state. Anecdotal evidence suggests that during the "special period," some relatives (mainly but not only the sons and daughters) of high-ranking Party cadres and other members of the government elite were allowed to establish their residency abroad without losing their right to return to the island, their citizen rights, or their residence there. This privilege, which is not available to most Cubans, seems to have been dispensed to individuals close to the elite as a way to shelter them from the deep economic crisis that Cuba was facing. Some have developed their own enterprises abroad, although it remains unclear in which cases the start-up capital came from their savings and in which cases it came from the Cuban government, which has been using this kind of "emigrant" as a way to expand its enterprises and capital sources abroad. Although this phenomenon exists, its magnitude is very hard to quantify, given the lack of transparency with which this kind of strategy is launched. In addition, since the Cuban government allows some foreign investors from Spain and other countries to conduct business with state enterprises in Cuba, any Cuban marrying this kind of entrepreneur also enjoys certain advantages in terms of being able to launch transnational strategies that improve his or her capacity to assist relatives on the island.

The women entrepreneurs who were interviewed had been living in Spain for a number of years, some of them with their nuclear families, , but they all had family members in Cuba whom they visited regularly and supported financially. They mentioned several factors that took them into self-employment and, in some cases, the development of successful enterprises. These include the barriers of the labor market in Spain combined with their desire to achieve "economic and personal independence." Although their enterprises were mostly built from scratch, two enjoyed the advantages of having married Spanish entrepreneurs who initiated them in business practices. This small number of women also reflected what seems to be a general trend. With the exception of the few who are backed up by the Cuban government in their business ventures, most Cubans in Spain are at a disadvantage in some respects compared to immigrant groups that come from societies in which significant amount of capital can be accumulated by them or their families before the migration experience, or who had prior entrepreneurial links with Spain.

There seems an anxiety about the process of integration into Spanish society among the owners of enterprises with whom I talked in Barcelona. In Barcelona, the pressure on immigrants to assimilate, which includes but is not limited to acquiring proficiency in Catalan, is greater, since there is an intense social consciousness shaped by years of social movements that have politicized bilingualism and the use of Catalan. The respondents who had enterprise outlets didn't have any display suggesting their Cuban background. They mentioned that they wanted to keep their business *a lo catalán* (the Catalan way). Some wanted to be eligible for the concessions and possibly financial assistance available from the local government to businesses in the service sector that show an effort to support the continuation of Catalonian traditions and culture in general. One of them mentioned that most of their clients speak Catalan and not Spanish with her, even though they know she is Cuban. She believes that they do so to see whether she is in tune with the local culture. The Cuban entrepreneurs with whom I spoke seem to be aware of pressure to assimilate, and they all showed a disposition to comply, applying the maxim "a donde fueres haz lo que vieres" (when in Rome, do as the Romans do).

Integration seems to be harder for Cubans of color regardless of their efforts, however, and particularly women, who face stereotypes based on sexism and racist attitudes. Under the post-1990s conditions in Cuba, the use of marriage strategies among Cubans with Spaniards and other foreigners to leave the island has been frequently related to *jineterismo* in the popular imaginary; although such a connection exists, it cannot be generalized as the universal pattern of behavior. However, such a stereotypical association particularly affects black and mulatto women in Spain. One of the entrepreneurs, a Cuban *mulata,* explained that she consciously makes an effort to avoid *el cubaneo* (which she defined as to be part of or identified with the popular imaginary about Cuban women as being too easygoing, ready to go dancing and the like) in order to avoid being identified as a *jinetera*. In her case, the interface of ethnicity, class, and skin color brings about a multilayered field of representations that is rooted in and incites prejudice. She seems very self-conscious about these dynamics and tries very hard to avoid the stereotype, which to some extent has led to a repression of some aspects of her Cuban culture.

It has been forcefully argued that the racist imaginaries associated with the transatlantic migrations during the colonial period still have a resonance among Caribbean diasporas in former metropolitan areas, where former colonial subjects not perceived as "white" are placed in a situation of multiple subordination as racialized immigrants and colonial subjects.[94] This pattern is apparent among Cubans in the United States as well when the number of blacks and mulattoes leaving the island recently experienced a dramatic increase.[95] Dark-skinned Cubans in Spain are facing similar experiences, although several factors have framed a complex societal perception about members of the group.

The strong historical links between Spain and Cuba, which include migration links, create a sense of closeness to members of the group. The exile condition of Cubans has also created an environment of empathy and solidarity in a society that has fresh memories of its own exiles during the Franco era. Cubans are also perceived as having some of the highest levels of education among immigrants arriving in Spain, which has also contributed to positive social attitudes toward members of the group. Although these perceptions are fluid, and prejudice against members of the group does exist, they have created a certain comfort zone for Cubans in their incorporation into Spanish society. Some of the aspects of the comfort zone also exist in the case of Cubans in the United States. However, racial prejudices are manifested differently in each society. Concerning the role of ethnicity, in contrast with Cubans in the United States, Cubans in Spain do not display their "ethnicity," nor do they encourage ethnic resilience as they do in Miami, where social mobility and ethnic resilience have gone together.[96] The differences between Spain and the United States in terms of the demographics of the group, spatial dispersion, the possibility of traveling to the island and maintaining links with relatives there, the cultural setting (including, but not limited to, the dominant language in the receiving society), and the ways in which ethnic relations are incorporated into politics are additional factors shaping the differences in the incorporation process.

Emigration to the United States in Recent Years

Not only has the United States been the main destination for Cuban migrants since the 1960s, but Cuba has also consistently been among the top countries of origin of the foreign-born population of the United States. In 1970, Cuba ranked eighth after Italy, Germany, Canada, Mexico, the United Kingdom,

Poland, and the Soviet Union. In 1980, Cuba ranked sixth after Mexico, Germany, Canada, Italy, and the United Kingdom; and in 1990, it ranked fourth after Mexico, the Philippines, and Canada. In the most recent census (2000), it ranked sixth after Mexico, China, the Philippines, India, and Vietnam.[97] According to census estimates for the year 2006, about 1.7 million Cubans reside in the United States. Of Caribbean countries, Cuba has had the second-highest number of people interdicted at sea by the U.S. Coast Guard. Between 1982 and September 2008, a total of 112,709 Haitians and 65,796 Cubans had been interdicted while attempting to reach U.S. shores, followed by Dominicans, with 34,974 interdictions.[98] Figure 4 shows the number of Cubans and Haitians interdicted by the U.S. Coast Guard between 1995 and 2007 by fiscal year. It shows that interdictions of the two groups have been erratic, with abrupt ups and downs—more so in the case of Haitians. The curve representing Cubans displays two peaks: 1999 and 2005. The number of interdictions of Cubans by the U.S. Coast Guard increased from 7,606 between 1983 and 1993 to 11,888 between 1995 and 2005.[99] This indicates that more Cubans were interdicted during the decade after the "rafter crisis" of 1994 and the subsequent bilateral agreement on migration than during the previous decade.

The Drain of Human Capital

One of the most salient characteristics of continuing emigration from Cuba has been the exodus of skilled workers and a dramatic drain of human capital in general. Tens of thousands of professionals and highly qualified workers, both men and women, have left Cuba since 1959. A recent study of "brain drain" conducted by the World Bank includes Cuba among the top thirty countries most affected by the emigration of skilled workers.[100] Census data by country gathered by the Latin American and Caribbean Demographic Center show that among the national groups for which the data are discussed, a high percentage of economically active Cuban immigrants work as managers, executives, directors, professionals, and technical personnel. According to census data corresponding to the years 2000 through 2002, the percentages of Cubans working in these occupations were 83 percent in Mexico, 73 percent in Chile, 52 percent in Costa Rica, 67 percent in Ecuador, and 50 percent in Panama. In countries for which information is available, a high percentage of Cuban immigrants have ten or more years of schooling: the highest proportions are found in Mexico (83 percent), Brazil (83 percent), Costa Rica (74 percent), and Panama (67 percent).[101] Data from member states of the Organization for Economic Cooperation and Development (OECD) on the educational attainment of the foreign-born population in these countries[102] show that 60 percent of Cubans residing in such countries around the year 2000 had a high-to-medium level of education, and 25 percent had a high level of education.[103] A United Nations report produced in 2005 indicates that 24.2 percent of Cuban expatriates in the OEDC countries were highly skilled workers.[104] Throughout these years, the extraordinary exodus of professionals and other skilled workers has also contributed to other societies, although the United States has benefited the most from Cuba's brain drain.

Figure 8 contrasts changes in levels of immigration of "professionals and technical personnel" with that of the total number of immigrants from Cuba admitted to the United States for several years between 1958 and 2001. Beginning in 1989, both the total number of immigrants to the United States and of Cubans in particular showed sustained growth in the proportion of highly skilled workers. In the case of Cubans, the increase in the proportion of highly

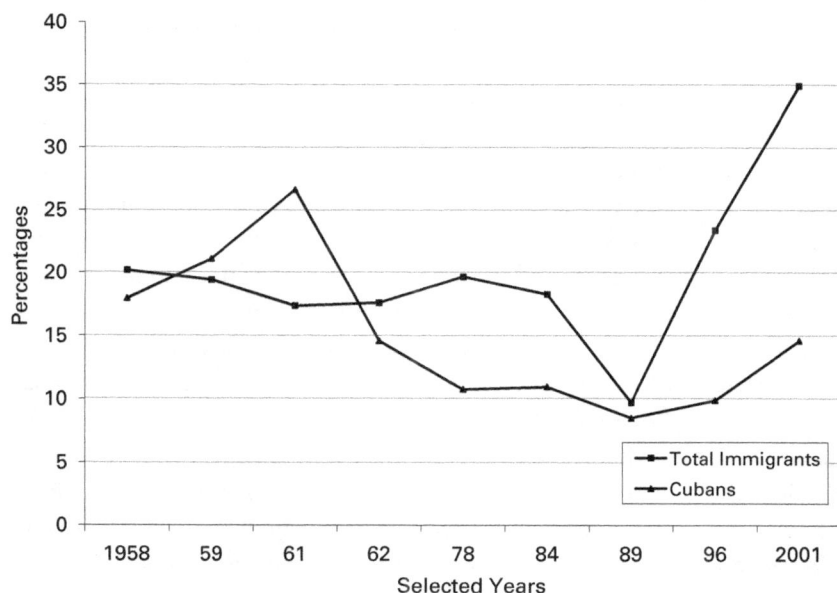

Fig. 8 Percentage of immigrants admitted to the United States in professional and technical occupations over the total declaring occupations (total and Cubans), 1958–2001 (selected years)

SOURCE: U.S. Department of Justice, INS (several editions).

skilled workers during this period points to the second most important period of brain drain from Cuba to the United States since the first years of the revolution.

Even though achievements in education cemented the legitimacy of the government for the most part, it also undermined it. Many Cubans have traveled to other countries for graduate degrees or to study for technical careers under scholarships provided by international organizations, foundations, the Cuban government, or other governments in the last fifty years. Because of the severe limitations on travel abroad that were imposed at the beginning of the revolution and which still exist for the most part, studying abroad has affected emigration directly and indirectly: directly, in that many Cubans have used this means to exit, and indirectly, insofar as studying abroad meant exposure to other societies; alternative literature, technological and political currents, and values; and greater individual freedom, to which they did not have access in their homeland. In addition, emigration became the unintended consequence of education in cases in which individuals returned after having completed their studies abroad but could not adjust to living in Cuba because of their new social and professional frames of reference. Tension created by the imbalance between the types of qualifications acquired abroad and what the labor market at home had to offer in terms of professional opportunities and social mobility has been a factor shaping brain drain in most underdeveloped societies[105] and has affected emigration from Cuba since the 1960s.

As is well known, the issue of brain drain is not unique to the Cuban case. For example, a World Bank report estimated that 14 percent of Mexican university graduates were living in other countries, and the percentage for Colombians was conservatively estimated at 11 percent.[106] It is also well known that societies that place a strong emphasis on education, such as India, Taiwan, and China, have lost many advanced students and professionals to the United States and western Europe. However, the high levels of human capital loss during the first years of the revolution, the continuing loss of human resources to the United States and other societies since then, and Cuba's restrictionist approach to immigration, transnational entrepreneurship among Cubans, and return migration hinder Cuba's potential to at least partially offset such losses in the near future. By contrast, some less-developed countries have launched aggressive incentive programs for their professionals and other skilled workers and entrepreneurs to return and invest in their homeland.

Many Cuban artists have arrived in the United States since the "special period," a fact that was highly publicized in the media. In 2004, the *New York*

Times announced "the largest mass defection of Cuban performers" to that date when forty-four dancers, singers, and musicians who had arrived in the United States to stage a revue requested political asylum.[107] However, this was just the tip of the iceberg of what became the most significant migration wave of Cuban intellectuals, writers, and artists since the first years of the revolution. Spain, Mexico, France, Colombia, Venezuela, Italy, and the United States, among other countries, have received them and benefited from their talents. Some among those who have established residence in countries other than the United States have been allowed to visit the island more systematically, keeping their professional links and even performing there. Government officials have promoted the presentation of works in Cuba of artists living abroad, although the process has been selective. Some, however, had to leave precisely because of their political activism or became actively involved in political activism once they left Cuba and have not returned. The so-called Mariel generation and those arriving in the 1990s have proven to be artistically and intellectually prolific in the United States. Many athletes and artists have used their competitions and performances abroad to "defect," which has also added to the drain of talented people.

Louis Pérez (1999, 43) reminds us that the links of Cuban musicians and performers to the United States via emigration, study, or temporary contracts are not new phenomena in Cuba's history. Some had moved to the United States at different times between the 1870s and the 1890s to advance their careers. The habit of searching for contracts and new artistic horizons in general outside the island grew stronger from that generation on, reaching a climax between the 1930s and 1950s. The global recognition and influence of Cuban music and international migration have gone hand in hand. Immigration of groups from different cultural backgrounds has enriched Cuban music since the colonial period, and the emigration of Cuban musicians and performers and their exposure to other cultural settings through their transnational livelihoods also contributed to the Cuban music and its dissemination. Furthermore, Cuba also experienced the emigration of artists, intellectuals, and professionals during periods of acute economic hardships or political repression, such as during the independence war and the turbulent hours of the Machadato and the Batistato. However, there are some features that make Cuba's migration context of the 1960s and beyond unique. Musicians and performers, artists of all types, and intellectuals do not return to their homeland once they have left the island as emigrants. Although in recent years there have been some efforts to try to develop cultural exchanges between Cubans residing on the island and abroad, these efforts do not change the context of "cultural exile" in which they take place. In addition to issue of censorship, the context is exilic if only because of the universal denial of the option of return.[108] The emigration of musicians, performers, artists, and writers has involved a dramatic severance of their professional links with the homeland, which has had long-lasting implications for the cultural production and the intellectual ambiance there. In this respect, Rafel Rojas (1998) asserts that it is hard to speak of a cultural exile in Cuban history the way it has manifested during the years following 1959. As he notes, the emigration of talented Cubans, and even their individual exiles during the republican period, tended to coexist with and even further develop the cultural and intellectual environment of the island through the fluidity of innovations, transnational partnerships, and other strategies and resources, which improved various cultural manifestations and impacted the publication of periodicals with alternative viewpoints on a wide spectrum of cultural topics, for example. Furthermore, prior to the 1960s, the demographic weight of the musicians, artists, performers, writers, and intellectuals leaving the island on a permanent basis was not as significant as it is now. Thus, more often than not, the artists and their fans have rediscovered themselves in the new spaces they inhabit, from Miami and New York to Mexico City, Madrid, and Paris.

The Dynamics of Growth of Cuba's Population

It has been estimated that the so-called emigration stock represented 11.5 percent of Cuba's population in 2005, while the "stocks of immigrants" represented only 0.7 percent of the population the same year.[109] These figures are in sharp contrast with the figures discussed earlier in this work about immigration to Cuba and Cuba's foreign-born population at the beginning of the twentieth century. By the last decades of the twentieth century that pattern had been reversed, and Cuba had become a net exporter of labor and a major source of refugees from the Americas, a pattern that continues today. Another major trend in Cuba's demography throughout the second half of the twentieth century and beyond has been a significant reduction of both the fertility and mortality levels and the aging of Cuba's population. Relatively low fertility and mortality levels are not new in Cuba's demographic profile; they respond to the long-term imbrication of socioeconomic and demographic processes that by the late 1950s had situated Cuba among the Latin American societies with the best educational attainment and health-related indicators as well as the lowest fertility and mortality levels. However, since the 1960s, Cuba has undergone a series of transformations in almost all social ambits that have impacted not only emigration but also reproductive behavior and demographic trends in general. Continuing emigration for half a century without a balancing counterpart in immigration, together with a sustained increased in the life expectancy of the population and a sharp reduction in the fertility rates to levels that have consistently been below the replacement level for several years, has led to an absolute reduction of the population, a process that started in the year 2006 and is expected to continue (see Table 2). Estimates by the United Nations Population Division indicate that Cuba's population will be less than 10 million by the year 2050, a figure that would place the population close to the level it had been in 1981 (see Table 2). Population projections by the Economic Commission of Latin America (CEPAL in Spanish) indicate that Cuba will consistently have the lowest population growth in Latin America and the Caribbean by the years 2025 and 2050,[110] which is consistent with the negative growth rates projected in Cuba and shown in Table 2. A closer look at Cuba's demographic trends since the 1950s in comparison with Latin America and the Caribbean in general (Table 3) shows some particularities in the Cuban case that are worth noticing.[111] In the period between 1955 and 1960, Cuba had indicators in mortality, fertility, and population growth that were moderate to low when contrasted with the Latin American and Caribbean averages. For example, life expectancy at birth was higher in Cuba (62.4) than in the region as a whole (54.7), while Cuba's infant mortality rate was well below the regional average (69.9 versus 114.3 per thousand). The gross reproduction rate[112] indicates that Cuban women were having, on average, fewer than two daughters in the second half of the 1950s, a fertility level that is rather low. The low-to-moderate levels in these demographic indicators also produced natural growth rates that were below the average for Latin America and the Caribbean (Table 3). While the region still had a gross reproduction rate value above 2 in 1980, Cuba's rate was well below replacement level by then, a low reproductive pattern that could jeopardize the population's natural reproduction levels. This is what has happened since the fertility levels continued to drop and emigration persisted. These demographic trends and low mortality rates have also shaped the aging of the Cuban population. Recent CEPAL (2007a) estimates indicate that for the year 2010, only 17.2 percent of the Cuban population will be fourteen or younger, while 26.8 percent of the Caribbean population will be fourteen years or younger. The share of the population sixty-five and over in Cuba's total population will be 12.4 percent in 2010, while the share of this age group in Latin America and the Caribbean will be much lower, 6.9 percent, and 8.5 percent of the Caribbean

Table 2 Cuba's population (all census years from 1774 to 2002, year estimates from 2003 to 2006, and projections until 2050)

	Population	Change (%)
Colonial period		
1774	171,620	
1792	273,979	59.64
1817	553,033	101.85
1827	704,487	27.39
1841	1,007,624	43.03
1861	1,366,232	35.59
1877	1,509,291	10.47
1887	1,609,075	6.61
U.S. military government		
1899	1,572,797	− 2.25
Republican period		
1907	2,048,980	30.28
1919	2,889,004	41.00
1931	3,962,344	37.15
1943	4,778,583	20.60
1953	5,829,029	21.98
After 1959 Revolution		
1970	8,569,121	47.01
1981	9,723,605	13.47
2002	11,177,743	14.95
2003	11,230,076	0.47
2004	11,241,291	0.10
2005	11,243,836	0.02
2006	11,239,043	− 0.04
Projections		
2010	11,257,000	
2015	11,250,000	− 0.06
2030	11,126,000	− 1.10
2035	10,929,000	− 1.77
2050	9,911,000	− 9.31

SOURCES: Census data from Oficina Nacional de Estadísticas 2008, table II.1; projections from Oficina Nacional de Estadísticas 2008 and United Nations, Department of Economic and Social Affairs, Population Division 2008b.

Table 3 Selected demographic indicators and subperiods, Latin American and Cuba, 1955–2020

	1955–1960	1960–1965	1965–1970	1970–1975	1975–1980	1980–1985	1985–1990	1990–1995	1995–2000	2000–2005	2005–2010	2010–2015	2015–2020
Gross reproduction rate													
Latin America	1.2	1.1	1	2.9	2.9	2.7	2.5	2,2	1.9	1.7	1.5	1.3	1.2
Cuba	1.8	2.3	2.1	1.8	1	0.9	0.9	0.8	0.8	0.8	0.7	0.8	0.8
Life expectancy at birth													
Latin America	54.7	57.7	59.1	61.2	63.4	65.4	67.3	69.1	70.8	72.2	73.4	74.5	75.5
Cuba	62.4	65.4	68.6	71	73.1	74.3	74.6	74.8	76.2	77.1	78.3	79.1	79.9
Infant mortality (per 1,000 births)													
Latin America	114.3	102.1	92.1	81.5	69.7	57.3	47.2	38.3	31.8	25.6	21.7	18.6	16
Cuba	69.9	59.4	49.7	38.5	22.3	17.4	15.9	15.3	9.6	6.1	5.1	4.5	3.9
Natural growth rate (per 1,000)													
Latin America	28.1	28.8	27	25.7	24.5	22.9	20.8	18.9	17.1	15.5	13.9	12.3	10.7
Cuba	19.2	26.9	24.3	20.1	11.5	10.2	10.7	7.9	5.6	4.4	2.9	2.4	1.9
Migration rate (per 1,000)													
Latin America	-0.4	-0.8	-0.9	-1.2	-1.8	-1.8	-1.6	-1.3	-2.3	-1.2	-1	-0.7	-0.6
Cuba	-1.6	-5.4	-6	-4.2	-3.3	-4.9	-0.7	-1.8	-2.2	-2.3	-2.8	-2.4	-2.1
Total growth rate (per 1,000)													
Latin America	27.7	28	26.1	24.8	23.3	21.1	19.1	17.3	15.8	13.2	12.7	11.3	10
Cuba	17.6	21.5	18.3	15.9	8.1	5.3	10	6	3.6	2	-0.1	-0.2	-0.3

SOURCE: CEPAL 2007a, tables 11b and 18b.

will be in that age bracket. Thus, Cuba will have a significantly older population and a net population loss in the next several years, which is at odds with regional trends. Neither the Caribbean nor Latin America is expected to have net population losses into 2020. To be sure, of all the forty-one countries and insular territories included in the most recent population growth estimates released by CEPAL, only Guyana and the Virgin Islands, along with Cuba, will experience negative growth rates in the 2015–20 period.[113] Although the emigration levels presented in Table 3 may be underestimated, as noted above, the longitudinal data sequence allows us to see that the whole region presents a consistent pattern and that the emigration levels from Cuba, compared to its immigration levels, have been consistently higher than the regional averages for almost all the five-year periods represented, with only one exception.

Several countries of the world are facing the socioeconomic challenges of projected population losses. One of these challenges is how they will deal with shortages of labor in key sectors of the economy caused by a low working-age population. However, this situation is not typical of less developed societies, such as Cuba, but has become a major issue in societies with the highest levels of development, such as some European countries, the United States, and Japan. In those cases, immigration from other countries is providing what has been termed a "replacement" for their declining population—hence the use of the term "replacement migration."[114] However, Cuba's labor absorption capacity at the beginning of the twenty-first century is far below what it was at the beginning of the twentieth. Thus, for the first time, Cuba is on the verge of a population and development dilemma: politico-economic problems lead to continuing population exodus, while the departure of qualified individuals, the low fertility levels, and the aging of the population also pose constraints to any prospect for social development. Any plausible solution in this area will require a change of attitude from the policymakers not only in terms of economic policies but also in terms of migration policy and the potential role of the migrants with respect to development strategies. As it happened with the emergence of current population dynamics, the impending correction of those negatively associated with socioeconomic development shall involve important sociopolitical transformations.

SIX

Transnational Social Fields Between Cuba and the United States at the Beginning of the Twenty-First Century

The Demographic and Other Foundations of Transnationalism

South Florida: The Epicenter of Cuban Migration

Estimates of the U.S. Bureau of the Census indicate that Latin American immigrants represented 73.7 percent of the foreign-born population of the state of Florida in 2006. This percentage places the state third in the national ranking after New Mexico and Texas, where Latin Americans constitute 78.9 percent and 74.6 percent of the foreign-born population, respectively.[1] The figures for Florida reflect continuing Cuban migration and the tendency of Cubans to concentrate in that state. The Cuban-origin population of the United States was estimated at 1,520,276 in 2006.[2] More than a million (1,054,371) live in Florida, making up close to 30 percent of the total Latino population of the state.[3] Within Florida, Cubans tend to concentrate in greater Miami or Miami–Dade County (MDC). MDC's population of 2,700,306[4] is slightly higher than that of the city of Havana, estimated at 2,168,255 in 2006.[5] MDC encompasses several cities: Miami itself, Coral Gables, Hialeah, Miami Beach, and El Doral, among others. The county is also an area of heavy immigration from abroad; half of its population in 2006 was born outside the United States. Of that group, 20 percent arrived after the year 2000, mostly from Latin America and the Caribbean.[6]

MDC's strong links to some of the largest Caribbean and Latin American cities involve trade, tourism, transportation, and communication as well as migration networks. In 1960, Dade County's Latino population represented 5.3 percent of the total population of the area; by 1990 it represented 49.2 percent.[7] Most of the residents of the area who speak a language other than

English speak Spanish. In fact, in 2006, only 646,467 residents of MDC declared that they only spoke English; by comparison, 1.39 million residents declared that they could speak Spanish.[8]

The U.S. Bureau of the Census estimates that 776,349 Cuban Americans were living in MDC in 2006, where they represented 52 percent of the Latino population and approximately 32 percent of the total population.[9] The immigration of Cubans continues to be a major factor contributing to the increase in the Latino population of MDC. Most Cuban Americans in the United States are foreign born (the proportion was 60 percent in 2005).[10] The number of Cuban immigrants admitted to the United States, which includes new immigrants admitted each year as well as adjustments of status, jumped from 67,751 in 1990–95 to 140,606 in 2000–2005.[11]

Table 4 contrasts the Cuban American population of the United States and MDC with the population of Cuba and Havana for the decennial years since 1960, plus the year 2006. The Cuban American population has experienced continuous growth, with greater dynamism during the first decades of the exodus. By contrast, Cuba's population growth has been much slower, and Havana experienced negative growth between 2000 and 2006. In the case of MDC, Cuban Americans equaled almost 36 percent of Havana's total population by 2006.

The last two censuses (1990 and 2000) show that Cubans in Florida have clustered principally in Hialeah and the city of Miami (Table 5). Yet these censuses show that the group has dispersed somewhat within the state: in 1990, approximately 62 percent of Cubans in Florida resided in the top locations, but ten years later, that number had dropped to 50 percent. Cubans have accounted for more than 50 percent of the foreign-born population in most of the areas in which they are numerous, and in some cases, they make up more than 70 percent (Table 5).

Labor Market Incorporation

As discussed earlier in this work, it is widely acknowledged that the context of Cuban migration right after the change of government in 1959 translated into a highly "selective" migration process. This selectivity is evident in the exceptionally favorable occupational and educational backgrounds of the migrants, which, combined with a relatively easy path to permanent immigration status and citizenship (compared to other immigrants from certain areas of the Caribbean and Latin America) had positive repercussions in terms of economic incorporation and social mobility. These and other aspects of

Table 4 A comparison of the population of Cuban Americans in the United States and Miami–Dade County with the populations of Cuba and Havana, 1960–2006

	Cuban Americans in the United States	Change (%)	Cuba's population	Change (%)	Cuban Americans as % of Cuba's population	Cuban Americans in MDC	Change (%)	Havana's population	Change (%)	Cuban Americans in MDC as % of Havana's population
1960	124,500		7,077,190		1.76			1,436,000		
1970	544,600	337.43	8,603,165	21.56	6.33	247,500		1,786,500	24.41	13.85
1980	927,995	70.40	9,693,907	12.68	9.57	405,810	63.69	1,929,400	8.00	21.03
1990	1,067,416	11.68	10,662,148	9.99	10.01	563,979	38.98	2,108,000	9.26	26.75
2000	1,315,346	23.23	11,146,203	4.54	11.80	681,032	20.75	2,187,000	3.75	31.14
2006	1,520,276	15.58	11,239,043	0.83	13.53	776,349	14.00	2,168,255	−0.85	35.81

NOTE: The 1980 figure for the Cuban American population in the United States represents the official census figure of 803,226 combined with the 124,769 Marielitos, who were not included in the census.

SOURCES: Boswell and Curtis 1984, tables 4.1 and 3.1; Comité Estatal de Estadísticas 1984, table 27; Mumford Report 2003, tables 2 and 6; Metropolitan Dade County Planning Department, Research Division 1994, table 12; Miami–Dade County Department of Planning and Zoning, Planning Research Section, 2003, Table 6; Oficina Nacional de Estadísticas 2008, tables II.1, II.4, and II.10; United Nations 2008a; U.S. Census Bureau, 2006a.

Table 5 Leading areas of concentration of Cubans in Florida

	1990			2000	
	As a percentage of the Cuban population statewide	As a percentage of the foreign-born population in that area		As a percentage of the Cuban population statewide	As a percentage of the foreign-born population in that area
Miami	23.11	53.7	Hialeah	16.7	73.3
Hialeah	19.53	73.4	Miami	14.7	50.3
Miami Beach	3.35	35.0	Tamiami	3.4	69.0
Westchester	3.01	75.7	Fountainbleau	2.6	44.3
Tamiami	2.79	67.4	Kendale Lakes	2.6	48.6
Coral Terrace	2.29	76.8	Westchester	2.4	79.9
Kendale Lakes	2.20	44.4	Miami Beach	2.2	31.1
Coral Gables	1.64	57.1	Kendall	1.9	32.0
Tampa	1.56	34.9	University Park	1.9	71.8
Sweetwater	1.35	63.2	Coral Terrace	1.8	76.9
Total	61.95		Total	50.2	
			Other areas		
			Tampa	1.7	23.8
			Pembroke Pines	1.5	17.9
			Coral Gables	1.4	51.5
			Total	54.8	

SOURCE: Computations based on U.S. Department of Commerce 1993, tables 19 and 168; U.S. 2000 Census, PUMS, electronic records.

Cuban migration, discussed above, have led to some disparities between the socioeconomic characteristics of the group with respect to the Latino population at large as well as to the majority (non-Latino white) population. While Cuban Americans do not reach the levels of the majority group in some socioeconomic indicators, they are still situated in a more advantageous position than most Latino groups (with the exception of some South American groups) in terms of educational attainment, incomes, and poverty levels, among other indicators. The mean earnings of Cuban Americans and Latinos in general were $13,567 and $9,432, respectively, in 2000; 25.2 percent of Latinos and 18.3 percent of Cubans lived below the poverty level, according to the last census.[12]

The 2000 census data on the distribution of the Cuban American workforce by occupational categories shows that at the national level, the percentages of Cuban American women and men employed in "management, professional and related occupations" are 34.50 percent and 29.39 percent, respectively (see Table 6). The numbers of people working in "management, professional and related occupations" are quite different among non-Latino whites, Latinos in general, and Cuban Americans in particular, although the gap is more pronounced between Cuban Americans and Latinos than between Cuban Americans and Anglos. Gender gaps are also found: non-Latino white men (34.50%); Latino men in general (14.58%); Cuban American men in particular (29.39%); non-Latino white women (38.64%); Latinas in general (22.93%); and Cuban American women (34.50%). While Cuban American men are more likely than Latinos in general to be employed in the "management, professional and related occupations," Latinos in general have a higher proportion of men employed in "production, transportation and materiel moving" (26.13%), a percentage that is much lower in the case of the non-Latino white and Cuban American groups (18.98% and 19.11%, respectively). The proportion of Latinas working in "service occupations" is significantly higher (25.63%) than the proportion of Cuban American women working in these occupations (16.18%), and both of these percentages are higher than the proportion of non-Latina white women (10.13%). Latinas, Cuban American women and Cuban American men have relatively high levels of people employed in "sales and office occupations," while the second most important occupation among Latino men in general is "construction, extraction, and maintenance."

In the case of MDC, the proportion of Cuban American women working in "management, professional and related occupations" drops to 30.49 percent with respect to their national average, while the proportion of Latinas

Table 6 Percentage of Cubans and other groups, by occupational categories, for the employed civilian population 16 years and over, 2000

	Male				Female			
	Total	Non-Hispanic White	Hispanic	Cuban	Total	Non-Hispanic White	Hispanic	Cuban
United States								
Management, professional, and related occupations	31.42	34.58	14.58	29.39	36.18	38.64	22.93	34.50
Sales and office occupations	17.86	18.23	14.79	21.02	36.75	37.66	34.84	39.70
Service occupations	12.08	10.13	19.01	13.10	18.03	16.15	25.63	16.18
Farming, forestry, and fishing occupations	1.09	0.80	3.56	0.54	0.33	0.23	1.42	0.19
Construction, extraction, and maintenance	17.08	17.27	21.93	16.85	0.75	0.74	0.86	0.69
Production, transportation, and materiel moving	20.47	18.98	26.13	19.11	7.96	6.60	14.33	8.75
Miami-Dade County								
Management, professional, and related occupations	28.71	46.49	24.04	25.86	31.87	46.82	26.98	30.49
Sales and office occupations	22.30	22.72	23.17	22.79	40.97	39.58	43.45	44.16
Service occupations	14.69	11.68	13.00	11.83	19.49	11.36	19.62	15.46
Farming, forestry, and fishing occupations	0.75	0.24	1.04	0.43	0.41	0.07	0.60	0.19
Construction, extraction, and maintenance	17.14	10.90	20.17	19.14	0.65	0.58	0.63	0.67
Production, transportation, and materiel moving	16.41	7.97	18.59	19.95	6.61	1.60	8.72	9.04

SOURCE: Computations based on U.S. 2000 Census, PUMS, summary File 4.

working in such occupations increases to 26.98 percent. The gap widens in the two cases with respect to the non-Latino white group, in which we find that almost 47% of non-Latina white women (and a similar percentage of white men) work in "management, professional and related occupations." The gap between the proportion of Latinas in general and Cuban American women in particular working in "sales and office occupations" and in "service occupations" narrows significantly. In MDC, Cuban American men and Latinos in general also have a more similar occupational structure than at the national level. However, the gap with regard to the non-Latino white group widens significantly. The occupational structure, then, shows that the gap between Cuban Americans and the Anglo group is more pronounced precisely in Miami–Dade County than at the national level, while the opposite occurs with respect to the gap between Cuban Americans and the Latino population in general. This is largely due to the fact that Cuban Americans make up much of the Latino workforce in MDC and their occupational and educational background tends to be more diverse in South Florida, where most of them reside. There is another characteristic of the incorporation of Cubans to the labor market that merits attention: the propensity of members of this group to be self-employed.

Cuban Americans in South Florida have developed a number of enterprises in MDC that have been socially clustered into an "ethnic enclave." In 1997, Cuban Americans owned 60 percent of all Latino-owned firms in MDC and employed about 67 percent of the workforce working for Latino-owned firms. Their sales represented 50 percent of the total.[13] The Cuban ethnic enclave in South Florida has cushioned the incorporation of many recent arrivals from the island in their transition into the U.S. labor market, while it has also facilitated further enterprise development among members of the group.[14] The significant levels of self-employment correspond to significant enterprise development by Cuban immigrants. According to the 2000 census (see Table 7), 11.44 percent of the foreign-born Cubans working in the United States were self-employed. This percentage was well above the average for Latinos (6.69 percent) and even above the national average for foreign-born workers (9.40 percent). Only Koreans had a higher percentage of self-employment. In MDC, 13 percent of the Cuban American workforce was self-employed, a percentage that is also above the total average for the foreign-born group and the Latino group. However, in MDC both Korean and Chinese immigrants had higher levels of self-employment than Cubans (Table 7). Cubans' incorporation as workers for local government agencies is well above that of the Latino group and the Asian groups represented and

Table 7 Foreign-born population by occupational category, United States and Miami–Dade County, 2000 (percentage)

Occupational category	All groups	Koreans	Chinese	Cuban	Hispanic
		United States			
Private wage and salary workers	75.46	69.98	76.55	76.53	81.76
Local government workers	6.87	2.77	4.18	6.79	5.71
State government workers	4.49	3.65	5.67	2.83	2.94
Federal government workers	3.38	3.74	3.21	2.10	2.52
Self-employed workers	9.40	18.25	9.65	11.44	6.69
Unpaid family workers	0.40	1.61	0.75	0.31	0.37
		Miami–Dade County			
Private wage and salary workers	76.09	57.69	70.71	76.63	79.23
Local government workers	7.49	0.00	4.70	6.65	5.34
State government workers	2.45	1.42	5.05	2.07	1.74
Federal government workers	1.93	4.36	2.79	1.34	1.34
Self-employed workers	11.65	33.49	16.45	13.00	11.94
Unpaid family workers	0.41	3.04	0.31	0.32	0.40

SOURCE: Computed based on U.S. 2000 Census, Summary table 4, electronic files.

close to the national average for immigrant workers. A similar pattern is found in MDC, although the gap with respect to the total average is more pronounced in MDC. Although this particular employment category does not distinguish between workers and elected and nonelected officials, it should be noted that Cuban Americans have a strong representation among government officials in MDC.[15]

Another way of looking at Cuban American entrepreneurship in the United States is through information about the firms owned by members of the group, such as sales and numbers of workers in areas where they have historically settled yet do not enjoy the same demographic and political representation. A survey by the Bureau of the Census (2006a) shows that in 2002, Cuban Americans owned most of the Latino firms in the Miami–Fort Lauderdale corridor, where their enterprises had significantly higher levels of sales (almost 60 percent in the Miami–Fort Lauderdale area and close to 48 percent in the Tampa-Clearwater area) and also employed most of the workers employed by Latino firms (over 62 percent in the Miami–Fort Lauderdale corridor, and about 36 percent in the Tampa-Clearwater corridor). Even if the number of firms owned by Cuban Americans in the two large combined statistical areas of the northeastern corridor included in the survey were significantly smaller than in areas where they have the highest concentration of numbers of the group, when compared to the other Latino groups represented, Cuban American firms tend to have higher percentages in terms of the number of employees and the dollar value of the sales of their firms. Such a gap suggests that although their firms are not as numerous, on average, in those areas, their economic impact is significant.

The general characteristics of labor market incorporation described above only begin to approach the complexities of Cuban Americans' economic situation in the United States. As the literature on immigration incorporation has extensively documented, many immigrants who are self-employed are not necessarily wealthy owners of successful enterprises. Among the self-employed are immigrants who, despite their qualifications, have found it hard to find jobs in the "first tier" of a labor market—that is, in occupations with good salaries and benefits. Instead, they have been forced to develop small enterprises that barely meet their families' needs.[16] To be sure, Cubans are no exception. However, entrepreneurship among Cubans is highlighted in this part of the analysis as a phenomenon that also points, as the enclave literature suggests, to the development of an economic base related to business ownership. When we examine this particular characteristic in historical and transnational perspective, we are able to see that such an economic base sharply contrasts with the economic decline of Cuba and the lack of economic opportunities in the island.

Family Remittances

Many Cuban families, like families in other countries of the periphery, depend on the participation of their members in foreign labor markets and the resulting remittances. Jorge Pérez-López and Sergio Díaz-Briquets (2005) estimated the remittance capacity of Cuban Americans to be between $600 million and $1 billion annually in 2005. There is consensus in the literature that monetary remittances sent by migrants from one country to another are hard to estimate because of several factors, ranging from the incompatibility of national accounting systems and the specific methodologies employed to study these flows to the fact that migrants tend to send money not only through formal channels (such as remittance agencies) but also, and sometimes even mainly, through their own family networks and other "informal mechanisms" that leave many money transfers unreported. Indeed, there are significant discrepancies in the estimates of the remittances sent by Cubans living abroad.[17] Nevertheless, scholars tend to agree that family remittances constitute "the most important source of dollars for monetary circulation."[18]

The International Fund for Agriculture and Development estimates that the dollar amount of the remittances sent to Cuba (from all over the world) in 2006 was $983 million.[19] Even under the assumption that the remittances sent to Cuba fall between $600 million and $1 billion per year,[20] it would be an impressive figure in any case, when contrasted with the number of workers in Cuba. Cuba's labor force (that is, the number of employed people) in 2008 was 4,948,200.[21] If we divide the low and the high estimates of the remittances by the number of workers actually employed in Cuba in 2006, under the hypothetical assumption that remittances were sent to workers and functioned as an additional source of income for them, then remittances would have added between $10 and $17.52 to each worker's salary each month. These are significant amounts; Cuba's mean monthly salary was approximately 450 Cuban pesos, or $20, in 2008.[22] Thus, hypothetically, if only the workers received the remittances, these would be a strong supplement to their monthly income. Certainly, not all Cuban workers receive remittances, and those receiving remittances include not only Cuban workers but also a number of people whose incomes tend to be considerably lower or nonexistent (e.g., retirees, the unemployed, and so on). These monetary transfers, then, are crucial to meeting the overall welfare of the population. The strategic importance of remittances for Cuban families is reinforced by the existing gap between the salaries paid to Cuban workers (mostly in pesos) and the prices they have to pay for consumer goods (set, for the most part, in CUCs). For instance, while the monthly average salary was officially reported at 415 Cuban pesos (19 CUCs) in 2008,[23] a one-kilogram package of powdered milk in the state stores cost 6.5 CUCs as of mid-December that year, and a can of sweetened condensed milk cost 1.3 CUC. A package of spaghetti cost 1 CUC, and a package of frozen chicken chunks cost 2.4 CUC per kg. It has been argued by Vidal (2007) that the stagnation of salaries, combined with the rising prices of consumer goods, has led to a drastic drop in the real salary between 1989 and 2006 (the last year for which real salary data is available).[24] The fact that the salaries paid to Cuban workers are extremely low is acknowledged by the Cuban government: "We are also conscious that in the midst of all the extreme objective difficulties that we are facing, the salary is clearly insufficient to satisfy the needs of the individual and therefore it has practically ceased to accomplish its role in securing the socialist principle 'from each according to his abilities, to each according to his work.'"[25] In addition to sending remittances, Cubans living in other countries also take considerable amounts of currency when they visit—thousands of U.S. and Canadian dollars, euros, Mexican pesos, and so on—which they use for home improvements and to assist Cubans trying to keep small enterprises afloat, including those operating in the underground economy, among other uses. They also take electronics and other household items, depending on Cuban customs regulations.

Remittances and Entrepreneurship

The dramatic situation that Cuba faced after the end of Soviet subsidies forced the government to make strategic decisions. Among the main measures deployed to fight the deep economic crisis that affected Cuba after the collapse of the Soviet bloc were the decriminalization of the use and possession of dollars, the opening of exchange bureaus where persons are permitted to purchase and sell U.S. dollars and other hard currencies at rates similar to those on the *mercado negro* (black market), and the legalization of transfers of dollars from relatives abroad. In addition, Cubans were granted access to the stores previously known as *diplotiendas,* where persons with dollars could purchase goods not available in regular stores. Since then, the remittances sent by Cubans living abroad to their relatives on the island have functioned as an important source of support for thousands of households there. In the summer of 1999 Western Union become the first global U.S.-based multinational company authorized by the U.S. State Department to handle family remittances to Cuba.[26] A number of smaller remittance agencies also offer this service from Miami and other locations. They are typically owned and operated by Cuban Americans and have been authorized by the two governments to handle this kind of transaction. Some of the remittance agencies operating from the United States also handle in-kind remittances or the sending of "humanitarian packages" that, complying with strict regulations, contain canned food, clothing, medicines, and other articles for personal use. More recently, after the lifting of certain bans, Cuban Americans have been sending cellular phones as well.

In September 1993, the Cuban government authorized a list of more than one hundred self-employment activities that Cubans could perform as part of a more general program of economic reforms designed to revitalize the economy. Since then, the number of self-employed individuals has fluctuated. It grew from approximately 151,000 in 1994 to approximately 208,500 in 1995, at which point it generally declined until 2007, when official figures placed the number at 138,400.[27] Despite the social and economic benefits of self-employment in Cuba—its cushioning of unemployment or generalized underemployment, the drop in the real salary, and the shortages of products and services—the state continues to be biased against it. Private entrepreneurs who try to gain greater levels of autonomy from the state apparatus encounter various obstacles. A fundamental obstacle faced by potential entrepreneurs and Cubans who already operate small enterprises, however, is the lack of political willingness to recognize independent entrepreneurship as an important socioeconomic force that can have a positive impact on the availability and quality of services and products and on the living conditions of the population. The state's biggest fear seems to be that independent entrepreneurs have the potential to become a social class (i.e., capitalists) that can eventually challenge the centralized control that a few state or mixed enterprises exercise over the most profitable activities of the economy.

It is in this context that what has been called "Cuba's second economy" is seen by rank-and-file Cubans as a sort of *economía del busque,* as more Cubans are pushed into performing economic activities that violate existing regulations. The second economy, which existed in Cuba before the "special period," refers to "activities outside the centrally planned economy (the 'first economy') on which Cuban citizens rely to 'resolve' their day-to-day economic needs . . . [some of which] are illegal and transgressors are subject to severe punishment if caught . . . [while] others are permitted forms of activities for private gain that nevertheless are discouraged by the government."[28] I heard the expression "Estamos en el busque" from a Cuban living on the island, and after inquiring further with other Cubans, I found out that for many Cubans the whole economy is *economía del busque:* the widespread practice of trying to use connections in or beyond the workplace to look for additional sources of income.[29] The real salary has dropped so dramatically since the late 1980s that the salaries Cubans receive in pesos are almost symbolic. This was not the case during previous stages of the "second economy." For most Cubans, the bulk of their everyday economic exchanges seem to depend on their capacity to build social networks that eventually facilitate a complex system of exchange through which they access construction materials, food, clothing, medicines, and quality services, including educational and health care services that they would not been able to access based on their salaries or what the state enterprises offer. However, such exchanges do not rely on bartering only; often, money is expected; and hence the importance of *el busque,* the ability to look for ways to supplement the extremely low income that a regular job in a state enterprise tends to generate. For example, in places where raw materials for the manufacturing of, say, cookware items are imported, some workers, including people in managerial positions, may develop a network to "divert" some resources to the underground economy for their own benefit.[30] The raw material is sold to other people who have small, clandestine, rudimentary shops where they manufacture the final products and sell them directly to the population by word of mouth through networks based on kinship and friendship. Enterprises that run import-export activities are also subject to the channeling of merchandise into the second economy through clandestine activities. Quality control operations, too; sometimes *el busque* consists of selling quality certificates to importers, among other activities.

Cubans also participate in activities that are considered legal yet remain highly regulated as additional sources of income. Renting rooms in one's living quarters for tourists, selling pizzas, hotdogs, and little boxes with typical Cuban meals (such as a combination of rice, beans, pork, and boiled malanga), selling crafts in craft markets, and using personal vehicles as taxis are among the limited number of enterprises Cubans can operate with government licenses. Indeed, renting rooms in their living quarters has become a major source of income for many families in Cuba. Currently, Cubans are allowed to rent such rooms to tourists and other visitors from abroad, charging rent in convertible currency, provided that they meet certain criteria, such as having the premises registered as their primary residence (where they have their rationing card registered) and paying taxes (a fixed rate is established, which they have to pay regardless of whether they can rent the rooms). Even though these small entrepreneurs are "truncated entrepreneurs," in the sense that they have very few options concerning the reinvestment of their profits and cannot hire workers legally, many of them are doing quite well. The most sophisticated ones, including professionals whose duties do not allow them to take care of the rentals, even hire friends or relatives underground to perform housekeeping and property-management functions. Some actually make much more money by renting part of their dwellings than by engaging in their professions. There is a sort of frenzy in the remodeling of dwellings for rental purposes. Sometimes the entrance of at least one of the rooms for rent is hidden in a creative way. The owners thus avoid government inspections and evade a taxation system that places a high burden when the rooms remain empty for several months—or simply bypass the rule on the number of rooms that can be rented. Since current rules establish that Cubans need to live in the premises where they have rooms for rent and regulate the number of rooms to be rented , sometimes a room is declared to be used by family members when in reality it is rented as well. The inspectors in charge of reporting any code or tax violation are often involved in *el busque* themselves and can be bribed.

Although we lack studies on this matter, my observations in Havana point to a connection between authorized entrepreneurship, the underground economy, and remittances and contacts with family members and friends abroad. For example, until recently Cubans were not allowed to have cell phones. Those wanting one had to use money and contacts with family and friends abroad to access cell phones and cell phone service, which small entrepreneurs use to coordinate their transactions. Now that Cubans have been allowed to purchase cell phones and service, they still rely for the most part on their relatives abroad to be able to acquire them. Remittances and business tips from relatives who live in other countries also help them structure income-generating activities such as running small beauty parlors, servicing taxis and *bicitaxis*,[31] running small eateries, renting rooms, and so on. It is hard for most Cubans living on a wage to purchase building materials in state stores and through the black market, and having access to remittances is critical for this purpose as well.

Transnational Livelihoods and Accumulation Strategies: The General and the Particular

The need to use family remittances to supplement household income is not exclusive to Cubans on the island. Immigrants from peripheral and semi-peripheral areas of the world, including the Caribbean islands, Mexico, Central America, and South America, have increasingly relied on transnational strategies that link their homeland to places where their family members have settled to be able to circumvent labor market disadvantages and improve their economic and social situation by securing additional sources of income. A recent report from the Inter-American Development Bank compares the flow of remittances to Latin America and the Caribbean with the financial flows related to foreign direct investment, tourism, and official assistance for development.[32] The comparison indicates that in several countries, the monies sent by individual migrants to their families and friends exceed the financial resources received from the other sources. The report states,

> In Latin America and the Caribbean, for example, individual migrants sent money home periodically, in amounts ranging from two dollars to three hundred dollars monthly. Yet when added up, these remittances total more than most countries receive in development assistance *plus* foreign direct investment. Over the years, fathers, mothers, sons, daughters, aunts, and uncles sent billions to loved ones across the Americas. Remittances are now a major source of foreign exchange for migrants' countries of origin.[33]

The sending of remittances is a global phenomenon that has been estimated to involve one person in every ten. There is indeed some empowerment associated with such practices, mainly when the options available to those receiving remittances are compared to the limited options of those who are not. Remittances have affected the rural and urban infrastructures and made homeownership and the development of small enterprises possible. Despite the fact that this is a global phenomenon, the Cuban has several specificities. To send remittances, Cubans have increasingly used private carriers, or *mulas,* who charge a fee for their services. The *mulas* proliferated due to the existing restrictions in terms of the amount of money that can be sent and the usual high fees charged by remittance agencies. As of early February 2007, sending $300.00 to Cuba through a Western Union office in Miami cost $25—

probably the highest cost in the region.[34] Lack of strong government regulations and the availability of a more extensive and reliable business infrastructure (including even online and phone transfers) lower the cost of this service for most Latin American and Caribbean countries. While money can be sent to Latin American and Caribbean societies from every state and city in which Western Union has offices, the same is not true for transactions with Cuba. Given U.S.-enforced rules that compel people sending money to close relatives in Cuba to sign an affidavit stating that they are sending the authorized amount to the authorized persons, Cubans in the United States need to send money in person, and not every Western Union office has been authorized to deal with Cuba. Cubans also pay higher prices and face more restrictions and difficulties associated with sending parcels. This is also true for long-distance calls in a context characterized by unreliable and expensive telecommunication services. In addition, the Cuban government charges an approximately 20 percent fee for converting U.S. dollars into CUCs. Since U.S. dollars cannot be used in Cuban stores, markets, hotels, restaurants, and the like that used to sell products in dollars, the tax becomes mandatory. All these regulations represent an additional burden on Cubans receiving remittances from abroad, since little or no accumulation is expected from the money sent, and its purchasing power is diminished by heavy taxation at the sending and receiving points in the form of fees related to the transaction. The costs for traveling to the island are exceptionally high as well. It has been reported that in 2000, the Cuban government charged more than $200 for a passport, $60 for a humanitarian visa, and $150 for a multiple-entry visa,[35] and the travel fees have experienced a significant increase since 2000. Persons born in Cuba who live permanently elsewhere should present a current Cuban passport to be able to enter Cuban territory, with the exception of those who emigrated before December 31, 1970, and have another citizenship. Currently, in theory, the Cuban passport is valid for up to six years. However, Cubans residing abroad need to obtain an approval from the Cuban government—the so-called *rehabilitación del pasaporte* (passport renewal)—twice within that period. The current fee to have the passport issued in the United States is $370 plus any additional fee the travel intermediary may request (typically about $35). In addition, within the six years from the issuing date, a fee of $360 ($180 each time it is renewed) should be paid to keep the passport current. Thus, the actual cost of keeping the Cuban passport current for the six-year period after the issuing date is not $370 but $730 (not including service fees). Cubans traveling to other countries need to request the exit permit (*tarjeta blanca*) from the government, which currently costs 150 CUCs. A person exiting Cuba on a temporary basis—say, to visit relatives abroad—may be absent from the country up to eleven months. However, the permit is not issued for eleven months at the time of departure; it is usually issued for one month, and from the second month to the eleventh, the individual pays a monthly fee to renew the permit. The fee is $150 monthly for those visiting relatives in the United States (not including service fees).

Until recently, the specificity of the Cuban case also pointed to the barriers imposed by the U.S. government to prevent the flow of currency from the United States to Cuba. Although some restrictions have been lifted under the administration of Barack Obama, the barriers imposed by the Cuban government concerning the productive use of remittances by private receivers (e.g., developing sustainable mid-sized or large enterprises) and the exclusion of Cubans sending remittances from abroad from any kind of authorized private business partnership with Cubans on the island are still enforced. Given the centralization of productive activities and most services in Cuba, remittances have not been used to promote home ownership, either. However, home improvement and construction using private resources, such as remittances, and state resources that are "deviated" from state enterprises takes place. Arguably, under new regulations allowing Cubans who meet certain requirements to build their own dwellings in certain areas designated for that purpose, remittances would increase their impact on home ownership, but this remains an isolated experiment.

Given the restrictions imposed by the Cuban government and labor regulations in Cuba, Cubans are less capable than other Latin American groups of challenging their subordinate position vis-à-vis the control of labor by the state and transnational corporations, which in their case is filtered through forms of state capitalism that include the development of state-owned enterprises and mixed enterprises (based on state partnership with selected foreign investors). While capital penetration takes place in Cuba through the mediation of the state, state regulations hinder Cubans from deploying a variety of strategies to avoid their subordination to those firms and enterprises in terms of labor rights, including the basic right to a salary with which to cover basic needs. The bias (and respective regulations) against the private sector also limits the capacity of Cubans on the island to use remittances and other resources to develop collective strategies, such as "hometown associations" (associations developed by migrants to assist their communities of origin), for the improvement of the service infrastructure, including transportation, water, electricity, and communication infrastructure in rural areas and even urban settlements, as migrants from peripheral societies tend to do.

Compared to their co-nationals residing on the island, Cubans in the United States of different class backgrounds (from small and mid-sized entrepreneurs to owners of large corporations) have had the advantage of being able to develop various modalities of economic transnationalism between the United States and countries where relatively significant Cuban communities exist, such as Mexico, Venezuela, Spain, and some Caribbean and Central American societies. However, economic transnationalism with their homeland, where the main recipients of their remittances are located, remains truncated. Thus, the restrictions of the Cuban context affect not only economic development and the entrepreneurial capacity of Cubans living on the island but also Cubans residing abroad who send an important part of their savings to a society where they cannot be fully involved as entrepreneurs.

While the reforms of the post-Soviet period brought a wave of restructuring of state-owned enterprises and the formation of joint ventures with foreign enterprises, they did not grant rank-and-file Cubans on the island the right to invest in their country, let alone in profitable enterprises directly linked to global circuits of accumulation. Such types of investment remain reserved for state-owned enterprises. Only very limited forms of entrepreneurship are allowed for rank-and-file Cubans living on the island. They may receive authorization to open small enterprises that can only be operated through self-employment by using a small number (typically no more than two) family members as assistants. These assistants also need to be registered for taxation purposes. Thus, the growth capacity of these enterprises is very limited, although some of them can be profitable, depending on the ability of their operators to mobilize material resources, attract clientele, and evade strict regulations. However, in all cases, the regulations ban franchising and transnational expansion, among other reproduction strategies. Within this context, the self-employed have remained truncated entrepreneurs for whom having family and friendship connections in the United States, Spain, Mexico, and other societies can significantly improve their ability to stay afloat and even prosper compared to those who do not enjoy this advantage. Yet the prevailing forms of social relations of production are regulated in ways that prevent them from becoming a social class or an autonomous economic force able to challenge the control of the state and transnational capital.

In this highly restrictive context, the transnational strategies related to income-pooling and social mobility have not led to the enhancement of citizenship rights, much less to "flexible citizenship."[36] The fields of governmentality

deployed by the two governments in this case represent the antithesis of flexible citizenship. Contrary to the case of Asian entrepreneurs, for instance, to
which most of Ong's work on flexible citizenship refers, holding more than
one passport under the conditions of dual citizenship (Cuban Americans,
Spanish Cubans, and so on) implies being subjected to an intricate web of
restrictions concerning their economic relationships with members of their
transnational households. For Cubans on the island, attempts at advancing
flexible citizenship strategies, such as trying to work in two labor markets
simultaneously, or profiting economically through membership in transnational social networks, often mean violating multiple rules and laws established by the Cuban government (and, in the case of U.S.-bound migration,
by the two governments) and being subjected to punishment. Nevertheless,
since the 1990s, a growing number of Cubans have been developing transnational livelihood strategies that involve acquiring another citizenship.

Changes in the Regulations in the United States

Regulations approved by the Bush administration in 2004 tightened the flow
of goods and money from Cubans in the United States to their relatives on
the island. Before the new regulations, Cubans aged eighteen or older were
allowed to send cash remittances not exceeding $300 per receiving household
over a three-month period and only under certain provisions. (The households of senior-level government and party officials in Cuba were exempt
from these regulations.) The allowed remittances remained at $300 every
three months per receiving household, but only "close relatives," defined as
parents, siblings, grandparents, grandchildren, and spouses in Cuba, were
entitled to receive them under the new law (which retained the provision
about government officials). The authorized per diem amount, or "the authorized amount allowed for food and lodging expenses for travel in Cuba,"
has been reduced from US$164 per day to US$50 per day for all family visits
to Cuba, "based on the presumption that travelers will stay with family in
Cuba."[37] These restrictions were essentially based on the belief that family
remittances are "a revenue generator for the Cuban government." In addition, the Bush administration tried to establish a strategy "to encourage law
enforcement" to deter the sending of remittances using "alternative channels." Thus, the new legislation also revoked "the existing general license provision in the Cuban Assets Control Regulations for banks to send individual

remittances to Cuba. Such transactions would require each bank to be specifically licensed as a remittance-forwarder service provider." This was done with the objective of facilitating "the oversight and effective enforcement of remittance regulations."[38] Family visits (to "immediate family") were reduced from one visit per year to one visit every three years for the purpose of visiting "close relatives."[39]

Regardless of their actual impact on the dollar amount sent to Cuba over the short term, the regulations concerning remittances and travel by family members were implemented through what is known as the "stick" and "carrot" mentality. The "stick" lies in the government's intent to control and discipline immigrants, who have been known to circumvent the travel ban to Cuba by traveling via "third countries" and not directly from the United States, as well as previous regulations concerning the sending of remittances. The "carrot" approach is also a mechanism designed to control Cubans—in particular, the Cuban American constituency, whose mainstream ideologues favor the restrictions. It includes a political message involving electoral politics and underscores President Bush's desire to show the Cuban American conservative constituency that he is determined to undermine the Cuban government with tougher economic sanctions.

After the enactment of the new regulations in question, the Miami-based newspaper *El Nuevo Herald* and, to a certain degree, the *Miami Herald* voiced the contrasting views of the rules by Cuban Americans in their respective opinion and editorial pages. For some, the measures would eventually curtail an important survival mechanism for the regime in Havana, while for others, they represented a violation of the rights of American citizens and the intrusion of government into private affairs, to the point of defining which family members are entitled to receive remittances. The new rules have brought to the surface existing tensions between the dominant political discourses about Cuban Americans and their rights as American citizens and workers (such as the right to travel to visit their relatives and the right to use part of their salaries and income to support their relatives) as well as their individual obligations in relation to family needs and expectations.

Some of these restrictions were lifted by the Senate in early 2009 under the administration of President Barack Obama. The definition of immediate relative was expanded to any individual related to the traveling individual by blood, marriage, or adoption within up to three generations. The restriction on frequency of visits was eliminated, and the limitation on the length of the stay was removed. The new approach addresses the humanitarian concerns of many Cuban Americans. However, important limitations remain, and the possibility that Cuban families might expand their transnational links will depend on greater political willingness on the part of both the U.S. and the Cuban governments to think more flexibly about the actual needs of Cuban families.

Informal Labor Circuits Between Cuba, the United States, and Other Societies

Several factors have been fueling the emergence of an informal labor circuit between Cuba and the United States since the 1990s. These include the dramatic shrinking of the purchasing power of the salaries and the limitations imposed on alternative sources of income through self-employment. Even the shrinking purchasing power of remittances due to the application of certain exchange rates and service fees, which makes it harder for working class emigrants to sustain their relatives in Cuba, may prompt Cubans to try to work at least temporarily abroad to supplement their family income in Cuba. Education and health are publicly funded services in Cuba. Cubans tend to pay reasonable fees for housing and public utilities, such as water and electricity, while there are social programs like those provided to the elderly and children which are provided at low or no cost at all. In theory, given the quality of such services, the low fees paid for them or the ability to access them at no cost should leave enough room for the salary to play a key role in the satisfaction of basic needs related to nutrition, clothing, and transportation. However, this is not the case. The salaries paid by the state to the vast majority of manual and professional workers in Cuba are not enough for them to satisfy such needs. Thus, Cubans need to look for additional sources of income within the island or abroad to be able to satisfy such needs. In addition, they need to procure medicines and other supplies that, even when they are prescribed, may not be available in Cuba. Even the quality of medical services and the typical time gaps between diagnosis and treatment have created an underground offer of better and faster medical services for a fee. The worsening of the quality of the educational system and its material conditions during the "special period" has also triggered the need to pay for private tutoring and look for textbooks and educational materials abroad or on the black market. The existence of more and better products in local agricultural markets and stores in recent years has propelled the search for alternative sources of income, because the products are there, but Cubans cannot afford them. The chronic deficit of housing units and the physical deterioration of existing ones due to lack of maintenance have also prompted many Cubans to search for alternative sources of income to improve their living conditions. Thus, not only emigration and a heavy reliance on remittances but also temporary participation in labor markets abroad have become the norm rather than the exception. However, Cuba's migration rules do not correspond to the requirements associated with the society's level of development and these social dynamics.

Conversations with Cubans in Cuba, the United States, and Spain suggest that a number of them residing on the island participate in an underground economy when they visit their relatives in other countries. Coming for an extended family visit in Miami to earn, say, $4.00 to $5.00 per hour at babysitting or janitorial jobs has become another way of coping with underemployment, unemployment, and the fact that while most products are sold for the new convertible currency on the island, most salaries are still paid in Cuban pesos. Cuban retirees who are in the first years of their retirement period and travel as much as possible to visit their relatives abroad seem to be an important segment of the population participating in labor markets abroad, either legally (as in the case of Cubans with residency permits in Spain who have decided to keep their residency in Cuba) or illegally. These retirees have greater flexibility, because they do not have work obligations in Cuba and it is easier for them to get permits from the Cuban government and other governments to stay abroad up to eleven months each time when they go as visitors. Based on the limited evidence available for this study, it seems accurate to say that Cuban retirees working in labor markets abroad while visiting their relatives seem to be playing a key role in sustaining their families in Cuba and improving their own living conditions there while helping their relatives with their household chores, such as helping to take care of newborns, running errands, and so on. Inquiries into the magnitude of this phenomenon and its social and individual implications are worth exploring. Their transnational livelihood strategies run parallel to those of Cubans who have been allowed to work formally and acquire residency and even citizenship in other countries while retaining their house and formal job connections to Cuba; this practice excludes Cuban Americans, though, given the nature of the bilateral relationship, and remains highly selective even with respect to other countries.

In addition to remittances sent by Cubans residing in the United States—and cash flows from participation in the Miami underground labor market by Cubans living on the island—another modality of economic transnationalism seems to be regular visits to relatives with bags full of easily portable items, such as accessories and clothing, that are in relatively high demand on Cuba's black market. Helping to set up a *paladar* (small restaurant) or other small enterprise by carrying necessary items, money, and business tips to relatives and friends on the island is another activity increasingly engaged in by Cuban migrants, despite governmental restrictions. What remains to be determined is the magnitude of the participation by Cubans in informal labor and entrepreneurial circuits connecting the island with other societies. For many Cubans, participation in transnational social fields that connect them to other Cubans abroad has become vital for their households' socioeconomic reproduction, but the Cuban government has been unwilling to recognize the importance of migrants as economic actors. Conversely, immigrants' participation in household-based transnational economic involvement with Cuba has been discreetly handled, at least in the core of Miami, since these transnational strategies are not only illegal but also run against the mainstream ideological construct that suggests the existence of a monolithic exile community aimed at keeping the embargo intact.

Contradictory Locations and Identities

Since the end of the Cold War, the "transformation" of the Cuban community in the United States from an exceptional "exile" group into an "immigrant group" is usually perceived as a major element of discontinuity in Cuban migration. Such a transformation is usually presented in relation to either policy shifts in Washington,[40] economic hardships in Cuba (widely held media perceptions about Cubans being "economic migrants" since the late 1980s), or sociopsychological shifts in Miami.[41] The revision of Cuban immigrants' "exceptionality" is hardly a new endeavor. The gradual transformation of Cuban exiles into another ethnic minority was anticipated more than twenty years ago and understood primarily as a consequence of the incorporation of the group into urban life characterized by "restless ethnic confrontation."[42]

The tension between "great transformation" (in Karl Polanyi's sense)[43] and "breakdowns" (in Donna Haraway's)[44] lies at the foundation of the exceptionality of the Cuban case and its commensurability with other cases. To analyze this tension we must consider the multiplicity of social ties involved in the changing dynamics of the immigration contexts and incorporation processes, including their transnational dimension. To be sure, Cubans in the United States have not been passive actors who only react to governmental policies. The group includes several "political generations,"[45] which adds complexity to their political and economic involvement.

There was an almost complete transplantation of the moneyed elite from Cuba during the first years of the exodus.[46] However, this phenomenon did not translate into the transplantation of class relations to the receiving country. The possibility of developing transnational class relations and referents in relation to the country of origin was curtailed as a result of the annihilation of the private sector in Cuba (the cornerstone of a complete transformation of the prerevolutionary class structure) and the emergence of a different system of social stratification in which power, prestige, and privilege were no longer meaningfully tied to private ownership but rather to political loyalty to the Communist Party/state structures. All this, compounded with the breaking of diplomatic relations between Cuba and the United States, meant that class relations of Cuban exiles in the United States had to be restructured without any meaningful class link to their homeland. In addition, many former members of the upper middle class experienced proletarianization and other forms of downward mobility in the United States. Many of them found themselves working in janitorial jobs, revalidating university degrees, and employing accommodating household strategies that often entailed the reversal of gender roles in income-pooling in their attempts at rebuilding an economic base and regaining social status.[47] Under such circumstances, class dislocation in exile created a tension between the historical referent that pointed to one's previous class location in Cuba and the subsequent repositioning into a new stratification system. Such a tension also informed class relocations of individuals who did not necessarily experience downward social mobility.

A wealthy Cuban sugar landholder might have been able to take with him enough money to start his exile experience as a wealthy sugar landholder. However, he was deprived of his class correlate in Cuba because the entire class system on the island had been disarticulated and transnational relations curtailed. Since he had no link to the class system of the society of origin, either through symbolic associations or tangible transactions, the development of solidarity ties with other members of the exile community (based on identification with a common political goal, to overthrow the government on the island, or the rejection of that system) faced less resistance than might have been the case had transnational class relations remained fluid.

Substantial class differences have always existed among Cubans in the United States. However, class surfaced as a social attribute of greater interest after the collapse of the Soviet bloc. There has been a significant growth in the number of Cuban immigrants who grew up after the revolution, which introduced new dynamics to the socioeconomic backgrounds represented among Cuban immigrants. In addition, since the "special period," the parameters of social positioning and status have been dislocated in Cuba, since neither party membership nor a professional title corresponded to greater status, as in earlier periods. Social status has increasingly been associated with access to hard currency, including transnational strategies to access it. This has contributed to the rise of a more pragmatic approach—not only to everyday life in Cuba, but to the migration experience as well—which is reflected in the higher priority of family roles and expectations than ideological discourses. Groups that have been in a disadvantaged position historically, including blacks, have increasingly participated in the immigration process, too, which has further accentuated class gaps as filtered through societal perceptions of "social distance," race, and actual discrimination. The embeddedness of class relations in Cold War ideological and political rationales reinforced exile and ethnic identities. However, after the collapse of the Soviet bloc, the cohesive mechanism that placed national identity, refugee identity, and exile identity over class identity as collective sources of meaning has been gradually eroded by multiple processes and social forces that operate in Cuba and beyond. The ideological construction of Cuban exiles by the U.S. government as escapees from and fighters against communism has distinguished Cubans from other Latin American and Caribbean groups for several consecutive decades. The U.S. government strongly emphasized a political assimilation strategy that included economic and social benefits toward members of the group in light of their ideological and symbolic value for the United States from the foreign policy perspective (which was relevant for domestic politics as well). Government assistance and the emphasis on Cubans as successful entrepreneurs have also served the ideological function of blaming the economic system in Cuba for economic failures on the island by demonstrating that Cubans working under capitalist conditions are able to create significant wealth.[48] The concentration of Cubans in Miami, where the media and leading political discourse tended to condemn the political system from which these immigrants escaped and hence legitimized their identity as refugees from communism, further reinforced their exile identity.[49] As with other immigrant groups, "an ultimate synthesis"[50] of the Cuban American group was created, one that can be directly traceable to the synergy between the formation of a community informed by the exile imaginary and the approaches toward the group by the two governments. Such a synthesis reinforces the idea of the Cuban community as a homogeneous and almost classless community of good entrepreneurs rather than union members,[51] and as exiles who have used their political leverage to ultimately frame Washington's policies toward the island. In addition, Cuban Americans are typically portrayed as active fighters against communism (or at least opposed to it) and practicing Catholics. Voting for Republicans also became part of this synthesis in the early years of exile. This portrayal of members of the group has been used as part of the mechanisms of "symbolic power"[52] employed to control the members of the group—and by members of the group to achieve certain goals. Both the refugee and the exile identities were reinforced under these circumstances.

However, the Cuban refugee/exile community has not been exclusively an "imagined community" tied to an assimilation project, a showcase experiment in Washington and a social experiment in Cuba. Since 1959, Cubans have left their country under exceptional conditions. Such conditions are far from ideal. Regardless of how one classifies them or how they regard themselves—as exiles, émigrés, refugees, or economic migrants—Cubans do not enjoy the right of return. Their transnational practices in relation to their homeland have been truncated by the fields of governmentality that control and regulate their migration experience. The centralized economy of the island and the bias against the diaspora and the private sector prevent the migrants from profiting from economic transnationalism, even though the remittances they send to their homeland are vital for their relatives and the government there. Abrupt halts to the migration flow, travel, telephone communications, and household-to-household economic transactions, as well as the requirement of exit permits for those with visas to emigrate to or visit other countries are some of the mechanisms employed that have led to the infringement of rights and further human suffering. Official representatives and common citizens have questioned the "exile" condition in the context of growing transnationalism. However, transnationalism has grown since the 1990s because of a combination of factors that go beyond political discourses and sources of meaning attached to them and enter into the realm of material needs, which explains to a large extent why the development of social reproduction fields that are transnational and exist to a large extent despite and against normative or legal dictums has gained centrality in the post–Cold War migration context. Within this context, Cubans' exile and refugee identities continue to evolve in complex ways that can be conceptually summarized by employing Manuel Castells's typology of major forms and sources of social identities, which he defines as (1) the "legitimizing identity," or that "induced by the dominant institutions of the society to extend and rationalize their domination"; (2) the "resistance identity," or that "generated by those actors that are in positions/conditions devalued and/or stigmatized by the logic of domination"; and (3) the "project identity," "a new identity that redefines their position in society, and by so doing seeks the transformation of the overall social structure" (in the exiles' case, the transformation of the social structure of the society of origin).[53] The Cuban exile identity has worked as a collective mechanism of ideological and political confrontation (resistance), social accommodation (resistance/legitimizing), and governmental control (legitimizing/disciplining). It is an identity that has been reinforced by the dominant political forces in Washington and Havana—one by inclusion and the other by exclusion. The exile identity has also worked as a legitimizing mechanism employed by the hegemonic fraction of the group who expect and demand political spaces for the realization of their political projects and economic strategies. The refugee and exile identities have been instrumentally employed by Cuban immigrants in general as a way to reposition themselves in the society of destination for the sake of social mobility there and social change in the homeland. They have worked to reaffirm "Cubanness" abroad through a national identity politically mediated by an exile condition and a utopian project of liberalization and return.[54] These identities have also worked for most Cuban Americans as a protective layer against the loss of rights and status vis-à-vis their society of origin and its state, related to their particular immigration context and minority status in the United States. They have also been employed to access scarce resources (material as well as symbolic) otherwise unavailable to them, not only as immigrants but also precisely because of the exceptionality of their migration experience.

Arguably, the exiles' ability to use the Cold War discourse as a mechanism to access resources otherwise unavailable to them proved to be counterhegemonic, to a certain extent, with respect to the two governments involved. Their refugee/exile condition was used by U.S. mainstream political actors at the peak of the Cold War to make a case against communism, and by the Cuban government to exclude the emigrants from the Cuban polity. Cuban Americans configured their refugee and exile identities to struggle for rights and recognition vis-à-vis the Cuban government both inside the United States and internationally by lobbying multilateral organizations and specific governments and world leaders to attract support to their cause. In the United States, these identities led to the acquisition of political clout and the opening of avenues to social mobility against the tide of the minoritization of the Latino groups in the United States. These mechanisms have produced "difficult identities"[55] that are nevertheless highly flexible in terms of their instrumental use. The maturation of the migration process within the post–Cold

War global context has brought about new twists to the construction of these identities. The exile and refugee identities are being reconfigured not only by statecraft and politics rooted in the Cold War mentality, but also by power relations and specific hegemonic/counterhegemonic practices related to exclusion and inclusion, as well as to ideologies and utopias enmeshed in a complex transnational system of expectations, interests, and strategies that range from families to enterprises. This system has been highly dynamic since the end of the Cold War. The ideological representation of the exile to advance political goals without regard for the transnational social dynamics of Cuban families in our time has led to an ideological disjuncture between the Cuban as exile, the Cuban as a working migrant, and Cuban households. Such a disjuncture has practical implications: the greater the political space the migrant worker claims as exile the greater the number of rights and obligations he/she has to give up as worker, family member, and citizen. This sort of zero sum game is framed by the rigidity of the dominant political discourses and practices in which the Cuban migration experience is embedded and their lack of correspondence with the pressing needs of most Cuban families both in the island and the United States. The process of alienation to which Cuban workers are subjected in their transnational spaces of socioeconomic and human reproduction is further exacerbated by this situation.

As seen before, in 1994 thousands of Cubans who were trying to reach U.S. shores were interdicted during what came to be known as the "rafter crisis." In addition to the tragic implications at the personal level, the rafter crisis produced important social and policymaking repercussions. It further reinforced the social distance(s) within the Cuban population in Miami that had intensified during the Mariel crisis in 1980 and beyond, when more and more Cubans, darker-skinned and educated in a different kind of system than their immigrant predecessors, arrived on Florida's shores in the space of a few months. The concentration of Cubans of visible African descent in areas such as Liberty City and Allapatah in South Florida, and similar areas with high concentrations of working-class African Americans, dark-skinned Dominicans, and Puerto Ricans in the Northeast, reveal deeper processes: darker-skinned Cubans, mostly from the Mariel and post-Mariel exoduses, are experiencing segregation, discrimination, and poverty related to a long transnational history of displacement ("structural displacements") and color/race/class divides.[56] The face of "the master status of race" in the United States, a phenomenon that constrains social mobility avenues for other Afro-Caribbean groups in the United States,[57] has become more palpable within the Cuban American experience since the 1980s. The pre-Mariel immigrant groups based their social relations mostly on ideological affinities created during the Cold War. This does not mean that the Cold War suppressed what Paul Gilroy called "the alignment of race and national belonging."[58] In this case, however, national belonging was also aligned with a particular global ideology, namely, anticommunist ideology. Their collective locations and sources of meanings attached to them placed Cuban Americans at a comfort zone within the triad of anticommunist ideology, racial constructs, and national belonging that prevailed during the Cold War in the United States. That comfort zone facilitated Cuban exiles' incorporation without consideration of their *Latinidad* (sense of belonging to the Latino group).

Even though many Cuban Americans participate in domestic politics guided by the consensus reached among Latino leaders concerning fair immigration policies, the defense of the civil and social rights of Latinos, and other major calls for the improvement of the status of Latinos in the United States, the group is not typically identified as a major bearer of the Latino imaginary or the political predicaments of the group.[59] Framed by power regimes, hegemonic systems, and symbolic means that blend the general and the particular in a specific context within the experience of Latin American and Caribbean groups in the United States, the participation of Cuban Americans in progressive domestic politics has materialized through "pockets of resistance." These include the Border Chicano movement, women's movements, gay and lesbian movements, the bilingual movement, and labor movements. As documented by María de los Angeles Torres (2004), the political situatedness of Cuban Americans in the United States has been framed by the Cold War politics and the identification of the hegemonic faction within the group with causes and leaders that were not popular among prominent leaders of the Latino community: from right-wing regimes in Central America and Africa to the Reagan administration in the United States. Conversely, pro-civil rights activities and other left-wing Latino activists in the United States were openly in favor of the Cuban government, and that compounded the tensions between the dominant views among each group and undermined any possibility for the integration of political agendas. The immersion of new generations of Cuban Americans in Latinos' political projects grew as the second and third generations gained political access. Generation gaps, in terms of "political generations," are playing a fundamental role in the reconfiguration of economic needs and political spaces among Cuban Americans.[60] From this perspective, generational gaps refer to substantial differences in terms of shared history and social expectations among Cuban immigrants concerning Cuba and the United States. They point to different "political generational experiences" that "are not entirely left behind with emigration" and that are shaped by previous and subsequent "transnational exposure."[61] In this context, communist or anticommunist grandiose narratives and prescriptions on "how to save the nation" have very little to do with the everyday needs of most Cuban families and their corresponding transnational strategies. Generational gaps and social distance(s) related to class, ethnicity, and racialization have produced contradictory locations within what is frequently portrayed as a monolithic exile community.[62] Since the 1990s, emigration to the United States has reflected the dual process of economic and political exhaustion in Cuba and the exhaustion of certain ideological and economic models beyond Cuba.

In South Florida, class, racial constructs, and generation-based experiences and interests are no longer blurred by the exile identity. Nor do these dimensions of the migration experience have to necessarily function in opposition to it and transnational strategies.[63] In Cuba, party membership is no longer incompatible with accumulation strategies, despite official anticapitalist discourses. As internal opposition grows in Cuba and the politico-economic elite on the island becomes more ingrained in capitalist ways of accumulation, including transnational strategies, and the business lobby favoring trade and other types of economic relations between the United States and Cuba expands, Cubans on the island and in the United States may be able to reposition themselves in ways that no longer align with traditional Cold War discourses, although such discourses still convey significant symbolic and political capital, authority, and prestige. The role of Cuban Americans in Cuba's rearticulation with the world economy in the future and the survival capacity of segments of the population with less access to material resources or political and symbolic capital are at stake as well. Their potential role is still clouded by political dynamics in which hostility in the bilateral relationship is intertwined with escalating repression. Major features of the political climate of Cuba include the imprisonment of members of the opposition without due process, tactics of social exclusion used against those who associate to demand greater democratization from within the system, the use of so-called rapid response brigades to intimidate the opposition, and severe restrictions on the circulation of information (including the use of the Internet). The most tragic episode of such repression was the imprisonment, without due process, of seventy-five human rights activists and others in what is known as "la primavera negra del 2003" (the black spring of 2003). Some events cause opposition groups to multiply and reinforce international solidarity with them, as in the case of the Las Damas de Blanco (Women in White), an association of women whose husbands and other relatives are in prison for their political positions. More recently, Cuban bloggers have emerged as an important political force.

The Other Logics of Transnationalism

Since the Clinton administration, it has become more difficult to distinguish between political transnationalism stemming from independent groups in Cuba and that sponsored by multilateral organizations in which the United States is highly influential or directly by the U.S. government for the purpose of rebuilding civil society in Cuba. The National Endowment for Democracy (NED), an organization that represents itself as an independent bipartisan organization and "a non-governmental organization that receives public funding to carry out democracy initiatives,"[64] has provided several grants to assist Cuban civil society groups and to promote discussions related to Cuba. The grants offered in 2005 ranged from $16,900 to the People in Peril Association (PIPA) to $663,690 to the Cuban Democratic Directorate, which operates in the United States but has members in Cuba as well. The grant to PIPA was to promote independent research on political and economic transitions. That to the latter organization was to promote "access to objective information and news in communities inside Cuba" through the establishment of a radio station "specializing in programming devoted to community development and community news."[65]

Other projects included support for the families of approximately three hundred political prisoners in Cuba through a grant of $55,000 to the Center for Free Cuba; the denunciation of human rights violations in Cuba through a grant of $65,000 to the Cuban Committee for Human Rights (CCHR); and the establishment of contacts with women's movements throughout the world and the initiation of training programs inside Cuba for independent women activists through a grant of $82,228 to Red Feminista (Feminist Network). Thus, the goals of governmental and nongovernmental organizations are sometimes blurred, as are the entanglements between Cuban Americans and nonmigrants who pursue certain goals concerning Cuba (e.g., humanitarian aid, greater cultural and academic exchanges, and the like) by employing transnational strategies.

Such links have tended to play a key role in developing initiatives and executing the projects that have involved the expansion of transnational social networks. The complex imbrication of exile groups with policymakers in Washington in the making of transnational politics finds its first conspicuous example in the Cuban American National Foundation's relationship with the Reagan administration, which sought to undermine the regime in Cuba. Government grants were also involved in this case.[66] Several groups of Cuban Americans that have established transnational links with opposition groups in Cuba have received funds from nongovernmental organizations based in the United States as well as from the U.S. government. They have acted as both transnational and policy entrepreneurs. For example, USAID granted more than $2 million to the University of Miami's Institute for Cuban American Studies as part of a $3 million commitment for the purpose of supporting the Institute's Cuba Transition Project. According to the USAID Web site, this grant assisted in the establishment of a "comprehensive database on transition issues and analysis materials that circulate in Cuba." It has been noted that "the Presidential Commission for Assistance to a Free Cuba, chaired by former Secretary of State Colin Powell, used the project's materials extensively in preparing a 400-page report to President George Bush,"[67] which led to the policy changes announced in 2004 and referred to earlier in this work. Thus the project sponsored by the National Endowment for Democracy not only received funds to advance certain initiatives that are in tune with mainstream approaches to U.S.-Cuban relations in the government, but they have also been instrumental in shaping policy.

The Transnationalization of the Media

Radio Martí started broadcasting to Cuba in May 1985, operating under the Act for Radio Broadcasting to Cuba of 1983, and TV Martí started its broadcasting in March 1990. The two projects were financed by the U.S. government in order to break the Cuban government's monopoly on information. These media systems have reached the Cuban audience on the island (more so Radio Martí) by offering viewpoints on Cuban issues that contrast with Cuba's official propaganda. However, Cubans living on the island have taken over the effort of breaking the monopoly of governmental views and information by intercepting satellite signals and have developed various mechanisms for their widespread diffusion across neighborhoods. These activities have become very profitable in the informal economy, but they also convey high risks, since they have been criminalized in Cuba's legal system. Presently, Cubans are avid "consumers" of news programs, *telenovelas,* and entertainment programs such as *Don Francisco* that are produced for the Latino population in the United States and the Spanish-speaking audience in general. Because of the island's proximity to the United States, Cubans have always been able to intercept signals. However, it was not until the mid-1990s that antennas and satellite dishes proliferated in Cuban households. As the *Miami Herald* assertively stated, such satellite dishes are "illegal but relatively widespread."[68] Cuban families willing to pay can have access to programs broadcast in the United States and other countries through various technological means. Typically, people pay $5 to $15 a month for illegal cable hookups—and risk losing their personal assets and even being imprisoned if discovered by the authorities. Yet the dense network of people involved in this activity has neutralized the state's ability to handle the situation. Cubans in the United States and other countries have played a key role in these developments, since in many cases they function as the main providers of the basic technology needed to capture the signals. According to Alberto, a Cuban American who recently visited Cuba:

> When I went to Cuba a couple of years ago, they told me that the policemen are the ones who have greater access to cable . . . a few months later I heard about the *redadas* against [police round-ups of] the networks of people involved in this. . . . The most innovative aspect of all this, aside from the technology that allows the hacking, is installation of the dish out of sight and the masking of the cables. Some of the common places to mask the dishes include plastic water tanks, the wall air conditioners. . . . Normally, they would be installed on the roof of the houses or buildings, but lately because of persecutions they are hidden behind the windows of houses. I have even seen them buried in the yard and covered with metallic covers used to protect underground water tanks—they pull them out when they want to watch TV and cover when they are not watching TV or when there are visitors in the house. . . . The cables are hidden in a variety of places—from government-owned telephone cables to false water tubes. . . . I was told that in La Lisa [a residential area on the periphery of Havana], some residents dug a tunnel and placed more than one hundred meters of cable underground. They are very poor people but they are willing to pay some money a month to watch *Sábado Gigante* and everything else.[69]

Alberto also notices that there is some "self-censorship," and sometimes programmers avoid the programs that are "very strong" politically. Another participant in the conversation added, "Sometimes the illegal programmers don't even want to transmit the news from channel 41 [a Miami station that has a program of interviews where high-ranking former Cuban officials who have defected tend to be interviewed]. The providers say that this is *candela* [very dangerous] because politically, these are 'very strong' programs. These programs are seen daily but mainly by consumers under category one [those who pay more]." Satellite signals can be received in different ways. The most expensive method involves a dish and a receiver, which gives access to many channels seen in Miami. Cubans who have a "free to air" programmable receiver, typically sold in the United States, can also access channels that have free transmission via satellite, such as PBS and other U.S. networks. The most common variant seems to be the systems of cables that are connected to a single receiver that tends to be located in "an unknown house." For those who use the cable system, the reception may not be very clear, though, and since the signal is distributed to several dwellings from a single one, the family who owns the receiver decides which programs will be seen, although apparently there is some coordination among the families enjoying the service.[70]

Musicians, painters, and other artists have also bridged the two societies more than ever since 1959. Literary narratives also reflect transnational social fields that tie Cuba with the United States.[71] However, strong tensions exist. In the United States, particularly in South Florida, performances by some invited Cuban musicians have been very controversial, while in Cuba only a handful of Cuban American artists, deemed "apolitical" or politically friendly with the government, have been able to perform there.

Multiple Transnational Actors and Projects

The Clinton administration promoted what were called "people-to-people contacts" in the expectation that "civil society" in Cuba would flourish and pose a challenge to the Cuban regime. In Cuba, El Decreto-Ley 54 de 1985 (Decree 54 of 1985) and its 1986 codification, La Ley de Asociaciones y Reglamento de la Ley de Asociaciones (The Law of Associations and its corresponding rules), permit the formation of NGOs, provided they are sponsored by a "state reference institution" and do not infringe on the area of responsibility of an already existing state-sponsored organization. Despite these restrictions, NGOs and social movements that have transnational links have proliferated in recent years. They prominently include groups whose members are subjected to persecution and harassment by the government, such as Las Damas de Blanco (Women in White), the Instituto de Economistas Independientes de Cuba (Institute of Independent Cuban Economists, or ICEI), the Asociación de Periodistas Independientes (Association of Independent Journalists, or APIC), the umbrella organizations Concilio Cubano (Cuban Concilium), La Asamblea para la Sociedad Civil en Cuba (Assembly for the Promotion of Civil Society), and El Proyecto Varela (Varela Project), among others. There are also grassroots groups, such as the Proyecto de Bibliotecas Independientes (Independent Libraries Project) and, more recently, independent bloggers' projects, which maintain that their goals are educational and humanitarian with no explicit political agenda. The above-mentioned organizations and groups do not enjoy official recognition, although they emphasize that they operate without violating constitutional law. Many organizations are nongovernmental in the sense that their missions are to create networks of support for groups that have been marginalized and even ostracized or persecuted by the government. Because of the perception in Washington that groups that either directly oppose the government or create alternative spaces for the Cuban population reinforce the civil society in Cuba, some of them have received funds from governmental and nongovernmental agencies abroad and enjoy ample recognition beyond Cuba. The organizations officially classified as NGOs and recognized as such tend to be subsidized by and support the Cuban government, such as the Federación de Mujeres Cubanas (Cuban Women's Federation).[72] There are also associations that predated the revolution, such as the Sociedad Económica Amigos del País, which was rehabilitated in 1994 as a "nongovernmental organization" that keeps an independent image but must abide by government and party rules.[73] This kind of "nongovernmental" organization is allowed to operate as long as the organizations' members and practices remain in tune with state regulations, policies, and strategies.

However, with the passage of the Cuban Democracy Act (also known as the Torricelli Bill) in 1992 and the Helms-Burton Act, which further codified economic sanctions, in 1996, it has become more difficult for companies with business links to the United States to build commercial ties with Cuba. Yet in the traditional "carrot/stick" approach, new avenues have also been opened since then to channel humanitarian aid to Cuba and support an array of humanitarian, cultural, political, and professional projects that do not receive governmental support on the island and are frequently subjected to state surveillance and persecution. Between 1992 and 2000, the United States authorized $897.4 million in humanitarian donations and $107 million in medical products or equipment as part of a policy designed to back the ideological axiom that the battle is against the Cuban government, not the Cuban people. These figures do not include the parcels of medicine and clothing regularly sent by Cuban immigrants and other residents of the United States to Cubans on the island. By 2008, Cuban imports from the U.S. constituted about 30 percent of all food and agricultural products. Despite the current restrictions on family remittances, a Department of State clarification on the rules governing trade and travel to Cuba establishes that NGOs willing to assist civil society organizations or their members may be granted permission provided that they apply for a specific license from Office of Foreign Assets Control.[74]

Religious networks, such as groups under the Church World Services umbrella, have been actively engaged in sending aid to Cuba in shipments licensed by the U.S. State Department. Shipments frequently include canned food, medicines, school supplies, soap, and blankets, among other items.[75] In its Web site on Cuba, the National Council of Churches details organization's recent steps in its relationship with Cuba.[76] Since Pope John Paul II's visit to Cuba and Clinton's policy of people-to-people contacts, Cubans in South Florida have been using religious channels to visit the island. Some are guided by their faith and willingness to assist members of either their former religious congregations on the island or newly formed ones. Other Cubans, motivated by personal, nonreligious reasons, simply use group licenses granted for religious activities to travel.[77] "Sister city" associations have also been establishing "meaningful, long term and sustainable relationships" with their "counterparts in Cuba."[78] As seen in the advertisements from the sister cities groups, "from liberal Berkeley to exclusive East Hampton," several city councils and independent groups in the United States have engaged in sister cities partnerships with cities in Cuba. Sister city associations have also been actively engaged in lobbying against the economic sanctions with their local representatives or directly in Washington. Since Cuban migrants in the United States face limitations that preclude their participation in "hometown associations" and other transnational arrangements to facilitate the channeling of humanitarian aid and the construction of social projects at the community level, nonmigrant transnational actors have taken the lead in recent years to channel aid and resources to benefit groups and projects at the community or other subnational scales. Thus, more often than not, the line between governmental and nongovernmental forms of transnational agencies has been blurred. The transnational social fields developed by nongovernmental actors tend to juxtapose and in some cases even get entangled with the transnational fields of governmentality in specific ways given the nature of the relationships between the Cuban and U.S. governments since 1961.

The transnational links between Cubans and their relatives have found new channels and forms of communication that did not exist some decades ago, and even when they started functioning globally, they were prohibited in the island. The Internet, the intranet variant, and the blogosphere have brought new dynamism to family, professional, cultural, economic, and political links between Cubans on the island with the rest of the world. Access to cyberspace is very limited in Cuba. The email system operates mainly through an intranet system, to which some groups, mainly Cuban medical personnel (those who have worked in internationalist medical brigades and a few others), have been given official access. Yet a growing number of Cubans have been contacting their relatives and friends abroad in recent years through that specific email system or through direct Internet accounts, which they access either through personal favors or for a high fee in hotels and other places or through Cuba's cyberspace black market. Some Cubans—particularly young Cubans—have been actively involved in the blogosphere as much as their limited resources and government censorship allows. One of them, Yoani Sánchez, made it to the list of *Time* magazine's most influential people in 2008, and she has received prestigious international awards and invitations. However, she has also been added to the list of Cubans who have been denied the exit permit from the Cuban government. Members of the blogosphere who are not supported by the government, some of whom have been even censored and have had their sites shut down, tend to receive technical assistance and some important services to be able to keep their transnational networks active from abroad. These transnational social actors have opened Cuba to the world and the world to Cuba in ways that were unimaginable a few years ago. Indeed, both the traditional transnational links among Cubans and the virtual ones, through the Internet, pose a significant challenge to Cuba's tight regulatory system in all spheres of life.

Conclusion

The capitalist system—a system of production for profit, rooted in private ownership, in which labor is a commodity, that uses multiple methods of surplus value appropriation and relies on global hegemonies, including their ideologies and myths—has shaped migration in Cuba from the sixteenth century to date. Even recent efforts aimed at detaching Cuban society from the forces of capitalism have not insulated the migration process from them, while attempts to build a radically different mode of production and social system have had profound repercussions for the process.

While the most enduring structures of capitalism appear to be immutable over the long term, they are constantly being modified by restructuring processes and social forces that cut across the units of the system.[1] This axiom has prevailed in approaches to international migration that are influenced by the longue dureé conceptualization of history and world-system analysis in particular. Building on these traditions and other conceptual frameworks (see Chapter 1), I undertook the study of international migration in Cuba from the colonial period to today by focusing on how the synergies between "cyclical history" and everyday life molded the process of international migration as part of a system that operates in the *longue durée*. Fernand Braudel's (1980) conceptualization of the *longue durée* provides an explicit path that bridges history and the social sciences by emphasizing the relevance of the analysis of social structures that cut across generations and even civilizations without neglecting what he calls "the dialectic of duration" and "the plurality of social time." By calling attention to the multiple movement of history, Braudel provides foundational conceptual and methodological tools that allow us to study migration in Cuba as a process shaped by the global structures of capitalism and social forces that operate transnationally and locally under a coherent historical narrative. Instead of fixed categories, Braudel invites us to approach the notions and concepts that he employs to illustrate "the dialectic of duration" as points of reference for historical inquiry.

The cycles and the intercycles can, in fact, have different durations and tend to operate at different scales.[2] In this particular study, "cyclical history" ranges from what Arrighi (1999) calls "systemic cycles of accumulation" to global and regional shifts in the division of labor and predominant labor supply systems, as well as geopolitical cycles involving shifts in international alliances and ideological and military reconfigurations (Wallerstein 1988), in their interrelations with "cycles" that have been specific to Cuba's direct relationship with the metropole or powerful states. An example of the latter is what Moreno Fraginals (2001) has documented as the two great cycles of Cuba's sugar industry: an earlier cycle, in which manufacturing prevailed, and a later one, characterized by dependent (with respect to the United States) industrial development, which started in the final decades of Spanish colonial rule and stretched to 1933 through two intercycles. Cuban historiography has also documented the cycles through which productive processes in Cuba related to the fusion of productive, commercial, and financial capital. At closer range, we see disparate forms of human agency—strategies, policy interventions, or simply reactions to catastrophic events. The latter include immigration, schemes aimed at profiting from the recruitment of laborers, changes in immigration policies, individual and family strategies that involved migration, bargains and conflicts between labor and capital over the use of immigrant labor, massive escape from social movements and revolutions, and so on.

International Migration in Cuba and Violence

International migration in Cuba reveals in a transparent way the structural link between migration and violence. In Cuba, the indigenous groups who managed to survive Spanish occupation by escaping to neighboring territories had ultimately been subjected to what today we call forced migrations, related in this case to the brutal violence of the conquest. Violent means were also deployed to meet labor requirements associated with the abrupt expansion of markets in different periods, as when hundreds of thousands of Africans, violently separated from their families and uprooted from their homelands, were forced into Cuba, either directly or through smuggling operations from neighboring areas. And violence also shaped the conditions under which Chinese indentured laborers were brought to Cuba, the regimes of labor exploitation to which they were submitted, and the human toll they paid. Military occupation and extreme forms of political turmoil, including revolutions, are among the major forces shaping international migration in Cuba since the colonial period. The takeover of Jamaica by the British in 1655 and the waves of violence that followed, which resonated throughout the region, brought Spaniards and other groups to Cuban shores. The military occupation of Havana by British forces for almost a year in the early 1760s also impacted immigration both directly and indirectly, including the opening of opportunities for the *negreros* to introduce more slaves. The War of the Spanish Succession and the independence of the Thirteen Colonies triggered population movements that affected Cuba directly, as did the confrontation between Spain and France from circa 1793 and 1795 that took place as part of more complex and prolonged struggles within and among European powers that had significant repercussions in the Caribbean. As a result of some of these events and the slave revolts in Saint-Domingue, the revolution, and the prolonged waves of turmoil that followed, thousands of French immigrants landed on Cuban shores between the late eighteenth century and the early nineteenth century. Although Cuba, still a Spanish colony, was not intensely affected by the non-Spanish European migrations generated by political turmoil in Europe in the nineteenth century, some of the migrants poured into the island. More migrants (with differing political tendencies) arrived on Cuban shores during the decolonization that swept through Latin America between 1810 and the 1820s and the conflicts that took place in the aftermath of decolonization, as well as during conflicts in Spain, such as the Carlist Wars. Spain's militarization of Cuba, with the aim of keeping its colonial rule of the island, brought hundreds of thousands of Spaniards—including, but not limited to, the large army mobilized to crush the independence movement. Many of them would eventually settle in the occupied territory. The Opium Wars also affected immigration to Cuba after the opening of several ports along China's Pearl Delta River for the trading of "coolies," starting in 1842 with the Treaty of Nanking.

Banishing members of the opposition from the island was a form of political control employed by Spain in Cuba. Even before the mid-1800s, there were some prominent Cuban intellectuals abroad who worked together in various ways against the colonial regime. However, the intensification of the struggle for independence from 1868 on and the growing risks associated with staying on the island forced more and more people to leave, many of whom cemented the tradition of "long-distance nationalism" related to political dynamics in Cuba.

The Spanish-American War opened up a new chapter in Cuba's history, one that would set the conditions under which the migration process would evolve under the direct tutelage of the United States. From then up to 1958, turmoil in several areas of the world brought hundreds of migrants to Cuba's shores as crumbling empires and regimes collapsed and new powers and borders emerged. Political violence also shaped migration at that time as the persecution of opposition groups by dictators and cycles of violence associated with the reaccommodation of political forces in the island forced a number of Cubans to leave in search of safe havens. Some of these emigrants would be involved in the organization of political and military resistance against those in power in Cuba. As early as 1917, Miami was emerging as an epicenter of Cuban exile politics, as these expatriates attempted to induce political changes on the island—a role that was reinforced during the revolts against Machado leading to the revolution of 1930. During the pivotal years before the overthrow of Fulgencio Batista, the Cubans' struggle once again took place in a sociopolitical continuum that stretched beyond the island. Underlying the nationalist discourses and the crusade against the regime's undemocratic and corrupt ways was the clash of the dominant ideologies of the Cold War. The powerful imprints of that global juncture would surface with particular force after 1959, when the revolution became fully subsumed into the global Cold War confrontation. Cuba's Cold War revolution led to a pattern of hostility between Washington and Havana that has long outlived the very existence of the Soviet Union as a political entity and has shaped migration since 1959. Repressive mechanisms involving various forms of violence meant to annihilate the private sector and control members of the opposition in Cuba, including forced physical exclusion from the island, and the systematic manipulation of migration for political purposes by the two governments have involved an array of forms of violence that have shaped the migration process for almost half a century. Cubans' systematic use of precarious means to exit the island, including rafts made of inner tubes and other floating objects, reveals a form of violence that reaches its highest expression in the formation of the "rafter phenomenon."

Accumulation in the Center and the Limits of Development in the Periphery

Of "the three hegemonies of historical capitalism" (Arrighi 1999)—the Dutch, the British, and the U.S.—the first two were filtered in Cuba through Spanish colonialism. As Arrighi highlights, the Dutch hegemony was short-lived in the long scheme of world history, yet it had a lasting resonance in the organization of the interstate system we know today. As a Spanish colony, Cuba was affected by the developments leading to this outcome, including the disruption that the rise of Dutch power created for Spain's imperial ambitions. The influence of British hegemony was felt more systematically and directly in Cuba, although it was also filtered through the Spanish colonial rule as well. What Arrighi (1999) identifies as the major aspects of the British hegemony—"settler colonialism, capitalist slavery, and economic nationalism"—molded international migration in Cuba with particular intensity. As Arrighi notes, the Spaniards themselves had pioneered the practice of settling conquered territories, which the British took to unprecedented levels in the Thirteen Colonies of North America. The tremendous demographic weight of the Spanish immigrants in Cuba and Spain's military settlements on the island, which were significantly expanded throughout the nineteenth century, and their social, cultural, economic, and political repercussions were major legacies of the Spanish colonial rule in Cuba. Particularly relevant were the large-scale transfers of labor and entrepreneurship from the metropole into the colony, transfers that responded both to geopolitical concerns and to expanding production on the island. "Slave capitalism" had equally enduring repercussions in Cuba. As manifested in Cuba, slave capitalism fed accumulation not only in the core economies of Europe but eventually in the United States as well, as the latter succeeded in integrating Cuba's sugar industry with that of the United States in conditions that favored accumulation in the North.[3] Spanish slave traders, in complicity with planters in Cuba, and the British importers of goods produced under conditions of slavery continued to introduce slaves in Cuba until well into the 1860s, well over several decades after the creation of a transatlantic regime for the purpose of ending the slave trade, which the British had formally championed since the early 1800s. Lastly, the practices and imaginaries associated with "economic nationalism" made significant inroads in Cuba as the nineteenth century advanced—in this case, through the Spanish idea of a national economy vis-à-vis its competitors and discourses and strategies supporting national economic projects in Cuba with various degrees of acceptance of the structures of colonialism. Discourses on nationalism and immigration were intertwined with influential political currents, class interests, and an overarching racist ideology.[4]

How the links between accumulation and imperial designs affected international migration in Cuba in the early stages of the transition from British-led global hegemony to U.S. global hegemony become more transparent as we focus on the period between the 1860s and 1930. Emigration to the United States from the 1860s to the end of Spanish colonialism on the island was largely determined by the repressive nature of the Spanish government and the struggle for independence. However, there was also a strong link between international migration in Cuba (either emigration from the island or immigration to the island) and capital accumulation in the United States.

The economic incorporation of Cuban workers and Spanish and Creole entrepreneurs from the island in the United States at that time allows us to see the role played by immigration in accumulation processes in the United States, mainly in the cigar industry and labor-capital relations associated with immigration from Cuba. Furthermore, migration played a key role not only in the transnationalization of political processes but also in the transnationalization of productive and labor processes that connected the two societies.[5] In addition, historical accounts on the transition experienced by Cuba's sugar industry since the 1860s to circa 1895, prominently the work of Manuel Moreno Fraginals, also show that accumulation in the sugar industry of the United States was benefiting indirectly from labor brought to Cuba from other societies as the island was increasingly being used as a major production platform for the inputs required by sugar refineries in the United States—a process that reached an institutional zenith with the enactment of the Sugar Act of 1871 in the United States.

By the early twentieth century, accumulation in the United States benefited from the recruitment of immigrant labor for the sugar industry in Cuba, including direct recruitment efforts made by U.S. companies operating there.[6] Thus, this kind of migration (which is conventionally portrayed as labor migration) was the continuation of a historical pattern that shows a link between international migration in Cuba with accumulation processes in the United States.[7] In the first period, the link was configured by the political migration that resulted from the struggle against Spanish rule and the growing penetration of U.S. interests in Cuba's sugar industry. Although both Cuba and the United States relied on a strong immigration regime associated with the expansion of productive processes in their respective economies, large-scale immigration did not imply large-scale accumulation in Cuba.

The issue of the transfer of entrepreneurship is more complex. It has been argued that one of the main characteristics of U.S. hegemony globally has been "the unilateral transfer" of both labor and entrepreneurship from the periphery.[8] This assertion is problematic, at least for the formative years of U.S. hegemony, if we take into consideration that one of the ways of advancing the economic interests of global corporations controlled by capitalists from the United States in Latin America was precisely the deployment of enterprises and entrepreneurship in the latter. In the particular case of Cuba, the control of accumulation processes in the island in the formative years of U.S. global hegemony involved the transfer of entrepreneurship from the United States mostly through direct investments but also through the exchange of technical expertise and the forging of business associations with entrepreneurs in Cuba, including many who were immigrants from Spain or second-generation immigrants and had economic interests in the United States as well. Moreover, it has been shown that the economic penetration of the United States in Cuba relied on a flexible immigration policy that left the doors open for the arrival of Spanish entrepreneurs and the retention and even expansion of immigrant enterprises in strategic sectors of the economy, including but not limited to the sugar industry, commerce, and the port economy, until the financial crash of 1920.[9] Even in periods of significant transfers of entrepreneurship to the United States, such as the period from the late 1860s to the end of the anticolonial struggle, it is hard to say that such transfers were unilateral precisely because of the transnational involvement of entrepreneurs at that time and the fact that entrepreneurs from the U.S. were also arriving in the island in different capacities, many of them as speculators to take advantage of the low prices of properties associated with the political instability in Cuba and even to circumvent the economic crises in the United States.[10] In the case of Cuba, the transfers of entrepreneurship would become unilateral only after 1959, for reasons that had little to do with accumulation processes in the United States.

However, the whole model of large-scale immigration associated with the expansion of strategic economic activities, mainly in the sugar industry, was exhausted by the end of 1920. From 1920 until 1958, Cuba gradually joined other societies of the periphery, including Caribbean societies that had been exporting labor during the beginning of the century. Cuba continued to receive immigrants from different areas of the world. Some escaped the redrawing of borders and political turmoil; others wanted to reunite with their families, sought jobs or investment opportunities, or simply hoped to use the island, often without success, as a stepping stone on the way to other countries, mainly to North America and South America. A number of Cubans went to live on a temporary basis in the United States, Mexico, and other countries in periods of increased political turmoil, including those involving significant violence in the final hours of the governments headed by Gerardo Machado and Fulgencio Batista. However, the accumulation-migration link pointed to the gradual reversal of a historical pattern: the emergence of Cuba as a labor exporter in the region, with the epicenter in the United States, a trend that had became clearer in the 1950s.

A lasting pattern of unilateral transfer of labor and entrepreneurship from Cuba to the United States unfolded only after 1959, when the United States lost direct control of accumulation circuits linked to productive processes in the island. This trend has prevailed for half a century now, creating an unprecedented loss of skilled workers and professionals to the United States and an unprecedented dependence of Cuban society on labor markets in the United States. These characteristics of the migration process have been determined not only by structural inequalities but also by specific migration policies that are hard to find in other cases of U.S.-bound migration, such as the bans placed on return migration and the limitations imposed upon the migrants' transnational economic relations involving their homeland. In this context, Cuba's migration policy has become a major factor widening the economic gap with the United States.

Although the United States has been actively involved in facilitating the transfer of labor and entrepreneurship from Cuba through its refugee policy toward Cuba and has been its main beneficiary, the transnational fields of governmentality upon which the regulation of the process is based—given the hostility in the bilateral relationship and Cuba's migration policy combined with the disarticulation of the private sector in Cuba, and the Cuban government's bias against the involvement of Cubans in autonomous forms of entrepreneurship, domestically and transnationally—have actively contributed to the sustained unilateral character of the transfers. A similar pattern exists with respect to most societies with which Cuba has had a significant migration link since 1959, although at smaller scales, compared to the case of U.S.-bound migration.

Given Cuba's highly restrictive immigration policy, only certain aspects of Cuban immigration rules and economic practices could have counterbalanced (to a very limited extent) the pervasive loss of labor and entrepreneurship to other countries. These include work-study programs involving contingents of foreign students who have worked in agricultural activities in Cuba, the use of foreign experts through consultancy agreements, the granting of resident status to immigrant groups who have been handpicked by the state (including exiles from right-wing regimes), and more recently, the limited imports of entrepreneurship (and very rarely workers) associated with investments conducted through mixed enterprises. However, other mechanisms, such as the exports of labor to other countries—including professionals and highly skilled manual workers recruited through the "international labor brigades"—have further deprived Cuba of much-needed expertise in the medical field and other areas. Although in theory these exports take place on a temporary basis (usually a few years) from the social perspective, in some countries, they have involved the continuous replacement of Cuban workers for relatively prolonged periods of time. In addition, the permits to work abroad issued by the Cuban government have been used by many Cubans to leave the island on a permanent basis.

The Migrants' Multiple Paths: Wealth, Alienation, and Social Exclusion

Immigration from Spain was the most complex type of all migrations affecting Cuban society in terms of the length of the process, its volume, the forces shaping the arrival of the migrants, their diversity in terms of demographic characteristics, class, occupational background, economic specialization of their regions of origin, the scale of their involvement in return migration and circular labor flows, and their impact on their society of origin. Furthermore, Spanish migrants' participation in transnational social fields was instrumental in shaping the multiple links that connected Cuba with Spain, the United States, other societies, and the structures of capitalism during the colonial period and beyond. The specialization of the areas of origin of Spanish migrants impacted their incorporation in Cuba and their socioeconomic roles there. Catalonians and immigrants from Seville, who were coming from regions with long-lasting specializations in trade, took on a somewhat different role than that played by immigrants from Galicia or the Canary Islands, where specialization in agricultural production prevailed. While the migration experience erased some existing differences among Spanish migrants, it reinforced others in terms of class location. For many of the Spaniards, immigration to the island represented a new stage in a long cycle of economic and social displacement that their families had endured in Spain. For others, immigration either served as a ladder of social mobility or represented the means through which their economic position, social status, and political influence had been reinforced. While some sent remittances and participated in transnational enterprises that allowed them to expand and even diversify their investments, others could barely send money to sustain their families in Spain. Many Spanish migrants settled in Cuba from the start and stayed there, but others worked seasonally on the island for a number of years without settling there, or moved from Cuba to other societies where they stayed for longer periods of time before they finally went back to Cuba, established their families elsewhere, or returned to Spain. Others simply lived in Cuba for a number of years and returned to Spain, some leaving family members and trusted individuals in charge of their property or enterprises in Cuba.

In the last decades of the nineteenth century, the transportation and communication technologies that enabled the transnational flows of people, information, capital, and ideas experienced significant improvement. Such progress facilitated the transnational involvement of migrants who worked seasonally in Spain, the United States, and other societies to supplement their incomes, while new frontiers opened up for the pursuit of accumulation. Often, Spaniards involved in transnational activities performed different (and sometimes overlapping) functions as merchants, bankers, industrialists, political activists, and so on. Their transnational strategies not only relied on but further propelled trade, investments, communications and transportation technologies, and other aspects of the growing articulation of the Atlantic economy at that time. The transnational involvement of Spanish migrants in Cuba was instrumental for the flourishing of the banking industry in Spain, to which they contributed with capital as investors, as depositors with monetary remittances, and by opening up markets in Cuba and the Americas in general. Spanish migrants forged transnational social relationships that included non-migrants, while institutions and strategies not necessarily rooted in migration framed their transnational practices.

Not only Spaniards but other migrants as well were actively involved in commercial and other investment activities and the circulation of monetary flows and capital, although these trends tend to be narrated as the outcome of impersonal forces and examined through metrics associated with the nation-state—for example, trade, international investments, and international monetary flows—when the migrants' transnational involvement is not factored in. French immigrants, Chinese immigrants, and other groups that had a minor demographic impact but important economic impact on Cuba, such as Germans, North Americans, Italians, and Middle Eastern and Eastern European immigrants, developed enterprises in Cuba and multistranded social relationships that linked Cuba with other societies. Caribbean laborers were instrumental in expanding transnational social fields that tied Cuba with neighboring islands while, as mentioned above, their labor was central in the articulation of Cuba with accumulation processes in the United States.

Thus, immigrants in Cuba played a key role in articulating the island with other societies and the structures of capitalism. However, they all were incorporated into a complex social fabric characterized by class differences, social inequality, and external dependency (to which they contributed and which affected most immigrants, particularly those on the lower rungs of the economic ladder and racialized groups). The most acute periods of economic crisis and the political dislocations and class struggle that affected Cuba at certain junctures were reflected in immigration debates and policies and the deportation waves that affected various groups. Right after the Spanish-American War, when the United States ruled the island and directly shaped immigration policy, the overall political climate was favorable to immigration, but the claim "Cubans for the Cubans" was occasionally voiced by pro-nationalist forces (prominently those representing national labor). Opposition to imported labor was mostly heard in contexts of acute labor confrontation. The importation of laborers from neighboring islands faced a particularly complex system of opposition. Influential groups rejected imported labor for various reasons, including racism—one of the pillars of Cuba's immigration debates since the colonial period. Opposition to the importation of labor increased as the economic and political climate of the island worsened after the crisis of 1920, and then again in the second half of the 1920s. As a result of policy bargains and institutional and political changes, by the mid-1930s a number of bills had been drafted by Cuban legislators, sometimes without success, and some laws had been enacted to protect domestic labor. New deportation procedures were established, mainly aimed at Haitians and other Caribbean groups in Cuba, but not sparing Spaniards either. Not only had an important number of enterprises owned by Spanish immigrants succumbed to the banking crash of 1920, but many Spanish workers suffered pauperism and involuntary repatriation then as well. Others would be forced to return to Spain as new economic crises emerged.

Free laborers arriving under various circumstances were subjected to forms of violence—symbolic and even physical violence, in extreme cases—associated with the process of alienation, understood as the objectification of human capacities.[11] For many migrants, alienation was compounded with prolonged periods of separation from their families. In extreme but not infrequent cases among certain immigrant groups, such as most Chinese men arriving in Cuba on their own, alienation associated with the selling of their labor power in a distant land was further aggravated by the fact that they never saw their family members again. As feminist theory shows, gendered forms of exploitation and antagonism shape alienation in specific ways.[12] Accumulation schemes based on sex trade and the individual need to make a living under difficult circumstances have historically pushed women into the hands of human trafficking rings associated with the sex industry. Certain groups of women arriving in Cuba since the early colonial period were subjected to these conditions, just as a number of Cuban migrants are today.

International Migration in Cuba Today and Cuba's Rearticulation with the Structures of Capitalism

During Cuba's most crucial historical periods, the process of international migration on the island has not been weightless. Today, Cuba is going through one such moment. Cuban society is taking a new path toward articulation with the global structures of capitalism, and international migration is, once again, a central aspect of this articulation.

After consistently negative net migration rates since the 1960s, and the collapse of the Soviet bloc almost two decades ago, at the beginning of the twenty-first century, international migration is tied to labor processes in Cuba and accumulation in the United States with singular intensity. The United States again functions as an epicenter of immigration from Cuba, but the diversification of the destinations of the migrants is a major characteristic of the process today. A growing number of Cubans are leaving for Spain, the former metropole. Many of them are using marriage and the consanguinity clauses of Spanish immigration law as migration strategies; others have procured Spanish residency and tourist visas to work on cyclical basis there.

Currently, the United States has more than 1.7 million Cuban Americans residing in the country, many of whom migrated after the 1980s and settled in South Florida. While at the beginning of the twentieth century Havana was a city of great demographic dynamism, much of which resulted from immigration, during the first years of the twenty-first century, from 2000 to 2006, Havana experienced a net population loss. The city had experienced a sharp decline in the growth rate since 1970, a trend that has been molded by emigration, among other factors. All in all, Cuban Americans in the United States represent approximately 14 percent of the total number of Cubans living on the island today. Historical coincidence has it that Spanish Cubans constituted 14 percent of Cuba's population in 1919.[13] The number of Cuban Americans living in the Greater Miami area represents approximately 36 percent of the total number of Cubans living in Havana today.

The United States cannot write Cuba's immigration law, as it did when it exercised full control of the island. However, its capacity to shape international migration in Cuba continues to be substantial. The post 1959 modalities of governing U.S.-bound migration have resulted in the development of transnational fields of governmentality that include the constant intervention of the two states for the purposes of controlling the process and the migrant population. These interventions include restrictions on the ways in which individuals and households in Cuba can benefit from the remittances received from family members working abroad. Since the disintegration of the Soviet Union, Cuban households have become increasingly dependent on transnational economic strategies as a way to supplement household incomes and improve families' social mobility and social reproduction on the island. This phenomenon is not unique to Cuba; rather, it is a universal characteristic of the role of migration in societies of the periphery. There is a sharp contrast, though, between the norms, interests, and values that guide Cuba's migration policy and the approach of the government toward the migrants compared to those prevailing in most countries of the periphery, particularly in the Latin American context. The regulatory system in place in the case of U.S.-bound migration also deviates from the norm in fundamental ways.

The protection of most Cuban migrants as refugees by the U.S. government continues to be justified by the specific conditions of the migration context. The Cuban government still denies Cubans such basic rights as freedom of speech and association, the right to exit without a permit from the government, and the right to return to their homeland after having lived on a permanent basis abroad—rights enjoyed by citizens of most democratic societies. The government's tendency to incarcerate or harass individuals who oppose it or who openly disagree with specific policies or aspects of the political system also justifies the granting of protection to individuals suffering from such repressive practices. Yet a major paradox faced by Cuban migrants today is that an overemphasis on Cubans as political refugees tends to obscure another, equally relevant fact: Cuba is a labor-exporting society of the periphery and many Cubans, like many other migrants from the periphery, need to sell their labor power in other societies to be able to satisfy the basic economic needs of their families. The alarming economic scenarios that Cubans are facing—a drastic drop of the real salary, the shrinking of meaningful employment and professional opportunities both in relative and absolute terms, acute housing problems, and other forces shaping migration—are not exclusive to the Cuban society. They are frequently found throughout the periphery. Furthermore, as has been extensively documented, many migrants around the world have been forced to give up nurturing their children during the most precious years of their growth precisely in order to sustain them economically. This phenomenon affects Cuban migrants and their families today.

These issues have been neglected in predominant narratives on Cuban migrants, which tend to emphasize aspects of their migration experience other than those related to the entanglements of Cuban migration with labor processes and the fact that most Cuban migrants are working-class migrants. Guillermo Grenier (1994), for example, has called our attention to the fact that even though most Cuban immigrants tend to work as salaried workers for enterprises that are not owned by Cubans, prevailing discourses tend to emphasize their migration experience as enterprise owners. As discussed in this work, entrepreneurship among migrants in Cuban society or migrants from Cuba in other societies, particularly the United States, has been central to the migration experience from the colonial period on. The same is true with respect to the active involvement of the migrants in political processes. Nevertheless, there has been a strong tendency in current dominant discourses to deemphasize Cuban workers as salaried workers and self-employment as successful entrepreneurship, even in cases in which it functions as a last-resort strategy of labor-market incorporation, when access to the first tier of the labor market is not possible, regardless of the qualifications of the migrant. This has led to an important gap between dominant discourses and the everyday practices of many (if not most) Cuban migrants arriving in recent decades.

Deemphasizing Cuban migrant workers as workers is a trend linked to discourses in which the *raison d'état* has prevailed, either directly or through what has been called the "seeing like the state" bias.[14] It has gone hand in glove with the suppression of class identity, which, compounded with the suppression of labor rights in Cuba in state enterprises and transnational enterprises, has led to the subordination of Cuban workers not only to capitalists but also to two powerful states. Family remittances offer a case in point. In 2004, Washington defined which members of Cuban families on the island were entitled to receive family remittances (the definition excludes cousins, aunts, and uncles, for example) and "regular" visits (once every three years). The amount of money that Cuban Americans can send, based on those regulations, was left at $300 every three months (as had been stipulated much earlier). The official argument guiding these restrictions is that the Cuban government benefits from the money that the migrants send to their relatives. Underlying this approach is the ideological construction of remittances as a state resource that can be politically manipulated, as is frequently done with foreign aid. In the case of remittances, such manipulation involves the infringement of the worker's basic right to use his/her wage to satisfy family needs. The severe restrictions imposed by the Cuban government on how such remittances can be used by Cubans on the island and Cubans sending them also demonstrate an understanding of remittances as a state resource and infringes on rights that have been historically recognized. An onerous exchange rate is imposed on remittances in Cuba, which, combined with the artificial depreciation of foreign currencies with respect to the Cuban peso, further reduces the purchasing power of the original amount sent. This affects Cuban workers and families on and off the island and severely constrains the economic impact of remittances on households and the society in general. The migrants have historically played a key role in assisting their relatives beyond subsistence through the development of family enterprises, a mechanism employed by many of them to compensate for or overcome the disruptive consequences associated with migration. Many migrants, including many Latin American migrants today, have been involved in projects of communal interest, such as those leading to the improvement of the living conditions of specific communities where neither government nor private sources have been effective, such as access to potable water, electricity, technological improvements in agricultural activities, and even the construction or remodeling of cultural, educational and recreational facilities. While these strategies for collective improvement are available to migrants in other labor-exporting societies, particularly in Latin America and the Caribbean, the sociopolitical structures in which Cuban migration is embedded tend to deny the migrants access to such strategies. Thus, instead of "insulating" them and their families from the disruptions of global capitalism and the pitfalls of national economic policies under totalitarianism, such structures have made them more vulnerable in many respects.

Any serious attempt at improving the situation of Cuban workers—and the standard of living and social development for the population on the island—calls for a revision of Cuba's migration policy and approaches toward the migrants. The migration policies of Cuba and the United States and its approaches to Cuban migrants should not be seen exclusively in a foreign policy context, then, but also examined from the perspective of how they improve the prospects for social and economic development within Cuba and preserve Cubans' labor rights and chances for human development and social mobility.

The current situation calls for a more humane, labor-friendly, and migrant-friendly migration policy in Cuba. The elaboration of such policy should be part and parcel of much needed sociopolitical and economic transformations in Cuba and it should incorporate as a major concern how it could facilitate the prospects for social and economic development in Cuba while preserving human, individual and other rights of Cubans on the island and those who reside abroad, including those who are contributing to Cuban society through social networks that prominently include but are not limited to family members.

Sample of Enterprises with Strong Links to Spanish Migrants in the Americas

Sample of Spanish Families in Cuba and Their Enterprises

Braga-Rionda family enterprises (sugar, financing, other)	circa 1850
Central Elena	1850
Central Tuinicú (under The New Tuinicú Sugar Company)	1889
Central Francisco (under The Francisco Sugar Company)	1901
Cuban-American Sugar Company (holding)	1906
Cuban Trading Company	1907
Central Manatí (under Manati Sugar Company)	1912
Czarnikow-Rionda Company of New York (brokerage)	1912
Cuba Cane Sugar Corporation (holding)	1915
Azucarera Céspedes S.A. Compañía	1923
Ganadera Becerra S.A. Compañía (under Manati Sugar Company)	1952
Flo-Sun Incorporated (holding)	current

The first immigrant was Joaquín Polledo (from the Rionda Polledo branch of the family, Asturias). He founded Polledo, Rionda & Company. Nephews Francisco, Joaquín, and Manuel followed him to the Americas. Francisco married the daughter of a Cuban sugar baron and founded Central Elena. Joaquín studied in Maine and married the daughter of a U.S. entrepreneur with whom he founded Bejanmin Rionda & Co. Manuel also studied in Maine and started working with Joaquín in New York. The three nephews eventually developed or worked in high corporate positions in transnational enterprises in the sugar industry. Investments in the United States and Cuba prominently included sugar mills, refineries, and brokerage firms. They had family members and property in Spain, where they assisted in social and educational projects in their hometown. The sons of the Rionda sisters followed in their uncles' steps. Two of them, Bernardo Braga Rionda (b. 1875) and Higinio Alberto Fanjul Rionda (b. 1877), continued working in the transnational investments of the family—the first from the United States and the second from Cuba. They were among the most successful investors of the second generation. Throughout the first three generations, the family become involved in the enterprises listed to the left, among other investments. The Cuban-American Sugar Company and then the Cuba Cane Sugar Corporation, which were organized as holdings for the acquisition of capital goods in the sugar industry, were considered the largest ones in the world within the sugar industry for a number of years until the latter was forced into restructuring after 1920. The closest foreign and local business partners of the family at some point included prominent elected officials in the United States and even a Cuban president (Mario Menocal). The son of Higinio

A. Fanjul Rionda, Alfonso G. Fanjul Estrada (b. 1909), established links by marriage with the family of another prominent family in the sugar industry, the Gómez Mena family.

Gómez Mena family enterprises (commerce, sugar, financing, other) — 1871

Central Gómez Mena (former "Santa Teresa") — 1902

Central Amistad (founded by another family in the early 1800s) — 1906

Central Mercedita (founded by another family in 1863) — 1925

General de Ingenios S.A. y Cía — 1940

Nueva Co. Azucarera Gómez Mena S.A. (holding) — 1950s

Industrial Arrocera de Mayabeque S.A. — 1953

Florida Holdings
Florida Crystals Corporation — current

Pedro and Andrés Gómez Mena, born in Burgos, Spain, founded several enterprises in Cuba in the nineteenth century. They were a commercial house founded by Pedro Gómez Mena in 1871, with activities in commerce and banking as well as investments in the sugar industry. In 1902 Andrés Gómez Mena bought a sugar cane mill, to which he gave the family name. From then on, the family would make significant investments in the sugar and banking industries, real estate, among others. A sample can be seen on the left. The Gómez Menas had business associates and close personal links in the United States and Mexico. Their networking reached the Cuban government. For example, José Gómez Mena was minister of agriculture and the family investment ventures were made through associations that included other political figures, such as Fulgencio Batista. José Gómez Mena lived part of his life in Mexico as well. Their business associates prominently included other Spanish-origin investors, some of whom also had developed family links with them through marriage. Descendants of the union of the Rionda-Fanjul and the Gómez Mena families married the Azqueta family (a wealthy Spanish-origin family with investments in sugar, banking, paper industries, and other enterprises). Some of the companies shown on the left represent the fusion of capital among these families. Brothers Alfonso Fanjul Jr. and José (Pepe) Fanjul (direct descendants of the Fanjul, Rionda, and the Gómez Mena families) are the chairman and vice-chairman and CEOs of Florida Holdings, an enterprise conglomerate that includes Florida Crystals Corporation. They were leading producers of refined sugar in the United States and the Dominican Republic. The family investments include the production of other crops, such as rice; real estate investments; and investments in renewable energy. The headquarters are in Florida and their investments are spread throughout the United States, the Caribbean, and beyond. Like their ancestors in Cuba, the Fanjuls have developed close links to influential politicians and political organizations in the United States.

N. Gelats y Compañía (trade, banking)	1876
Banco Gelats S.A.	1940

Narciso Gelats was a Spanish immigrant who arrived in Cuba in 1857. He moved to Cuba to assist an uncle with his enterprises, which included lending activities. The family founded Banco Gelats, one of the largest banks owned by Spaniards in Cuba and one of the main investors in Spain. It was involved in mortgage lending and commercial lending, among other financial activities. The Gelats were linked to other Spanish-origin investors through many business channels. Partnerships included the Braga-Rionda and the Gómez Mena families, among others.

Bacardi-Boutellier	1862
Bacardi family and enterprises (production of rum, commerce, other)	1862
Bacardi y Compañía	1875
Cervecería Modelo	1946
Miguel y Bacardí Ltd. (urban transportation)	1946
Molinera Oriental S.A.	1958
Bacardi and Co. Limited	1960
Bacardi Limited	current

The origin of the Bacardi enterprises in Cuba has been traced to 1838 to the Bacardi-Boutellier partnership. Facundo Bacardi Maso took ownership of what would be known as the Bacardi Company in 1862. He was a wine merchant from Catalonia whose family started settling in Cuba in the 1830s. The Bacardi family is known for their participation in the struggle against Spanish colonialism. During the U.S. military occupation, Emilio Bacardi, the eldest son of Facundo, was appointed mayor of Santiago de Cuba, where the family enterprise had been established. Their ties with other immigrant groups included Spanish, Italian, and French families. Their personal and business links grew particularly strong with the Bosch family, also from Barcelona. The Bacardi enterprises remained for the most part in the beverage and food industries, although they also had investments in other enterprises. Like other Spanish-origin investors in Cuba, they had investments in companies controlled by U.S. investment groups, such as the Rockefellers. The Bacardis left Cuba after 1959 and rooted the global expansion of their enterprises in some Caribbean islands, the Bermudas, Mexico, and the United States. (They had opened companies in some of these areas as early as the 1920s.) Currently, Bacardi Limited bills itself as "the largest privately held spirits company in the world" (http://www.bacardilimited.com/heritage_6.html).

Marimón, Bosch y Compañía S en C. (commerce, sugar, financing, other)	1863
Bergnes y Compañía S. en C.	1865
Mercadé, Bergnes y Compañía S. en C.	1915
Central Esperanza	1915
Minera Occidental Bosch, S.A.	1952
Motel Rancho Luna	1953
Azucarera Oriental Cubana S.A. Compañía	1920s

Marimón Juliah, and Clixto Bergnes Soler arrived from Catalonia in the nineteenth century. They would develop various business ventures together and on their own. By the early 1900s, theirs were among the most influential Spanish-origin families in Cuba. Most of the companies listed on the left exemplify either the ties among Spanish-origin families or the evolution of enterprises as a result of transactions among them. Sometimes more than three family enterprises would be linked as a result of marriage strategies, as in the case of Venancio Mercadé (who, by marrying a sister of José Bosch, connected the Bosches, the Mercadés, and the Bergneses). José Marimón had been president of the Banco Español de la Isla de Cuba since 1906, and in 1914, when the Spanish Chamber of Commerce was founded, he was its president as well. The Bosch family cultivated strong business and personal links with several Spanish-origin entrepreneurs beyond the first generation, including the Bacardis. In the 1920s, Jose M. Bosch (Pepín), who had worked in his family enterprises and for a branch of a U.S. bank in Cuba, married Enriqueta Shueg Bacardi, daughter of Enrique Schueg, a French national who had married a Bacardi sister and became the president of the company in the early 1920s. Pepín Bosch, who had been minister of the treasury in Cuba, worked as the president of the Bacardi corporation between 1951 and 1976 and died in Miami in 1994.

Herrera-Blanco family (commerce, sugar, other)	1823
Empresa de Vapores Correos y Transportes Militares (Vapores Herrera)	1850
Compañía de Vapores de Ramón Herrera	1870
Compañía Cubana de Vapores de Sobrinos de Herrera S and C	1886
Nueva Fabrica de Hielo S.A.	1888
Havana Brewery (beer factory)	1909

The Herrera and Blanco family has its origins in Santander. Ramón Herrera San Cibrián arrived in Cuba in 1829; his brother Cosme also went to Cuba. After having worked for a commercial and maritime transportation house owned by a Spanish family and then as the main representative and investor of a maritime transportation company, Ramón Herrera San Cibrián founded the Vapores Herrera company, which received contracts and subventions from the Spanish government to transport military personnel and official cargo and correspondence. He was also one of the founders of the Spanish Bank in Havana. Ramón Herrera San Cibrián and his family in Cuba developed a diversified investment portfolio that included commercial, financial and industrial

La Tropical and La Trívoli (beer and soft drink factories)	1916

activities, and some farms, among other investments. Their investments were spread across Spain, the United States, and Cuba. He was president of El Casino Español and the Chamber of Commerce, Industry, and Navigation in Cuba.

Three of his nephews had arrived in Cuba between 1859 and 1865. After his death in 1885, the nephews created Compañía de Vapores Sobrinos de Herrera. Cosme's son, Julio, took control of the Compañía de Vapores in 1903, and it was sold in 1916.

The Nueva Fabrica de Hielo, founded in 1888, was controlled by the family Blanco Herrera and included other Spanish investors, such as Narciso Gelats, who took control of the enterprise circa 1818. In 1930, Julio Blanco Herrera became the president of the company. Marriage strategies and political involvement were instrumental in the family's economic ascendancy. Their involvement in Spanish clubs and investments in the influential newspaper *Diario de la Marina* (in which many wealthy Spanish entrepreneurs invested throughout the newspaper's history) also shaped their economic success.

Argüelles y Hermanos	1849
Caminos de Hierro de la Habana	1881
Hijos de Argüelles	1896

Argüelles y Hermanos was led by Ramón Argüelles Alonso, who was born in Asturias. The company became one of the main lenders in the tobacco industry in Cuba and a major investor in trade, banking, and transportation. Ramón Argüelles invested heavily in Spain and had investment interests in the United States and London. He was president of the company Ferrocarriles Unidos y Almacenes de Regla, S.A. (a railroad transportation and warehouse company); Hijos de Argüelles specialized in banking and finance. Ramón Argüelles's sons continued investing in various enterprises in Cuba, including sport facilities, restaurants, etc. Despite the family's initial prominence among Spanish entrepreneurs in Cuba, it privileged its investments in Spain, and its economic prominence in Cuba faded away in the 1920s.

Banco del Comercio	1919

The Banco del Comercio was founded by Spanish immigrants. In 1955, it merged with the Trust Company of Cuba (TCC). The TCC was linked to the Sucesion de L. Falla Gutierrez, one of the most powerful investment groups originating in immigrant enterprises. It included Cuban politicians, such as Fulgencio Batista, as investors, and its business networks included the Gómez Mena family as well.

Enterprises in Spain with Strong Links to Spanish Migrants or Founded by Migrants

Banco Hispano Americano	1900	The Banco Hispano Americano was the first large transnational banking institution in Spain. Among its founders were Spanish migrants from Asturias and the Basque country who had made their fortunes in Cuba and Mexico. Florencio Rodríguez, a wealthy returnee from Cuba, was a member of the executive committee. He was the brother-in law of Antonio Basagoiti, the bank's first chairman. A number of Spanish migrants were either partners or clients.
Banco Central	1919	Founded in Madrid.
Banco Santander	1857	The financing of trade between Spain and Latin America was a major activity of Banco Santander.
Banco Santander Central Hispanoamericano (BSCH)	1991	The BSCH resulted from the fusion of Banco Santander and Banco Central. The BSCH has recently acquired several Latin American banks and has a strong presence in Latin America. It is at the core of Grupo Santander, one of the most powerful Spanish global corporations today.
Casa de Banca Gijón	1894	Florencio Rodríguez founded Casa de Banca Gijón after his return to Spain. Its operations prominently involved Cuba, Mexico, and Spain.
Banco Gijón	1899	Recorded at some point as Casa de Banca Florencio Rodríguez, Banco Gijón was controlled by Spaniards with investments on both sides of the Atlantic.
García-Calamarte y Cía (trade, banking)	1865	García-Calamarte y Cía was founded in Madrid by returnees from Cuba. It offered services related to lending to large commercial firms and the transfers of remittances.
Banco Calamarte	1920	In the twentieth century, investments and transactions involving Cuba and Latin America in general continued to be one of the bank's major functions.

Herreo y Compañía (trade, banking)	1841	Oviedo. By 1890 its representative in Barcelona was a major broker in monetary transfers from Cuba.
Banco Herrero S.A.	1912	Oviedo
Casa de Comercio Pedro Masaveu Rovira	1867	Oviedo
Pedro Masaveu y Compañía	1892	Oviedo
Grupo Masaveu	Current	Trade and banking were at the origins of the Banca and the Masaveu Group; they had strong links with Spanish migrants, including returnees. The Masaveu Group is one of the largest financial/industrial corporations in Spain today.
Juliana y Compañía	1899	Gijón
Banco Gijonés de Crédito	1926	Gijón
Vidal Cuadras Hermanos	1846	Barcelona. The Bank Vidal Cuadras Hermanos evolved to become an important banking institution in Barcelona.
Banco da Coruña (banking)	1857	Coruña
Caixa de Aforros e Monte de Piedade (banking)	1876	Galicia
Banco de Vigo (banking)	1900	Vigo

NOTE: Restructuring companies under different names was not infrequent. Not all restructurings are reflected in the company names presented below. Only a sample of the most representative enterprises are listed. The appendix emphasizes the social aspects of the evolution of the enterprises and the transnational involvement of their members. Given such emphasis, the sizes of their enterprises and their specializations vary.

SOURCES: Jenks 1970; Pederson 1997, 2000, and 2001; García Alvarez 1990; Foster 1990; García López 1992; Bahamonde 1992; Jiménez 2000; Florida Crystals 2001; *El Mundo* 2001; Collazo Pérez 2002; McAvoy 2003; Rodrigo 1998 and 2004, and Marqués Dolz 2006.

APPENDIX B

Chronology of Major Events, Agreements, Laws, and Regulations Affecting Cuban Migration to the United States, 1959–2009

January 1959

The revolutionary forces take over the government. The United States recognizes the new government.

May 1959

Land reform limits private ownership and prohibits foreign ownership.

1960

Confiscation and nationalization of large enterprises. It affects mostly U.S.-based companies. In October, the United States imposes a trade embargo except for certain foods and medicines. The "urban reform law" ends most private practices in real estate. The state is pronounced the sole entity allowed to lease real estate.

January 1961

The United States breaks off diplomatic relations with Cuba.

April 1961

Bay of Pigs military expedition by Cuban exiles. The United States sets Cuban sugar quota to zero for 1961 and the first half of 1962.

December 1961

Official proclamation of the "Marxist-Leninist" character of the revolution by the Cuban government.

February 1962

Total prohibition of exports to Cuba from the U.S. except for food and medicine.

March 1962

The "rationing card" is instituted as the main mechanism for the distribution of food and other items for consumption.

October 1962

Cuban Missile Crisis. Additional U.S. trade sanctions include parties in third countries.

November 1962

Prohibition of direct flights between Cuba and the United States.

November 1960–1962

U.S.-sponsored "Pedro Pan Operation" brings 14,000 unaccompanied Cuban children and teenagers to the United States.

February 1963	Travel to Cuba is prohibited for U.S. citizens unless special permits are issued.
July 1963	Cuban assets in the United States are frozen. Economic transactions are virtually prohibited.
October 1963	Second land reform further lowers the ceiling on private ownership.
September 1965	The Cuban government announces that Cubans with relatives in the United States will be allowed to leave using the port of Camarioca.
October 1965	The Camarioca boatlift. More than five thousand Cubans picked up by relatives are taken to the United States.
November 1965	Bilateral "memorandum of understanding" establishes procedures for the exodus.
December 1965–1971	The "freedom flights," an open-ended airlift, is used by more than 340,000 Cubans to leave for the United States between 1965 and 1971.
November 1966	The Cuban Refugee Adjustment Act is passed in the United States. It allows inspected and admitted or paroled Cubans to apply for permanent residence after being physically present in the United States for at least one year and a day. (This remains the main law regulating Cuban immigration.)
1968	The urban private sector is annihilated through the state confiscation of more than 50,000 mid-sized to small enterprises. By this time the state already controls wholesale, banking, foreign trade, and other strategic sectors and industries.
March 1971	Bilateral "memorandum of understanding" allows two daily flights between Miami and Varadero.
February 1973	Signature of a bilateral anti-hijacking agreement.
May 1973	The Cuban government unilaterally terminates the agreement.
1977–1979	The two governments open "Interest Sections" in their respective capitals to handle migration and other issues.

A group from the Cuban diaspora meets in Havana with the Cuban government to discuss issues concerning migration and political prisoners. The meeting is known as "The Dialogue."

Flexibilization of exiles' visits to relatives in Cuba ("community flights").

Negotiations for the release of 3,000 political prisoners and their resettlement in the United States with their families.

Permits are issued for a greater number of Cuban Americans to visit Cuba. Approximately 100,000 Cubans living in the United States visit relatives in Cuba.

April 1980	Approximately 10,000 Cubans occupy the Peruvian embassy in Havana as a way to leave the island. The port of Mariel is opened by the Cuban government for Cuban Americans to pick up relatives on the island on the condition that they take other Cubans designated by the government with them; 124,769 Cubans arrive in Florida in approximately three months during this "Mariel Crisis."
December 1980	Official meeting to discuss the repatriation of "Marielitos" that were "excludable."
April 1982	Charter air links between Cuba and the United States are halted by the U.S. government.
July 1984	Bilateral talks on immigration.
December 1984	Migration agreement. Cuba accepts repatriation of 2,746 Marielitos imprisoned in the United States. The United States promises to issue up to 20,000 visas annually under the preference system and an unrestricted number of visas to immediate relatives of U.S. citizens outside the quota.
May 1985	The U.S. government authorizes the anti-Castro station, Radio Martí, to broadcast to Cuba. Cuba suspends the migration agreement.
November 1987	Reinstatement of the 1984 agreement.
1988	Beginning of the "Exodus Program" sponsored by the Cuban American National Foundation (CANF) with the intention of taking Cubans residing in third countries to the United States.

| November 1989 | The Treasury Department further limits travel expenses for U.S. citizens authorized to travel to Cuba. |

1990–1991 Some modifications are proposed and introduced in Cuban law pertaining to the minimum age to emigrate and other issues related to work and visit abroad.

1991–1996 Cubans suffer the worst economic crisis since 1959 (and one of the worst in history) as the Soviet subsides cease.

October 1992 The commercial volume of food and medicines sent to Cuba through U.S. subsidiaries rises to US$770 million.

The Cuban Democracy Act is passed, strengthening United States sanctions, restoring direct phone services, and allowing media bureaus to operate from the island.

October 1993 Cuba legalizes the circulation of dollars and stimulates direct receipt of remittances.

October 1993 Agreement on the repatriation of 1,500 Cubans who did not qualify to remain in the United States.

April 1994 A conference called "La Nación y la Emigración" is held in Cuba as a follow-up to the "Dialogue" held in 1978 between the Cuban government and some members of the Cuban diaspora.

August 1994 The Cuban government proclaims an "open door" policy after a series of incidents in embassies in Havana and boat hijackings by Cubans attempting to leave the island. In March 2004, more than seventy Cubans had tried to leave in a tugboat. The government prevented their exit using water hoses. More than forty people, including children, died during the action.

The United States launches "Operation Distant Shore," involving forty federal agencies. Some are in charge of a "picket line" established to patrol the Florida Straits. Cuban rafters leave in increasing numbers. The United States bans travel to Cuba to pick up Cubans and suspends remittances. The "rafter crisis" leads to 37,191 interdictions by the U.S. Coast Guard.

September 1994 Migration accord. The United States agrees to issue 20,000 visas yearly. The visas would be made available through various mechanisms, including special lottery drawings conducted by U.S. officials in Havana (the

	Special Cuban Migration Program). The Cuban government agrees to cooperate to assure orderly, legal emigration.
October 1994	The United States agrees to receive more than 20,000 Cubans detained in refugee camps and increases the number of refugee admission slots for Cuba to include not only political prisoners but also those in other categories defined by the 1953 U.N. Refugee Convention. Another session of the conference "La Nación y la Emigración" is held in Cuba.
May 1995	Migration accord. Cubans interdicted at sea or entering Guantánamo Naval Base illegally will be returned to Cuba if they cannot prove asylum cases. Cuba agrees not to impose sanctions on those being repatriated and to patrol its coasts to deter illegal emigration. Cubans already in Guantánamo will be processed to enter into the United States on humanitarian claims.
October 1995	The U.S. government announces further relaxation of people-to-people contacts.
February 1996	Cuban MIGs shoot down two aircraft of the Miami-based organization "Brothers to the Rescue." Four Cuban Americans (including three American citizens) are killed.
March 1996	The Cuban Liberty Solidarity Act (Helms-Burton Act) is signed by the U.S. president. It establishes a cap in the amount of remittances allowed per month to Cuba, strengthens the policy of "people-to-people contacts," and imposes sanctions against foreign subsidiaries dealing with U.S. properties in Cuba confiscated after 1959.
November 1996	The Illegal Immigration Reform and Immigration Responsibility Act is passed, raising economic standards for sponsoring relatives for immigration. This and other provisions affect Cubans and other immigrants. This law does not override the Cuban Refugee Adjustment Act of 1966.
November 1997	The Nicaraguan Adjustment and Central American Relief Act. It helps undocumented Cubans adjust their status under special provisions.
1998–2002	John Paul II visits Cuba. The United States lifts the ban on allowing Cubans to send remittances to their

relatives in Cuba, explores ways to increase humanitarian aid, and allows sales of agricultural and medical products to "independent entities." Flights to Cuba from Miami are restored with flights from other cities added.

Early 2000	The agribusiness and other lobbies intensify their campaign to have the embargo lifted. Cubans continue to arrive legally while human smuggling operations also intensifies.
Spring 2003	The Cuban government imprisons seventy-five human rights activists, members of the opposition, and punishes most of them with long prison sentences. This period is known as Cuba's "Black Spring" (la Primavera Negra).
October 2003	The Presidential Commission for Assistance to a Free Cuba is created under the George W. Bush administration.
May 2004	The Presidential Commission for Assistance to a Free Cuba issues a report that includes recommendations to further regulate Cuban Americans' family visits to the islands and transactions with their relatives. The following recommendations are approved for 2004: remittances allowed per receiving household remain at $300 every three months, but only "close relatives," defined under the new rules as parents, siblings, grandparents, grandchildren, and spouses in Cuba, are entitled to receive them. The authorized "per diem amount" to spend in Cuba is reduced from US$164 per day to US$50 per day for all family visits. Another "La Nación y la Emigración" conference is held in Cuba.
November 2004	The Cuban government bans the use of U.S. dollars to purchase goods and services; only the local convertible currency (CUC) or the Cuban peso may be used. This rule forces those receiving remittances to exchange them into local currency for consumption purposes. The Cuban government implements exchange rates and service taxes that allow it to retain approximately 20 percent of each U.S. dollar received by Cubans at the time of exchange.
2006	The United States announces new regulations that reduce the backlog of family visas, ease access to U.S. visas for Cuban physicians in "third countries," deny

visas to Cuban violators of human rights, and pledges the U.S. government to alert Cuban families in the United States if any of their relatives have been stopped at sea in interdiction operations.

Mid-2008   The average nominal salary is 436 Cuban pesos, or approximately 18 CUCs (a similar amount in U.S. dollars based on Cuba's official exchange rate). For most Cubans, the salary is not enough to cover the basic alimentary and clothing needs of their families. Family remittances remain the main source of income for many Cuban households.

March 2009   Under the administration of Barack Obama, the Senate approves new rules concerning visits of Cuban Americans to their relatives. The definition of "immediate relative" is expanded to include any individual related to the traveling individual by blood, marriage, or adoption, within up to three generations. The maximum per diem rate is expanded to $179. The frequency of visits is set to once every twelve months, and the limitation on the length of the stay is removed.

April 2009   The U.S. government lifts bans on travel to the island by Cubans with relatives there as well as existing bans on the amount of money to be sent as remittances. U.S. companies are allowed to establish fiber-optic and satellite connections with Cuba to provide their services to the Cuban population.

May 2009   The Obama administration proposes to reopen discussions with Cuba on immigration issues to address the two governments' commitment to "safe, legal and orderly migration." In addition, it proposes to review trends in undocumented Cuban migration to the United States and coordinate operations on migration issues. (These talks had been halted since they were last held in mid-2003.)

SOURCES: University of Miami 1967; Boswell and Curtis 1983; Portes and Bach 1985; Bach 1988; Editora Política 1994a and 1994b; Pérez 1999; U.S. Department of State 2004; U.S. Department of Justice, INS *Statistical Yearbook* 2003; U.S. Department of Homeland Security 2006a, 2006b, and 2007; U.S. Coast Guard 2005 and 2008; and additional sources cited throughout Chapter 5.

NOTES

Preface

1. My translation from Spanish ["las personas cuyo padre o madre hubiese sido originariamente español" and "los nietos de quienes perdieron o tuvieron que renunciar a la nacionalidad española como consecuencia del exilio"]. "Información General Explicativa sobre la opción de la nacionalidad española de origen, en la aplicación del la 'Ley de la Memoria Histórica'" (brochure from the Ministerio de Asuntos Exteriores y de Cooperación, España, available at the Spanish Consulate in Miami, January 2009). The exilic condition is presumed for the case of Spaniards who left Spain between July 18, 1936, and December 31, 1955 (ibid.). The grandsons and granddaughters of Spaniards who left after December 31, 1955, or after the Amnesty Law passed in October 1977 are also considered in the legislation, but they need to present additional documentation. Other groups can benefit as well, but the greatest impact on Cuba and other Latin American societies is expected to derive from what is popularly known as *la ley de abuelos* (the grandparents' law).

2. "Cubanos nietos de españolas se topan con una norma discriminatoria del franquismo," *Cubaencuentro*, April 24, 2009.

Introduction

1. Look Lai 1989.

2. "Teniendo en cuenta las dimensiones del fenómeno, y su importancia numérica en relación con la población total, Cuba aparece como el único territorio latinoamericano receptor de un movimiento migratorio masivo a lo largo de todo el siglo XIX y primer tercio del XX" (Maluquer de Motes 1992, 15–16; my translation).

3. For theoretical syntheses focused on the links between global and regional changes in the division of labor and migration, see Sassen-Koob 1980; Portes and Walton 1981.

4. For discussions of different aspects of the political economy of Cuba's transition into production and accumulation schemas that relied on immigrants from Spain, the Caribbean, Asia, and to a lesser extent other areas at the beginning of the twentieth century, see López Segrera 1975; Le Riverend 1974; Pérez de la Riva 1975; Guerra and Pulpeiro 1976; Knight 1977; Moreno Fraginals 2001; Richardson 1989, 1992.

5. Ortiz López 1998.

6. Ortiz 1975, 53. The term *bozales* was also used in other areas of the Caribbean. In Haiti even today a section of Port-au-Prince is still called "Croix des Bossales." In an email communication, Georges Fouron indicated that there was a slave market in that area during the colonial period and explained that the term "Nègre bossale" is still used in Haitian Creole to refer to a black Haitian who is regarded as not having acquired "European ways."

7. Saco 1879, 68–70; cited in Klein 1967, 67.

8. For a discussion about the emergence of the transnational perspective, several approaches to transnationalism in relation to power and hegemony, how such approaches complement world-systems analysis, and an earlier formulation of the comprehensive transnational perspective employed in this work, see Cervantes-Rodríguez 2002 (partially reproduced in Chapter 1 with the permission of Greenwood Publishing Group, Inc., Westport, Connecticut). For an earlier application to the case of Spanish migration to Cuba, see Cervantes-Rodríguez 2003 and 2005 (partially reproduced in Chapter 3 with the permission of Biblioteca Nueva, Madrid).

9. Braudel 1980.

10. Ibid., 27.

11. In Chapter 1, I discuss how the conceptualization of the *longue durée* has influenced migration studies and how it has been combined with several ways of addressing transnational relations and processes. I further theorize Braudel's dialectical conceptualization of history as an explicit path to bridge history and the social sciences in light of its relevance for the study of international migration in Cuba.

12. I discuss key concepts employed in this work, including the concept of social fields, in Chapter 1. It suffices for now to say that "social fields" are understood as "networks of [social] networks," with social networks being "chains of social relations specific to persons" (Glick-Schiller 2003, 104).

13. The typology of "the hegemonies of historical capitalism" and their corresponding "systemic cycles of accumulation" offered in Arrighi 1999 is relevant for the study of international migration in Cuba in light of the global and historical conceptualization employed in this work. This argument is developed in Chapter 1.

14. Arrighi 1999.

Chapter 1

1. Conventionally, Cuban historiography distinguishes four major periods: (1) the colonial period, which began in the sixteenth century and ended at the conclusion of the Spanish-American War; (2) the period of U.S. military occupation and administration, which began in December 1898 and ended on May 20, 1902, with the inauguration of the first elected president in Cuba, Tomás Estrada Palma, a Cuban general in the independence wars; (3) "the republican period," which began with the inauguration of the first elected president and ended on December 1958; and (4) the revolutionary period, which began in January 1959. "The revolution" and "the revolutionary period" are terms that conventionally allude to the period starting in 1959 and not just the upheaval, although there are divergent opinions concerning when the actual revolutionary process yielded the formation of a political establishment that was not revolutionary any longer. Although that issue is beyond the scope of this book, I agree that the post-1959 period should not be treated monolithically as "the revolutionary period." I examine the transformations that started in 1959 in terms of the depth of the changes involved and their entanglements with the migration process and identify some subperiods for analytical purposes.

2. University of Havana's Centro de Estudios Demográficos (CEDEM), founded in 1976 with the mission of becoming the leading university research center for the study of major demographic and population processes in general, did not include international migration among its major research lines until the 1990s. By then, other centers, such as Centro de Estudios sobre los Estados Unidos (CESU) and Centro de Estudios de Alternativas Políticas (CEAP) were already producing scattered studies on emigration from Cuba after 1959. A sample of representative works produced in the early 1990s by Cuban researchers on the island shows an emphasis on the topics of migration and U.S. policy toward Cuba and Cuban Americans in the United States, and includes a call for the systematic analysis of individual motivations to migrate (see Martín 1995). However, it was not until after the foundation of the Centro para el Estudio de la Migración Internacional (CEMI) in 1989 that a scholarly center was vested with a mandate to focus on the topic of international migration. The Web site of the CEMI (last consulted in early 2008; my translation) referred to the mandate in question as follows: "Currently, the Center is recognized as the executor of the investigations on Cuban emigrants [or emigration from Cuba] that are conducted in the country" [En la actualidad [el centro] es reconocido como ejecutor de las investigaciones que acerca de la Emigración Cubana se realizan en el país]. The emphasis is on "la Emigración Cubana," a term that can refer to both Cuban emigrants and emigration from Cuba, suggests a focus on the post-1959 period. The mission statement further clarifies that CEMI focuses "essentially on the migration process and the changes in the migration pattern, Cuban settlements abroad, and Cuba's policy toward its emigrants [or emigration]." It also alludes to the polemical nature of the lines of inquiry associated with the topics dealt with, which makes

clear the political sensitivity toward them: "These topics are necessarily polemical and provoke debates, inside and outside Cuba, when analyzed and researched" [Las líneas abordadas por el CEMI están esencialmente referidas al proceso migratorio y las tendencias cambiantes del patrón migratorio, los asentamientos de cubanos en el exterior y la política de Cuba hacia su emigración, temáticas cuyo análisis e investigación provocan, necesariamente, debate y polémica, dentro y fuera de Cuba]. In 2008, CEDEM, whose current director is the former director of CEMI, hosted a conference on international migration in which representatives of research centers and the ministries of foreign relations and the interior participated, which suggests the growing institutionalization of the topic as a major research area favored by the state.

3. Gilroy 1999, chap. 1.

4. De la Fuente 1996, 164; my translation.

5. I discuss this issue in Chapters 4 and 5.

6. Deschamps Chapeaux and Pérez de la Riva 1974.

7. Wimmer and Glick-Schiller 2003, 576; also see Glick-Schiller 1999.

8. Wimmer and Glick-Schiller 2003.

9. Braudel 1980.

10. Wimmer and Glick-Schiller 2003.

11. For example, Cuban historian Oscar Zanetti Lecuona (1995, 119; my translation) argues that the prolonged struggle for Cuba's independence and then against U.S. domination "made the national question the articulating axis of Cuban historiography, even perhaps in a more accentuated fashion than in other Latin American countries" [Las largas décadas de combate por la independencia y la igualmente prolongada lucha posterior contra el dominio norteamericano, hicieron del problema nacional el verdadero eje de la historiografía cubana, de un modo probablemente más acentuado que en otros países de Latinoamérica].

12. Franc Báez Evertsz (1986, 27; my translation) argues that "the explanation of structural disparities and the economic dynamics of the Antillean countries as part of a unitary context influenced by a common general process, has been a constant concern among the authors of [focused on] the area" [la explicación de las disparidades estructurales y de dinámica económica de los países antillanos, en el marco unitario de un proceso común, ha sido una preocupación constante para los autores del área].

13. Matos 1999.

14. See ibid.

15. Ortiz 2002.

16. Mignolo 2000, 168.

17. The Annales school, a major forerunner of the world-systems perspective, has its institutional roots in the journal *Les annales d'histoire économique et sociale,* founded in 1929. Through this and other publication outlets, Annales scholars advocated a multidisciplinary approach to history by incorporating the methods and conceptual frameworks of sociology, geography, and history for the study of "social history," as opposed to the study of history through political events, diplomacy, war, and the role of extraordinary leaders, a tradition that dominated among historians. Fernand Braudel's work was instrumental in advancing this tradition.

18. N. Miller 2003. See also Pérez 1995a.

19. See Wallerstein 1974 and 1979.

20. In the next chapters I discuss specific contributions of these and other authors whose contributions to the understanding of international migration in Cuba were molded by historical structural traditions.

21. Portes and Walton 1981, 13.

22. Ibid., 19.

23. See, for example, Sassen-Koob 1980 and Light and Bonacich 1988.

24. Wallerstein 1974, 1979.

25. Amin 1974; Portes and Walton 1981; Richardson 1992; Sassen 1996.

26. Portes and Walton 1981, chaps. 1 and 2.

27. Pessar 1997; see also Basch et al. 2000.

28. Basch et al. 2000, 7.

29. Smith and Guarnizo (1999) offer a collection of articles representative of this tradition. For a summary of theoretical debates, see Portes (2001); see also Levitt 2001.

30. Basch et al. 2000, 7.

31. See Bourdieu 2001 and Thomson 2001.

32. Long 2000, 196–97.

33. Glick-Schiller and Fouron 2001a. For a detailed explanation of the concept of "long-distance nationalism," see Glick-Schiller and Fouron 2001b.

34. By the late 1990s, several academic programs had been rebranded as "international studies" largely because of the influence of the transnational perspective.

35. See, for example, Rosenau 1980 and Keohane and Nye 1981.

36. See, for example, Cox 1981, Ashley 1986, Van der Pijl 1998, and Robinson 2000 and 2003.

37. Cox 1986, 246–47.

38. Arrighi 1999, 29–30.

39. Ibid.

40. Ibid., 25.

41. See, for example, Keck and Sikkink 1998, Guarnizo and Smith 1999, Mahler 1999, Kyle 2000, Glick-Schiller and Fouron 2001a, Smith 2001.

42. Grewal and Kaplan 1999; Pettman 1996.

43. Ong 1999, 6.

44. Harvey 1996, chaps. 14–16.

45. Foucault 2000, 219–21.

46. Torres (2004) offers an enlightening account of Cuban American politics and the politics toward members of the group that explicitly challenges the rigidity of the state-centric perspectives. The topic of the systematicity, tensions, and complementarity involved in the two governments' approaches to migration has also been emphasized from other theoretical quarters: see Pedraza-Baley 1985; Colomer 1998.

47. Building on Yaganisako and Delaney (1995) and focusing on the experience of the Chinese migrants who move across societies regularly, Ong (1999, 68) calls attention to the importance of claiming the entrepreneurial nature of a group as practices of regulation and control. Croucher (1996) emphasizes the ideological force of the discourses about Cuban American entrepreneurship.

48. For similar practices in Puerto Rico, see Briggs 2002.

49. See Grosfoguel 1999a and 1999b.

50. Grosfoguel 1999a and 1999b.

51. Quijano 1991; Mignolo 2000 and 2003.

52. Mignolo 2000, 6.

53. Grosfoguel 1999a, 1999b, and 2003. For a recent volume on Caribbean migration that combines this conceptualization and the transnational perspective, see Cervantes-Rodríguez, Grosfoguel, and Mielants 2009.

54. Briggs 2002, 16.

55. Ibid. For theoretical discussions (rooted in the coloniality of power concept) about the links among capitalism, colonialism, and modernity, and the importance that the hegemonic manipulation of the concepts of race and culture have in molding such links, see Quijano 1991; Mignolo 2000.

56. Braudel 1980, 34.

57. Ibid., 26–32.

58. Ibid., 28.

59. Ibid., 29.

60. Ibid., 32.

61. Ibid., 40.

62. Immanuel Wallerstein (1988) calls our attention to the fact that although the term "conjoncture" is usually translated as "conjuncture," its translation as "cyclical history" is more in

tune with the meaning given by Braudel. From this perspective, "conjuncture" suggests both "fluctuations" as well as "the structural similarities" of "seemingly different dynamics" (e.g., the structural similarities of global hegemonic stages) (Wallerstein 1988; Arrighi 1999).

63. Wallerstein 1988, 293–94.

64. Arrighi 1999.

65. For the notion of "patterned migrations," see Sassen 1996.

66. An extensive body of literature on capitalist accumulation, the penetration of the capitalist mode of production in societies where it was nonexistent or had limited presence, and forms of surplus value appropriation and transfer has shed light on the centrality that labor migration has had in these dynamics and how specific processes operating at different scales (global, regionally, within nations, in specific localities) have molded such links (e.g., Furtado 1963; Emmanuel 1972; Amin 1974). Building upon this tradition, a series of theoretical syntheses on labor migration rescued these topics in light of additional theoretical contributions on the systemic nature of capitalism as enunciated by world-systems analysis (e.g., Wallerstein 1974; 1982). These works emphasized the dialectical interplay between global structures of accumulation and politico-economic processes that operate at different scales. See Portes 1977; Sassen-Koob 1980; Portes and Walton 1981.

67. See Sassen-Koob 1980.

68. See Poyo 1989, 1991; Pérez 1995b; Rivero Muñiz 1976; Casanovas Codina 1999; Casasús 1953. As shown in this volume, works on the Caribbean and other regions have documented the key role played by migrants in the development of multiple forms of exchange and relationships, such as trade, monetary flows, and investments. Although this issue is extensively discussed in reference to the literature on Spanish and other groups of migrants to the island and migrants from Cuba and elsewhere, the literature on other cases has tended to shed light on the multiple roles played by migrants historically. See, for example, Manners 1965, Gabaccia 2000, Mustafa 2001, Dunlevy and Hutchinson 1999, Díaz-Alejandro 1970.

Chapter 2

1. Mignolo 2000, 131.

2. Mignolo 2000; see also Kennedy 1987 and Arrighi 1999.

3. For recent theoretical syntheses on the links between imperial designs, colonialism, the institution of slavery, modernity, and capitalism as manifested in the Americas, and their relevance in the constitution of the global structures of the modern capitalist world-system, see Quijano 1991; Quijano and Wallerstein 1992; Mignolo 2000. The following works constitute a sample of analyses that offer relevant insights on specific aspects of these links as manifested in the Cuban case: Guerra 1964; López Segrera 1985; Le Riverend 1974; Moreno Fraginals 2001; Pérez de la Riva 1978; Klein 1986; Ortiz 2002; González-Ripoll 2004; de la Fuente 2008.

4. See Marrero 1972; Le Riverend 1974; Gott 2004.

5. Livi-Bacci 1997, 55; citing Thomas 1994, 96–98; for alternative estimates, which nevertheless also pointed to depopulation, see Marrero 1972; López Segrera 1973; and Gott 2004 (who disputes the thesis of complete extermination of the indigenous population).

6. Livi-Bacci 1997. The Spaniards had been bringing African slaves with them since their first arrival. This issue and the introduction of members of the indigenous population from Yucatan are discussed later in this work.

7. Torres-Cuevas 2002a. Torres-Cuevas agrees with other historians that De Soto's expeditions into "Florida" (as all the territories touching the Gulf of Mexico on the north and east were known at the time) deprived Cuba of precious resources and depressed Cuba's population growth.

8. Marrero 1972; Le Riverend 1974; and Sosa Rodríguez and Bojóquez 1991.

9. Marrero 1972.

10. Marrero 1972; Le Riverend 1992a 1992b.

11. Building upon historical structural analyses on these matters, Báez Evertsz (1986) offers an insightful theoretical synthesis on the role played by the production of tobacco in the penetration of the rivals of Spain in the Caribbean and the expansion of the production of sugar in the British Caribbean toward the end of the seventeenth century.

12. For analyses on the dynamics shaping immigration in Cuba during the first centuries of colonization, see Guerra 1964; Marrero 1972; Moreno Fraginals 2001 and 2002; Ortiz 2002; Morse 1984; Le Riverend 1992a 1992b, and 1994; Pérez Guzmán 1997; Pérez de la Riva 2004; de la Fuente 2008.

13. Leal 1988; Pérez Guzmán 1997.

14. Marrero 1972; Leal 1988; Pérez Guzmán 1997; Le Riverend 1992b; de la Fuente 2008.

15. Detailed analyses about the functions performed "from and by Havana" for the Spanish crown and the infrastructure developed in relation to its defense capabilities are offered in McNeill 1985; Leal 1988; Pérez Guzmán 1997; García González 1998; Pérez de la Riva 2004; Alvarez Estévez 2001; Moreno Fraginals 2002; de la Fuente 2008.

16. McNeill 1985.

17. Özveren 1994, 26. A "commodity chain" is "a network of labor and production processes whose end result is a final commodity." See Hopkins and Wallerstein 1986, 159.

18. McNeill 1985, 173.

19. Moreno Fraginals 2001; Báez Evertsz 1986.

20. Le Riverend (1974); Moreno Fraginals (2001); Báez Evertsz 1986.

21. For studies about or referring to various aspects of the evolution of Havana in the early colonial period, see Roig de Leuchsenring 1963; Leal 1988; Le Riverend 1992a; Pérez Guzmán 1997; Pérez de la Riva 2004; Kapcia 2005; de la Fuente 2008.

22. The SEAP survived under different names and mandates until it ceased to function after 1959. In 1994 the Cuban state inaugurated an organization under the same name as an NGO. A brief history of the SEAP is found at http://www.seap.cult.cu/.

23. For discussion on the roles played by the SEAP and the interests represented, see Moreno Fraginals (2001); Kapcia 2005.

24. Cited by García Díaz and Guerra Vilaboy 2002, 15.

25. Sánchez-Albornoz 1974, 127.

26. Ibid., 127–28.

27. Roig de Leuchsenring 1963; Le Riverend 1992.

28. Roig de Leuchsenring 1963, 14. See also Abdala 2003, 38.

29. Francisco López Segrera (1985) calls attention to the socioeconomic contrast between the western and eastern parts of the island by referring to "the east -west contradiction." Works on the history of Havana tend to emphasize its global projection and external links rather its links with other cities of Cuba's urban system.

30. Arrighi 1999, 32–43.

31. Gott 2004, 13.

32. Kennedy 1987; Arrighi 1999.

33. Friedlaender 1978.

34. Carreras 1985. For immigration of French subjects to Cuba in that period, see also Alvarez Estévez 1988.

35. García Díaz and Guerra Vilaboy 2002, 15.

36. McNeill 1985, 170.

37. Moreno Fraginals 2001, 23–24; my translation.

38. Ibid.; see also Portell-Vilá 1994; Knight 1977.

39. McNeill 1985.

40. Moreno Fraginals 2001; D'Estéfano Pisani 1988; Carreras 1985.

41. D'Estéfano Pisani 1988; Carreras 1985.

42. R. Morris and J. Morris 1976, 259.

43. Ibid.

44. Padrón 2005.

45. Deive 1989; Padrón 2005; D'Estéfano Pisani 1988. *Proceedings of the International Colloquium "Les Français dans l'Orient cubain"* (1993) also contains valuable analyses of the factors leading to the migration of French-origin groups to Cuba's eastern territories and its implications.

46. Moreno Fraginals 2001; Carreras 1985; Báez Evertsz 1986.

47. The estimates on the number of arrivals associated with turmoil in Hispaniola frequently include just those coming as a direct result of the Haitian revolution, while a few works include people from the whole of Hispaniola as turmoil became widespread, and even other French territories after the French revolution. The estimates range from 20,000 to 34,000 people. Lacking consensus on this matter, it should be noted, however, that any figure within these ranges is significant if we take into consideration that according to the census of 1792, Cuba's total population was 272,300 inhabitants. For a discussion on estimates on arrivals of French subjects at that time, see Padrón 2005. For a discussion of estimates of people leaving from Hispaniola at different stages, see Deive 1989.

48. Although under the Treaty of Fontainebleau (1762) France had ceded Louisiana to Spain, a treaty signed in 1800 had returned it to France. The pressure stemming from revolution in Haiti and from other geopolitical crises, and the pressures exerted by the United States, led to the purchase by the latter for 60 million francs (or about $15 million), an amount that included both the price for the territory and the debts of the French with the United States (see R. Morris and J. Morris 1976, 158).

49. Carreras 1985; Padrón 2005.

50. Padrón 2005, 35; citing Portuondo n.d., 111.

51. Padrón 2005; *Proceedings of the International Colloquium "Les Français dans l'Orient cubain"*; Sonesson 1995.

52. Butel 1993, 162.

53. Ibid., 168.

54. García Díaz and Guerra Vilaboy 2002, 15; my translation.

55. Sonesson 1995.

56. Moreno Fraginals and Moreno Masó 1993.

57. McNeill 1985, 89; see also Moreno Fraginals and Moreno Masó 1993.

58. McNeill 1985, 101.

59. Carreras 1985; Moreno Fraginals and Moreno Masó 1993.

60. Moreno Fraginals and Moreno Masó 1993.

61. Maluquer de Motes 1992; Moreno Fraginals and Moreno Masó 1993; Sánchez Alonso 1995.

62. See Gott 2004.

63. "Compared to the encomienda, which was mainly a tributary and service system imposed upon Indians, usually in exchange for their productive use of the land, repartimiento was a more flexible labor procurement system that relied on the territorial mobility of groups of Indians that were usually recruited from areas that were quite distant from production centers. Repartimiento was more common in regions of the Americas where indigenous labor was relatively abundant, and highly mobile cuadrillas of indigenous laborers were formed to meet labor demand in different areas. The allocation of labor was based on a draft system that was granted from Spain: . . . in general, the Crown compromised with the settlers' urgent need for Indians by extending its system of drafting Indians for specific tasks. This draft system came to be known as repartimiento" (MacLeod 1973, 207–8). For the combination of these two systems of labor use in Cuba, see Le Riverend 1992b and MacLeod 1973.

64. Levine (1993) notices that since the early official recognition by the pope that the Catholic monarchs of Spain had indisputable jurisdiction over religious affairs in Cuba, no official document ever challenged the power of the Roman Catholic faith on the island. Not even the Cadiz Constitution, he also notes, considered one of the most liberal and progressive constitutions in Spain, challenged the prohibition to profess a faith other than Roman Catholicism in Spanish-dominated territories. For other works with information on the topic of Spain's restrictions on immigration based on religion and other considerations, including the issue of the bans

imposed on the introduction of certain slave groups in the colonies based on their rebellious behavior and religious (mainly Muslim) background, see Franco 1974, Carreras 1985, Menéndez Paredes 1999, and de la Fuente 2008.

65. Ortiz 2002.

66. Ibid. See also Le Riverend 1974; Carreras 1985, and McNeill 1985.

67. Moreno Fraginals (2001) refers to this first boom in the production of sugar as the first "danza de los millones" (literally translated as "the dance of the millions"), an expression frequently used in Cuban historiography to refer to the periods of economic boom related to the expansion of the sugar industry.

68. De la Fuente 2008.

69. Gott 2004, 24; de la Fuente 2008.

70. For a comprehensive analysis of the use of the slave workforce in different activities as the urban and rural economies of Cuba diversified, see Klein 1967; Le Riverend 1974.

71. As cited by Friedlaender 1978, 208.

72. McNeill 1985, 170.

73. Ibid.

74. González-Ripoll 2004, citing Curtin 1969. For alternative estimates, see Pérez de la Riva 1979; Klein 1967.

75. Sánchez-Albornoz 1974, 126.

76. J. Franco 1996, chap. 1.

77. Moreno Fraginals 2001; Friedlaender 1978.

78. Knight 1977; J. Franco 1996; Moreno Fraginals 2001.

79. Carreras 1985.

80. Ferguson 2003, 166.

81. See, for example, Le Riverend 1974.

82. McNeill (1985) refers to the participation of merchants from Cuba in smuggling when analyzing the crucial role that "covert trade" played in connecting the island with global trade circuits. Torres-Cuevas (2002a) documents the involvement of Spanish authorities and members of the clergy in clandestine trade with buccaneers, particularly in Bayamo where the economy was flourishing by the early seventeenth century as a result of such activities. He also notices the imbrications of smuggling and the rise of a sort of territorially bounded patriotic consciousness advocated by the Creoles. Immanuel Wallerstein has also referred to the involvement of European authorities in smuggling and other "extra-imperial" activities.

83. Knight 1977, 52.

84. For a detailed analysis on the role of manumission and *coartación* in the links between slavery and the integration of the freed groups in Cuba and figures on the participation of "colored" people in the army by periods, see Klein 1967, chap. 3.

85. Moreno Fraginals 2001.

86. De la Fuente 2008.

87. Ibid., 168.

88. Montejo Arrechea 1993, 31, citing the Salvat Dictionary: "Lugar destinado a reuniones de negros Bozales de cada nación africana. Reunión de personas ineptas donde hay desorden"; my translation.

89. Ibid., 43. In the late nineteenth century, Spain still prohibited the gathering of Africans and Creoles (including blacks and mulattoes) in the *cabildos* even though this rule was frequently violated. See also Scott 1985.

90. For insights on the black population's strategies of organization, accommodation, and resistance in Cuba, see Scott 1985, Montejo Arrechea 1993. De la Fuente (2008) offers a focus on Havana's slaves and black population in general in the earliest stage of the colonial period.

91. Richardson 1992, 76–77. For a systematic analysis of the transnational tangible and intangible connections forged by slaves and "people of color" and other subaltern groups in Cuba, see Scott 2005.

92. "Queda autorizado el Gobierno para decretar en plazo breve la libertad de los actuales patrocinados de Cuba, dentro y bajo la jurisdicción de la ley de 1880" (Carreras 1985, 124; my

translation). Carreras 1985 and Klein 1986 document the legislation under which *patronato* was established in Cuba. For the complexity and time/space difference in the nature of abolition in Cuba, see Scott 1985.

93. Gilroy 1999.

94. Scott 1985; Louis Pérez 1983.

95. Mignolo 2000, 13. On the synergy between Occidentalism and capitalism from an alternative perspective, see Arrighi 1999.

96. Mignolo (2000) shows that such a disparate application of standards concerning what is progress and which groups deserve human dignity led to the silencing of the Haitian revolution by the advocates of the ideologies on rights, justice, and independence. González-Ripoll et al. (2004) offer in-depth analyses of how the fear that the Haitian revolution had instilled in the Spanish authorities reflected on Cuban society.

97. Ibid.

98. Cepero Bonilla 1948, Moreno Fraginals 2001, Bergard 1989, and Corbitt 1971 shed light on the class interests and ideologies involved in the debates on slave trafficking and abolition and their implications for the adoption of certain immigration policies. Rebecca Scott (1985) offers a comprehensive discussion on different interpretations of the rationales behind abolition, including her own, which is based on a detailed analysis of the spatial and temporal dimensions of pro-abolitionist stances and practices.

99. Pérez de la Riva 1978; Humboldt 1930.

100. For discussion of aspects of the political environment in relation to the development of conspiracies and the complicity and/or reaction of the Spanish authorities, political currents in the second half of the nineteenth century, and related topics, see Cepero Bonilla 1948; Pérez de la Riva 1978; Carreras 1985; Torres-Cuevas 2002b.

101. Carreras 1985.

102. Naranjo Orovio 1996a and 1996b, Corbitt 1971; Carreras 1985; González-Ripoll 2004; Gott 2004.

103. Bureau of the American Republics n.d.; Sánchez-Albornoz 1974.

104. Wittke 1952.

105. Moreno Fraginals 2001, 142.

106. Máquez Sterling 1969, 145.

107. Del Monte y Aponte 1929; my translation.

108. "Real Cédula del 21 de Octubre de 1817," document consulted at the Rare Books Collection, New York Public Library.

109. "In its simplest form, the term *colono* refers to 'small-scale farmer.' However, in most instances it is used to describe a cultivator of sugar cane specifically. Furthermore, the term was expanded in nineteenth-century Cuba, when the cultivation of cane became separated to some extent from its processing. Thereupon independent cane-growers entered into contractual grinding agreements with particular mills to which they delivered their cane when it was cut. Normally, such colonos owned their own land. Soon a new practice developed by which the central [mill], which had large tracts of owned or rented land, contracted with landless individual farmers, by what were essentially sharecropping or tenant agreements, to grow cane. Thus a colono can be a small-scale farmer, a landowning sugar cane farmer who has a grinding contract with a mill, or a tenant producing cane on land owned or rented by the mill" (R. Guerra 1964, 209–10).

110. See De la Sagra 1831, 339.

111. See De la Sagra 1831. Additional information on the evolution of this settlement is available at http://www.cienfuegoscuba.galeon.com/.

112. Ibid.

113. For a detailed analysis of the rationales of the colonizing projects in these areas, see ibid., 339–45. For other analyses on colonizing projects related to geopolitical and racist ideologies, see Lecuyer 1987, Carreras 1985, Naranjo Orovio 1996b, and Corbitt 1971.

114. Cagiao 1992.

115. For the demographics of immigration from Spain, see Maluquer de Motes 1992.

116. Guiteras 1927–28.

117. Roselló Socorro 2002; Benigni Lauder 2002.

118. Roselló Socorro 2002; Benigni Lauder 2002.

119. Benigni Lauder 2002. A general argument on the link between the Italian diaspora and the Italian government can be found in Gabaccia 2002.

120. Carreras 1985; see also Friedlaender 1978.

121. Briggs 2002 explains this tendency for the case of Puerto Rico.

122. De la Sagra 1831, table titled "resúmenes generales de los cuatro censos."

123. Cuban census data cited in Friedlaender 1978 and Bureau of Foreign Commerce 1957, table 85.

124. Livi-Bacci 1997.

125. Ibid., 104, citing McEvedy and Jones 1978, 279.

126. Moreno Fraginals 2002, 57. An alternative estimate focused on Havana suggests a lower figure (see de la Fuente 2008).

127. These included sailors, merchants with no more than two assistants bringing commodities, public servants, military personnel, and members of the clergy (Sonesson 1995, 14).

128. Maluquer de Motes 1992; Durán 1992; Sánchez Alonso 1995.

129. The estimates presented below are drawn from Naranjo Orovio 1992 and the percentages calculated based on that data unless otherwise specified. For alternative estimates and analyses on the demographics of Spanish migration, see Palazón Ferrando 1995 and Maluquer de Motes 1992.

130. Núñez 1996.

131. Look Lai 1989, 117; see also Corbitt 1971.

132. Trolliet 1994, 12 n. 2: "n'est pas un terme chinois mais une transcription phonétique anglicisée du tamil *kúli* (salaire) a moins que ce ne soit du turk *kuli* (esclave)"; my translation.

133. Look Lai 1989.

134. Official data cited by Corbitt 1971; Córdova 2001, 205. For the inhuman conditions in which Chinese migrants traveled and worked, see Look Lai 1989.

135. Look Lai 1989, 117.

136. Trolliet 1994. For the issue of the high geographical concentration of the exit districts or counties, see Look Lai 1989.

137. Corbitt 1971, 4.

138. Look Lai 1989, 124.

139. Moreno Fraginals 2001.

140. Herrera Jerez and Carillo Santana 2003; Abdala 2003.

141. Knight 1977, 34.

142. Look Lai 1989, 125.

143. Ibid., 126.

144. For a detailed analysis of each of these forms of resistance, see Helly 1979.

145. Richardson 1992, 74–75.

146. Baltar Rodríguez 1997; see also Pérez de la Riva 2000 and Herrera Jerez and Castillo Santana 2003.

147. Mignolo 2000.

148. Baltar Rodríguez 1997.

149. Louis Pérez 1999; Pérez de la Riva 2000, 2004; Moreno Fraginals 2001; Vega Suñol 2004.

150. Louis Pérez 1999, 74–75.

151. Ibid., 20.

152. Ibid.; Vegal Suñol 2004.

153. Alonso and Chávez Alvarez 1978, table 34.

154. Sosa Rodríguez and Bojóquez 1991.

155. See Moreno Fraginals 2001, 260; Córdova 2001, 182–88; Lecuyer 1987.

156. Moreno Fraginals 2001, 259.

Chapter 3

1. De la Fuente 2008, 88.
2. Harvey 1996, 264–65.
3. Macías Hernández 1988.
4. Conversation with a descendant of an immigrant family to Santiago de Cuba in Barcelona, June 2005.
5. These strategies are documented by Rueda (1993) through interviews and other evidence.
6. Ibid., 73; citing a 1916 report by the Consejo Superior de Emigración.
7. See Durán 1992, 413–18.
8. Mustafa 2001.
9. Chin, Yoon, and Smith 1996.
10. Moreno Fraginals 2001; Báez Evertsz 1986.
11. For syntheses of the links between migration and economic changes, such as trade and long-distance investments, see Díaz-Alejandro 1970; Dunlevy and Hutchinson 1999; Gould 1995.
12. Losada Alvarez 1995.
13. Ibid.
14. Miguel Donozo to Frederick Huth and Co., La Coruña, October 11, 1826, in "Letters to Frederick Huth and Co." n.d., Guildhall Library, London, MS 25050.
15. See the Frederick Huth and Co. Archives at University College London.
16. EFE 2002.
17. For a discussion of the involvement of Catalonian merchants and other entrepreneurs in economic activities in Spain and Cuba, see Rodrigo 1998, 359. For a discussion of the role of merchants from the Peninsula in general and Catalonia in particular in the sugar industry in the 1840s, see Marqués Dolz 2006 (see also Moreno Fraginals 2001). Rodrigo and Marqués Dolz debate the emphasis of Bahamonde and Cayuela (1992) on the significance of the transfers of capital of wealthy Spaniards to Spain. Their works indicate that, in fact, while large sums of capital were transferred to Spain by the *Indianos* after having made their fortunes in Cuba, their transfers did not always imply abandonment of their investments in the island. Quite the opposite: often their investments in Spain continued to be supported to a large extent by their economic involvement in Cuba (see Rodrigo 1998, 2004). Wealthy Spaniards, including rich merchants who had profited from the slave trade and other transactions, were actively involved as financiers to the *hacendados* and in the development of various types of enterprises in Cuba (Marqués Dolz 2006). In addition, many Spaniards who did not accumulate significant wealth were nevertheless involved in the creation of new small and mid-sized enterprises (ibid.).
18. Maluquer de Motes 1992, table 15.
19. Ibid.; Sonesson 1995; Palazón Ferrando 1995.
20. Sonesson 1995; Palazón Ferrando 1995.
21. Rodrigo 2004; see also Sonesson 1995.
22. Rodrigo 2004; Sonesson 1995.
23. Piqueras 2003, 127–28.
24. Rueda 1993, 61.
25. Rodrigo 2004, 22; my translation.
26. Ibid. See also Sonesson 1995.
27. Sonesson 1995, 166–67; my translation. See also Cerutti 1995.
28. My notes from the international colloquium "Cuba: De colonia a república" in Barcelona at the Universitat Pompeu Fabra, June 16–17, 2004.
29. Rodrigo 2004, 17. The term *Indiano* refers to Spaniards who migrated to the Americas and returned to their homeland with considerable wealth.
30. Bahamonde and Cayuela 1992.
31. García López 1992.
32. See, for example, Cagiao 1992; García López 1992; Sonesson 1995; Morales Saro 1992; Macías Hernández 1992.

33. Cagiao 1992.
34. Bahamonde 1992; Bahamonde and Cayuela 1992; García López 1992.
35. García López 1992, 125, citing a study by Rafael M. Labra (1915) about remittances from the United States paid through major Spanish banking institutions.
36. Cagiao 1992.
37. On conditions leading to emigration from Galicia and the use of remittances, see Sánchez 1995, Cagiao 1992, and Losada Alvarez 1995.
38. Naranjo Orovio 1992, 188.
39. Macías Hernández 1992, 98.
40. Maluquer de Motes 1992, 66–67.
41. Census data cited in Macías Hernández 1988, 96.
42. For the demographics of immigration from the Canary Islands and patterns of labor market incorporation, see Maluquer de Motes 1992, 66; Durán 1992; Hernández García 1992. A sample of enterprises developed by Spanish families in Cuba that were still operating in 1958 indirectly suggests that women tended to inherit and became involved in their husbands' enterprises when they became windows (see Jiménez 2000).
43. Rueda 1993, 58.
44. Cited in García Hernández 1992, 126; my translation.
45. Macías Hernández 1992, table 5.9, 209.
46. García López 1992.
47. Marx 1974.
48. Piqueras 2003, 108; my translation.
49. Second article of the BHC's statutes, cited in S. Fernández 2002, 108; my translation.
50. Bahamonde 1992; see also S. Fernández 2002.
51. For a discussion on the involvement of the United States in the migrants' remittances, see García López 1992. For economic and social aspects of the Spanish presence in the United States, see Fernández-Shaw 1987.
52. García López 1992, 104–5.
53. *El Mundo* 2001.
54. See García López 1992.
55. Naranjo Orovio 1988.
56. Ibid.
57. Cagiao 1992, 293–316.
58. "Yo tengo un periódico consagrado a defender los intereses de Galicia, Cee es un pueblo de Galicia, y como se halla perjudicado por la grave conducta de Baldonedo y Zabala, me creo en el imprescindible deber de atacarlos rudamente, ya que de las templadas exhortaciones no han hecho caso." *Opinión en Galicia* 2005; my translation.
59. *El Mundo* 2005.
60. Macías Hernández 1992.
61. Soldevilla and Rueda 1992.
62. See Macías Hernández 1992; Morales Saro 1992; Durán 1992; Cabrera Deniz 1996.
63. Costa 2004.
64. See Monge Muley 1953, Soldevilla and Rueda 1992, Morales Saro 1992, and Cagiao 1992.
65. Macías Hernández 1992, 1988.
66. Ibid.
67. Azcona 1992.
68. Morales Saro 1992; Monge Muley 1953.
69. Morales Saro 1992.
70. Cagiao 1992; Monge Muley 1953.
71. Azcona 1992.
72. Rueda 1993, 105.
73. See Rodríguez 1996.
74. R. Scott 2005, 2.

75. Cerutti 1995, 47.
76. Moreno Fraginals 2001, 421.
77. S. Fernández 2002, 40.
78. Moreno Fraginals 2001.
79. Louis Pérez 1999, appendix, table 1.1; Moreno Fraginals 2001.
80. Cerutti 1995, 47.
81. Poyo 1991; Rivero Muñiz 1976.
82. Arnao 1877; my translation.
83. Aguilera Rojas 1909; my translation.
84. Poyo 1989.
85. Rueda 1993, 75.
86. See Casasús 1953.
87. The insights on the political involvement of Cubans in the United States and their links with Cuba have been drawn from Casasús 1953; Poyo 1989; Louis Pérez 1995a and 1999; Loyola Vega 2002; and Torres-Cuevas 2002b, unless otherwise specified.
88. Louis Pérez 1995b.
89. Martí 1995.
90. Louis Pérez 1995a.
91. For a general argument about how the attempts of exiles and refugees to oust governments in their countries of origin can be regarded by the governments from which they operate as a potential threat to their national security, see Zimmerman 1995.
92. Rueda 1993, 109.
93. See ibid., Casasús 1953, Poyo 1989, and Casanovas Codina 1999.
94. Casanovas Codina 1999.
95. Rivero Muñiz 1976; Poyo 1989; Casanovas Codina 1999.
96. Rueda 1993, 104.
97. U.S. Census Bureau 2000.
98. See http://martimaceo.org/default.aspx.
99. The discussion in this section about Spanish-enterprises is based on the sources presented in Appendix A.

Chapter 4

1. Keal 1986, 128.
2. Keal defines "sphere of influence" as "a definitive region within which a single external power exerts a predominant influence, which limits the independence or freedom of action of states within it" (ibid., 124).
3. Dumoulin 1980; Eferén 1995.
4. Bejarano 1993.
5. Statistics from the Secretaría de Hacienda de Cuba, cited in Maluquer de Motes 1992, 55.
6. On the impact of immigration on general demographic trends at the beginning of the twentieth century, see Hernández Castellón 1984, 139–48.
7. Maluquer de Motes 1992, table 32.
8. Sánchez Alonso 1995; Naranjo Orovio 1992.
9. Maluquer de Motes 1992; Naranjo Orovio 1992.
10. Naranjo Orovio 1992, table 2; Maluquer de Motes 1992.
11. On the political economy of sugar production at that particular juncture, see González 1978; Dumoulin 1980; López Segrera 1975; Moreno Fraginals 2001.
12. Maluquer de Motes 1992, 748.
13. Brooke 1899.
14. Immigration Law of 1906, cited in Secretaría de Hacienda 1907.

15. On "assisted migrations" and the handling of Spanish immigrants by recruiters, Spanish organizations, the role of the Triscornia center, and related topics, see Naranjo Orovio 1988; Palazón Ferrando 1995.

16. Immigration Law of 1906, cited in Secretaría de Hacienda 1907.

17. Ibid.

18. Cited by Macías Martín 2002, 298; my translation.

19. Richardson 1989 and 1992. On the arrival of temporary workers and immigrants from neighboring islands and the conditions of their incorporation into Cuban society, see Pérez de la Riva 1979, Dumoulin 1980, Knight 1985, and McLeod 1998.

20. Pérez de la Riva 1979. Some researchers are hesitant to accept this estimate. See, for example, Knight 1985. Others, such as McLeod 1998, accept it as fact.

21. See Farnós and Cervera 1976, table 15; Castellón 1986.

22. Dumoulin 1980.

23. Ibid.

24. S. Guerra and Pulpeiro 1976.

25. Palazón Ferrando 1995, 151.

26. S. Guerra and Pulpeiro 1976.

27. Brooke 1899, 31.

28. Ibid.

29. The "certificates" were petitions for references about the potential entrants' character, values, and economic means.

30. "Cualquier individuo de la raza amarilla susceptible, por sus características étnicas, de confundirse con un chino"; my translation.

31. For information on specific laws and rules affecting Chinese immigration and immigrants, see Carreras 1985, Jiménez Pastrana 1963, and Herrera Jerez and Carillo Santana 2003.

32. See Herrera Jerez and Carillo Santana 2003, 33–35.

33. Ibid., table 4.

34. Baltar Rodríguez 1997, table 4.

35. Look Lai 1989.

36. Ibid., 42.

37. Ibid.

38. Cited by Alvarez Estévez and Guzmán Pascual 2002, 26.

39. Ibid.

40. Naranjo Orovio 1992, table 2.

41. Ibid.

42. Ibid.

43. Pollitt 1984, 3.

44. González 1978; Louis Pérez 1983.

45. González 1978; Carrillo 1994.

46. For in-depth analyses of this period and the revolution of 1933 in Cuba, see Carrillo 1994 and Pérez-Stable 1998.

47. Córdova 1995; Carrillo 1994.

48. See, for example, Jiménez Pastrana 1963; Soler Martínez 1993; Carrillo 1994; and Herrera Jerez and Castillo Santana 2003.

49. For bills introduced between 1921 and 1930 that reflected the prevailing pro-nativist atmosphere, see Macías Martín 2002 and Carrillo 1994.

50. For insights on how the United States influenced Cuba's approach to immigration and national security, see Bejarano 1993.

51. For laws reflecting labor rights, see Carrillo 1994; see also Carreras 1985.

52. Carrillo 1994, 217.

53. Ibid., 290.

54. Carreras 1985, 470; my translation.

55. Telegram No. 148 from the Spanish ambassador in Havana to the Spanish secretary of state, December 23, 1933, cited in Macías Martín 2002, 395; my translation.

56. Dirección General del Censo 1945.

57. Palazón Ferrando 1995, 302. Scattered notes in the literature refer to foreigners being forced to leave their descendants in Cuba, which raises a whole set of questions concerning to what extent deportations were associated with the development of transnational household strategies instead of radical departures. I have not found enough evidence to open up this inquiry as part of this work, yet it deserves future attention.

58. Bejarano 1996.

59. Ibid.

60. Bejarano 1993.

61. Levine 1996, 265.

62. Ibid.

63. Levine 1993; Pava 2001.

64. Cited in Bejarano 1993, 8.

65. Ibid., 7. On the experience of the Jewish immigrants with the Cuban government in different periods, see Levine 1996.

66. See Avni 1996.

67. Ibid.; Menéndez Paredes 1999.

68. See Ruz and Lim Kim 2000.

69. Dirección General del Censo 1945, table 11.

70. Ibid., 747.

71. Ibid., 748.

72. Ibid., 749–50.

73. Ibid., table 11, 878, 879.

74. See Naranjo Orovio 1988 and Maluquer de Motes 1992.

75. Dirección General del Censo 1945, 765–57.

76. Ibid., 788. Note that approximately 17.5 percent of the active foreign-born population and 20 percent of the native population worked in activities that were classified as "unspecified."

77. Dirección General del Censo 1945.

78. Ibid., 790.

79. Ibid., 780–801.

80. Louis Pérez 1999, 20. For detailed accounts of the economic and social links between the United States and Cuba at that time, see Portell-Vilá 1994, Moreno Fraginals 2001, and Louis Pérez 1983 and 1999.

81. Fraginals 2001; Louis Pérez 1999.

82. Louis Pérez 1999, 30–31.

83. U.S. Department of Commerce and Labor 1904, 499.

84. INS 1962.

85. Ibid., table 16.

86. See Pérez-Stable 1998, Rojas 1998, and Louis Pérez 1999.

87. Louis Pérez 1999, 417.

88. Carrillo 1994.

89. Ibid.

90. The data are from the Bureau of Foreign Commerce 1957 unless otherwise specified.

91. Pérez-Stable 1998, 64.

92. Louis Pérez 1983.

Chapter 5

1. For the broader Caribbean and Latin American migration contexts at that time, see Zolberg 1989; Zolberg, Suhrke, and Aguayo 1989; Sassen-Koob 1986; and Portes and Rumbaut 1996.

2. The percentages of immigrants admitted from Latin America and the Caribbean by subregions and subperiods since 1901 were computed by the author based on the data provided

by INS *Statistical Yearbook* 1994, table 2, which is available online at http://www.dhs.gov/xlibrary/assets/statistics/yearbook/1999/FY99Yearbook.pdf. The data for the whole region were computed based on the total number of immigrants admitted from the Americas minus those admitted from Canada and Newfoundland, when applicable.

3. Castañeda 1993.

4. Pastor 1985; Portes and Rumbaut 1996.

5. For analyses of the processes and policies shaping U.S.-bound Caribbean migration during the Cold War, see Pastor 1985; Zolberg, Suhrke, and Aguayo 1989; Sassen-Koob 1986; Portes and Rumbaut 1996; Maldonado 1979; Pedraza-Bailey 1985; Torres-Saillant and Hernández 1998; and Grasmuck and Pessar 1991.

6. See Pedraza-Bailey 1985; García 1996.

7. See Deere 1984, 24.

8. Aranda 1980, 172; my translation.

9. Deere 1984; Pérez-Stable 1998.

10. Pérez-Stable 1998, 62.

11. Mesa-Lago 1989.

12. Deere 1984, table 3.

13. Pérez-López 1995, 36. For the role of small and medium-size producers and the state in agricultural production and land ownership at the beginning of the revolution, see Deere 1984 and Aranda 1980. For later stages, see Mesa-Lago 1989 and Pérez-López 1995.

14. Such measures ranged from the fumigation of their crops in order to annihilate their productive capacity to threatening mechanisms (Clark 1992).

15. The notions of "exit" and "voice" are employed here following Hirschman's (1970) model.

16. For a detailed analysis of movements of resistance against the new regime and the repercussions for the participants, including imprisonment, executions, and exile, see Clark 1992 and Encinosa 1995.

17. The official discourses in Cuba tend to present population movements as a result of development strategies. This tells only part of the story. The relationship between forced displacements, the general population's territorial mobility in general, and security rationales has not been sufficiently studied.

18. X. Franco (1982, 27) indicates that the rural population dropped in all provinces between 1970 and 1980, although in the case of Havana the number of inhabited rural places ("lugares habitados rurales") did not decrease in that period. Another estimate (CEE 1983) indicates that the rural population declined in all provinces except Havana between 1970 and 1981.

19. X. Franco 1982, 26.

20. Ibid., 26–27.

21. "Teniendo en cuenta el alto grado de especialización agrícola así como el alto grado de urbanización (Camagüey ocupa el tercer lugar en el país excluyendo Ciudad de la Habana), todo parece indicar que se está produciendo un movimiento contradictorio, no favorable al desarrollo económico-social de esta provincia." Ibid., 27; my translation.

22. García Pleyán 1980, 28.

23. García Pleyán 1986, table 1.

24. See Mesa-Lago 1982, 1987, 1989.

25. Vega 1986.

26. Pérez-López 1995, 36.

27. Ibid., 37–38, citing Mesa-Lago 1969, 62.

28. See Portes and Bach 1985.

29. Ibid.

30. Levine 1993, 269.

31. M. García 1996, 14.

32. Salazar-Carrillo 1989.

33. Ritter 2004, 4.

34. García Reyes and López de Llergo 1997, table II.4.

35. "The stage of import substitution prevalent in Cuba at the beginning of this decade was predicated upon consumer and light goods industries, a profile outgrown by most Latin American economies by the early to mid-seventies. These characters clearly derive from a classical-neoclassical development strategy, one that in terms of political economy fits the figure of a colonially dominated country emphasizing static comparative advantage, the expansion of agriculture, and a gradualist approach to modernization." Salazar-Carrillo 1989, 230.

36. Hernández Castellón 1984, tables IV-32 and IV-33.

37. Ibid.

38. The idea of producing 10 million tons of sugar in 1970 was launched by the government. Despite the opposition it faced on professional and technical grounds, the government mobilized extraordinary human and material resources to accomplish such an ambitious goal. The goal was never reached and several economic activities were significantly slowed down as a result.

39. Rosenberg 1992.

40. Ibid.; see also Mesa-Lago 1989.

41. Rosenberg 1992; Mesa-Lago 1989.

42. It has been argued that the "parallel market" was created by the government in 1973 "to increase the variety of consumer products, reduce the substantial monetary surplus built up, and compete with a thriving black market" (Pérez-López 1995, 47). It was revitalized in the 1980s to exercise greater control of the distribution system. For further information on the evolution of the distribution systems through different "market" initiatives, at the different stages of the revolution, see Pérez-López 1995; Zimbalist 1989; Rosenberg 1992; and Mesa-Lago 1989.

43. For an analysis of this stage, its antecedents, and its implications, see Pérez-López 1995, Zimbalist 1989, Mesa-Lago 1989, Clark 1992, and García Reyes and López de Llergo 1997.

44. G. Fernández 2002, 20.

45. The data includes Pine Island, although it played a much more minor role compared to the city of Havana (Hernández Castellón 1984, table IV-18, 156).

46. Oficina Nacional de Estadísticas 2008, table II.21.

47. Rodríguez Chávez 1997, 22.

48. This trend and emigration to other countries (either with or without documents) is a topic that merits future attention.

49. Pedraza-Bailey 1985; Bach 1988, 2; Domínguez 1992.

50. For samples of earlier chronologies and others that have been built upon them, see University of Miami 1967, Boswell and Curtis 1984, and Pedraza-Bailey 1985.

51. "Generally, then, this has been a golden exile for the Cuban refugees. Seldom has a foreign group come to the United States so well prepared educationally and occupationally and seldom has this country received one so well" (Portes 1969, 508).

52. Bach 1988, 2. For analyses of the links between migration and foreign policy, see also Domínguez 1992; Pedraza-Bailey 1985; Colomer 1998.

53. The threat of hostile action by exile groups against regimes in their homelands has been a security concern for hosting states in several immigration contexts, U.S.-bound Cuban migration among them. See Zimmerman 1995.

54. University of Miami 1967.

55. Cuban Refugee Adjustment Act, Public Law 89–732, November 2, 1966, as amended in 1976.

56. Pedraza-Bailey 1985; Bach 1988; Roberts 1995; Colomer 1998.

57. Boswell and Curtis 1984; Portes and Bach 1985.

58. Author's computations based on historical series from different editions of the INS *Statistical Yearbook*.

59. Editora Política 1994b.

60. For an insightful analysis of this dialogue, the actors involved, and the state actions behind the scenes, see Torres 2004, 97.

61. For general figures on the Mariel exodus, see G. Fernández 2002. For figures on the number of children, see Silva 1985, 14.

62. Torres 2004.

63. For the forces shaping the Mariel exodus, see G. Fernández 2002, M. García 1996, Torres 2004, and Bach 1987.

64. G. Fernández 2002, table 2.

65. For a detailed analysis of these episodes, see M. García 1996, 76–77.

66. Ibid.; G. Fernández 2002, 74.

67. Bach 1987; Domínguez 1992; Colomer 1998.

68. Pedraza-Bailey 1985.

69. Dilla 1999.

70. Escaith 1999, 58; Economist Intelligence Unit 2001; Hegeman 1997.

71. United Nations, General Assembly 2004, 13.

72. Jatar-Hausmann 1999.

73. Rodríguez Chávez 1997, 70.

74. Cancio Isla 2004.

75. U.S. Coast Guard 2008.

76. For detailed analyses on policy issues related to the "rafter crisis" and the living conditions of the rafters at the detention camps, see Ackerman and Clark 1995, F. Guerra and Alvarez-Detrell 1997, Campisi 2005, Henken 2005, and Lisandro Pérez 1999. The author has also taken into consideration the experiences of Cubans who came on rafts at that time, based on informal conversations with some of them.

77. U.S. Coast Guard, "Alien Migrant Interdiction: Frequently Asked Questions," "feet wet/feet dry," http://www.uscg.mil/hq/g-o/g-opl/AMIO/amiofaq.htm.

78. U.S. Department of State 2004.

79. Ibid.

80. Foucault 2000, 221.

81. Ibid., 206.

82. Ibid., 217–18.

83. These data on the Cuban-origin population in Latin American countries were retrieved from CELADE 2006. They are based on the Cuban-origin population reported in the census of each country. Therefore, they underestimate the actual numbers because they do not refer to the most recent population and do not include the undocumented one. Nonetheless, they shed light on the main countries where Cubans tend to reside currently as well as on their sex ratios. (For various reasons, official data in general tend to underestimate the foreign-born population and international migration trends.)

84. CELADE 2006.

85. Agence France Presse 2006.

86. Discussions of these patterns and issues related to migration from the Caribbean societies to their former metropolitan areas in Europe can be found in Cervantes-Rodríguez, Grosfoguel, and Mielants 2009.

87. Dirección General del Instituto Español de Emigración 1987; Ministerio del Interior 1992, 1996; Ministerio de Trabajo y Asuntos Sociales 2000, 2001.

88. Dirección General del Instituto Español de Emigración 1987; Ministerio del Interior 1992, 1996; Ministerio de Trabajo y Asuntos Sociales 2000, 2001.

89. For the Madrid figures, see Comunidad de Madrid 2007, 82. For Cubans in Spain, see Secretaría de Estado de Inmigración y Emigración 2007, 4. Alternative sources indicate a larger number of Cubans in Spain, which might be due to differing methodologies.

90. The evidence about qualitative aspects of the incorporation of Cuban migrants in the city of Barcelona discussed in this section is drawn from recorded interviews and informal conversations conducted by the author there between 2003 and 2005. See "Research Methods and Strategies" in Chapter 1.

91. Interview with immigration attorney, Barcelona, Summer 2005: "Los cubanos utilizan básicamente a la familia, hubo un miembro de la familia que consigue salir, ya sea por matrimonio—que evidentemente es el sistema más usado por los cubanos, el matrimonio. Alguien de su

familia se ha casado con un español, viene y a través de ese matrimonio, vienen los padres, o los hijos o los hermanos. Ese es el mecanismo"; my translation.

92. Ibid.

93. Ministerio de Trabajo y Seguridad Social 1991, table 2b (historical series 1980–1989), Spain; Ministerio de Trabajo y Asuntos Sociales 2000, 271.

94. Grosfoguel 1999a.

95. Ibid.; Croucher 1996.

96. For the case of Cubans in the United States, see Portes and Stepick 1993.

97. INFOPLACE 2007.

98. U.S. Coast Guard 2008.

99. Ibid.

100. Özden and Schiff 2006.

101. CELADE 2006.

102. Organization for Economic Cooperation and Development (OECD) Database on Immigrants and Expatriates, http://www.oecd.org/document/51/0,2340,en_2825_494553_34063091_1_1_1_1,00.html. The OECD comprises thirty countries, mostly European, but also Japan, Korea, Mexico, the United States, and Canada. The data on Cuba were processed by the author, omitting countries with very low levels of immigration from Cuba.

103. The OECD (ibid.) defines a low level of education as "less than upper secondary," medium as "upper secondary and post-secondary non-tertiary," and high as "academic" or "vocational" tertiary or "advanced research."

104. "Expatriates" in the report refers to people living outside their country of origin regardless of the length of their stay in other countries (see also United Nations 2005).

105. Portes and Walton 1981.

106. Oppenheimer 2005.

107. *New York Times* 2004.

108. "The realization that our place will be constructed in and by both countries does not deny the exile component of out reality" (Torres 2004, 198). For the conditions under which many Cuban artists and writers work in the island, see Ripoll 1989.

109. See Rathat and Xu 2008.

110. CEPAL 2007b.

111. The migration rates by subperiods may be underestimated. For example, a conservative estimate by the United Nations placed Cuba's and the Latin American and Caribbean net external migration rates at -2.9 and -1.5 per thousand, respectively, for 2000–2005, but CEPAL estimates for the same period indicate -2.3 and -1.2 per thousand, respectively. See United Nations, Department of Economic and Social Affairs, Population Division 2006.

112. The gross reproduction rate refers to the average number of daughters per woman. This indicator is one of the most refined ones when measuring fertility levels, for it eliminates the biases related to the age structure of a given population at different points in time or differences in the age structure between or among the populations that are being compared.

113. CEPAL 2007a, table 1.1.2.

114. The term "replacement migration" has been used in United Nations reports to refer to immigration as a mechanism to counterbalance population losses in countries with fertility rates that are below the replacement level (see United Nations, Department of Economic and Social Affairs 2000). The term is used for highly industrialized societies that have problems in reproducing their native workforce and would be experiencing net population losses as a result of low fertility levels and the aging of their population.

Chapter 6

1. U.S. Census Bureau 2006g.

2. U.S. Census Bureau 2006h.

3. U.S. Census Bureau 2006b.

4. U.S. Census Bureau 2006e.

5. Oficina Nacional de Estadísticas 2008, table II.5, http://www.one.cu/aec2006/anuariopdf 2006/capitulo2/II.5.pdf.

6. U.S. Census Bureau 2006f.

7. Portes and Stepick 1993, table 8.

8. U.S. Census Bureau 2006f.

9. U.S. Census Bureau 2006d.

10. U.S. Census Bureau 2005.

11. U.S. Department of Homeland Security 2006b, table 3.

12. A summary of socioeconomic characteristics of Cuban Americans and other Hispanic groups can be found in Mumford Report 2003.

13. Based on 2001 data from the U.S. Census Bureau cited in Miami–Dade County 2002, table 15.

14. For the social and economic characteristics of the Cuban ethnic enclave in Miami, see Portes and Bach 1985.

15. On Cuban American's political power in South Florida, see Portes and Stepick 1993.

16. See Light and Bonacich 1988.

17. For a detailed discussion of estimates and methodologies, see Pérez-López and Díaz-Briquets 2005.

18. Ritter and Rowe 2002, 8. See also Pérez Rodríguez 2003.

19. United Nations, International Fund for Agriculture and Development 2006.

20. Detailed discussions on low and high estimates can be found in Archibald and Rowe 2002 and Pérez-López and Díaz-Briquets 2005.

21. Oficina Nacional de Estadísticas 2008, table VI.2.

22. Ibid., table VI.4.

23. Castro 2007.

24. Vidal 2007.

25. Castro 2007. ["Somos conscientes igualmente que en medio de las extremas dificultades objetivas que enfrentamos, el salario aún es claramente insuficiente para satisfacer todas las necesidades, por lo que prácticamente dejó de cumplir su papel de asegurar el principio socialista de que cada cual aporte según su capacidad y reciba según su trabajo."]

26. Although Moneygram, another major remittance company headquartered in the United States, was allowed to send money to Cuba in the year 2000 through a Canadian partner, it has not offered service continuously.

27. For a discussion of estimates of the self-employed population, see Cervantes-Rodríguez 2008. For the official estimate for 2007, see Oficina Nacional de Estadísticas 2008, table 7.2.

28. Until recently, Cubans were not allowed to purchase cell phone connections; they had to ask friends and family members who visited the island to establish the connections for them (sometimes they paid a fee to Cubans with such contacts if they had visitors). The rules have changed; now Cubans can connect their lines directly through the state-owned communication company.

29. Cervantes-Rodríguez 2008.

30. For the definition of the "second economy," see Pérez-López 1995. Alternative analyses of the underground or second economy in Cuba are in Ritter 2004 and Roque n.d.

31. A *bicitaxi* is a two-person cart pulled by a bicycle, usually ridden by young men. The ride usually costs between fifteen and forty Cuban pesos depending on the distance and the weight of the items carried by the passenger.

32. Inter-American Development Bank 2006.

33. Ibid., introduction.

34. At the same time, it cost $11.99 to send the same amount to Jamaica; approximately $12.00 to El Salvador, Honduras, and Nicaragua; $14.99 to Mexico; and still only $15.00 to Argentina (two Western Union offices in Miami confirmed these rates by telephone on February 7, 2007). A regional report produced in 2006 documents that the costs of sending remittances to

Cuba have been consistently among the highest in Latin America and the Caribbean (see Orozco 2006).

35. Eckstein and Barberia 1992, 819.

36. Ong 1999.

37. U.S. Department of State 2004.

38. Ibid.

39. Ibid.

40. See, for example, Lisandro Pérez 1999.

41. See, for example, Forteaux 1999.

42. Portes 1984.

43. Polanyi 1944.

44. Haraway 2000.

45. Maurice Zeitlin (1966, 495) applied Rudolf Heberle's (1951) definition of "political generations"—"individuals of approximately the same age who have shared, at the same age, certain politically relevant experiences"—to the study of Cuban politics. Eckstein and Barberia 2002 and Torres 2004 offer fresh insights on how "the political generations" of Cuban Americans are influenced by their transnational experiences.

46. Portes and Bach 1985.

47. Ibid.

48. On the political and symbolic importance of Cubans for the United States in the midst of the Cold War, see Pedraza-Bailey 1985 and Grosfoguel 1995. For the role of Cuban Americans in shaping U.S. policy toward Cuba, see D. Fernández 1987 and Torres 2004.

49. For the factors leading to form of identities, see Pedraza-Bailey 1985; Portes and Stepick 1993; Torres 2004.

50. K. Miller (1990, 124) refers to "the ultimate synthesis" of "a good Irish American" as including being "a good democrat, a practicing Catholic, a good family man or devoted wife and mother, in most cases a loyal union member, and nearly always at least a passive supporter of Ireland's sacred cause."

51. Although the ethnic enclave argument has shed light on important social and economic aspects of Cubans' incorporation into the U.S. labor market, some authors have warned that it is an inadequate when conceived of as the only form of incorporation or even the prevailing one. For example, Guillermo Grenier notes that by the early 1990s, even though no more than 5 percent of working Cuban Americans in the Greater Miami area were employed in the enclave economy, scholarly works dealing with the economic incorporation of the group would typically refer almost exclusively to the ethnic enclave while neglecting the migrants' incorporation outside the enclave and even their participation in the labor movement. See Grenier 1992 and Grenier and Stepick 1992; see also Croucher 1996.

52. See Pierre Bourdieu's 1978 essay, "Sur le pouvoir symbolique," in Bourdieu 2001.

53. Castells 1999, 208.

54. See Torres 2004.

55. Grosser 1996.

56. See Croucher 1996; Grosfoguel 1999a; Skop 2001; Ojito 2000; and Sporn 2000.

57. Basch et al. 2000, 65.

58. Gilroy 1999b, 10.

59. Torres 2004.

60. Ibid.; Eckstein and Barberia 2002.

61. Eckstein and Barberia 2002, 800; see also Torres 2004.

62. Croucher 1996; Grosfoguel 1999a; Torres 2004; Skop 2001; Eckstein and Barberia 2002.

63. For the compatibility and tensions between the exile identity and transnational strategies, see Torres 2004.

64. Lowe 2005.

65. National Endowment for Democracy 2005.

66. "One particularly lucrative State Department contract was awarded [under the Reagan administration] to the Cuban American National Foundation. Under this 1.7 million deal CANF

would establish a program for Cubans held in third countries to be relocated to the United States. CANF would screen the applications, make a recommendation to the Immigration and Naturalization Service on whether or not to issue a visa, relocate the exile, and provide basic services during the period of transition. From this program other émigré businesses received subcontracts to provide health care and employment counseling to the new arrivals" (Torres 2004, 122). This program was celebrated mainly as a program that allowed many Cubans to reunite with their relatives in the United States. It also had some important political undercurrents attached to it, namely, the expansion of the political base of CANF in Miami and even Cuba, since the program would be widely known among dissident groups on the island (Torres 2004; see also Portes and Stepick 1993).

67. USAID 2005.

68. *Miami Herald* 2006.

69. Informal conversation among friends.

70. Ibid.

71. For a collection of papers on this topic, see D. Fernández 2005.

72. For a discussion of the role and types of nongovernmental organizations in Cuba, see Espinosa 1999.

73. For more information, visit http://www.seap.cult.cu/.

74. U.S. Department of State 2007.

75. National Council of Churches n.d.

76. Ibid.

77. Mahler and Hansing 2005.

78. Valanti 2001.

Conclusion

1. Wallerstein 1974; see also Sassen-Koob 1980.

2. Braudel 1980; see also Wallerstein 1988, 1993; Arrighi 1999.

3. Moreno Fraginals (2001) forcefully argues that the United States managed to force Cuba into exporting less value-added sugar to the refineries of the United States. This process of "industrial downgrading" would be followed by a series of mechanisms that reinforced U.S. control over production in Cuba, such as direct investments and the signing of highly protectionist commercial treaties, which some Cuban historians tend to depict as a cornerstone in the establishment of "the main characteristics of the Cuban economy during the republican stage," including dependence on the U.S. sugar market, mono-exporting, and heavy dependence on the imports of manufactures (García Alvarez 1990, 21).

4. See Chapter 2 for a comprehensive discussion.

5. See Casasús 1953, Rivero Muñiz 1976, Poyo 1989 and 1991, Pérez 1995, and Casanovas Codina 1999, among other authors discussed in Chapters 2 and 3.

6. For the case of Cuba specifically, see López Segrera 1973 and 1985, de la Riva 1975, Moreno Fraginals 2001, and Guerra and Pulpeiro 1976, among other authors discussed in Chapters 2 and 3. Other works that systematically include other cases in the Caribbean allow us to see the link of the Cuban case with regional trends more clearly (e.g., Báez Evertsz 1986 and Bonham 1992).

7. For works that shed light on the issue of historical continuity, see, for example, López Segrera 1973 and de la Riva 1975.

8. Arrighi 1999.

9. For the role of Spanish entrepreneurs as both facilitators and competitors in relation to U.S. companies in Cuba, and the periods and industries involved, see García Alvarez 1990. For additional insights on issues pertaining to the transfer of labor and entrepreneurship at that time, see García and Zanetti 1976, Guerra and Pulpeiro 1976, Louis Pérez 1983 and 1999, and García Rodríguez 2006.

10. Louis Pérez 1983 and 1999.

11. Marx 1974; see Chapter 1.

12. Bartky 1982; Slagter 1982.

13. García Alvarez (1990, table 2) estimates that the total number of the Spanish-origin population in Cuba (immigrants and second-generation Spaniards) represented 14 percent of Cuba's total population in 1919.

14. Abraham and Schendel (2005) argue that the "seeing like a state" bias permeates the use and re-creation of constructs that hinder our ability to see the nuances of illegality and even the involvement of the state in practices that are officially declared as illegal. In the case of international migration, it also hinders our ability to see beyond what hegemonic discourses define as the fundamental aspects of the process as a way to justify policy interventions. Such aspects can be (and often are) relevant. The recognition that some aspects are important should not lead us to deny the importance of other aspects for certain groups the hegemonic fractions claim to represent. The neglect by political leaders of the migrants' need to support their families on the island and have regular personal contacts with them, in times in which other forms of exchange are encouraged, and their neglect of the negative effects that strict regulations on remittances have on households and Cuban society in general can only be justified beyond the state apparatus when the "seeing like a state" bias prevails.

REFERENCES

Abdala, Oscar Luís. 2003. *Los chinos en el oriente cubano*. Santiago de Cuba: Ediciones Santiago.

Ackerman, Holly, and Juan M. Clark. 1995. *The Cuban Balseros: Voyage of Uncertainty*. Miami: Cuban American National Council.

Agence France-Presse. 2006. "Misiones médicas enfrentan oposición." May 28 (Havana).

Aguilera Rojas, Eladio. 1909. "Francisco Vicente Aguilera y la revolución cubana de 1868." Havana. Reprinted in *Revista Cubana* 1, no. 1 (January–July 1968): 171–74.

Alarcón, Norma, Caren Kaplan, and Minoo Moallen. 1999. "Introduction: Between Woman and Nation." In *Between Woman and Nation: Nationalisms, Transnational Feminisms, and the State*, ed. Norma Alarcón and Minoo Moallen, 1–16. Durham: Duke University Press.

Alfonso, Pablo. 1998. "Fundaciones dan millones para levantar el embargo." *El Nuevo Herald*, July 6.

Alonso, Gladys, and Ernesto Chávez Alvarez, eds. 1978. *Memorias del censo de 1931*. Havana: Editorial Ciencias Sociales.

Alvarez Estévez, Rolando. 1988. *Azùcar e inmigración, 1900–1940*. Havana: Editorial Ciencias Sociales.

———. 2001. *Huellas francesas en el occidente de Cuba, siglos XVI–XIX*. Havana: Editorial José Martí.

Alvarez Estévez, Rolando, and Marta Guzmán Pascual. 2002. *Japoneses en Cuba*. Havana: Fundación Fernando Ortiz.

———. 2004. *Alemanes en Cuba: Siglos XVII al XIX*. Havana: Editorial Ciencias Sociales.

Amaro, Nelson. 1989. "Mass and Class in the Origins of the Cuban Revolution." In *Cuban Communism*, 6th ed., ed. Irving Louis Horowitz, 13–36. New Brunswick, N.J.: Transaction Publishers.

Amin, Samir. 1974. *Modern Migrations in West Africa*. New York: Oxford University Press.

Aranda, Sergio. 1980. *La revolución agraria en Cuba*. Mexico: Siglo Veintiuno Editores.

Arnao, Juan. 1877. *Páginas de la historia*. New York. Reprinted in *Revista Cubana* 1, no. 1 (January–July 1968): 168–69.

Arrighi, Giovanni. 1999. *The Long Twentieth Century: Money, Power, and the Origins of Our Times*. London: Verso.

Ashley, Richard. 1986. "The Poverty of Neorealism." In *Neorealism and Its Critics*, ed. Robert Keohane, 204–54. New York: Columbia University Press.

Avni, Haim. 1996. "Postwar Latin American Jewry: An Agenda for the Study of the Last Five Decades." In *The Jewish Diaspora in Latin America*, ed. Lois Baer Barr, 13–14. New York: Garland Publishing.

Azcona, José Manuel. 1992. "La participación vasca en la empresa colonial y migratoria americana (1492–1992)." In *Historia general de la emigración española a Iberoamérica*, ed. Pepa Vega, Pedro A. Vives, and Jesús Oyamburu, 469–99. Madrid: Closas-Orcoyen.

Bach, Robert. 1987. "The Cuban Exodus: Political and Economic Motivations." In *The Caribbean Exodus*, ed. Barry B. Levine, 106–30. New York: Praeger.

———. 1988. "Migration as an Issue in U.S.-Cuban Relations." Occasional Paper Series, The Central American and Caribbean Program, School of Advanced International Studies, Johns Hopkins University, March 1988.

Báez Evertsz, Franc. 1986. *La formación del sistema agroexportador en el Caribe: República Dominicana-Cuba, 1515–1898.* Santo Domingo: Editora Universitaria, UASD.

Bahamonde, Angel. 1992. "Los dos lados de la migración transoceánica." In *Historia general de la emigración española a Iberoamérica*, ed. Pepa Vega, Pedro A. Vives, and Jesús Oyamburu, 93–134. Madrid: Closas-Orcoyen.

Bahamonde, Angel, and José Cayuela. 1992. *Hacer las Américas: Las elites coloniales españolas en el siglo XIX.* Madrid: Alianza Editorial.

Bahar, Ruth, ed. 1995. *Bridges to Cuba, Puentes a Cuba.* Ann Arbor, MI: The University of Michigan Press.

Baltar Rodríguez, José. 1997. *Los chinos de Cuba: Apuntes etnográficos.* Havana: Colección Fuente Viva.

Barkan, Elliott R. 2004. "America in the Hand: Transnational and Translocal Immigrant Experiences in the American West." *Western Historical Quarterly* 35, no. 3 (Autumn): 331–54.

Bartky, Sandra. 1982. "Narcissism, Femininity and Alienation." *Social Theory and Practice* 8:127–143.

Barrett, John. 1920. *Argentine Republic: General Descriptive Data.* Washington, D.C.: Pan American Union.

Basch, Linda, Nina Glick Schiller, and Cristina Szanton Blanc. 2000. *Nations Unbound: Transnational Projects, Postcolonial Predicaments, and Deterritorialized Nation-States.* Langhorne, Pa.: Gordon and Breach. [Orig. pub. 1994.]

Bastos de Avila, Fernando. 1964. *Immigration in Latin America: A Study.* Washington, D.C.: Pan American Union.

Bejarano, Margalit. 1993. "La inmigración a Cuba y la política migratoria de los EE.UU. (1902–1933)." *Estudios Interdisciplinarios de América Latina y el Caribe* (Universidad Hebrea de Jerusalén) 4, no. 2 (Julio–Diciembre). http://www.tau.ac.il/eial/IV_2/bejarano.htm.

———. 1996. *La comunidad hebrea de Cuba: La memoria y la historia.* Jerusalem: Universidad Hebrea.

Benigni Lauder, Loredana. 2002. "Sociedades italianas en Cuba." In *Emigrazione e presenza italiana in Cuba*, ed. Domenico Capolongo, 1:79–105. Roccarainola, Italy: Circolo Culturale B.G. Duns Scoto.

Bergard, Laird W. 1989. "The Economic Viability of Sugar Production Based on Slave Labor in Cuba, 1859–1878." *Latin American Research Review* 24, no. 1: 95–113.

Black, George. 1988. *The Good Neighbor: How the United States Wrote the History of Central America and the Caribbean.* New York: Pantheon Books.

Boswell, Thomas, and James R. Curtis. 1984. *The Cuban-American Experience: Culture, Images, and Perspectives.* New Jersey: Rowman and Allanheld.

Boswell, Thomas D., and Emily Skop. 1995. *Hispanic National Groups in Metropolitan Miami.* Miami: Cuban American National Council.

Boulding, Elise. 1991. "The Old and New Transnationalism: An Evolutionary Perspective." *Human Relations* 44, no. 8: 789–806.

Bourdieu, Pierre. 2001. *Langage et pouvoir symbolique.* Paris: Éditions Fayard.

Braudel, Fernand. 1972–73. *The Mediterranean and the Mediterranean World in the Age of Philip II.* 2 vols. New York: Harper and Row, 1972–73.

————. 1980. *On History.* Chicago: University of Chicago Press.

Brenner, Philip, Patrick J. Haney, and Walter Vanderbush. 2002. "The Confluence of Domestic and International Interests: U.S. Policy Toward Cuba, 1998–2001." *International Studies Perspectives* 3, no. 2: 192–208.

Briggs, Laura. 2002. *Reproducing Empires: Race, Sex, Science and U.S. Imperialism in Puerto Rico.* Berkeley and Los Angeles: University of California Press.

Brooke, John R. 1899. "Civil Report of Major General John R. Brooke, Governor of Cuba, 1899." New York Public Library Archives.

Bureau of Inter-American Affairs. Office of the Coordinator for Cuban Affairs. 1998. "Implementing Procedures for Family Remittances to Cuba." May 13. http://www.state.gov/www/regions/wha/fs_980513_charterflights.html.

Bureau of the American Republics. n.d. *Laws of the American Republics Relating to Immigration and the Sale of Public Lands.* Bulletin 53. Washington, D.C.: U.S. Government Printing Office.

Butel, Paul. 1993. "Relations commerciales entre la France et Cuba sous la Restauration." In *Proceedings of the International Colloquium "Les Français dans l'Orient Cubain."* Bordeaux: Maison des Pays Ibériques.

Cabrera Deniz, Gregorio. 1996. *Canarios en Cuba: un capítulo en la historia del archipiélago (1875–1931).* Las Palmas de Gran Canaria: Ediciones del Cabildo Insular de la Gran Canaria.

Cagiao, Pilar. 1992. "Cinco siglos de emigración gallega a América." In *Historia general de la emigración española a Iberoamérica,* ed. Pepa Vega, Pedro A. Vives, and Jesús Oyamburu, 293–316, Madrid: Closas-Orcoyen.

Campisi, Elizabeth. 2005. "Guantanamo: Safe Heaven or Traumatic Interlude?" *Latino Studies* 3, no. 3: 375–92.

Cancio Isla, Wilfredo. 2004. "Inician viajes con 'pasaporte habilitado.'" *El Nuevo Herald,* June 2.

Carranza, Julio, Luis Gutiérrez, and Pedro Monreal. 1999. "Le petite et moyenne entreprise à Cuba: Le point de vue de trois économistes cubains." *Cahiers des Amériques Latines* 31/32: 103–20.

Carreras, Julio. 1985. *Historia del estado y el derecho en Cuba.* Havana: Editorial Ciencias Sociales.

Carrillo, Justo. 1994. *Cuba 1933: Students, Yankees, and Soldiers.* New Brunswick, N.J.: Transaction Publishers.

Casanovas Codina, Joan. 1999. "La nación, la independencia y las clases." *Encuentro de la Cultura Cubana* (15): 177–86.

Casasús, Juan. 1953. *La emigración cubana y la independencia de la patria.* Havana: Editorial Lex.

Casaús, Marta E. 1992. "Planteamiento general del contexto socioeconómico: España e Iberoamérica." In *Historia general de la emigración española a Iberoamérica,* ed. Pepa Vega, Pedro A. Vives, and Jesús Oyamburu, 151–76. Madrid: Closas-Orcoyen.

Castañeda, Jorge G. 1993. *Utopia Unarmed: The Latin American Left After the Cold War.* New York: Knopf.

Castellano Gil, José. 1990. *Quintas, prófugos y emigración: La Laguna (1886–1935).* Santa Cruz de Tenerife, Canary Islands: Centro de la Cultura Popular Canaria.

Castells, Manuel. 1999. *The Power of Identity.* Oxford: Blackwell Publishers.

————. 2000. *The Rise of the Network Society.* Oxford: Blackwell Publishers.

Castro, Raúl. 2007. "Trabajar con sentido crítico y creador, sin anquilosamientos ni esquematismos." Speech delivered on July 26. *Granma* 11, no. 207 (July 27).

CEE. See Comité Estatal de Estadísticas de la Republica de Cuba.

CELADE (Centro Latinoamericano de Demografía). 1996. *Statistics on population.* http://www.cepal.org/1996.

————. 2006. *Banco de datos en línea de investigación de la migración internacional en América Latina y el Caribe.* Proyecto IMILA. http://www.eclac.cl/Celade/proyec tos/migracion/IMILA00e.html.

CEPAL. 1997. *Balance preliminar de la economía de América Latina y El Caribe, 1997.* Santiago de Chile: Comisión Economómica para América Latina.

————. 2007a. *Anuario Estadístico para América Latina y el Caribe, 2007: Estadísticas Sociales.* http://www.eclac.cl/publicaciones/xml/6/32606/LCG2356B_1.pdf.

————. 2007b. "Demographic Trends in Latin America." *América Latina y el Caribe: Observatorio demográfico,* no. 3 (April). http://www.eclac.org/publicaciones/ xml/0/32650/OD-3-Demographic.pdf.

Cepero Bonilla, Raúl. 1948. *Azúcar y abolición. Apuntes para una historia crítica del abolicionismo.* Havana: Editorial Cenit.

Cerutti, Mario. 1995. *Empresarios españoles y sociedad capitalista en México (1840–1920).* Gijón, Spain: Fundación Archivo de Indianos.

Cervantes-Rodríguez, Ana Margarita. 2002. "Transnationalism Power and Hegemony: A Review of Alternative Perspectives and Their Implications for World-Systems Analysis." In *The Modern/Colonial/Capitalist System in the Twentieth Century,* ed. Ramón Grosfoguel and Margarita Cervantes-Rodríguez, 47–78. Westport, Conn.: Greenwood Press.

————. 2003. "Atlantic Countercurrents: Spanish Migration and Transnationalism, Empirical Evidence and Theoretical Insights." Paper presented at the International Conference of the Immigration and Ethnic History Society, "Transcending Borders: Migration, Ethnicity, and Incorporation in an Age of Globalism," New York City.

————. 2005. "El transnacionalismo entre España y las Américas durante finales del siglo XIX y principios del siglo XX: La conexión cubana." In *Cuba de Colonia a Republica,* ed. Martín Rodrigo. Madrid: Biblioteca Nueva.

————. 2008. "The Informal Economy in Cuba." Unpublished paper discussed at the Center for Migration and Development, Princeton University, November, 2008.

Cervantes-Rodríguez, Ana Margarita, Ramón Grosfoguel, and Eric Mielants, eds. 2009. *Caribbean Migration to the United States and Western Europe: Essays on Incorporation, Identity, and Citizenship.* Philadelphia: Temple University Press.

Cervantes-Rodríguez, Ana Margarita, and Amy Lutz. 2003. "Coloniality of Power, Immigration and the English-Spanish Asymmetry in the United States." *Nepantla* 4, no. 3: 523–60.

Chin Ku-Sup, Yoon In Jin, and David Smith. 1996. "Immigrant Small Business and International Economic Linkage: A Case of the Korean Wig Business in Los Angeles, 1968–1977." *International Migration Review* 30, no. 2: 485–509.

Clark, Juan M. 1992. *Cuba, mito y realidad: Testimonios de un pueblo.* Caracas: Saeta Ediciones.

Collazo Pérez, Enrique. 2002. "Empresas asturianas en Cuba (1840–1920)." *Revista de Indias* 62, no. 225: 535–58.

Colomer, Josep. 1998. "Salida, voz y hostilidad en Cuba." *América Latina, Hoy,* no. 18: 1–41.

Comité Estatal de Estadísticas de la Republica de Cuba (CEE). 1976. *Boletín Estadístico.* Havana: CEE.

———. Instituto de Demografía y Censos. 1983. *Censo de población y viviendas, 1981: Evolución de la urbanización en Cuba, 1907–1981.* Havana: CEE.

———. Oficina Nacional del Censo. 1984. *Censo de población y viviendas, 1981, República de Cuba, Vol. 16.* Havana: Combinado Poligráfico Alfredo López.

———. 1987. *Principales aspectos demográficos de la población de Cuba en el año 1986.* Havana: CEE.

Comunidad de Madrid. 2007. Observatorio de Inmigración. "Informe demográfico de la población extranjera en la Comunidad de Madrid, Abril 2007." http://www.madrid.org/cs/Satellite?blobtable = MungoBlobs&blobcol = urldata&blobkey = id&blobwhere = 1181238216525&ssbinary = true&blobheader = application %2Fpdf.

Corbitt, Duvon Clough. 1971. *A Study of the Chinese in Cuba, 1847–1947.* Wilmore, Kent.: Asbury College.

Córdova, Efrén. 1995. *Clase trabajadora y movimiento sindical en Cuba, 1819–1959.* Vol. 1. Miami: Ediciones Universal.

———. 2001. *El trabajo forzoso en Cuba: Un recorrido amargo de la historia.* Miami: Ediciones Universal.

Costa, Lluís. 2004. "La difícil construcció d'un projecte periodistic catalá a Cuba." Paper presented at the international colloquium "Cuba: De Colonia a República," Barcelona, Universitat Pompeu Fabra, June 16–17.

Cox, Robert. 1981. "Labor and Transnational Relations." In *Transnational Relations in World Politics,* ed. Robert Keohane and Joseph Nye, 554–84. Cambridge: Harvard University Press.

———. 1986. "Social Forces, States, and World Orders: Beyond International Relations Theory." In *Neorealism and Its Critics,* ed. Robert Keohane, 204–51. Columbia University Press.

Croucher, Sheila. 1996. "The Success of the Cuban Success Story: Ethnicity, Power, and Politics." *Identities* 2, no. 4: 351–84.

Cuban Economic Research Project. 1993. *Labor Conditions in Communist Cuba.* Miami Beach: University of Miami Press.

Curtin, Philip. 1969. *The Atlantic Slave Trade: A Census.* Madison: University of Wisconsin Press.

Davie, Maurice R. 1936. *World Immigration: With Special Reference to the United States.* New York: Macmillan.

Deere, Carmen Diana. 1984. "Agrarian Reform and the Peasantry in the Transition to Socialism in the Third World." Working Paper 31, The Helen Kellogg Institute for International Studies, December.

———. 1990. *Household and Class Relations: Peasants and Landlords in Northern Peru.* Berkeley and Los Angeles: University of California Press.

Deive, Carlos Esteban. 1989. *Las emigraciones de dominicanos a Cuba (1795–1808).* Santo Domingo: Fundación Cultural Dominicana.

de la Fuente, Alejandro. 1996. "Negros y electores: Desigualdad y políticas raciales en Cuba (1900–1930)." In *La nación soñada: Cuba, Puerto Rico y Filipinas ante el 98,* ed. Consuelo Naranjo, Miguel Puig, and Luis Miguel García, 161–91. Madrid: Doce Calles.

———. 2008. *Havana and the Atlantic in the Sixteenth Century.* Chapel Hill: University of North Carolina Press.

Del Aguila, Juan M. 1994. "The Party, the Fourth Congress, and the Process." In *Cuba at a Crossroads: Politics and Economics After the Fourth Party Congress,* ed. Jorge Pérez-López. Gainesville: University Press of Florida.

De la Sagra, Ramón. 1831. *Historia Económico-política y estadística de la isla de Cuba.* Havana: Imprenta de las Viudas de Arazoza y Soler.

Del Monte y Aponte, Domingo. 1929. "Estado de la población blanca y de color de la isla de Cuba." In *Escritos de Domingo del Monte y Aponte (tomo I).* Colección Libros Cubanos 12. Havana: Cultural S.A.

Department of State. "Cuba: Issues in the News" (November 1999).

Deschamps Chapeaux, Pedro, and Juan Pérez de la Riva. 1974. *Contribución a la historia de la gente sin historia.* Havana: Editorial Ciencias Sociales.

D'Estefano Pisani, Miguel Antonio. 1988. *Cuba en lo internacional.* Havana: Editorial Ciencias Sociales.

Díaz-Alejandro, Carlos. 1970. *Essays on the Economic History of the Argentine Republic.* New Haven: Yale University Press.

Díaz-Briquets, Sergio, and Lisandro Pérez. 1981. "The Demography of the Revolution." Population Reference Bureau, vol., 36, no1. (April 1981): 1–41.

Díaz-Briquets, Sergio, and Jorge Pérez-López. 1994. "Cuba's Labor Adjustment Policies During the Special Period." In *Cuba at a Crossroads: Politics and Economics After the Fourth Party Congress,* ed. Jorge Pérez-López. Gainesville: University Press of Florida.

———. 1997. "Refugee Remittances: Conceptual Issues and the Cuban and Nicaraguan Experiences." *International Migration Review* 31, no. 2: 411–37.

———. 1998. "The Determinants of Hispanic Remittances: An Exploration Using U.S. Census Data." *Hispanic Journal of Behavioral Sciences* 20, no. 3: 320–48.

Dilla, Heroldo. 1999. "Camarades et investisseurs: Cuba, une transition incertaine." *Cahiers des Amériques Latines* 31/32: 83–102.

Dirección General de Expansión Comercial. 1966. *Estudio económico de Cuba.* Madrid: Ministerio de Comercio.

Dirección General del Censo. República de Cuba. 1945. *Censo de 1943.* Havana: P. Fernández y Compañía.

Dirección General del Instituto Español de Emigración. 1987. *Agenda 1987.* Madrid: Dirección General del Instituto Español de Emigración.

Documentos Políticos. 1966. *Política internacional de la revolución cubana.* Vol. 1. Havana: Editora Política.

Dodd, Nigel. 1994. *The Sociology of Money: Economics, Reason, and Contemporary Society.* Cambridge: Polity Press.

Domínguez, Jorge I. 1992. "Cooperating with the Enemy? U.S. Immigration Policies Toward Cuba." In *Western Hemisphere Immigration and United States Foreign Policy,* ed. Christopher Mitchell. University Park: Pennsylvania State University Press.

Duany, Jorge. 1997. "From the Cuban Ajiaco to the Cuban-American Hyphen: Changing Discourses on National Identity on the Island and in the Diaspora." *Cuban Studies Association Occasional Paper Series* (University of Miami) 2, no. 8 (October).

Dumoulin, John. 1980. *Azúcar y lucha de clases, 1917.* Havana: Editorial Ciencias Sociales.

Dunlevy, James, and William Hutchinson. 1999. "The Impact of Immigration on American Import Trade in the Late Nineteenth and Early Twentieth Centuries." *Journal of Economic History* 59:1043–62.

Dupuy, Alex. 1976. "Spanish Colonialism and the Origins of Underdevelopment in Haiti." *Latin American Perspectives* 2:5–29.

Durán, José Antonio. 1992. "Repatriación, emigración temporal y retornos de la larga duración." In *Historia general de la emigración española a Iberoamérica*, ed. Pepa Vega, Pedro A. Vives, and Jesús Oyamburu, 410–25. Madrid: Closas-Orcoyen.

Eckstein, Susan, and Lorena Barberia. 2002. "Grounding Immigrant Generations in History: Cuban Americans and Their Transnational Ties." *International Migration Review* 3, no. 36: 799–837.

Economist Intelligence Unit. 2001. *Cuba, Country Profile 2001*. London. http://www.eiu.com/schedule.

Editora Política. 1994a. *Conferencia "La nación y la emigración" (abril 22, 23 y 24)*. Havana: Editora Política.

———. 1994b. *Diálogo del gobierno cubano y personas representativas de la comunidad cubana en el exterior (1978)*. Havana: Editora Política.

EFE. 2002. "Caixanova inaugura en Miami sede para América Latina." *Finanzas*. June 5. http://www.finanzas.com/id.3784495/noticias/noticia.htm.

El Mundo. 2001. "El BCH, un banco en permanente transición." *El Mundo* (Special Reports). http://www.elmundo.es/especiales/2001/08/economia/bsch/bch.html.

———. 2005. "La Quinta provincia Gallega." June 20.

Encinosa, Enrique. 1995. *Cuba en guerra: Historia de la oposición anticastrista, 1959–1993*. Miami: Endowment for Cuban American Studies.

Escaith, Hubert. 1999. "Cuba pendant la 'Période spéciale': Ajustement ou transition?" *Cahiers des Amériques Latines* 31/32: 55–82.

Espino, María Dolores. 1994. "Tourism in Cuba: A Development Strategy for the 1990s." In *Cuba at a Crossroads: Politics and Economics After the Fourth Party Congress*, ed. Jorge Pérez-López. Gainesville: University Press of Florida.

Espinosa, Juan Carlos. 1999. "Civil Society in Cuba: The Logic of Emergence in Comparative Perspective." Cuba in Transition 9 (Association for the Study of the Cuban Economy). http://lanic.utexas.edu/la/cb/cuba/asce/cuba9.

Farnós, Alfonso, and Sonia Catasús Cervera. 1976. "Las migraciones internacionales." In *La población de Cuba*, ed. CEDEM, 65–84. Havana: Centro de Estudios Demográficos.

Ferguson, Niall. 2003. *Empire: The Rise and Demise of the British World Order and the Lessons for Global Power*. London: Basic Books.

Fernández, Alejandro E. 1992. "Mutualismo y asociacionismo." In *Historia general de la emigración española a Iberoamérica*, ed. Pepa Vega, Pedro A. Vives, and Jesús Oyamburu, 331–57. Madrid: Closas-Orcoyen.

Fernández, Damián. 1987. "From Little Havana to Washington, D.C.: Cuban-Americans and U.S. Foreign Policy." In *Ethnic Groups and U.S. Foreign Policy*, ed. Mohammed E. Ahrari, 115–34. Westport, Conn.: Greenwood Press.

———, ed. 2005. *Cuba Transnational*. Gainesville: University Press of Florida.

Fernández, Gastón. 2002. *The Mariel Exodus: Twenty Years Later, a Study on the Politics of Stigma and a Research Bibliography*. Miami: Ediciones Universal.

Fernández, Susan. 2002. *Encumbered Cuba: Capital Markets and Revolt (1878–1895)*. Gainesville: University Press of Florida.

Fernández-Shaw, Carlos M. 1987. *Presencia española en los Estados Unidos*. Madrid: Instituto de Cooperación Iberoamericana, Ediciones de Cultura Hispánica.

Florida Crystals. 2001. *Florida Crystals International Directory of Company Histories*. Vol. 35. Detroit: St. James Press.

Foner, Philip S. 1978. *La guerra hispano-cubano-norteamericana y el surgimiento del imperialismo yanqui.* Vol. 1. Havana: Editorial Ciencias Sociales.

Forteaux, Michel. 1999. "La communauté cubaine des États-Unis: D' 'exilé' à 'immigré,' une nouvelle identité." *Cahiers des Amériques Latines* 31/32:197–210.

Foster, Peter. 1990. *Family Spirits: The Bacardi Saga.* The Braga-Rionda Collection. Toronto: MacFarlane Walter and Ross.

Foucault, Michel. 2000. "Governmentality." In *Michael Foucault: Power. Essential Works of Foucault 1954–1984,* ed. James D. Faubio and Paul Rabinow, 3:201–22. New York: The New Press. [Orig. pub. 1978.]

Fragomen, Austin T., Jr. 1997. "The Illegal Immigration Reform and Immigrant Responsibility Act of 1996: An Overview." *International Migration Review* 31, no. 2 (Summer): 438–60.

Franco, José Luciano. 1974. *Ensayos históricos.* Havana: Editorial Ciencias Sociales.

———. [1980] 1996. *El Comercio Clandestino de Esclavos.* Havana: Editorial Ciencias Sociales.

Franco, Mario. 1989. "An Analysis of the Black Market of Foreign Exchange in Computable General Equilibrium." Ph.D. diss., Department of Economics, University of Massachusetts.

Franco, Xiomara. 1982. *Proceso de concentración y urbanización de la población rural, 1970–1980.* Havana: JUCEPLAN.

Friedlaender, Heinrich. 1978. *Historia económica de Cuba.* Vol. 2. Havana: Editorial Ciencias Sociales.

Gabaccia, Donna. 2000. *Italy's Many Diasporas.* Seattle: University of Washington Press.

García, Alejandro, and Oscar Zanetti. 1976. "La Organización." In *United Fruit Company: Un caso de dominio imperialista en Cuba,* ed. Oscar Zanetti and Alejandro García. Havana: Editorial Ciencias Sociales.

García, María Cristina. 1996. *Havana-USA: Cuban Exiles and Cuban Americans in South Florida, 1959–1994.* Berkeley and Los Angeles: University of California Press.

García Alvarez, Alejandro. 1990. *La gran burguesía comercial en Cuba (1898–1921).* Havana: Editorial Ciencias Sociales.

García Díaz, Bernardo, and Sergio Guerra Vilaboy. 2002. "Introducción." In *La Habana/Veracruz Veracruz/La Habana, las dos orillas,* ed. Bernardo García Días and Sergio Guerra Vilaboy, 13–20. Mexico City: Universidad Veracruzana.

García González, Ivette. 1998. *La Habana: tiempo de conflictos.* Havana: Verde Olivo.

García López, José Ramón. 1992. *Las remesas de los emigrantes españoles en América, siglos xix y xx.* Gijón, Spain: Ediciones Jucar, Fundación Archivo de Indianos.

García Pleyán, Carlos. 1980. *La transformación de la estructura urbana en Cuba (1959–1975).* Havana: Instituto de Planificación Física (June).

———. 1986. *La transformación de la estructura de las ciudades principales en Cuba.* Extended summary of Ph.D. diss., Instituto de Planificación Física, Havana.

García Reyes, Miguel, and Guadalupe López de Llergo. 1997. *Cuba después de la era soviética.* Mexico City: El Colegio de México.

García Rodríguez, Mercedes. 2006. *Las industrias menores: Empresarios y empresas en Cuba (1880–1920).* Havana: Editorial de Ciencias Sociales.

Gay, Enrique, and Herminia Rodríguez. 1946. *A Statement of Cuban Law in Matters Affecting Business in Its Various Aspects and Activities.* Washington, D.C.: Interamerican Development Commission.

Gelabert-Navia, José A. 1996. "American Architects in Cuba: 1900–1930." *Journal of Decorative and Propaganda Arts* 22:132–49.

Gereffi, Gary, Miguel Korzeniewicz, and Roberto P. Korzeniewicz. 1994. "Introduction: Global Commodity Chains." In *Commodity Chains and Global Capitalism*, ed. Gary Gereffi and Miguel Korzeniewicz, 1–14. Westport, Conn.: Praeger Press.

Gibson, Campbell, and Kay Jung. 2006. "Historical Census Statistics on the Foreign-Born Population of the United States, 1850–2000." Working Paper 8, Population Division, Bureau of the Census, Washington D.C., February.

Gilroy, Paul. 1999. *The Black Atlantic: Modernity and Double Consciousness.* Cambridge: Harvard University Press.

Glick-Schiller, Nina. 1999. "Transmigrants and Nation-States: Something Old and Something New." In *The Handbook of Immigration: The American Experience*, ed. Charles Hirschman, Philips Kasinitz, and Josh DeWind, 94–119. New York: Russell Sage Foundation.

———. 2003. "The Centrality of Ethnography in the Study of Transnational Migration: Seeing the Wetland Instead of the Swamp." In *American Arrivals*, ed. Nancy Foner, 99–128. Santa Fe, N.Mex.: School of American Research.

———. 2005. "Transnational Social Fields and Imperialism: Bringing a Theory of Power to Transnational Studies." *Anthropological Theory* 5:439–61.

Glick-Schiller, Nina, and Georges Fouron. 1999. "Transnational Lives and National Identities: The Identity Politics of Haitian Immigrants." In *Transnationalism from Below*, ed. Michael P. Smith and Luis E. Guarnizo, 130–63. New Brunswick, N.J.: Transaction Publishers.

———. 2001a. "All in the Family: Gender, Transnational Migration, and the Nation-State." *Identities* 7, no. 4: 539–82.

———. 2001b. *Long-Distance Nationalism and the Search for Home.* Durham: Duke University Press.

González, Nelson H. 1978. "Las relaciones económicas Cuba-Estados Unidos, 1902–1958." *Economía y Desarrollo* 46 (March–April): 123–36.

González-Ripoll, María Dolores. 2004. "Desde Cuba, antes y después de Haití: Pragmatismo y dilación en el pensamiento de Francisco Arango sobre la esclavitud." In *El rumor de Haití en Cuba: temor, raza y rebeldía, 1789–1844*, ed. González-Ripoll, Consuelo Naranjo, Ada Ferrer, Gloria García y Josef Opatrný, 9–81, *El rumor de Haití en Cuba: Temor, Raza y Rebeldía, 1789–1844*, Madrid: CSIC.

Gott, Richard. 2004. *Cuba: A New History.* New Haven: Yale University Press.

Gould, David. 1995. "Immigrants Links to the Home Country: Empirical Implications for U.S. Bilateral Trade Flows." *Review of Economics and Statistics* 76, no. 2: 302–16.

Grasmuck, Sherri, and Patricia Pessar. 1991. *Between Two Islands: Dominican International Migration.* Berkeley and Los Angeles: University of California Press.

Greenbaum, Susan D. 2002. *More than Black: Afro-Cubans in Tampa.* Gainesville: University Press of Florida.

Grenier, Guillermo. 1992. "The Cuban-American Labor Movement in Dade County: An Emerging Immigrant Working Class." In *Miami Now: Immigration, Ethnicity, and Social Change*, ed. Guillermo Grenier and Alex Stepick, 33–159. Gainesville: University Press of Florida.

Grenier, Guillermo, and Alex Stepick. 1992. "Introduction." In *Miami Now: Immigration, Ethnicity, and Social Change*, ed. Guillermo Grenier and Alex Stepick, 1–17. Gainesville: University Press of Florida: 1992.

Grewal, Inderpal, and Caren Kaplan. 1994. *Scattered Hegemonies: Postmodernity and Transnational Feminist Practices*. Minneapolis: University of Minnesota Press.

Grosfoguel, Ramón. 1995. "Global Logics in the Caribbean City System: The Case of Miami." In *World Cities in a World System*, ed. Paul Knox and Peter Taylor, 156–70. Cambridge: Cambridge University Press.

———. 1999a. "Cultural Racism and Colonial Caribbean Migrants in the Core of the Capitalist World-Economy." *Review* 22, no. 4: 409–34.

———. 1999b. "Puerto Rican Labor Migration to the United States: Modes of Incorporation, Coloniality, and Identities." *Review* 22, no. 4: 505–24.

———. 2003. *Colonial Subjects: Puerto Ricans in a Global Perspective*. Berkeley: University of California Press.

Grosser, Alfred. 1996. *Les identités difficiles*. Paris: Presses de la Foundation Nationale de Sciences Politiques.

Guarnizo, Luis E. "The Economics of Transnational Living." *International Migration Review* 37, no. 3: 666–99.

Guarnizo, Luis E., and Michael P. Smith. 1999. "The Locations of Transnationalism." In *Transnationalism from Below*, ed. Michael P. Smith and Luis E. Guarnizo, 3–34. New Brunswick, N.J.: Transaction Publishers.

Guerra, Felicia, and Tamara Alvarez-Detrell. 1997. *Oral History of the Cuban Exodus of '94*. Colección Cuba y Sus Jueces. Miami: Ediciones Universal.

Guerra, Ramiro. 1964 [1928]. *Sugar and Society in the Caribbean: An Economic History of Cuban Agriculture*. New Haven: Yale University Press.

Guerra, Sergio, and Rosa Pulpeiro. 1976. "La región." In *United Fruit Company: Un caso de dominio imperialista en Cuba*, ed. Oscar Zanetti and Alejandro García. Havana: Editorial Ciencias Sociales.

Guiteras, Pedro José. 1927–28. *Historia de la isla de Cuba*. Vols. 1–3. Havana: Cultural.

Habel, Janette. 1999. "Cuba dix ans après la chute du mur de Berlin." *Cahiers des Amériques Latines* 31/32:35–53.

Hall, Peter. *The World Cities*. 1968. New York: McGraw-Hill Book Company, World University Library.

Haraway, Donna. 2000. *How Like a Leaf: An Interview with Thyrza Nichols Goodeve*. Routledge: New York.

Harper, Paula. 1996. "Cuba Connections: Key West–Tampa–Miami, 1870 to 1945." *Journal of Decorative and Propaganda Arts* 22:278–91.

Harvey, David. 1996 [1990]. *The Condition of Postmodernity: An Inquiry into the Origins of Cultural Change*. Cambridge, Mass.: Blackwell.

Heberle, Rudolf. 1951. *Social Movements*, New York: Appleton-Century Crofts.

Hegeman, Roxana. 1997. "Exiles Prop Up Cuban Economy by Sending Money to Families." Associated Press.

Helly, Denise. 1979. *Idéologie et ethnicité: Les Chinois Macao à Cuba*. Montreal: Les Presses de l'Université de Montreal.

Henken, Ted. 2005. "Balseros, Boteros, and El Bombo: Post-1994 Cuban Immigration to the United States and the Persistence of Special Treatment." *Latino Studies* 3, no. 3: 393–416.

Hernández, José Manuel. 1998. "The Politics of Wishful Thinking: Precedents of the Bay of Pigs." *Cuban Studies Association* (University of Miami) 3, no. 3 (April).

Hernández Aguilar, Prócoro. 1992. "Quinientos años de historia catalana en América." In *Historia general de la emigración española a Iberoamérica*, ed. Pepa Vega, Pedro A. Vives, and Jesús Oyamburu, 237–60. Madrid: Closas-Orcoyen.

Hernández Castellón, Raúl. 1984. *El proceso de la revolución demográfica en Cuba.* Havana: Centro de Estudios Demográficos.

Hernández-Catá, Ernesto. 2001. "The Fall and Recovery of the Cuban Economy in the 1990s: Mirage or Reality?" Working Paper 1/48, International Monetary Fund.

Hernández García, Julio. 1992. "Panorámica de la emigración a Iberoamérica de las Islas Canarias, siglos XVI–XIX." In *Historia general de la emigración española a Iberoamérica,* ed. Pepa Vega, Pedro A. Vives, and Jesús Oyamburu, 115–45. Madrid: Closas-Orcoyen.

Herrera Jerez, Miriam, and Mario Carillo Santana. 2003. *Identidades, espacios y jerarquías de los chinos en La Habana republicana (1902–1958).* Havana: CIDCC.

Hirschman, Albert. 1970. *Exit, Voice, and Loyalty: Responses to Decline in Firms, Organizations, and States.* Cambridge: Harvard University Press.

Homer-Dixon, Thomas. 1995. "The Ingenuity Gap: Can Poor Countries Adapt to Resource Scarcity?" *Population and Development Review* 21, no. 3 (September): 587–612.

Hopkins, Terence K., and Immanuel Wallerstein. 1986. "Commodity Chains in the World-Economy Prior to 1800." *Review* 10, no. 1: 157–70.

Hughes, Jeffrey. 1986. "Historical Comparability." In *Dominant Powers and Subordinate States: The United States in Latin America and the Soviet Union in Eastern Europe,* ed. Jan Triska, 336–56. Durham: Duke University Press.

Humboldt, Alejandro de. 1930. *Ensayo político sobre la isla de Cuba.* Colección Libros Cubanos 17. Havana: Cultural.

INFOPLACE. 2007. "Countries of Birth of the Foreign-Born Population, 1850–2000." http://www.infoplease.com/ipa/A0900547.html.

INS. *See* U.S. Department of Justice, Immigration and Naturalization Service.

Inter-American Development Bank. 2004. *Sending Money Home: Remittance to Latin America and the Caribbean.* http://www.iadb.org/mif/v2/files/StudyPE2004eng.pdf.

Inter-American Development Bank, Multilateral Development Fund. 2006. *Promoting Financial Democracy.* Washington, D.C. http://www.iadb.org/am/2006/doc/StatisticalComparisons.pdf.

Jatar-Hausmann, Ana Julia. 1999. *The Cuban Way: Capitalism, Communism, and Confrontation.* West Hartford, Conn.: Kumarian Press.

Jenks, L. H. 1970. *Our Cuban Colony: A Study in Sugar.* New York: Arno Press.

Jiménez, Guillermo. 2000. *Las empresas de Cuba.* Miami: Ediciones Universal, 2000.

Jiménez Pastrana, Juan. 1963. *Los chinos en la liberación cubana.* Havana: Instituto de Historia.

Joppke, Christian. 1999. *Immigration and the Nation-State: The United States, Germany, and Great Britain.* Oxford: Oxford University Press.

Jorge, Antonio. 1989. "Ideology, Planning, Efficiency, and Growth: Change Without Development." In *Cuban Communism,* 6th ed., ed. Irving Louis Horowitz. New Brunswick, N.J.: Transaction Publishers.

Kapcia, Antoni. 2005. *Havana: The Making of Cuban Culture.* Oxford: Berg.

Kaplan, Caren, and Inderpal Grewal. 1999. "Transnational Feminist Cultural Studies: Beyond the Marxism/Poststructuralism/Feminism Divides." In *Between Woman and Nation: Nationalisms, Transnational Feminisms, and the State,* ed. Norma Alarcón and Minoo Moallen, 349–63. Durham: Duke University Press.

Keal, Paul. 1986. "On Influence and Spheres of Influence." In *Dominant Powers and Subordinate States: The United States in Latin America and the Soviet Union in Eastern Europe,* ed. Jan F. Triska. Durham: Duke University Press.

Kean, Christopher. 1992. *Diez días en Cuba: Mensaje de la disidencia a la diáspora.* New York: Freedom House; Washington, D.C.: Of Human Rights.

Kearney, Michael. 1995. "The Local and the Global: The Anthropology of Globalization and Transnationalism." *Annual Review of Anthropology* 24:547–65.

Keck, Margaret E., and Kathryn Sikkink. 1998. *Activists Beyond Borders: Advocacy Networks in International Politics.* Ithaca: Cornell University Press.

Kennedy, Paul. 1987. *The Rise and Fall of the Great Powers: Economic Change and Military Conflict from 1500 to 2000.* New York: Vintage Books.

Keohane, Robert, and Joseph Nye. 1981. "Introduction." In *Transnational Relations and World Politics,* ed. Keohane and Nye, xii–xvi. Cambridge: Harvard University Press.

Klein, Herbert S. 1967. *Slavery in the Americas. A Comparative Study of Virginia and Cuba.* Chicago: University of Chicago Press.

———. 1986. *African Slavery in Latin America and the Caribbean.* New York: Oxford University Press.

Knight, Franklin. 1977. *Slave Society in Cuba During the Nineteenth Century.* Madison: University of Wisconsin Press, 1977.

———. 1985. "Jamaican Migrants and the Cuban Sugar Industry, 1900–1934." In *Between Slavery and Free Labor: The Spanish-Speaking Caribbean in the Nineteenth Century,* ed. Manuel Moreno Fraginals, Frank Moya Pons, and Stanley L. Engerman. Baltimore: Johns Hopkins University Press.

———. 1994. "The New Caribbean and the United States." *The American Academy of Political and Social Science* 533 (May): 33–47.

Knox, Paul, and Peter Taylor, eds. 1995. *World Cities in a World System.* Cambridge: Cambridge University Press.

Koehn, Peter H. 1991. *Refugees from Revolution: U.S. Policy and Third-World Migration.* Boulder, Colo.: Westview Press.

Krasner, Stephen D., ed. 1983. *International Regimes.* Ithaca: Cornell University Press.

Kunz, E. F. 1973. "The Refugees in Flight: Kinetic Models and Forms of Displacement." *International Migration Review* 7:125–46.

Kurth, James R. 1986. "The United States, Latin America, and the World: The Changing International Context of U.S.–Latin American Relations." In *The United States and Latin America in the 1980s: Contending Perspectives on a Decade of Crisis,* ed. Kevin J. Middlebrook and Carlos Rico. Pittsburgh: University of Pittsburgh Press.

Kyle, David. 2000. *Transnational Peasants: Migrations, Networks, and Ethnicity in Andean Ecuador.* Baltimore: Johns Hopkins University Press.

Laclau, Ernesto. 2000. *La guerre de identities: Grammaire de l'emancipation.* Paris: Éditions La Découverte.

Lambie, George. 1998. "Cuban-European Relations: Historical Perspectives and Political Consequences." *Cuban Studies Association* (University of Miami) 3, no. 4 (May).

Leal, Eusebio. 1988. *La Habana, ciudad antigua.* Havana: Letras Cubanas.

Leckie, Robert. 1992. *The Wars of America.* New York: HarperCollins.

Lecuyer, Marie-Claude. 1987. *Immigration blanche à Cuba: L'expérience galicienne (1853–1855).* Paris: Publications de l'Equipe de Recherche de l'Université de Paris.

Lee, Everett S. 1970 [1965]. "A Theory of Migration." In *Population Geography: A Reader,* ed. George J. Demko, Harold M. Rose, and George A. Schnell. New York: McGraw Hill.

Lefebvre, Henri. 1996. *Writings on Cities.* Edited and translated by Eleonore Kofman and Elizabeth Lebas. Cambridge: Blackwell Publishers.

Lemus, Encarnación, and Rosario Márquez. 1992. "Los precedentes." In *Historia general de la emigración española a Iberoamérica,* ed. Pepa Vega, Pedro A. Vives, and Jesús Oyamburu, 37–91. Madrid: Closas-Orcoyen.

Le Riverend, Julio. 1974. *Historia económica de Cuba.* Havana: Instituto Cubano del Libro.

———. 1992a. *La Habana, espacio y vida.* Madrid: MAPFRE.

———. 1992b. *Problemas de la formación agraria de Cuba: siglos XVI–XVII.* Havana: Editorial Ciencias Sociales.

———. 1994. *Debate en soliloquio y otros ensayos sobre Cuba.* Mexico City: Instituto Mora.

"Letters to Frederick Huth and Co. from Spanish Merchants and Bankers, 1812–1848." n.d. Guildhall Library, London. MS 25050.

Levine, Robert M. 1993. *Tropical Diaspora: The Jewish Experience in Cuba.* Gainesville: University of Florida Press.

———. 1996. "Jews Under the Cuban Revolution: 1959–1995." In *The Jewish Diaspora in Latin America,* ed. David Sheinin and Lois Baer Barr. New York: Garland Publishing.

Levitt, Peggy. 2001. "Transnational Migration: Taking Stock and Future Directions." *Global Networks* 1, no. 3: 195–216.

Lewis, W. Arthur. 1978. *The Evolution of the International Economic Order.* Princeton: Princeton University Press.

Light, Ivan, and Edna Bonacich. 1988. *Immigrant Entrepreneurs: Koreans in Los Angeles, 1965–1982.* Berkeley and Los Angeles: University of California Press.

Livi-Bacci, Massimo. 1997. *A Concise History of World Population: Second Edition.* Malden, Mass.: Blackwell Publishers.

Loescher, Gil, and John A. Scanlan. 1986. *Calculated Kindness; Refugees and America's Half-Open Door, 1945 to the Present.* New York: Free Press; London: Collier Macmillan.

Long, Norman. 2000. "Exploring Local/Global Transformations: A View from Anthropology." In *Anthropology, Development, and Modernities: Exploring Discourses, Countertendencies, and Violence,* ed. Alberto Arce and Norman Long, 184–201. New York: Routledge.

Look Lai, Wally. 1989. "Chinese Indentured Labor: Migrants to the British West Indies in the Nineteenth Century." *Amerasia* 15, no. 2: 117–38.

López Segrera, Francisco. 1973. *Capitalismo dependiente y subdesarrollo, 1510–1959.* Mexico City: Editorial Diógenes, S.A.

———. 1975. "La economía y la política en la república neocolonial (1902–1933)." In *La república neocolonial,* ed. Juan Pérez de la Riva and Grupo de Estudios Cubanos de la Universidad de La Habana. Havana: Editorial Ciencias Sociales.

———. 1985. "Cuba: Dependence, Plantation Economy, and Social Classes, 1762–1902." In *Between Slavery and Free Labor: The Spanish-Speaking Caribbean in the Nineteenth Century,* ed. Manuel Moreno Fraginals, Frank Moya Pons, and Stanley L. Engerman, 77–93. Baltimore: Johns Hopkins University Press.

Losada Alvarez, Abel. 1995. *As relacións económicas entre Galicia e os países de destino da emigración. A Coruña.* Galicia: Xunta De Galicia.

Lowe, David. 2005. "Idea to Reality: A Brief History of the National Endowment for Democracy." http://www.ned.org/about/nedhistory.html.

Lowenthal, Abraham F. 1990. *Partners in Conflict, the United States and Latin America.* Baltimore: Johns Hopkins University Press.

Macías Hernández, Antonio M. 1988. "Un Siglo de Emigración Canaria a América: La Importancia de los Factores de Atracción." In *Españoles hacia América: Una emigración en masa, 1880–1930,* ed. Sánchez Albornoz, 110–35. Madrid: Alianza.

———. 1992. *La migración canaria, 1500–1980.* Columbres, Asturias: Júcar and Fundación Archivo de Indianos.

Macías Martín, Francisco. 2002. *Cuba: Crisis política, crisis económica y emigración (1920–1935).* Santa Cruz de Tenerife, Canary Islands: Ediciones de Baile del Sol.

MacLeod, Murdo J. 1973. *Spanish Central America: A Socioeconomic History, 1520–1720.* Berkeley and Los Angeles: University of California Press.

Mahler, Sarah. 1999. "Theoretical and Empirical Contributions Toward a Research Agenda for Transnationalism." In *Transnationalism from Below,* ed. Michael P. Smith and Luis E. Guarnizo, 64–102. New Brunswick, N.J.: Transaction Publishers.

Mahler, Sarah, and Katrin Hansing. 2005. "Toward a Transnationalism of the Middle: How Transnational Religious Practices Help Bridge the Divides Between Cuba and Miami." *Latin American Perspectives* 32, no. 1 (January): 121–46.

Maingot, Anthony. 1992. "Immigration from the Caribbean Basin." In *Miami Now: Immigration, Ethnicity, and Social Change,* ed. Guillermo Grenier and Alex Stepick, 18–40. Gainesville: University Press of Florida.

Maldonado, Edwin. 1979. "Contract Labor and the Origins of Puerto Rican Communities in the United States." *International Migration Review* 13:103–21.

Maluquer de Motes, Jordi. 1992. *Nación e inmigración: Los españoles en Cuba (ss. xix y xx).* Gijón, Spain: Ediciones Jucar, Fundación Archivo Indianos.

Manners, Robert A. 1965. "Remittances and the Unit of Analysis." *Southwestern Journal of Anthropology* 21, no. 3: 179–95.

Máquez Sterling, Carlos. 1969. *Historia de Cuba desde Cristóbal Colón a Fidel Castro.* Madrid: Las Américas.

Marcané, Luis Fernández. 1924. *Contribución al estudio de la doble nacionalidad de los hijos de españoles nacidos en América: La ley de 18 de julio de 1917 ante el tribunal supremo.* Havana: El Siglo Veinte.

Marquis, Christopher. 2002. "It's Republican vs. Republican on Cuba." *New York Times,* July 28.

Marrero, Levi. 1972. *Cuba: Economía y sociedad.* Vol. 2. Río Piedras, Puerto Rico: Editorial San Juan.

Martí, José. [1893] 1995. "Mi Raza." In *José Martí: Obras completas,* 2:298–99. Havana: Editorial Ciencias Sociales. Originally published in *Patria* (New York), April 16.

Martín, Consuelo. 1995. "Al rescate de la subjetividad: los estudios de la emigración." *Temas,* no. 1 (January–March): 50–56.

Marx, Karl. [1867] 1974. *Capital, a Critique of Political Economy, Vol. 1.* New York: International Publishers.

Massey, Douglas, et al. 1987. *Return to Aztlan: The Social Process of International Migration from Western Mexico.* Berkeley and Los Angeles: University of California Press.

Matos, José Antonio. 1999. *La historia en Fernando Ortiz.* Havana: Colección Fernando Ortiz.

McAvoy, Muriel. 2003. *Sugar Baron: Manuel Rionda and the Fortunes of Pre-Castro Cuba.* Gainesville: University Press of Florida.

McEvedy, C., and R. Jones. 1978. *Atlas of World Population History.* Harmondsworth, U.K.: Penguin.

McLeod, Marc. 1998. "Undesirable Aliens: Race, Ethnicity, and Nationalism in the Comparison of Haitian and British West Indian Immigrant Workers in Cuba, 1912–1939." *Journal of Social History* 31, no. 3 (Spring): 599–623.

McNeill, John R. 1985. *Atlantic Empires of France and Spain: Louisbourg and Havana, 1700–1763.* Chapel Hill: University of North Carolina Press.

Menéndez Paredes, Rigoberto. 1999. *Componentes árabes en la cultura cubana.* Havana: Ediciones Boloña.

Mesa-Lago, Carmelo. 1969. "The Revolutionary Offensive." *Trans-Action* 6, no. 6 (April): 22–29.

———. 1989. "The Cuban Economy in the 1980s: The Return of Ideology." In *Cuban Communism,* 6th ed., ed. Irving Louis Horowitz, 187–26. New Brunswick, N.J.: Transaction Publishers.

———. 1995. "Cuba's Raft Exodus of 1994: Causes, Settlement, Effects, and Future." *North-South Agenda* 12 (April).

———. 1998. "Hacia una evaluación de la actuación económica y social en la transición cubana de los años noventa." *América Latina, Hoy* (Universidad Complutense de Madrid, Spain), no. 18.

Mészáros, István. 1970. *Marx's Theory of Alienation.* London: Merlin Press.

Metropolitan Dade County Planning Department, Research Division. 1994. *Hispanics in Dade County.* Miami: Metropolitan Dade County Planning Division.

Miami Dade County, Department of Planning and Zoning. 2002. *Profile of Hispanic-Owned Businesses in Miami-Dade County, Fl., 1997.* Miami: Miami Dade County.

Miami Dade County, Department of Planning and Zoning, Planning Research Section. 2003. *Demographic Profile of Miami Dade County, Florida, 1960–2000.* Miami: Miami Dade County. http://www.miamidade.gov/planzone/Library/Census/demographic_profile.pdf.

Mignolo, Walter. 2000. *Local Histories, Global Designs: Coloniality, Subaltern Knowledges, and Border Thinking.* Princeton: Princeton University Press.

———. 2003. "'Un paradigma otro': Colonialidad global, pensamiento fronterizo y cosmopolitismo critico." Unpublished manuscript.

Miller, Kerby. 1990. "Class, Culture, and Immigrant Group Identity in the United States: The Case of Irish-American Ethnicity." In *Immigration Reconsidered: History, Sociology, and Politics,* ed. Virginia Yans-McLaughlin. New York: Oxford University Press.

Miller, Nicola. 2003. "The Absolution of History: Users of the Past in Castro's Cuba." *Journal of Contemporary History* 38, no. 1: 147–62.

Ministerio del Interior. Various years. *Anuario Estadístico de Extranjería.* Madrid: Ministerio del Interior.

Ministerio de Trabajo y Asuntos Sociales. Various years. *Anuario de Migraciones.* Madrid: Ministerio de Trabajo y Asuntos Sociales.

Ministerio de Trabajo y Seguridad Social. 1991. *Anuario de Emigración.* Madrid: Ministerio de Trabajo y Asuntos Sociales.

Mintz, Sidney W. 1974. *Caribbean Transformations.* Chicago: Aldine.

Monge Muley, George M. 1953. *Centros españoles (Libro Primero). Obra Póstuma de Don Serrato Morge.* Barcelona: Bigay y Bononova.

Montejo Arrechea, Carmen V. 1993. *Sociedades de instrucción y recreo de pardos y morenos que existieron en Cuba colonial: Período 1878–1898*. Veracruz: Instituto Veracruzano de Cultura.

Morales, Salvador. 1984. *Conquista y colonización de Cuba, Siglo 16*. Havana: Editorial Ciencias Sociales.

Morales Saro, M. Cruz. 1992. "La emigración asturiana a América." In *Historia general de la emigración española a Iberoamérica*, ed. Pepa Vega, Pedro A. Vives, and Jesús Oyamburu, 51–85. Madrid: Closas-Orcoyen.

Moreno Fraginals, Manuel. 2001. *El ingenio: Complejo económico social cubano del azúcar*. Havana: Editorial Ciencias Sociales. [Orig. pub. 1978.]

———. 2002. *Cuba/España, España/Cuba: Historia común*. Barcelona: Crítica.

Moreno Fraginals, Manuel R., and José J. Moreno Masó. 1993. *Guerra, migración y muerte: El ejército español en cuba como vía migratoria*. Gijón, Spain: Fundación Archivo de Indianos.

Morner, Magnus. 1992. *Aventureros y proletarios: Los emigrantes en Hispanoamérica*. Madrid: MAPFRE.

Morris, Emily. 1998. "La recuperación de la economía cubana desde 1993: su estructura, desempeño y política económica." *América Latina, Hoy*, no. 18.

Morris, Richard B., and Jeffrey B. Morris. 1976. *Encyclopedia of American History, Bicentennial Edition*. New York: Harper and Row.

Morse, Richard. 1984. "The Urban Development of Colonial Latin America." In *The Cambridge History of Latin America*, ed. Leslie Bethell, 67–104. Cambridge: Cambridge University Press.

Mumford Report. 2003. "Hispanic Populations and their Residential Patterns in the Metropolis." http://mumford.albany.edu/census/HispanicPop/HspReportNew/page1.h tml.

Mustafa, Sam. 2001. *Merchants and Migrations: Germans and Americans in Connection, 1776–1835*. Aldershot: Ashgate.

Naranjo Orovio, Consuelo. 1988. *Del campo a la bodega: Recuerdos de gallegos en Cuba*. La Coruña, Galicia: Ediciones de Castro.

———. 1992. "Análisis cuantitativo." In *Historia general de la emigración española a Iberoamérica*, ed. Pepa Vega, Pedro A. Vives, and Jesús Oyamburu, 177–200. Madrid: Closas-Orcoyen.

———. 1996a. *Medicina y racismo en Cuba: La ciencia ante la inmigración canaria en el siglo XX*. Las Palmas: Centro de la Cultura Popular Canaria.

———. 1996b. *Racismo e inmigración en Cuba en el siglo XIX*. Madrid: Ediciones Doce Calles, Fundación de Investigaciones Marxistas.

National Council of Churches. n.d. "The NCC and Cuba." http://www.ncccusa.org/news/cuba/cubaindex.html.

National Endowment for Democracy. 2005. "Latin America and Caribbean Program Descriptions." http://www.ned.org/grants/05programs/grants-lac05.html#Cuba.

New York Times. 2004. "Members of Cuba Troupe Say They Will Seek Asylum." November 15. http://query.nytimes.com/gst/fullpage.html?res=9904E1D8143FF93 6A25752C1A9629C8B63&sec=&spon=&pagewanted=2

Núñez, Rafael. 1996. "Los otros españoles que se fueron a Cuba: El drama de los repatriados." In *La nación soñada: Cuba, Puerto Rico y Filipinas ante el 98*, ed. Consuelo Naranjo, Miguel Puig, and Luis Miguel García, 597–609. Madrid: Ediciones Doce Calles.

Office of Global Analysis. 2008. FAS, USDA "Cuba's Food & Agriculture Situation Report" (March). http://www.fas.usda.gov/itp/cuba/CubaSituation0308.pdf.

Oficina Nacional de Estadísticas, República de Cuba. 2007. *Anuario estadístico de Cuba 2006.* http://www.one.cu/aec2006/anuariopdf2006.

———. 2008. *Anuario estadístico 2007.* Havana. http://www.one.cu/aec2008.htm.

———. 2009. *Anuario Estadístico de Cuba 2008.* http://www.one.cu/aec2008.htm.

Oficina Nacional de los Censos Demográficos y Electoral. 1953. *Censo de la población 1953.* Havana: Tribunal Supremo Electoral de la República de Cuba.

Ojito, Mirta. 2000. "How Race Is Lived in America." *New York Times,* June 5. http://www.nytimes.com/library/national/race/.

Ong, Aihwa. 1999. *Flexible Citizenship: The Cultural Logics of Transnationality.* Durham: Duke University Press.

Opinión en Galicia. 2005. "Fundación Fernando Blanco de Lema, Ayuntamiento de Cee." October 17. http://www.galiciadigital.com/opinion/opinion.1017.php.

Oppenheimer, Andrés. 2005. "Latin 'Brain Drain' May Be Net Positive in the End." *Miami Herald,* July 17.

Organization for Economic Cooperation and Development (OECD). *Database on Immigrants and Expatriates.* http://www.oecd.org/document/51/0,2340,en_2825_494553_34063091_1_1_1_1,00.html.

Orozco, Manuel. 2006. "International Flows of Remittances: Costs, Competition, and Financial Access in Latin America and the Caribbean—Toward an Industry Scorecard." Report presented at the Meeting on Remittances and Transnational Families sponsored by the Inter-American Development Bank and the Annie Casey Foundation, May 12. http://americas.fiu.edu/events/2007/international%20flows%20of%20 remittances.p df.

Ortiz, Fernando. 1975 [1946]. *El engaño de las razas.* Havana: Editorial Ciencias Sociales.

———. 2002 [1940]. *Contrapunteo cubano del tabaco y el azúcar.* Havana: Editorial Ciencias Sociales.

Ortiz López, Luis. 1998. *Huellas etnolingüísticas bozales y afrocubanas.* Madrid: Vervuert Verlag Iberoamericana, 1998.

Özden, Çaglar, and Maurice Schiff, eds. 2006. *International Migration, Remittances and Brain Drain.* New York: Palgrave Macmillan.

Özveren, Eyüp. 1994. "The Shipbuilding Commodity Chain, 1950–1790." In *Commodity Chains and Global Capitalism,* ed. Gary Gereffi and Miguel Korzeniewicz. Westport, Conn.: Praeger Press.

Packenham, Robert A. 1989. "Cuba and the USSR Since 1959: What Kind of Dependency?" *Cuban Communism,* 6th ed., ed. Irving Louis Horowitz, 135–65. New Brunswick, N.J.: Transaction Publishers.

Padrón, Carlos. 2005. *Franceses en el suroeste de Cuba.* Havana: Ediciones Unión.

Palazón Ferrando, Salvador. 1995. *Capital humano español y desarrollo económico latinoamericano: Evolución, causas y características del flujo migratorio (1882–1990).* Valencia: Institut de Cultura Juan Gil-Albert.

Pastor, Robert A. 1985. "Introduction: The Policy Challenging in Migration and Development in the Caribbean." In *Migration and Development in the Caribbean: The Unexplored Connection,* ed. Robert A. Pastor. Boulder, Colo.: Westview Press.

Pava, Richard. 2001. *Les juifs de Cuba, 1492–2001.* Nantes: Éditions du Petit Véhicule.

Pederson, Jay. 1997. *International Directory of Company Histories.* Vol. 18. Detroit: St. James Press.

————. 2000. *International Directory of Company Histories.* Vol. 32. Farmington Hills, Mich.: St. James Press.

————. 2001. *International Directory of Company Histories.* Vol. 37. Farmington Hills, Mich.: St. James Press.

Pedraza-Bailey, Silvia. 1985. *Political and Economic Migrants in America: Cubans and Mexicans.* Austin: University of Texas Press.

Pérez, Lisandro. 1992. "Cuban Miami." In *Miami Now: Immigration, Ethnicity, and Social Change,* ed. Guillermo Grenier and Alex Stepick. Gainesville: University Press of Florida.

————. 1999. "The End of Exile: A New Era in U.S. Immigration Policy Toward Cuba." In *Free Markets, Open Societies, Closed Borders? Trends in International Migration and Immigration Policy in the Americas,* ed. Max Castro, 197–209. Coral Gables, Fla.: North-South Center.

Pérez, Louis A., Jr. 1983. *Cuba Between Empires, 1878–1902.* Pittsburgh: University of Pittsburg Press.

————. 1995a. *Essays on Cuban History, Historiography, and Research.* Gainesville: University Press of Florida.

————, ed. 1995b. *José Martí in the United States: The Florida Experience.* Arizona: Arizona State University.

————. 1999. *On Becoming Cuban: Identity, Nationality, and Culture.* Chapel Hill: University of North Carolina Press.

Pérez de la Riva, Juan. 1975. "Los recursos humanos de Cuba al comienzo de siglo: Inmigración, economía y nacionalidad (1899–1906)." In *La república neocolonial,* ed. Juan Pérez de la Riva and Grupo de Estudios Cubanos de la Universidad de la Habana. Havana: Editorial Ciencias Sociales.

————. 1978. *El barracón: Esclavitud y capitalismo en Cuba.* Barcelona: Crítica.

————. 1979. *El monto de la inmigración forzada en el siglo XIX.* Havana: Editorial Ciencias Sociales.

————. 2000. *Los culíes chinos en Cuba.* Havana: Instituto Cubano del Libro.

————. 2004. *La conquista del espacio cubano.* Havana: Fundación Fernando Ortiz.

Pérez Guzmán, Francisco. 1997. *Habana: Clave de un imperio.* Havana: Editorial Ciencias Sociales.

Pérez-López, Jorge F. 1995. *Cuba's Second Economy: From Behind the Scenes to Center Stage.* New Brunswick, N.J.: Transaction Publishers.

Pérez-López, Jorge F., and Sergio Díaz-Briquets. 1990. "Labor Migration and the Offshore Assembly in the Socialist World: The Cuban Experience." *Population and Development Review* 16, no. 2: 273–99.

————. 2005. "Remittances to Cuba: A Survey of Methods and Estimates." Cuba in Transition 16 (Association for the Study of the Cuban Economy). http://lanic.utexas.edu/project/asce/pdfs/volume15/pdfs/diazbriqu etsperezlopez.pdf.

Pérez Rodríguez, Joaquín. 2003. "El remitente cubano: Algunas características particulares." Cuba in Transition 13 (Association for the Study of the Cuban Economy). http://lanic.utexas.edu/project/asce/pdfs/volume13/perezrodriguez.pdf.

Pérez-Stable, Marifeli. 1998. *La revolución cubana: Orígenes, desarrollo y legado.* Madrid: Colibrí.

Pessar, Patricia. 1997. "Introduction: New Approaches to Caribbean Emigration and Return." In *Caribbean Circuits: New Directions in the Study of Caribbean Migration,* ed. Pessar, 1–12. New York: Center for Migration Studies.

Pettman, Jan. 1996. *Worlding Women: A Feminist International Politics*. London: Routledge.

Pichardo, Hortensia. 1977. *Documentos para la historia de Cuba*. Vols. 1, 2, and 3. Havana: Editorial Ciencias Sociales.

Piqueras, José Antonio. 2003. *Cuba, colonia y emporio de un mercado interferido (1878–1895)*. Madrid: Fondo de Cultura Económica.

Polanyi, Karl. 1944. *The Great Transformation: The Political and Economic Origins of Our Time*. Boston: Beacon Press.

Pollitt, Brian H. 1984. "The Cuban Sugar Economy and the Great Depression." *Bulletin of Latin American Research* 3, no. 2: 3–28.

Portell-Vilá, Herminio. 1994. *Nueva historia de la República de Cuba*. Miami: La Moderna Poesía.

Portes, Alejandro. 1969. "Dilemmas of a Golden Exile: Integration of Cuban Refugee Families in Milwaukee." *American Sociological Review* 34, no. 4 (August): 505–18.

———. 1976. "Determinants of Brain Drain." *International Migration Review* 10:489–508.

———. 1977. "Labor Functions of Illegal Aliens." *Society* 14, no. 6: 31–37.

———. 1984. "The Rise of Ethnicity: Determinants of Ethnic Perceptions Among Cuban Exiles in Miami." *American Sociological Review* 49 (June): 383–97.

———. 2001. "Introduction: The Debates of Significance on Immigrant Transnationalism." *Global Networks* 1 (July): 181–93.

Portes, Alejandro, and Robert L. Bach. 1985. *Latin Journey: Cuban and Mexican Immigrants in the United States*. Berkeley and Los Angeles: University of California Press.

Portes, Alejandro, and Rubén Rumbaut. 1996. *Immigrant America: A Portrait*. Berkeley and Los Angeles: University of California Press.

Portes, Alejandro, and Alex Stepick. 1993. *City on the Edge: The Transformation of Miami*. Berkeley and Los Angeles: University of California Press.

Portes, Alejandro, and John Walton. 1981. *Labor, Class, and the International System*. New York: Academic Press.

Portuondo, Olga. n.d. "Santiago de Cuba, desde su fundación hasta la Guerra de los Diez Años."

Poyo, Gerald. 1989. *With All, and for the Good of All: The Emergence of Popular Nationalism in the Cuban Communities of the United States, 1848–1898*. Durham: Duke University Press.

———. 1991. "The Cuban Experience in the United States, 1865–1940: Migration, Community, and Identity." *Cuban Studies* 21:19–36.

Préstamo, Felipe J. 1996. "The Architecture of American Sugar Mills: The United Fruit Company." *Journal of Decorative and Propaganda Arts* 22 (1996): 82–103.

Proceedings of the International Colloquium "Les Français dans l'Orient Cubain." 1993. Bordeaux: Maison des Pays Ibériques.

Quijano, Anibal. 1991. "Colonialidad y Modernidad/Racionalidad." *Perú Indígena* 29:11–21.

Quijano, Anibal, and Immanuel Wallerstein. 2002. "Americanity as a Concept, or The Americas in the Modern World-System." *International Journal of Social Sciences* 134 (November 1992): 500–527.

Rathat, Dilip, and Shimei Xu. 2008. "Migration and Remittances in Cuba." In The World Bank, "Migration and Remittances Factbook, 2008." March 18. http://

siteresources.worldbank.org/INTPROSPECTS/Resources/334934-1181678518183/
Cuba.pdf.

Real Academia Española. 1950. *Diccionario manual de la lengua española*. Madrid: EPASA CALPE.

"Real Cédula de 21 de octubre de 1817 sobre cómo aumentar la población blanca de la isla de Cuba." 1818. Havana: Oficina de Arazoza y Soler.

Richardson, Bonham. 1989. "Caribbean Migrations, 1838–1985." In *The Modern Caribbean*, ed. Franklin W. Knight and Colin A. Palmer, 203–28. Chapel Hill: University of North Carolina Press.

———. 1992. *The Caribbean in the Wider World, 1942–1992*. Cambridge: Cambridge University Press.

Ripoll, Carlos. 1989. "Writers and Artists in Today's Cuba." In *Cuban Communism*, 6th ed., ed. Irving Louis Horowitz, 499–514. New Brunswick, N.J.: Transaction Publishers.

Ritter, Archibald R. M. 1994. "Cuba's Economic Strategy and Alternative Futures." In *Cuba at a Crossroads: Politics and Economics After the Fourth Party Congress*, ed. Jorge Pérez-López, 67–93. Gainesville: University Press of Florida.

———. 2004. "Cuba's Underground Economy." Carleton Economic Papers 4–12, Carleton University, Department of Economics.

———. 2006. "Economic Illegalities and the Underground Economy in Cuba." *Focal*, March, 1–19.

Ritter, Archibald R. M., and Nicholas Rowe. 2002. "Cuba: From 'Dollarization' to 'Euro-ization' or 'Peso Re-Consolidation'?" March. http://www.carleton.ca/economics/cep/cep00-13update.pdf.

Rivero Muñiz, José. 1976. *The Ybor City Story, 1885–1954*. Translation of *Cubanos en Tampa* by Eustasio Fernández and Henry Beltran. Tampa: n.p.

Roberts, Bryan. 1995. "Socially Expected Durations and the Economic Adjustment of Migrants." In *The Economic Sociology of Immigration*, ed. Alejandro Portes. New York: Russell Sage Foundation.

Robinson, William. 2000. "Capitalist Globalization and the Transnationalization of the State." Paper presented at the Annual Meeting of the International Studies Association, Los Angeles, March 14–18.

———. 2003. *Transnational Conflicts, Central America, Social Change, and Globalization*. New York: Verso.

Roca, Sergio. 1989. "State Enterprises in Cuba Under the New System of Planning Management." In *Cuban Communism*, 6th ed., ed. Irving Louis Horowitz. New Brunswick, N.J.: Transaction Publishers.

———. 1994. "Reflections on Economic Policy: Cuba's Food Program." In *Cuba at a Crossroads: Politics and Economics After the Fourth Party Congress*, ed. Jorge Pérez-López. Gainesville: University Press of Florida.

Rodrigo, Martín. 1998. "Con un pie en Cataluña y otro en Cuba: La familia Samá, de Villanova." *Estudios Històrics i Documents dels Arxius de Protocols* 61:359–95.

———. 2004. "'Quiero más uno aquí que diez allí': De hacendados en Cienfuegos a inversores en Barcelona." *Revista de Historial Industrial* 22:1–38.

Rodríguez, Eduardo Luis. 1996. "The Architectural Avant-Garde: From Art Deco to Modern Regionalism." *Journal of Decorative Propaganda Arts* 22:254–77.

Rodríguez Chávez, Ernesto. 1997. "El flujo emigratorio cubano, 1984–1995: Balances y perspectivas." *Revista de Ciencias Sociales Nueva Época* 3 (June): 37–82.

Roig de Leuchsenring, Emilio. 1963. *La Habana: Apuntes históricos*. Havana: Consejo Nacional de Cultura.

———. 1973. *Historia de la Enmienda Platt*. Havana: Editorial Ciencias Sociales.

Rojas, Rafael. 1998. *La isla sin fin, contribución a la crítica del nacionalismo cubano*. Miami: Ediciones Universal.

Roque C., Marta Beatriz. n.d. "Economía informal en Cuba." Unpublished paper.

Roselló Socorro, Richard. 2002. "Presencia italiana en Cuba: 1492–1902." In *Emigrazione e presenza italiana in Cuba*, ed. Domenico Capolongo, 1:15–30. Roccarainola, Italy: Circolo Culturale B.G. Duns Scoto.

Rosenau, James. 1980. *The Study of Global Interdependence: Essays on the Transnationalization of World Affairs*. New York: Nichols.

———. 1990. *Turbulence in World Politics: A Theory of Change and Continuity*. Princeton: Princeton University Press.

Rosenberg, Jonathan. 1992a. "Cuba's Free-Market Experiment: 'Los mercados libres campesinos, 1980–1986.'" *Latin American Research Review* 27, no. 3: 51–90.

———. 1992b. *Politics and Paradox in the Liberalization of a Command Economy: The Case of Cuba's Free Peasant Markets, 1980–1986*. Ph.D. diss., University of Miami.

Rueda, Germán. 1993. *La emigración contemporánea de los españoles a los Estados Unidos, 1820–1950*. Madrid: MAPFRE.

Ruz, Raúl, and Martha Lim Kim. 2000. *Coreanos en Cuba*. Havana: Fundación Fernando Ortiz.

Saco, José Antonio. 1879. *Historia de la esclavitud de la raza africana en el nuevo mundo y en especial en los países Américo-hispanos*. Barcelona: Jaime Jesús.

Salazar-Carrillo, Jorge. 1989. "Interdependence and Economic Performance in Cuba." In *Cuban Communism*, 6th ed., ed. Irving Louis Horowitz, 227–34. New Brunswick, N.J.: Transaction Publishers.

———. 2006. "Las remesas dichosas." *El Nuevo Herald*, March 22.

Sánchez-Albornoz, Nicolás. 1974. *The Population of Latin America: A History*. Berkeley and Los Angeles: University of California Press.

Sánchez Alonso, Blanca. 1995. *Las causas de la emigración española (1880–1930)*. Madrid: Alianza Editoral.

San Martín, Nancy. 2002. "Empresas de Miami participan en feria agrícola en la Habana." *El Nuevo Herald*, September 13.

Sassen, Saskia. 1991. *The Global City: New York, London, Tokyo*. Princeton: Princeton University Press.

———. 1996. *Losing Control? Sovereignty in an Age of Globalization*. New York: Columbia University Press.

Sassen-Koob, Saskia. 1980. "The Internationalization of the Labor Force." *Studies in Comparative International Development* 15, no. 4: 3–25.

———. 1986. "New York City: Economic Restructuring and Immigration." *Development and Change* 17 (January): 85–120.

Scott, James, ed. 1998. *After the End: Making U.S. Foreign Policy in the Post–Cold War World*. Durham: Duke University Press.

Scott, Rebecca. 1985. "Explaining Abolition: Contradiction, Adaptation, and Challenge in Cuban Slave Society, 1860–1886." In *Between Slavery and Free Labor: The Spanish-Speaking Caribbean in the Nineteenth Century*, ed. Manuel Moreno Fraginals, Frank Moya Pons, and Stanley L. Engerman, 25–53. Baltimore: Johns Hopkins University Press.

————. 2005. *Degrees of Freedom: Louisiana and Cuba After Slavery.* Cambridge: Harvard University Press.

————. 1998. "Building, Bridging, and Breaching the Color Line: Rural Collective Action in Louisiana and Cuba, 1865–1912." In *Democracy, Revolution, and History*, ed. Theda Skocpol, with the assistance of George Ross, Tony Smith, and Judith Eisenberg Vichniac. Ithaca: Cornell University Press.

Secretaría de Estado de Inmigración y Emigración. 2007. "Boletín estadístico de extranjería e inmigración no. 14, Octubre 2007: Participación de la población extranjera en la sociedad española." http://extranjeros.mtas.es/es/InformacionEstadis tica/Boletines/Ar chivos/Boleti nindexExtranjeria-num-14-Web.pdf.

Secretaría de Hacienda. 1907. *República de Cuba: Disposiciones relativas a la inmigración.* Havana: Imprenta y Papelería de Rambla y Bouza.

————. n.d. *Inmigración y movimientos de pasajeros, 1902–1936.* Havana.

Silva, Helga. 1985. *The Children of Mariel: Cuban Refugee Children in South Florida Schools.* Washington, D.C.: CANF.

Skop, Emily. 2001. "Race and Place in the Adaptation of Mariel Exiles." *International Migration Review* 35, no. 2: 449–71.

Slagter, Janet T. 1982. "The Concept of Alienation and Feminism." *Social Theory and Practice* 8:155–64.

Smith, Jackie, Charles Chatfield, and Ron Pagnucco. 1998. *Transnational Social Movements and Global Politics: Solidarity Beyond the State.* New York: Syracuse University Press.

Smith, Michael Peter. 2001. *Transnational Urbanism.* Malden, Mass.: Blackwell Publishing.

Smith, Murray. 1994. "Alienation, Exploitation, and Abstract Labor: A Humanist Defense of Marx's Theory of Value." *Review of Radical Political Economics* 26, no. 1: 110–33.

Soldevilla, Consuelo, and Germán Rueda. 1992. *Cantabria y América.* Madrid: MAPFRE.

Soler Martínez, Rafael. 1993. "Francia y los revolucionarios del oriente cubano." In *Proceedings of the International Colloquium "Les Français dans l'Orient Cubain,"* 67–74. Bordeaux: Maison des Pays Ibériques.

Sonesson, Birgit. 1995. *Catalanes en las Antillas: Un estudio de casos.* Colombres: Archivo de Indianos.

Sosa Rodríguez, Enrique, and Carlos E. Bojóquez. 1991. *Habanero campechano.* Mérida: Ediciones Universidad Autónoma de Yucatán/Universidad de la Habana.

Sporn, Pam. 2000. *Cuban Roots/Bronx Stories.* Produced and directed by Pam Sporn. Narrated by Pablo Eliott Foster Carrión. Latino Public Broadcasting, Third World Newsreel.

Stepick, Alex. 1992. "The Refugees Nobody Wants: Haitians in Miami." In *Miami Now: Immigration, Ethnicity, and Social Change*, ed. Guillermo Grenier and Alex Stepick, 57–82. Gainesville: University Press of Florida.

Stowers, Genie N. L. 1990. "Political Participation, Ethnicity, and Class Status: The Case of Cubans in Miami." *Ethnic Groups* 8:73–90.

Sullivan, Kevin. 2001. "Americans Defy Cuba Embargo." *Washington Post*, October 13.

Tablada Pérez, Carlos. 1987. *El pensamiento económico de Ernesto Che Guevara.* Havana: Ediciones Casas de las Américas.

Teitelbaum, Michael. 1985. *Latin Migration North: The Problem for U.S. Foreign Policy.* New York: Council on Foreign Relations.

Theriot, Lawrence. 1989. "Cuba Faces the Economic Realities of the 1980s." In *Cuban Communism*, 6th ed., ed. Irving Louis Horowitz, 257–76. New Brunswick, N.J.: Transaction Publishers.

Thomas, Hugh. 1994. *La conquista de México*. Barcelona: Planeta.

Thomson, John B. 2001. "Preface." In *Pierre Bourdieu: Langage et pouvoir symbolique*. Paris: Éditions Fayard.

Torres, María de los Angeles. 2004. *In the Land of Mirrors: Cuban Exile Politics in the United States*. Ann Arbor: University of Michigan Press.

Torres-Cuevas, Eduardo. 2002a. "Conquista y colonización en los albores de la Edad Moderna: La experiencia cubana." In *Historia de Cuba: Formación y liberación de la nación*, ed. Eduardo Torres-Cuevas and Oscar Loyola Vega, 27–72. Havana: Pueblo y Educación.

———. 2002b. "Las patrias de los criollos." In *Historia de Cuba: Formación y liberación de la nación*, ed. Eduardo Torres-Cuevas and Oscar Loyola Vega, 73–98. Havana: Pueblo y Educación.

Torres-Saillant, Silvio, and Ramona Hernández. 1998. "Escape from the Native Land." In *The Dominican Americans*. Westport, Conn.: Greenwood Press.

Trolliet, Pierre. 1994. *La diaspora chinoise*. Paris: PUF.

United Nations, Department of Economic and Social Affairs, Population Division. March 17, 2000. "Replacement Migration: Is It a Solution to Declining and Ageing Populations?" http://www.un.org/esa/population/publications/migration/migration.htm.

———. 2006. "International Migration 2006." October. http://www.un.org/esa/population/publications/2006Migration_Chart/2006IttMig_wallchart.xlsby.

———. 2008a. "Cuba: Population of Urban Agglomerations with 750,000 Inhabitants or More in 2007 (thousands), 1960–2000." *World Urbanization Prospects, the 2007 Revision Population Database*. http://esa.un.org/unup/p2kodata.asp.

———. 2008b. *World Population Prospects: The 2006 Revision and World Urbanization Prospects: The 2005 Revision*. http://esa.un.org/unpp.

United Nations, General Assembly. 2004. "Necessity of Ending the Economic, Commercial, and Financial Embargo Imposed by the United States of America to Cuba." Report of the Secretary General, A/59/302 (June).

United Nations, International Fund for Agriculture and Development. 2006. "Sending Money Home: Remittances Flows to Developing and Transition Countries." http://www.ifad.org/events/remittances/maps/brochure.pdf.

United Nations High Commissioner for Refugees (UNHCR). 1997. *The State of the World's Refugees: A Humanitarian Agenda*. Oxford: Oxford University Press.

University of Miami. The Research Institute for Cuba and the Caribbean Center for Advanced International Studies. 1967. "The Cuban Immigration, 1959–1966, and Its Impact on Miami–Dade County, Florida: A Study for the Department of Health, Education, and Welfare, United States Government." Coral Gables: University of Miami.

U.S. Agency for International Development (USAID). 1995. *Latin America and the Caribbean Selected Economic and Social Data*. Washington, D.C.: U.S. Agency for International Development (USAID).

———. 2005. "USAID Extends Support to University of Miami's Cuba Transition Project." March 31. http://www.usaid.gov/locations/latin_america_caribbean/country/cuba/cubatransition2.html.

USAID. *See* U.S. Agency for International Development.

U.S. Census Bureau. 1991. *Census of Population and Housing, 1990, Summary Tape File 1-A, Florida.* Metro-Dade Planning Department, Research Division.

———. 1992. *Census of Population and Housing, 1990, Summary Tape File 3-A, Florida.* Metro-Dade Planning Department, Research Division.

———. 1993. *1990 Census.* Washington, D.C.: U.S. Government Printing Office.

———. 1999. *Region and Country or Area of Birth of the Foreign-Born Population.* http://www.census.gov/population/www/documentation/twps0029/tab04.html.

———. 2000. *2000 Census.* PUMS, Summary File 4. Population and Housing Tabulations.

———. 2006a. "2005 American Community Survey." http://factfinder.census.gov/serv let/DatasetMainPageServlet?_program = ACS&_submenuId = datasets_2&_lang = en&_ts.

———. 2006b. "Florida, ACS Demographic and Housing Estimates." *2006 American Community Survey.* http://factfinder.census.gov/servlet/ADPTable?_bm = y&- geo_id = 04000US12&-qr_name = ACS_2006_EST_G00_DP5&-ds_name = ACS_ 2006_EST_G00_&-_lang = en&-_sse = on.

———. 2006c. "Hispanic-Owned Firms, 2002." Washington D.C.: Bureau of the Census.

———. 2006d. "Miami Dade County, Florida." *2006 American Community Survey.* http://factfinder.census.gov/servlet/ADPTable?_bm = y&-geo_id = 05000US12086 &-qr_name = ACS_2006_EST_G00_DP5&-ds_name = ACS_2006_EST_G00_&- _lang = en&-redoLog = false&-_sse = on.

———. 2006e. "Miami Dade County Florida, Demographic and Housing Estimates." *2006 American Community Survey.* http://factfinder.census.gov/servlet/ADP Table?_bm = y&-qr_name = ACS_2006_EST_G00_DP5&-geo_id = 05000US120 86&-ds_name = &-_lang = en&-redoLog = false.

———. 2006f. "Miami Dade County Florida, Selected Social Characteristics." *2006 American Community Survey.* http://factfinder.census.gov/servlet/ADPTable?_ bm = y&-geo_id = 05000US12086&-qr_name = ACS_2006_EST_G00_DP2&-ds_ name = &-_lang = en&-redoLog = false.

———. 2006g. "Percent of People Born in Latin America." *2006 American Community Survey.* http://factfinder.census.gov/servlet/GRTTable?_bm = y&-_box_head_ nbr = R0504&-ds_name = ACS_2006_EST_G00_&-_lang = en&-format = US- 30&-CONTEXT = grt.

———. 2006h. "United States, ACS Demographic and Housing Estimates." *2006 American Community Survey.* http://factfinder.census.gov/servlet/ADPTable?_bm = y&-qr_name = ACS_2006_EST_G00_DP5&-geo_id = 01000US&-ds_name = &-_lang = en&-redoLog = false.

———. 2007. "2006 American Community Survey." http://factfinder.census.gov/jsp/ saff/ SAFFInfo.jsp?_content = su2_new_features_10_6.html.

U.S. Coast Guard. 2005. "Alien Migrant Interdiction: Total Interdictions, Calendar Year 1982 to Present." http://www.uscg.mil/hq/g-cp/comrel/factfile/index.htm.

———. 2008. "Alien Migrant Interdiction: Total Interdictions, Fiscal Year 1982 to Present." http://www.uscg.mil/hq/cg5/cg531/AMIO/FlowStats/FY.asp.

U.S. Department of Commerce, Bureau of Foreign Commerce. 1957. *Investment in Cuba: Basic Information for United States Businessmen.* Washington, D.C.: U.S. Government Printing Office.

U.S. Department of Commerce and Labor, Bureau of Statistics. 1904. *Statistical Abstract of the United States.* Washington, D.C.: Government Printing Office.

U.S. Department of Homeland Security, Office of Immigration Statistics. 2006a. *2004 Yearbook of Immigration Statistics.* January. http://www.dhs.gov/xlibrary/assets/statistics/yearbook/2004/OIS_2004_Yearbook.pdf.

———. 2006b. *2005 Yearbook of Immigration Statistics.* November. http://www.dhs.gov/xlibrary/assets/statistics/yearbook/2006/OIS_2005_Yearbook.pdf.

———. 2007. *2006 Yearbook of Immigration Statistics.* September. http://www.dhs.gov/xlibrary/assets/statistics/yearbook/2006/OIS_2006_Yearbook.pdf.

U.S. Department of Justice, Immigration and Naturalization Service. 1958–79. *Annual Report of the Immigration and Naturalization Service.* Washington, D.C.: U.S. Government Printing Office. [Each annual report is published after the close of the year to which it pertains.]

———. Various years. *Statistical Yearbook of the Immigration and Naturalization Service.* Washington, D.C.: U.S. Government Printing Office. [The 1981 yearbook was published in 1984, the 1993 and 1997 yearbooks in 1994 and 1998, the 1998 yearbook in 2000. The dates in the citations refer to the years of publication.]

U.S. Department of State. 2004. "Executive Summary." In *Report to the President from the Commission for Assistance to a Free Cuba.* Office of the Press Secretary, Washington, D.C., May 6. Available at http://www.cafc.gov/rpt/index.htm. Also available in *Federal Register,* June 16, 2004.

———. 2007. "Summary on New Rules on Travel and Exports to Cuba." http://www.state.gov/p/wha/rls/fs/34617.htm.

Valanti, Lisa. 2001. "Sister Cities Make Links." *Resist, Inc.,* July. http://www.resistinc.org/newsletter/issues/2001/07/valanti.html.

Valdés, Nelson P. 1979. "Revolutionary Solidarity in Angola." In *Cuba in the World,* ed. Cole Blasier and Carmelo Mesa-Lago, 87–117. Pittsburgh: University of Pittsburgh Press.

van der Pijl, Kees. 1998. *Transnational Classes and International Relations.* London: Routledge, 1998.

Van Sertima, Ivan. 1998. *Early America Revisited.* New Brunswick, N.J.: Transaction Publishers.

Vega, Juan. 1986. *Comentarios a la Ley General de la Vivienda.* Havana: Editorial Ciencias Sociales.

Vegal Suñol, José. 2004. *Norteamericanos en Cuba: Un estudio histórico.* Havana: La Fuente Viva.

Venegas Fornias, Carlos. 1996. "Havana Between Two Centuries." *Journal of Decorative and Propaganda Arts* 22:12–35.

Verdonneaud, Catherine. 1993. "Del sur de Francia a Santiago de Cuba." In *Proceedings of the International Colloquium "Les Français dans l'Orient cubain,"* 89–98. Bordeaux: Maison des Pays Ibériques.

Vertovec, Steven. 1999. "Conceiving and Researching Transnationalism." *Ethnic and Racial Studies* 22, no. 2 (March): 447–62.

Vidal A., Pavel. 2007. "La inflación y salario real." February. http://www.nodo50.org/cubasigloxxi/economia/vidal-300607.pdf.

Wallerstein, Immanuel. 1974. *The Modern World-System: Capitalist Agriculture and Origins of the European World-Economy in the Sixteenth Century.* New York: Academic Press.

————. 1982. "World-Systems Analysis: Theoretical and Interpretative Issues." In *World-Systems Analysis: Theory and Methodology,* ed. Terence K. Hopkins and Immanuel Wallerstein, 219–135. Beverly Hills, Calif.: Sage Publications.

————. 1988. "The Inventions of TimeSpace Realities: Towards an Understanding of Our Historical Systems." *Geography* 63, no. 32: 289–97.

————. 1993. "The TimeSpace of World-Systems Analysis: A Philosophical Essay." *Historical Geography* 23:5–22.

Weiner, Myron. 1985. "On International Migration and International Relations." *Population and Development Review* 11, no. 3 (September): 441–81.

————. 1992–93. "Security, Stability, and International Migration." *International Security* 17:91–126.

Wennerlind, Carl. 2002. "The Labor Theory of Value and the Strategic Role of Alienation." *Capital and Class* 26, no. 2: 1–21.

The White House. Office of the Press Secretary. 1999. "Statement by the President." January 5. http://www.state.gov/www/regions/wha/990105_clinton_cuba.html.

Wilson, K. L., and Alejandro Portes. 1980. "Immigrant Enclaves: An Analysis of the Labor Market Experiences of Cubans in Miami." *American Journal of Sociology* 86:295–319.

Wimmer, Andreas, and Nina Glick-Schiller. 2003. "Methodological Nationalism, the Social Sciences, and the Study of Migration: An Essay in Historical Epistemology." *International Migration Review* 37, no. 7: 576–610.

Wittke, Carl. 1952. *Refugees of Revolution: The German Forty-eighters in America.* Philadelphia: University of Pennsylvania Press.

World Bank. 1994. *World Tables.* Baltimore: Johns Hopkins University Press.

————. 1996. *World Debt Tables 1996, External Finance for Developing Countries.* Vol. 1. Washington, D.C.: World Bank.

Wright, Eric Olin. 1955. *Classes.* London: Verso.

Yanagisako, Sylvia, and Carol Delaney, eds. 1995. *Naturalizing Powers: Essays in Feminist Cultural Analysis.* New York: Routledge.

Zanetti Lecuona, Oscar. 1995. "Realidades y urgencias de la historiografía social en Cuba." *Temas,* no. 1 (January-March): 119–28.

Zeitlin, Maurice. 1966. "Political Generations in the Cuban Working Class." *American Journal of Sociology* 71, no. 5 (March): 493–508.

————. 1970. *Revolutionary Politics and the Cuban Working Class.* New York: Harper and Row.

Zimbalist, Andrew. 1989. "Incentives and Planning in Cuba." *Latin American Research Review* 24, no. 1: 65–93.

————. 1994. "Reforming Cuba's Economic System from Within." In *Cuba at a Crossroads: Politics and Economics After the Fourth Party Congress,* ed. Jorge Pérez-López, 220–37. Gainesville: University Press of Florida.

Zimmerman, Warren. 1995. "Migrants and Refugees: A Threat to Security?" In *Threatened Peoples, Threatened Borders,* ed. Michael Teitelbaum and Myron Weiner, 88–116. New York: W. W. Norton.

Zolberg, Aristide R. 1989. "The Next Waves: Migration Theory for a Changing World." *International Migration Review* 23 (Fall): 403–30.

Zolberg, Aristide R., Astri Suhrke, and Sergio Aguayo. 1989. *Escape from Violence: Conflict and the Refugee Crisis in the Developing World.* New York: Oxford University Press.

racism (*continued*)
  immigration policy and, 9, 33, 66–75, 78, 119, 122, 124, 127, 129, 246. See also *blanquea-miento*; colonizing projects
Radio Martí, 174, 230, 261
rafter crisis, 6, 33, 172, 175, 178–81, 190, 226, 239, 262
rationing card, 165, 173, 212, 259. See also *libreta de abastecimiento*
Reagan administration, 227, 230, 288 n. 65
remittances, Cuban migration after 1959 and, 208–13
  informal labor circuits and, 219–21
  regulations by the U.S. government, 217–19
  Spanish migrants and, 89, 95–99, 101, 244, 245, 256. See also Argentina; Asturias; Canary Islands; Catalonia; Galicia
  transnational economic strategies and, 213–17
revolutionary offensive, 161, 166
Richardson, Bonham, 38
Roberts, Bryan, 171. See also socially prescribed durations
Rodrigo, Martín, xvii, 92, 94, 277 n. 17
Rodríguez, Florencio, 102, 256. See also *Indianos*

Saco, José Antonio, 6
Santander, 100, 104, 254
Santiago de Cuba
  strategic importance and global links, 44–45, 152
  immigrants and migrant workers in, 54, 80, 92, 134, 139, 253
  transnationalism by migrants, 56, 88, 91, 93, 104
Sassen-Koob, Saskia. See Sassen, Saskia
Sassen, Saskia, 34, 37–38
Scott, Rebecca, 63, 65, 107
Seville, 60, 64, 71, 86
sister-city associations, 234
slave society in Cuba. See African slaves in Cuba; capitalist slavery; structural displacement
  anti-slavery regime and trafficking, 61–62, 79, 240
  coartación, 62–63
  debates about, 66–67, 69, 70, 71, 79
  formation of associations by African-origin groups, 63–65
  Haitian revolution and, 66–67
  manumission, 62–63
  patronato, 65

social contrasts, 47, 48, 106
southern states of the United States and, 53
socially prescribed durations, 171. See also Cuban Adjustment Act
Sociedad Asturiana de Beneficencia, 105. See also Covadonga Clinic in Tampa; *Nuestra Señora Covadonga Principado de Asturias*; *Quinta Covadonga*
Sociedad Económica Amigos del País (SEAP), 47, 233
Sociedad de Socorros Mutuos, 74
Sociedad Italiana de Beneficencia, 74
Sociedad Libanesa de Cuba, 139
Sociedad Palestino-Arabe, 139
Sociedad Siria, la, 139
Sociedad Unión Martí-Maceo, 113–14
Sonesson, Birgit, 93
sourjournerism, 88–89, 97, 98
South Florida, Cubans in, 205, 226, 228, 234, 247. See also Key West; Miami
Soviet Union
  Cuba's economic dependency to, 163, 175–76. See also special period
  disintegration of and Cuba's socioeconomic conditions, 175–78, 209, 248, 262, 286 n. 24. See also rafter crisis; special period
Spanish-American War, 3, 87, 116–17, 119, 124, 239, 246
Spanish immigrants in Cuba, 3, 9, 42, 57, 73, 77, 92, 97, 118, 120, 122, 240, 251. See also Alicante; Almería; Andalucía; Asturias; Basque Country; Barcelona; Canary Islands; Catalonia; Galicia; Madrid; Santander; Seville
Spanish immigrants and temporary workers in the United States, 58, 85, 89, 106, 112–13, 251. See also Key West; Philadelphia; Tampa; Ybor City
Spanish militarization of Cuba and migration, 56–57
Spanish wealthy returnees, 94, 99–102, 106, 277 n. 17. See also Hispanic-Antillean Bourgeoisie; *Indianos*
special period (*período especial en tiempo de paz*), 168, 176, 187, 193, 219, 223. See also Soviet Union
structural displacement, 15, 66, 226
Syria, migrants from in Cuba, 135, 138–39

Tampa
  clubs and associations formed by Cuban migrants, 109–14
  Cuban and Spanish migrants in the cigar industry, 112–13

Cubans in after 1959, 202, 207
Italian immigrants in, 113. *See also* Italians
José Martí political activism in, 110–13. *See also* Martí, José
Spanish immigrant associations, 106
tarjeta blanca, 115, 155, 215. *See also* exit permit
Ten Year War, 108. *See also* independence wars in Cuba
Torres, María de los Angeles, 32, 227, 285 n. 108
Torricelli Bill. *See* Cuban Democracy Act
trade and migration. *See also* banking industry and migration
  Chinese and other migrants, 127, 136
  French migrants, 54, 56
  German migrants, 83–84, 89–90
  Spanish migrants, 90–95, 97, 108
transculturation, 20
transnational fields of governmentality and U.S.-bound Cuban migration, 33, 168–69, 180–81, 217, 234, 243, 245, 248
  perspective, xiv, 8, 24, 25, 27, 207. *See also* comprehensive perspective on transnationalism
  processes and migration, 6, 8, 87, 112, 245. *See also* banking industry and migration; trade and migration
  strategies of livelihoods, 10, 12, 13, 26, 86, 122, 193, 213, 217, 220
Treaty of Nanking, 79, 238. *See also* Opium Wars
Triscornia, 120
Turkey, migrants from in Cuba, 85, 136–37

Unión Libanés-Siria, 139
Unión Murgadesa de Beneficencia y Recreo, 105
United Fruit Company (UFCO), 123

United States
  bilateral relation with Cuba after 1959 and migration, 259–65. *See also* Bush, George W.; Cuban Refugee Adjustment Act; Obama, Barack; Presidential Commission for the Assistance to a Free Cuba; transnational fields of governmentality
  citizens and U.S.–born population in Cuba, 83, 110, 135, 141, 152
  Cuban-origin population in, 145–49, 199–201
  migrants from Cuba and Cuban Americans in. See Florida; Key West; Miami; New York; Philadelphia; Tampa; Ybor City
  migrants from Spain in. *See* Spanish immigrants and temporary workers in the United States
  role in shaping Cuba's migration policy, 75, 117, 119, 123–25, 135, 138, 246. *See also* transnational fields of governmentality
Unión Libanés-Siria, 139
urban reform, 160, 259
Uruguay, 73, 103, 118, 129

Venezuela
  Cuban migration and, 108, 161–62, 181–82, 193, 216
  Spanish migration and, 98, 103–4, 134
Veracruz, 52, 90, 108

Wallerstein, Immanuel, 36, 38, 236
wet feet–dry feet rule, 179
Wimmer, Andrea, 17, 269
White Population Board (*Junta de Población Blanca*), 71. See also *blanqueamiento*
Women in White. *See* Damas de Blanco

Ybor City, 113
Yucatan, 41, 58, 84, 128

www.ingramcontent.com/pod-product-compliance
Lightning Source LLC
Chambersburg PA
CBHW021849020426
42334CB00013B/258